The Life of the Mind in America

BOOKS BY PERRY MILLER

PERRY MILLER

THE LIFE
OF THE MIND
IN AMERICA

FROM THE REVOLUTION TO THE CIVIL WAR

BOOKS ONE THROUGH THREE

A HARVEST BOOK
HARCOURT, BRACE & WORLD, INC.
NEW YORK

For Marie-Louise and Samuel Rosenthal

Foreword

Some seven or eight years before his death in 1963, when Perry Miller began thinking of how he would go about presenting an account of the development of an American "mind" in the new nation, he was principally engaged in an examination of the writers of what is usually considered the "classic" period of American literature. Brief though the time had been between the Revolution and their day, Emerson and Thoreau, Hawthorne and Melville, observing the headlong course on which the country was embarked, found themselves virtually united on one basic theme: the judgment of Nature upon that society. "Things" were in the saddle, and Nature's nation could bring forward no Newton, could hail no voice "greater than Shakespeare."

Just as, in examining the New England Mind, he had found it necessary to backtrack to the English—and Continental—Reformation, so the writer now returned to the first days of the Republic, to begin, as he hoped, to distinguish the various strands of intellectual experience that went into the establishing of an American identity. While the grand design was completed, the present volume constitutes all that was written.

Book One, with its examination of the manner in which the churches, through the mechanism of the Revival, found a means by which they could both prosper and preserve a unity of mission despite sectarian multiplicity, had been completed and had undergone thorough revision. Book Two, on the truly heroic exertions of jurists to construct a legal system, to establish courts for the new nation, had undergone considerable revision. Of Book Three, on science and technology, only the first chapter had been completed, but the final working outline of what was to follow is included. The intention was that these books, together with a Prologue, "The Sublime in America," and another book on education, would constitute the first volume of the work as a whole.

vii

For those Americans who figure in this story, two considerations were always present to their vision: the challenge of the vast territory, its limitless prairies, its great rivers, its sublime mountains, all waiting to be explored, to be mastered, to be mined; and the uniqueness of the new man, the American republican, who would indubitably achieve marvels in the governance of society, in science, in letters and the arts, indeed, who could, unlike the weary and debauched citizen of the Old World, legitimately aspire to the moral sublime. That part of the life of the mind in America that went on in Concord, Massachusetts, was often skeptical of such grandiose projections, but it should be remembered that even Henry Thoreau could say, "With a little more wit we might use these materials so as to become richer than the richest now are, and make our civilization a blessing."

ELIZABETH W. MILLER

Cambridge, Massachusetts
May 13, 1965

Contents

CONTENTS

BOOK ONE

THE EVANGELICAL BASIS

CHAPTER ONE

The Intellect of the Revival

But as yet the state of the Christian world is such, that to expect to promote religion without excitements is unphilosophical and absurd. The great political, and other worldly excitements that agitate Christendom, are all unfriendly to religion, and divert the mind from the interests of the soul. Now these excitements can only be counteracted by *religious* excitements. And until there is religious principle in the world to put down irreligious excitements, it is in vain to promote religion, except by countering excitements. This is true in philosophy, and it is a historical fact.

—CHARLES GRANDISON FINNEY, 1835

1.

THE GRAND ERA OF THE REVIVAL

"A revival of Religion," proclaimed the Reverend Finney, "presupposes a declension." The religious leaders of the new United States were almost immediately convinced that the political achievement of federal union had been accompanied by a spiritual deterioration hardly to be equaled in the darkest chapters of Christian history. Indeed, they so strongly imposed their horrid vision of a country hovering in the 1790's on the brink of ruin that for the next six decades they could unfailingly rouse the nation by abjurations against falling again into that abyss. In all the land, no voice was to be heard, from 1800 to 1860, to salute—and mourn—America's momentary chance to escape its Christian specificity; no spokesman, whether Finney or William Ellery Channing, to deny that around 1800 the community had been rescued, just in the nick of time, from a descent into atheism.

Heretics are undoubtedly much more fascinating than the orthodox. Perhaps it is for this reason that secular historians, in seeking motivations, or causations, for the crisis, have given exaggerated emphasis to the notion that the mighty revivals of the turn of the century were chiefly reactions against the Enlightenment. True, several surviving leaders of the Revolution, most conspicuously Jefferson, were rationalistic to the point of overt Deism; it is also true that Tom Paine's *The Age of Reason* (1795) circulated among village dissidents, and especially among the rude settlements of the frontier, and in 1795 the blind ex-Baptist preacher Elihu Palmer did gather an out-and-out Deistic Society in New York. The clergy could paint horrendous tableaus of "the Bavarian Illuminati" as well as of other lurid plots to subvert the churches; and in New Haven President Timothy Dwight of Yale College assured posthumous notoriety by predicting that were Jefferson elected in 1800 his villains would deflower the female population of Connecticut. All these alarms were intensified because, as the great Presbyterian Robert Baird put it in his analysis of *Religion in America* (1844), the federal government was barely established "when the French Revolution burst forth like a volcano and threatened to sweep the United States into its fiery stream."

There survives out of the years 1790 to 1815 an immense (considering the meager population) American literature of denunciation of the French Revolution, with proportionately almost nothing on its behalf. In 1831 John Quincy Adams explained to Alexis de Tocqueville that forty years previously the philosophy of Voltaire and the school of Hume were influential in America: "Since then the crimes of the French Revolution have made a strong impression on us; there has been a reaction of feeling, and this impulse still makes itself felt." This was Adamsish understatement. Students at Yale—so ran the endlessly repeated *exemplum*—had become dreadfully corrupted by their smatterings of Paine, Voltaire, d'Alembert, but were dramatically redeemed from frivolity by the boldness of Timothy Dwight, who allowed them to debate with him the inspiration of the Bible against their rational prophets, and in "fair fight" defeated them.

None the less, I believe it is unrealistic to represent the majority of Christian Americans (and the majority of the country was, to some degree or other, Christian) as primarily worried in the 1790's about a threat from European infidelity. And, as it seems to me, it is still more unrealistic to suppose that the memory of the revivals in the minds of the faithful had, as chief ingredient, the belief that the nation had been rescued from eighteenth-century rationalism. Nor can we further suppose that either participants in the Second Great Awakening or those who carried it on for the next thirty or forty years conceived of

4

their work in this limited frame of reference. To do so were to mistake entirely the structure of the popular sentiment.

For one thing, Federalist attacks on the infidelity of Jeffersonians backfired on such fantastics as Timothy Dwight; Republicans learned to discount their vehemence, and to vote for Jefferson and Madison. More importantly, the churches themselves resisted the attempt to make them pawns in a political game, and obstinately insisted that the danger threatening the country was not the sophistication of a few but the lassitude of the many. This was the version of their achievement which the pioneer revivalists passed on to their followers; this was the pattern which for the next sixty years defined the task. This was the conception, only peripherally concerned with the French Revolution, which dictated Finney's prescription of the necessity of meeting excitement with more excitement.

There is of course no gainsaying that American Protestants were profoundly disturbed by the news from France, or that they took tales of antireligious conspiracies very much to heart. Still, the central fact is that the disturbing bulletins from Europe fed an appetite for self-examination and self-recrimination which had been born in America long before the fall of the Bastille. In 1795 the militant Methodist Church could call for a day of fasting among its converts without mentioning Paris, but concentrating entirely on the sins and iniquities of America—"our growing idolatry, which is covetousness and the prevailing love of the world," manifested in profanations of the Sabbath, disobedience to parents, and increase of drunkenness. The General Assembly of the Presbyterians in 1798 would list as a preliminary consideration the unexampled scenes of devastation and bloodshed in Europe, but get down to serious business with a recital of "a general dereliction of religious principle and practice among our fellow-citizens." In Connecticut, the same year, a Baptist association, still struggling to get out from under the "Standing Order," rejoiced that all denominations were concurring in lamentation about the "melancholy and truly alarming situation of the United States."

In time, accounts of the Second Awakening, brought out in the early years of the nineteenth century to stimulate the continuation of the Revival, put less and less emphasis upon what had been the danger of a French or Deistic invasion, until at last the concept virtually disappeared. This fact in itself tells much about the magnificent era of revivals inaugurated in or around 1800: it was in great part an internal convulsion, and it progressively endeavored to conceive of itself as exclusively internal. Indeed, one can almost say that the steady burning of the Revival, sometimes smoldering, now blazing into flame, never quite extinguished (even in Boston) until the Civil War had been fought, was a central mode of this culture's search for national identity. The task was to ascertain just what were the sins of the community that needed reforming, what were its own defects, not those contracted from Europe.

Thus A. P. Marvin, in *Bibliotheca Sacra* of April, 1859—in the midst of what he considered the Third Great Awakening of America— looked back to 1800, to the Second, and found the efficient provocation of that upsurge in the worldliness and pride which came with the providentially secured independence and consequent prosperity. Hence that revival, as contrasted with the First (of 1740), had been primarily concentrated on the doctrine of divine sovereignty, whereas Edwards, Whitefield, and Gilbert Tennent had dedicated their attention to the issue of justification by faith. To be sure, all accounts of the New England aspect of the 1800 movement show that it was essentially a recapitulation of the Edwardsean revival. Thanks to Dwight and the emerging "New Haven theology," certain shifts in emphasis prevented the enthusiasm from flaring into the violences which so rapidly had discredited 1740. The Connecticut sector of the Second Awakening dampered down the noise and confusion, so that the resurgence could go on quietly for some twenty years. Except for those presided over by Asahel Nettleton, who never undertook a revival in any community uninvited, the ceremonies were under the direction of "settled" ministers, who marvelously combined stimulation with restraint, and of whom the supreme artist in the art of balancing these contradictions was Lyman Beecher. New Englanders had been severely scarred by criticisms of the First Awakening—all Calvinists had read Charles Chauncy—and were resolved never again to let emotions get so out of control as to provoke ridicule. So, though the Second Awakening in Connecticut and in other New England states is an integral part of the story—and out of it were to come energies that worked throughout the nation—it is a local phenomenon, and by itself would not have captivated the imagination of the expanding country. The image that would dominate the popular mind had, inevitably, to come from the West itself. Kentucky provided it.

The men who set the volcano in action were mostly Presbyterians in the Appalachian mountains, though they worked in co-operation with Baptists, and in general seem barely distinguishable from their Methodist colleagues. The biographies of the chief actors, such men as James McGready, Barton W. Stone, William McGee, as recounted by their adherents provide little for the historian of ideas to work with.

6

The powerful fact about these protagonists is that, in relation to the accumulated wisdom of Protestant theology, they had few ideas and were little capable of cerebration. They were all intensely concerned with "salvation," either of themselves or of everybody around them, and they had a social situation made to their hands. They invented the camp meeting. They held their first one at Gaspar River Church in July, 1800; but for decades thereafter the archetypal session, the one that dominated the American vision, was the performance they staged at Cane Ridge, in Kentucky, commencing on August 6, 1801. Here was enacted a religious revolution. Tom Paine may have penetrated a few log cabins, but this orgy had little or nothing to do with him. It was a spasm among the populace, a violent explosion of emotions which for long had been seeking release, an overwhelming portent for the future of the continent.

There was not merely one preacher, but a score—Baptist, Methodist, Presbyterian—and they held forth not in rotation but simultaneously, in all corners of the enclosure. The people literally "fell" in droves. Here first erupted on a mass scale the incredible array of "exercises" —falling, barking, catalepsy, rolling, running. There were shrieks, laughter, outcries, incantations. From Cane Ridge, said Peter Cartwright (for whom it always remained a mark to shoot at), "the news spread through all the Churches, and through all the land, and it excited great wonder and surprise; but it kindled a religious flame that spread all over Kentucky and through many states."

It brought also controversies, schisms, separations, all of which denominational historians recount. Quarrels about, let us say, the proper "means" often sounded so envenomed that an outside observer might suppose revivalism about to be dissipated by fragmentation. (Alexis de Tocqueville never understood its dynamic force in the society.) Actually, in the larger perspective of American thinking, these divisions —though frequently argued with dismaying ferocity—are of little importance before the terrific universality of the Revival. In fact, the dominant theme in America from 1800 to 1860 is the invincible persistence of the revival technique, coming to its resplendent triumph in the Third Awakening, of 1857–58. We can hardly understand Emerson, Thoreau, Whitman, Melville, unless we comprehend that for them this was the one clearly given truth of their society. By its basic premise, revivalism required—indeed demanded—that between outbursts there come lulls, which would shortly thereafter be denounced as "declensions." This was the accepted assumption, and for the mass of the American democracy, the decades after 1800 were a continuing, even though intermittent, revival.

It may be said that the torch lit at Cane Ridge in 1801 was kept short of holocaust by political and military pressures. At any rate, the "work" was phenomenally renewed upon the end of the war with England, in 1815. Especially was this reinvigoration evoked by the awareness that, with the floodgates of migration opened, the "West" threatened to become a vast amphitheater of barbarism. There was no hope for it unless religion could be thrust violently into the desert by means of the revival and the camp meeting. Beginning with Schermerhorn and Mills's *A Correct View of that Part of the United States which lies West of the Allegheny Mountains with regard to Religion and Morals* (1814)—the authors were profoundly pessimistic—the older America commenced a gigantic campaign to enlist the new into Christian culture. The details of this story—the organizations, the orations, the contributions, the missionaries—need not concern us other than to note that such "missionary" societies were as active in Charleston as in Boston, and that they were a major factor in the thinking of the country. The thesis that only Christianity could save Ohio and Alabama from barbarism became a staple of American literature. Hundreds contributed to the formulation, but the gist of the argument may for us appear in William Cogswell's *The Harbinger of the Millennium* (1833):

The Great Valley of the Mississippi (twenty-four hundred miles in length, and twelve hundred in breadth) may be said, in general terms, to be little better than one immense field of moral desolations. A contemplative view of this is enough to make heaven weep, if weeping could be there; enough to break any heart unless harder than adamant, and to rouse it into holy action, unless colder than the grave.

Taking for granted, as we may, the numerous organizations which proposed to evangelize the West, we should note that a great incentive to Eastern activity was, as Cogswell put it, that "moral desolations have a baneful influence upon contiguous societies." By their efforts to convert the West, Easterners were as much vaccinating themselves as they were seeking to rescue perishing pioneers. To the end of their days, those who had sweated in the camp meetings would remain assured "that the astonishing physical phenomena which attended them were a necessary means of arresting the popular attention."

Yet it is a mistake to think of revivalism in this era as only a frontier phenomenon. As Cogswell intimates, the belief that a revival is "contagious"—that it can spread—quickly became an *idée fixe* of the Second Awakening. It could reach as easily backward to the East as it could expand toward the Mississippi. Risings and fallings, followed by

8

revisings, went on as solidly in New England and Pennsylvania as in Illinois. Isabella Bishop asserted in 1859 that in the South the prayers of Christians "have not been answered by any marked outpouring of the Holy Spirit." Possibly there were peculiar circumstances (not unconnected with the "peculiar institution"?) why massive camp meetings were less frequent there; still, the literature adequately reveals that the pattern of the Revival took over the rural localities, and that in time the slaves were indulging themselves in it. However, there can be no doubt that in the 1820's the area in which revivals grew to the rankest luxuriance was the state of New York. By 1830 the region between Troy and Buffalo was already known as the "burned-over district," though for another two decades it could still find fuel to keep the furnace roaring.

Out of this cauldron emerged the figure who supremely—more than Nettleton, Beecher, or such Methodists as Cartwright—incarnated the aspiration and the philosophy of the revival, Charles Grandison Finney. The narrative of his violent conversion in 1821—how he literally saw a vision of Christ in the main street of Adams, how he "penetrated into the woods," wrestled with the Lord until "I could feel the impression, like a wave of electricity going through and through me"; how he immediately gave up his lucrative law practice to become the most spectacularly successful of American evangelists—all this was as familiar to the pious of his era as the story of St. Paul on the road to Damascus. Yet what makes Finney the central character in this chapter is that while he could say, "I had been brought up mostly in the woods," and while he resisted any formal theological education, he did have a vigorous mind. Not only could he slay his thousands in the frenzy of a revival, but in 1835 could articulate his *Lectures on Revivals of Religion,* indisputably the most powerful theoretical statement of the significance of the titanic enterprise. Overnight it sold 12,000 copies in America, soon was translated into Welsh, French, German. No religious leader in America since Edwards had commanded such attention; no one was to do it again until Dwight Moody. Hence Finney's book stands—though many of his fellow-revivalists disagreed with him, though many attacked his methods—as the key exposition of the movement, and so a major work in the history of the mind in America. Its study is imperative if one wishes to pursue the mental adventure of the country.

2.

THE ASPIRATION OF THE REVIVAL

By 1831, *The Spirit of the Pilgrims* (the magazine Lyman Beecher founded in Boston in 1827 as a weapon against Unitarianism) could complacently reflect that the cause of Christ in America had marched from conquest to conquest as "the result of those revivals of religion which for thirty years have been enrolling, augmenting and disciplining the sacramental host." There was no need for apology. As Calvin Colton asserted in 1833, ministers now know by experience: "They go to work with as full and as undoubting confidence, as men apply themselves to any enterprise whatever, and in the career of which they have realized repeated and uniform earnests of success." Which is to say that before the Panic of 1837, a revival in America had become as sure a thing as a real-estate venture or as a pioneer investment in railroads.

We may thus legitimately ask what, in the decades since Cane Ridge, had become the criterion of success? The naïve might suppose it would be the number of scoffers, tavern-keepers, riotous river-boat men brought suddenly to their knees. Indeed, the narratives of evangelists, Finney and Cartwright most conspicuously, are studded with many startling victories over open enemies. But in fact this was the lesser department of the endeavor. The object of a revival, said the mighty Methodist Bishop McIlvaine in 1832, is only in part the conversion of sinners—though often treated as if the sole end; the more important objective is, and has always been, *"the quickening of the people of God to a spirit and walk becoming the gospel."* We miss entirely the dynamics of the great revivals of the early nineteenth century if we suppose them missions to the heathen: they got their demonic power because they were addressed to those already more or less within the churches, because they operated in a society where a general consent to the principles of Protestant Christianity was taken for granted. They were not so much aimed at subjugating a wilderness as at reinvigorating the force of what was already professed. The town atheist might come to scorn and remain to pray; the finely coiffed Episcopalian lady might end by jerking so violently that her hairpins fell out, and the revivalist would chronicle his victories. But the mass of those he preached to, whom he humbled and "converted," were those who offered no ideological opposition, who wanted the "wave of electricity" to flow through them. And the ritual required a Finney, a Beecher, or a Cartwright to set the wave in motion.

In 1800 and even in 1830 memories of 1740 persisted (Finney constantly cited Edwards) ; but the appeal of that Awakening had been to the individual shut up in his closet, even though the more celebrated manifestations took place among crowds. After 1800, the vast literature in defense of the Revival is unabashedly communal. Naturally, both Finney and Beecher tell of private conversations and of particular persons with whom they prayed in private, but these are side forays along the highway of an immense social progress. By 1830 a writer in *The Christian Spectator* has no hesitation in defining a revival as "the increase of holiness among a people."

The stages by which the intransigent individualism of Edwards's preaching moved into the mass exhortation of Cane Ridge are almost imperceptible. But by 1830, by the great days of Finney, the transformation is complete. The *Spectator* agrees that individuals, under these "impressions," may retire from the "assemblies to commune with their hearts," but the writer's real concern is about an influence which suddenly pervades "a congregation or neighborhood." Repeated phrases show how thoroughly in this period a hope of regenerating sinners had become one with the expectation of redeeming communities en bloc. Thus in 1829 another writer in the *Spectator* had already discerned the path of modern revivalism: just as the Gospel can rescue individuals, he said, so also "it can renew the face of communities and nations. The same heavenly influence which, in revivals of religion, descends on families and villages . . . may in like manner, when it shall please him who hath the residue of the Spirit, descend to refresh and beautify a whole land."

The whole land—the whole beautiful, terrible, awesome land! The pathetic thousands who camped and writhed at Cane Ridge were not consciously thinking in any such terms. Had some Walt Whitman arisen prematurely among them to recite strophes on the destiny of America, they would have shouted him down. They had congregated there from everywhere and nowhere; they were not a settled congregation, like Jonathan Edwards's in Northampton; most of them knew not to what church they belonged, or which they would join, and accepted Baptist, Methodist, Presbyterian alike. They were not preaching nationalism, they were enacting it. Even in tight-lipped Connecticut, the revival took on a tone unprecedented in 1740, and by 1818 the establishment had to yield. To be sure, denominational rivalry seemed often to be aggravated, and after a revival there was frequently an ignominious squabble for the converts. Still, these were comic, incidental accompaniments. From 1800 onward, either in New England or the West, the driving concern was that the ecstasies had to assure, not only the conviction of innumerable individuals, but the welfare of the young country. This unvoiced but compelling motive finds expression not so much in occasional moments of triumph, but in the cold appraisals which revivalists themselves penned between their peaks of excitement. So, for instance, a writer in *Bibliotheca Sacra* of 1845 (a dull moment in the Revival) asked for a stocktaking, and in these astonishing terms:

Still, do they [revivals] pervade the masses of society? Do they touch the springs of our political movements? Can we trace their influence in any perceptible degree among the great body of the members of two of the learned professions? Till something like this is effected, how can we remain satisfied with these partial and entirely inadequate exhibitions of divine grace? In the degree in which they have been enjoyed, can they save the country?

There we have it—"save the country"! Did the country need saving? Why the urgency? It is a shallow view of the social situation which regards the revivals as only a device in the capitalistic expansion —as though revivals did no more than set Max Weber's "Protestant Ethic" on fire in primitive America and so give added incentive to the pious to work in their callings of building up a new country, even though there is, I agree, some such aspect to the movement. On the other hand it is equally unperceptive to take the Revival as solely a religious outburst unrelated to national and economic concerns. In every cataclysm there were hundreds who asked only, "What shall *I* do to be saved?" But over and over again, when the workers in the vineyards could be induced for a moment to lay aside their pruning shears and explain what they were about, they came back to the *communal* effect of their exertions. Not only the moral but the physical aspect of a community is changed by a revival, said Sprague: it ". . . has encouraged industry, and has caused the social virtues to look forth in smiles, where chilling selfishness, or hateful discord, or unblushing crime, seemed to have established a perpetual reign."

Whether revivals actually so transformed communities, or whether the effect was at all lasting, or whether indeed the communities needed any such transformation, is not a matter of such importance as the fact that in these terms the revivalists conceived their function. In 1851 the Reverend David Riddle, raising money in New York for the American Home Missionary Society, made the point wonderfully clear:

Yes! American Christians, in the nature of the case and from the analogies of the past, it is safe to conclude that we must be a great people, but not necessarily or universally a holy people. . . . For, let no man delude himself with the dream, alike contrary to fact and philosophy, that without evangelical influences and institutions, any thing else, however excellent, will preserve us as a people from ruin. . . . It is not enterprise, or physical improvements, or a glorious constitution and good laws, or free trade, or a tariff, or railroads and steamships, or philosophy, or science, or taste; but the grace of God, that bringeth salvation, appearing to every man, and inwrought into the heart of every man, that can save us from the fate of former republics, and make us a blessing to all nations.

Hence, when we ask to what the Revival really aspired, we are obliged to recognize that in the early nineteenth century it was accepted as a uniquely *American* ritual, and that its aims were molded accordingly. Robert Baird addressed his book to English and European Protestants, and so was careful to make explicit many things which Americans took for granted; he explained, as though he were speaking of some obscure rite in the African jungle, how revivals have been found "most effectual" in America because "of those principles in our mental constitution which are appealed to with peculiar power by these seasons of concentrated religious interest." This was tantamount to asserting that the "principles" of the American mentality were somehow basically different from the European; as Baird flatly declared, "Christians on one side of the Atlantic expect them, and on the other they do not." Baird could only dismiss as hardly worth answering the European sneer that "Americanism" in religion consisted of ignorant and ranting preachers: the European who were to denounce the United States as uncivilized because it does not offer everywhere the luxuries of Paris "would display no more ignorance of the world, nor a greater want of common sense, than were he to despise the plain preaching of a man who enters the pulpit with a mind replete with Scriptural knowledge."

From the time of the Wesleys and Whitefield there had been in England preachings out of doors to large concourses of people; these were conveniently forgotten, or else overshadowed, by the noise, blare, and persistence of American revivals. European visitors were in constant amazement. "America," said the English Isabella Bishop, "presents a spectacle foreign to our practice if not to our notions of bold evangelization." The people are too energetic "to pardon dreary platitude or vague and glittering generalities"; they demand something lifelike, "something which removes them from their sordid six-day cares into an atmosphere of holiness and perchance of hope." To achieve this aspiration, it took the sledge-hammer blows of a revival. And it took the gifts of a revivalist like Finney, in a country devoted to "business," to gain attention for the interests of eternity. Hence the particularly American character of the phenomenon, and the otherwise inexplicable identification of patriotism with it. For as Baird concluded, while there exist differences in the philosophy of conducting revivals, especially as between Connecticut and Kentucky, yet all "agree that such a revival is an inestimable blessing: so that he who should oppose himself to revivals *as such,* would be regarded by most of our evangelical Christians as *ipso facto,* an enemy to spiritual religion itself."

3.

ENEMIES OF THE SPIRIT

Incredible though it might seem to the evangelicals, there was stubborn opposition to the work of God. Had this resistance come only from lingering eighteenth-century rationalists like Jefferson, or from village adherents of Tom Paine, we might discount it as a minor aberration which could be dismissed. What was galling to the revivalists, at the height of their triumph, was the rise of a strong *religious* critique. To be sure, there was never anything like an organized counterattack; the assaults came from too disparate quarters—the "Old School" Presbyterians of Princeton, the Episcopalians, from the German Reformed Church, the "sober-side" Congregationalists, and most articulately from Boston Unitarians. Still, they did establish the fact of a basic division in the mind of the country.

Generally considered, the period following 1800 was, for about forty years, one of massive revivals. They give a special tone to the epoch; through them the youthful society sought for solidarity, for a discovery of its meaning. Yet disruptive forces were at work. Had the controversy been only one of Christianity versus Deism, Cane Ridge would have sounded a conclusive answer. But the problem was not so simple. It was of the essence of the Revival that it conquer everything in sight; by its very nature it could brook no opposition. If it could not humble its opponents, then the great issue would remain unsolved. Could the nation remain a nation if Christian bodies were so separated by manners and modes?

The evangelical thrust was not, naturally, discouraged because the Episcopal Church stood aloof from the Revival. In 1800 it was still so bedraggled as a consequence of the Revolution, still so branded as a "British" institution, that its barbs at Cane Ridge were utterly without effect. Even after the church regained coherence, even in the days of Bishop Hobart, it remained, in the view of most Americans, a sanctuary for the comfortable, for the genteel, so that its comments on the Revival seemed not worth the revivalists' notice. Episcopalians after the Revolution, cautiously decorous, seldom indulged in polemic, but in 1816 Rayner Menzies did bring out a *Dissertation on Awakenings,* which may be celebrated as the first consistent, albeit exasperated, assault upon the whole idea. Despite its Anglican prejudice, it is a readable book. Menzies has fun noting that during Connecticut revivals young persons overcome with a sense of guilt go apart in meadows to pray, "but they have been careful to utter their groans and prayer so loud, that persons passing at a considerable distance, might hear them." Menzies argued the superior virtue of set prayers over perfervid spontaneous whines, and even entered into a fairly learned argument to prove that regeneration is gradual and progressive, not instantaneous. He went back to 1740, to brand Whitefield as indeed the instigator of "enthusiasm." Such distaste might be never so strong among the Episcopalians, many of whom were effective in business, the law, and even in politics; it remained true that the great Revival had nothing to fear from them. "It may be well to state," said Henry Caswall in 1839, ". . . that religious mania is said to be the prevailing form of insanity in the United States." This was perhaps an accurate sociological observation, but what effect could it have upon Charles Grandison Finney!

As for the German churches, the issue of the Revival set off controversy both within and between the two major confessions, which in turn had repercussions among the four evangelical churches. The Reformed Church, from its theological citadel at Mercersburg, Pennsylvania, resisted the intrusion. The explanation perhaps lies in Philip Schaff's description of it as not so much Calvinistic as "Melanchthonian." Schaff, a profound scholar in the grand German tradition, had come to Mercersburg in 1844. Before he came to America, he romantically dwelt on the idea of a great assembly "in the forest by moonlight, and under heaven's blue, starry dome of peace," devoutly listening to solemn warnings and filling the silence of nature with praises of Christ, imagining the scene as "sublime and captivating." But experience convinced him that much which is human and impure mingles itself with these excitements, that they nourish a distrust of calm preaching, and that after the straw fire has burned itself out, "it has left a complete desolation, with frivolous mockery of all religion."

Schaff's disillusionment was hastened by the impact upon him, as upon the Reformed Church and many in other churches, of one of the most trenchant books of the period, *The Anxious Bench* (1843; second edition, 1844), by his colleague at Mercersburg, John Williamson Nevin. Oddly enough, Nevin came of Scotch-Irish stock, and had been a Presbyterian until he migrated to this "German" institution. His book was credited with rescuing the Church from a contagion of "Puritan and Methodistic modes of thought," of redirecting it toward an "organic" polity. What seemed his most telling maneuver was to accuse all revivals of being essentially Methodist: "Wesley was a small man as compared with Melanchthon." He concentrated his fire upon Finney's anxious bench, with all its "solemn tricks for effect," a monstrous machine imparting "justification by feeling rather than faith," conveying only "fanatical impressions." Finney's was the old heresy that conversion is "the product of the sinner's own will, and not truly and strictly a new creation in Christ Jesus by the power of God." Finney himself brushed aside these criticisms, but Nevin's attack crystallized a minority opinion which stubbornly resisted the dominant spirit of the times.

The Revival caused greater disruptions within the German Lutheran community, splitting it into factions, one of which, for a time calling themselves "the New Lutherans," experimented with the "new measures," especially the anxious bench. In 1843, one of this group, Reuben Weiser, angrily replied to Nevin with *The Mourner's Bench,* saying that none "but Infidels, or Formalists will be found in the present day, fighting against Revivals, unless their theory of Religion is of such a character as to set aside all efforts to awaken impenitent sinners." Calvinism, he sneered, may sit in professorial chairs and prate of moral inability, while the new measures are running away with the world and doing the work of the Master. As for there being no Biblical authorizations for the anxious bench, there are also none "for Theological Seminaries—for Colleges, or even for Common Schools—none for Sabbath Schools, or Temperance Societies, or Bible, or Missionary or Tract Societies—none for the many Benevolent institutions of our day, which are the chief ornaments of the nineteenth century!" But a decade later Schaff was happily able to report in Berlin that though one might fill a book on the anxious-bench controversy in both the German Churches, by this time the "healthy tendency" had prevailed among the Lutherans as well, and that "the system of new measures has already outlived itself." Whatever good there had been "in this Methodistic thunder-storm and whirlwind, has remained, and been taken up into a sound churchly life." This might be reassuring news to Prussian theologians, but in America it meant that from these bastions the Revival had been repulsed.

Nevin was effective outside the German communions in part because he had been trained at Princeton. That Seminary, with its learned and mighty faculty—Charles Hodge (who boasted that in his fifty years of teaching he had never broached a new or original idea), Albert Dod, J. W. Alexander—had been distrustful of the Revival from the beginning, and became openly hostile when Finney propagated his new measures. The tension between this "Old School" mentality and the revivalist wing of the Presbyterian fellowship, basically a matter of their attitudes toward the method, was gradually exacerbated by theological doctrines that grew from these premises, and finally by the slavery question, until in 1837 the Church was split asunder. For a movement which sought the union in fellowship of all Protestants, this was indeed a defeat. The Seminary kept up a drumfire upon the evangelicals, Hodge scoring several hits, as for instance in 1847 by deriding the claim that these revivals were "American": there is nothing national in true religion, nor should there be. The very fact "that these revivals are *American*," that the Spirit of God does not ordinarily carry on His work elsewhere by this means, "should convince us that it is neither the common, nor the best mode in which the cause of religion is to be advanced."

Yet in a sense, neither Nevin nor Princeton did ever quite rend the seamless garment: they never condemned the principle of the Revival *in toto,* but simply objected (however strenuously) to inflated eloquence, to a neglect of theology, to allowing emotions to run away with logic. Had the Revival encountered no more formidable opposition than this, it could have moved confidently, as indeed it did, to the conquest of America. But what threw a harpoon into its vitals, and caused it ceaseless anxiety, was the attack of the Unitarians. Not that they were so numerous, outside Massachusetts, as to cause serious alarm, but that by employing a learning and a prose which were bound to have effect, the Unitarians set up and maintained the truly divisive argument within the Protestant churches.

Only when one appreciates the hunger both of the lonely spirit and of the whole society which brought crowds of simple citizens to Cane Ridge, to the Methodist camp meetings, to the halls where Finney welded them (momentarily) into communities, can one perceive the skill of the Unitarian attack. These disputants had inherited from debates over the Great Awakening a method of argument trained to go for the jugular. They had sharpened their claws on the granite of

Jonathan Edwards, and had practiced their logic upon the "ortho-dox" in the first decades of the century. Though the generation who gathered around William Ellery Channing were not always so "rationalistic" as they have been accounted—they carried a sense of the strenuous life and the proverbial New England conscience into the meadows of "liberal Christianity"—still they were outraged both as theologians and as gentlemen by the violence of the Revival. When, as Ephraim Perkins charged in 1826, they found themselves proscribed as "heirs of hell, children of the devil, and enemies of all righteousness, traitors to the cause of religion, and the enemies and opposers of God, and denounced as the enemies of mankind and the bane of Christian society," they struck back, and struck hard.

The literature of Unitarian antirevivalism makes lively reading even today. It is filled with a sense of urgency, for as *The Christian Examiner* reported in 1827, Finney and his cohorts have a deliberate system, are resolved to introduce it into every city and village, "until they shall have the satisfaction of beholding the fires of religious frenzy which have flashed up in particular places, spread through the land, to use their own expression, 'as fires spread and roar through the parched forests.' " At once the most effective and the most irritating to the revivalists was Orville Dewey's masquerade, *Letters of an English Traveller to His Friend in England on the 'Revivals of Religion' in America,* printed at Boston in 1828. Indeed, one might say that Dewey was the one Unitarian who most carried into liberalism the passion of his Calvinistic heritage, and who, because of the adeptness of his disguise as a foreign observer, could hit the revivalists on all their most vulnerable or exposed points.

Dewey did more than mirror the frown of Boston's disapproval. He knew his Calvin, and he worked for a "Revival of Religion" far grander than the paltry shows enacted by Finney and Beecher. Loftily condescending, his discourse embellished by quotations from Wordsworth, he had words of pity for the people in country villages: "who meet with but little to arouse and quicken the mind, where a general stagnation and stupor of mind is the thing most to be feared, it is not so much amiss that *religion* should come in the form of excitement."

So much for Finney's argument that excitement qua excitement was justification enough! Dewey's fictional Englishman explained that the American theory of revival presupposed utter passivity of mind, that the notion of sudden infusion upset normal social relations, that the tumult of these meetings obscured any sense of the cosmic majesty of God, and that in the end of all, the judgments of revivalists defied those of ordinary common sense. Then getting down to the climactic argument, Dewey contended that out of these excitements grew "an idea akin to that of the old pagan philosophy, that religion is some divine *afflatus*—breathed into the mind—having nothing in common with it—existing independently and alone—not incorporated with the mind and dwelling in the most intimate friendship with it, but maintained within it, as an abstract principle or etherial essence, by a foreign and preternatural influence."

Well, these were the fighting words: a "foreign" influence! Going on to delineate the social hazards of persuading carpenters they knew as much as theologians, marshaling proofs that in conversion no miracle need be interposed, Dewey repeated the by then standardized arguments against the intrusion of itinerants (the greatest of these was Finney) into settled parishes. Then the final charge: the revivalists were betraying their people by imposing upon them, through factitious means, a bogus and so an un-American ideology. They might genuinely feel that old things have passed away, "but it is not so much in the habits or even the dispositions of their minds, as in the new objects which have been brought distinctly and vividly before their minds." In the end—or indeed as early as Ezra Stiles Gannett's pamphlet of 1831 (*Good and Evil of Revivals*)—the Unitarian dissent was codified: revivals, said Gannett, are completely artificial, "inasmuch as particular means devised by human ingenuity, and forced into action according to prescribed rules or for a special purpose, are brought to bear upon a community."

We come back to the magic words, and they all depend upon "community." Although the revivals, whether in Rochester or Lexington, were engulfed in a morass of local passion and recrimination, the *idea* of the work, *pro* or *con,* had relevance for the community, so that even the most ignorant, even the most illiterate, had to ask themselves dangerous questions, not about how they responded to Christ Crucified, but about how they conceived the American psychology. Ostensibly, revivals were populated with sinners converted to Christ: actually, they were nothing of the sort. The question before each community was whether it was acting as a community. The force of the revival would, of course, have evaporated had Finney or Beecher ever presented this as the actual concern. But indirections frequently find out directions, most of all in social history. Orville Dewey had accused the revivalists of falsifying the psychological nature of man. And so the massive authority of American Protestantism (leaving aside the Episcopalians, the Quakers, Princeton Seminary) had no alternative but to reinforce its assertions that it not only comprehended the scheme of universal salvation, but that it—and it alone—understood the psychology of man. Oddly, fantastically, in an era devoting its major energies to discussion of the nature of supernatural grace, every event, including the premises of its own theological discourse, conspired to focus attention upon the nature of man.

4.

THE COMPLEXITIES OF REBUTTAL

The simplest, most obvious, and apparently the conclusive answer of the Revival to its critics was that it gave the masses the sort of religion they wanted, and, to a great extent, apologists relied on this brute fact. In 1831 *The Spirit of the Pilgrims* thought it sufficient refutation of Ezra Stiles Gannett to proclaim:

Let him mingle with it enough to feel its influence upon his heart; let him go himself to the inquiry meeting, and pass from seat to seat and listen to the relations there given; let him become minutely acquainted with the anxieties of awakened souls, and with the views, feelings, and joys of new converts; let him pass through a season of such as this; — and we are persuaded he will burn his tract, and lament before God that he ever wrote it.

Unfortunately neither Ezra Gannett nor John Nevin was disposed to do anything of the sort, but had curiosity thus moved them, what they saw could only have confirmed their abhorrence. It becomes increasingly patent that the defense would require more sophisticated arguments in rebuttal.

Lyman Beecher's magazine, in its angry retort to Orville Dewey, revealed the social motivation at work within the revival. Defense on such grounds had to be manipulated skillfully, for already, by 1828, those devoted to the "social problems" of the society—prison reform, women's rights, vegetarianism, poor relief, and ultimately, of course, abolition of slavery—were denouncing the revivals not only for distracting interest from these projects but indeed for hindering them. By 1854 Charles Loring Brace would exclaim that Finney or any of the champions might hold forth for a whole winter at the Broadway Tabernacle without a word he uttered reaching the nearby Five Points, center of New York's poverty and vice.

The revivalists chose to ignore such strictures. At least in the early stages, they tended to pass over as rapidly as possible the self-sufficient rewards of a change of heart and emphasized, though always in conveniently vague terms, the advantages that accrued to society: "a more comprehensive and impartial benevolence, which, while it does not

overlook the family, extends to God, and pervades his kingdom."
Upon conversion, said Mark Tucker in 1833, Christians "begin to live,
for a time, as they ought *always* to live." And haunting all these
defenses, though never becoming explicit, is the furtive implication
that without it posterity is in danger; in fact, it soon becomes evident,
though seldom acknowledged, that anxiety over the future, not of the
individual soul in heaven, but of this nation on earth, lies at the
center of the movement. "Besides these immediate results," said *The
Spirit of the Times* to Orville Dewey (another example of how "immediate results" were played down in these apologetics), "we are to
remember that the public sentiment of the nation generally, and of
coming generations, must be affected by the present discussions of the
great subject of revivals of religion."

The thousands of pages which religious periodicals devoted to
proving the validity of revivals are in themselves remarkable evidence
of how, progressively, the business became self-conscious rather than
naïvely spontaneous. Two treatments stand out as respectable intellectual replies to Nevin, Dewey, or Gannett: William Sprague's *Lectures
on Revivals of Religion* in 1833, and the pages on this issue in Robert
Baird's *Religion in America.*

Sprague's book is addressed to Americans, whereas Baird's is a lecture to Europeans. Sprague starts, significantly, with the problem of
distinguishing a true revival from a spurious one; he then delivers a
systematic, clinical discourse on the symptoms of authentic experience.
What is astonishing is how little it owes, or even pretends to owe, to
the psychological analyses of Jonathan Edwards or to eighteenth-century authorities. Sprague's every care is devoted to preventing "a gust
of animal passion" from embarrassing a genuine revival. "Instances
have occurred," he severely admonishes, "in which Jehovah, who has
declared himself a God of order, has been professedly worshipped in
scenes of utter confusion; and impiety has been substituted for prayer;
and the wildest reveries of fanaticism have been dealt out, instead of
the sober and awful truths of God's word." Wherefore, without en-
tangling himself in any labyrinth of psychological theory, Sprague
asserts that the best proof of the validity of a revival is the extent to
which, after the excitement has gone by, the fruits of holiness persist
in the community. The "means" should always be characterized by
seriousness, order, simplicity, honesty, affection, at the same time
firmly presenting the fearful doom of sinners. In the process there is as
little need for troubling "awakened sinners" with the complexities of
Protestant theology as with psychological niceties: "Show him, at the
same time, that the secret purposes of God do not in the least infringe

the moral agency of man." As *The Christian Spectator* said in commending Sprague's volume, "The grand result to which revivals are here tending, is the complete moral renovation of the world," which is to be accomplished by elevating "the intellectual, spiritual, and social condition of men."

Robert Baird had to contend with the impression generally prevailing among European Protestants that American revivals were no better than orgies. He was a wise and a just man, and freely admitted that there had been abuses—camp meetings were unduly prolonged, et cetera—but upon the whole, he insisted, American revivals exhibit order, uniformity, sanity. No more ready than Sprague to get involved in psychological disputes, Baird touches lightly upon the widely accepted principles of "common sense," and so, since "the power of fixed and continuous attention in deepening the impressions of any subject is one of the familiar principles of mental science," he claims for the minister only the function of holding the mind of his listeners to the subject. "Here, then, is the great principle of revivals." Remarking that social sympathy within a community helps to make a revival effective, what, he disarmingly asks, could be "more natural"? He denies the widely held European notion that a minister who depends upon revivals rather than upon the state or upon national custom will become the sycophant of his congregation. Emphasizing always that our churches are not official institutions, but living bodies of believers, he can conclude: "In this opinion, I am sure, Christians of all denominations in the United States sincerely and entirely concur."

Certainly the hope of the Revival cut across denominations; the defense again and again insisted that it was an *American* method, perfected there, vindicated there. But unhappily there was not always fundamental agreement among revivalists about the philosophy and methods of the movement. And what, ghastly thought, would be the situation if revivalists disagreed among themselves?

Here Charles Grandison Finney was invaluable. If the Revival was something peculiarly American, he was the most American of them all, in vigor, in mind, in ruthlessness, in passion. If he turned the vast arena of revivalism into internecine strife, brought down upon himself the hostility not so much of Unitarians as of fellow-evangelicals, was he an irresponsible disturber of the peace—a blind Sampson, as some believed, wrecking the temple in a mad fury—or was he, and he above all the rest, the one who most surely executed the essential American impulse of the Revival?

That a great revival should cause divisions within a particular religious communion—that in fact it was virtually bound to do so—had become a commonplace of American experience. Everyone knew that 1740 had shattered the religious uniformity of New England, both in doctrine and in polity, and had for two decades riven the Presbyterian Church of New Jersey and Pennsylvania. In the West, in the wake of Cane Ridge, the Presbyterian Church was again fragmented. The Cumberland Presbytery seceded and became a separate body; Stone led his followers into a "Christian" body which by 1832 joined with a dissident group recruited by Thomas and Alexander Campbell out of disparate Baptist and Methodist elements, and so established the "Disciples of Christ." The Methodist Episcopal Church, as is well known, held together, thanks to its marvelous discipline, its circuit riders, and its frankly Arminian theology. But it is correct to say that all these organizational conflicts, though they make up the substance of denominational histories, were not of great importance in the area of what I term the religious mentality. There, the simple fact of the Revival, under whatever auspices—and indeed often under several auspices at once (as at Cane Ridge)—was central. Whether it produced formal unity or created new churches was of less import than the omnipresence of the Revival. Finney proved to be the greatest radical of the lot simply because he clearly realized this truth and operated upon it.

Almost all revivalists of the period display traits which a "romantic" age recognized as demonic. While Lord Byron was regularly denounced as a corrupter of youth, Lyman Beecher was fascinated by him, recognizing in him an alter ego. Nettleton was perhaps too melancholy a being to play the role, and Nathaniel W. Taylor too professorial; but Timothy Dwight was a man of passion, and the pioneer Westerners—McGready, Cartwright, Stone—were vehement men. The deviationists who emerged out of the movement—one thinks especially of Brigham Young—carried into their heresies the frenetic compulsiveness of the movement. But as compared with Finney, they all seem pallid. This is not necessarily because he possessed (in the phrase of the time) more "animal spirits" than they (Lyman Beecher was a man of tremendous physical vigor), but because all the others, whether in Connecticut or Kentucky, were linked with the eighteenth century, striving to enact anew the Great Awakening of 1740. Finney's pre-eminence lies in his embracing the Revival out of no academic theological training, but fully imbued with the spirit of the nineteenth century. Not for him the charge and countercharge of Beecher against Orville Dewey. The most demonic of the whole fraternity, possessed of the shrewdness that enabled him to win such battles for the Lord as no other could match, Finney among the evangelicals was a Napoleon among his marshals.

The story of his whirlwind deeds across northern New York, in New York City and Philadelphia, and even in Boston, has often been told, but it is still difficult for us to conceive how revolutionary he loomed. He imposed "new measures." Finney "prolonged" his meetings, not only into the small hours of the morning, but for day after day, so that all business was brought to a standstill. More outrageously, he had the unconverted in every town he visited prayed for "by name." He allowed women to pray in public. Above all, he devised "the anxious bench"—so reprehended by John Nevin—a space kept empty in front of the meeting, to which penitents could walk (or stumble) in full view of the society, and there be interrogated, criminals on their own admission, by God's attorney, Charles Grandison Finney, named for a sentimental eighteenth-century hero but employing the most unsentimental of nineteenth-century techniques for cross-examination. Not Thomas Jefferson, or Madison, or Monroe led America out of the eighteenth century. Lyman Beecher was a spiritual grandson of Edwards, as Timothy Dwight was in the flesh; neither of them ever faintly glimpsed the possibility that the battle would not still be fought in inherited terms. So, Beecher attacked Finney's "methods," and made a great show of bringing him to reason. Actually, Beecher did nothing of the sort. The famous New Lebanon Conference, on July 18, 1827, where Beecher and Nettleton attempted to repel the Finney invasion of New England, was, like many later diplomatic arrangements, one in which the rebel seemed submissive, only to continue upon his original course, never again to be challenged. Nettleton withdrew to the seminary in East Windsor, and poor Beecher, magnificent though he was, in so far as he was related to the Revival, for the rest of his life remained a tail to the Finney kite.

For Finney had, as his *Memoirs* reveal, the advantage of having come "out of the woods," and he had undergone the tough training of the law. He was both Natty Bumppo and Judge Jeffrey. His "new measures" were minor tactics: what told upon the populace was his tone. He would not go to Princeton; its graduates "were not ministers that met my ideal of what a minister of Christ should be." Once he was converted, he went to Parson Gale, a graduate of Princeton, who told him he should respect the weighty, sustained theological arguments elaborated by great and good men—greater than he and possibly better. He was amazed to find that the theologian did not interpret the Bible "as I would have understood the same or like passages in a law book," but insisted upon running it through the sieve of preconceived "theory." Should one deal with the Constitution of the United States in this manner—this obviously alien manner? Finney had only one answer: "I had no where to go but directly to the Bible, and to the philosophy or workings of my own mind, as revealed in consciousness."

Consciousness! We shall have more to do with it. It is a magic word in the early Republic. Finney's rejection of academia might have been absurdity without the prestige he invoked by employing this term. Finney the master evangelist would never submit to becoming one of the ministerial fraternity: "I was bred a lawyer. I came forth from a law office to the pulpit, and talked to the people as I would talk to a jury." He wanted decisions, here and now, not in some endless metaphysical realm. He got his decisions, and if the jury were convinced, why question his methods? What is fascinating about him is that he is not a bully, but the advocate at the bar.

Not only folklore but history has exaggerated the momentousness of Beecher's and Nettleton's confrontation with Finney at New Lebanon in July, 1827. Most students know about it from Beecher's so-called *Autobiography* (this was compiled by his children, but there is so much of the old man in it that, like Finney's *Memoirs*, it is a central narrative for American history). What actually happened was that colonial forms of American Protestantism here encountered the nineteenth century. At the time, Beecher and Nettleton were already collecting documents, and magisterially corresponding with each other, preparatory to the publication of a book of *Letters*. In it they proposed to efface the wild man.

Nobody ever stole a march on Finney. At Troy, on March 4, he preached upon the text "can two walk together except they be agreed?" He had it printed well before July 18. Ostensibly, the sermon is a defense of emotion in religion; in design, it is a lawyer's brief, precluding the New Englanders from bringing Jonathan Edwards into court. Finney knew how to cite precedents which the simple might suppose damaging to his client. He utilized "President Edwards" with the same freedom that Mr. Justice Story would employ Lord Ellenborough, and to the complete bewilderment of Nettleton and Beecher.

Finney's basic theorem was that everybody can agree upon intellectual propositions. The difference is that some grasp them with the heart, others with only the mind. Thus at Troy and New Lebanon Finney proposed a disjunction which—though it had long figured in literary metaphor and had been dealt with by Edwards—had acquired a new vitality in romantic literature and in religious exhortation, that of the head versus the heart, of intellect versus emotion. Beecher was perfectly familiar with the verbal distinction; he never could comprehend that at New Lebanon he met a creature prepared to say, in language later used by Herman Melville, "To the dogs with the Head."

"We have reason to believe," said Finney on March 4, "that holy angels and devils apprehend and embrace *intellectually* the same truths, and yet how differently are they affected by them!" The difference between damnation and salvation is not one of doctrinal definition: it consists "in the different manner in which the heart or affections receive these truths, or act in view of them." As he went triumphantly on, Finney insisted that all pleasure and pain, like all sin and holiness, have the seat entirely in the *"heart."* So the heart, not the mind, was the battlefield. Strip a revival of "animal feeling," and the carnal heart will be sure to revolt. And this will make the real distinction, that which Edwards strove in vain to establish, despite his immense piety; for he was crushed under the weight of mind. Since the distinction exists only in the realm of the affections, not in that of intellect and theology, we confront the fact that the two sorts (divided in heart even though united in formal profession) *"cannot* walk together, because they are not agreed: and the more holy and heavenly the saints become in their affections and conduct, the farther apart they will be, until the light of eternity will set them, in feeling and affections, as far asunder as heaven and hell."

It is difficult for us to comprehend how such pronouncements wrung the heart of Asahel Nettleton, confused Lyman Beecher, and scandalized Professor Taylor. Finney seemed wantonly to throw away everything that the students of Jonathan Edwards had been patiently gathering together, the success of which endeavor they could prove by their decorous conduct of the Second Awakening in Connecticut. Finney damned them as ritualists and intellectuals. To push the dagger home to aroused sinners, Finney would say in his *Lectures,* "requires nerve." Without nerve enough to bring them to the point of instant and absolute submission, "How unfit is such a man to be trusted in a case like this?" Beecher thought himself man enough for the job, and repeatedly proved that he could be, but most of New England Congregationalism, including Nettleton, withered under the blast.

However, in 1827 Beecher and Nettleton put up the best fight they could by publishing their *Letters.* Much in their book has to do only with the rivalry of New England against New York (then conceived of as the "West"); all this is tedious and irrelevant. The importance lies in its revelation of the basic, philosophical divergences about the Revival: in thus proposing a disunity in the phenomenon considered both by friends and by foes the distinctively American achievement—

by first protesting, and then effectively underscoring, the controversy within the ranks of the sanctified—these *Letters* prefigure the future course of intellect in America in a way that bewildered Nettleton and Beecher never consciously intended.

Nettleton, we suppose, was endeavoring to defend New England by all the lights given him, namely those supplied by Jonathan Edwards. One may well speculate whether Mr. Edwards would have acknowledged that either Nettleton or Finney really grasped his delicate integration of mind and emotion. But Nettleton went after Finney's thesis in the March 4 sermon with what he thought was Edwardsean logic: if some, he protested, having equal comprehension of the truth, respond more emotionally than others, then "they cannot walk together." "On Brother Finney's principles it is *impossible* to keep the unity of the spirit in the bond of peace." The fatal difficulty with Finney, insisted the *Letters,* is that "he uses *feeling* and *heart* as synonymous terms." This was a startling, and might have been a devastating charge. But suppose Finney is right? Was there anything in the intellectual atmosphere of the early nineteenth century (let us forget Mr. Edwards) which would lead any clear-thinking man to make a distinction between "feeling" and "heart"? Obviously, the old discrimination, whether it ever had been valid, was outmoded. There was indeed still a viable controversy as to whether in the glow and warmth of the revival "nothing more is meant than mere animal feeling, of the martial kind, applied to the subject of religion." Nettleton asked the question. Very early on, and more and more frequently as time went on, Finney perfected, in his *Memoirs,* the all-powerful answer to such objections, even as metaphysical ones as those of Nettleton: "the results justify my methods."

5.

SOLITUDE AND SOCIETY

It is a commentary on the period that the general public were not hugely aroused by arguments between revivalists and antirevivalists, but that they were endlessly occupied with arguments among revivalists about the true nature of the phenomenon and how it should be conducted. In the 1820's the mass of this literature became a discussion of Charles Grandison Finney.

As we have seen, the flow of condemnation emanating from the theologians of Princeton Seminary, learned and powerful though they were, had not the slightest effect on Finney. By the time Alexander Blaikie's *The Philosophy of Sectarianism*, which contained the substance of their position, was published in 1855, Finney had become a national institution. In his volume, Blaikie went back to Finney's incendiary sermon of 1827, and once again "proved" that since two cannot walk together except they be agreed, the only way to get agreement is not to trust any unanimity of the heart but to build upon a solid, factual, systematic creed. Through the use of any other means, the sensibilities of men are aroused to imaginary visions of glory which are "too often mistaken for the renewing of the Holy Ghost."

Leaders of the Awakening in Connecticut, which still, after its local standards, was progressing in the 1820's, were in a more difficult position, for they passionately believed in the Revival and for years had argued that it should not be questioned simply because in it "natural means" were used. In 1833 Calvin Colton confidently argued that while formerly, indeed, a revival was thought to be a community visitation, "unexpected, and apparently unasked," we are now assured that it is a divine blessing "upon measures concerted and executed by man, where the instruments are obvious." So the only objection New Englanders could make to Finney's triumphs was that his methods were vulgar. They were, then, in the difficult position of having to trot out against him the very argument Unitarians had advanced against themselves. Edward Griffin had turned from the law to preaching when he had been converted back in the 1790's, but by 1832 he was troubled by the news from York State. Truth, he would now declare, has to do with reason and conscience, whereas the "tactics" employed in those parts arouse only imagination and passion and so inevitably lead to a stupid reliance on forms: "The frequent repetition of these imposing ceremonies will destroy their effect, and leave us with forms instead of feelings." Lyman Beecher was even more the equivocator. At New Lebanon he had told Finney, as he loved to retell the story, that if Finney tried to invade New England, "as the Lord liveth, I'll meet you at the state line, and call out all the artillerymen, and fight every inch of the way to Boston, and then I'll fight you there." But Beecher's enmity was mainly envy; Finney did come to Boston in 1831, not over Beecher's dead body, but at Beecher's invitation!

The Spirit of the Pilgrims in this year strove to be judicious about Finney, to jump to no rash conclusions. We must remember, it cautioned, that the Holy Spirit "operates *through the medium of our faculties,* and *in conformity with the established laws of the human mind.*" So whatever the theoretical objections may be against protracted meetings, for instance, experience has shown them to be useful, which is not surprising, for these long observances "restrain and hold in check, for a time at least, that overflowing tide of worldliness, by which serious impressions ordinarily are swept away." A great many New Englanders or New England–trained ministers found such talk confusing. In England in 1834 Calvin Colton valiantly defended the American revival system before all sorts of critics, but when he returned in 1836 to a Protestantism dominated by Finney, the experience so shocked him that he became an Episcopalian and took orders! He had been defending in England "revivals of the original type," where pastors were sober guides for inquiring minds, but now, he found, the churches had surrendered to "extravagant and disastrous measures." Like Fenimore Cooper, he felt that a revolution had taken place in the country during his absence. As Cooper fulminated against the degradation of democracy in *Home As Found,* Colton arraigned the evangelical churches in *Thoughts on the Religious State of the Country* for having degenerated into a mob. There was no question for Cooper as to who was primarily to blame for the debacle—Andrew Jackson. There was equally no difficulty for Calvin Colton to name his villain—Charles Finney.

According to Colton, the Revival had got so far out of hand that the clergy were subservient to their congregations, that ministers were "run over and trampled under foot by fanaticism." Churches had become plague spots of "meddling, tattling, slander, scandal" (we remember Cooper's description of sanctimoniousness in *Home As Found*). Serious charges these; they could not be laughed away as could those of Cooper, because they came not from a disgruntled landlord who felt that the democracy no longer treated him with proper deference; these accusations came from the heart of the church, and from one who had been a promoter of revivals. If a major, though tacit, premise of the revival had always been that in the mass phenomenon of revival disparate peoples and competing churches might find a social cohesion which could dispense with such corrupt European institutions as an Established Church or an ecclesiastical levy, then the threat of the splintering, the shattering, of the movement was a serious concern for the very life of the Republic. Fears increased as the age seemed to veer more and more toward dangerous reform movements, toward radical ideas. It was a telling, a dreadful blow, when the Reverend Richard W. Dickinson declared in 1839: "No man can surrender his judgment to the wisdom of our modern expedients for facilitating the conversion of the world, without exhibiting in the pulpit . . . the ultraism of an Agent, the fanaticism of a Revivalist, or the imbecile conscientiousness, coupled with the pride and dogmatism of a Reformer."

So in the 1820's and 1830's much depended, for the health and future development of the Revival, upon what sort of man Finney was, and on what vision of the nation he possessed. Again the analogy with Jackson forces itself upon us. With it comes an urgent reflection: a revival in Connecticut, under the sober control of settled pastors, could suit with a Federalist temper in politics, could bridge the transition to the Whig Party. But the kind of revival stimulated by Finney in upstate New York, though it refrained from politics and was not necessarily confined to Democrats, was a mass uprising, a release of energy, a sweep of the people which made it an expression of that energy we call Jacksonian America.

On the subject of the Old School Calvinism and of Princeton Seminary, Finney is brash, comic, the spokesman for something we should not ticket anti-intellectualism, but which is a form of revolt against intellect. Finney was licensed by a presbytery in 1823; upon being asked whether he subscribed to the Westminster Confession, he said he had never read it. We may doubt that ever in his life he really did read it.

Finney began with a realization that the complexities of Protestant theology—Lutheran or Calvinist—had no relation to the actualities of American life. This is not to say that his was a variant of "pietistic" revolt against abstractions, as we might describe the Quaker movement, or Fénelon, or the theology of Halle. Indeed, crudely verbalized as his thinking was, he is at the opposite pole from Schleiermacher. To Finney the mighty edifices of Protestant theology seemed as baroque as the cathedrals of France to Gibbon: the theologians "often seemed to me to state one thing and prove another, and frequently fell short of logically proving anything." While he would say, in what seems the spirit of pietism, that without the direct teachings of the Holy Spirit, a man never makes progress in preaching the Gospel, he protested that experience is all, and then qualified his assertion by adding, it is "a matter of consciousness." What made Finney the primary power in American revivalism was his ability to make this large, reiterated assumption as to what constitutes "consciousness," and thereafter never to descend into metaphysical speculation about his meanings. In the name of it, he could defy Princeton, and thus put aside, with a single gesture, the weight of historical theology.

Always he professed, and showed, that he was no enemy to education; he separated himself from Pietism by never declaring war on systematic theology, and indeed eventually tried his hand at it himself.

What he attacked was the effeminacy of seminary graduates. "Young men are shut up in their schools, confined to books and shut out from intercourse with the common people, or contact with the common mind." His particular target was Princeton, but professors at Mercersburg, Yale, Andover, or Bangor could take his blasts as directed at them (the Harvard Divinity School was, of course, so far beneath his contempt that he hardly bothered to include it):

Those fathers who have the training of our young ministers are good men, but they are ancient men, men of another age and stamp, from what is needed in these days of excitement, when the church and world are rising to new thought and action. . . . Some of them are getting back toward second childhood, and ought to resign, and give place to younger men, who are not rendered physically incapable by age, of keeping pace with the onward movements of the church.

How could those who never mingled with the church train young men for "the field"? It was a shame and a disgrace that professors in their studies should write letters "advisory, or dictatorial" to those in the heat of battle.

Hence it is an essential aspect of the revolution Finney wrought that he provided it with a rhetoric. Seminaries teach elegance, but as for real eloquence—"that gushing, impressive, and persuasive oratory, that naturally flows from an educated man whose soul is on fire with his subject, and who is free to pour out his heart to a waiting and earnest people"—of this they learn nothing. Lyman Beecher had a colloquial vein, the tang of Connecticut meadows, but he had been taught by Timothy Dwight, and seldom did his pulpit utterances convey (as his children lamented) the raciness of his conversation. Even Beecher could not rock an audience with such irony as, for instance, Finney's characterization of seminary-produced prayers:

Some pray out a whole system of divinity. Some preach, some exhort the people, till every body wishes they would stop, and God wishes so too, undoubtedly.

While Finney preferred the sermons of "formerly ignorant" Methodists or earnest Baptists to those of learned theologians, he himself strove, with remarkably good taste, to avoid vulgarity. He was nothing of a ranter or a play-actor. He was superbly conscious of his audience: "I tried also to use such language as they would understand. . . . I sought to express all my ideas in few words, and in words that were in common use." His ideal of "gushing" oratory was what would come from an intense but "educated" man. When such preachers are in earnest, "Their language is in point, direct and simple. Their sentences are short, cogent, powerful. The appeal is made directly for action; and hence all such discourses take effect." In an age that luxuriated in the rotund paragraphs of Daniel Webster, or in the lush sentimentality of gift-book prose, Finney's simplicity of style stands out. In this respect he is a transmitter of the Puritan doctrine of the "plain style," and a prophet of the revolt against the romantic.

Finney's sense of style is central to his whole conception of his mission; over and over he revealed that his inspiration was the courtroom. Suppose, he would say, I go into court to argue a case and my witnesses contradict me? Just so, a preacher speaking before a cold, stolid congregation meets contradiction from those who ought to be his witnesses. Or, Finney would vary the figure, the church is a jury: "A minister ought to do as a lawyer does when he wants to make a jury understand him perfectly. He uses a style perfectly colloquial. This lofty, swelling style will do no good." Finney scorned preaching from notes, insisted on the importance of repetition, and conceived every sermon as an occasion to "anticipate the objections of a sinner, and answer them." When accused of fanaticism or Arminianism, he never stooped to argue: he just said "Nonsense," and pressed his case the harder. "It is enough to make humanity weep, to see the fog and darkness, that have been thrown around the plain directions of the gospel, till many generations have been emptied into hell."

In the large perspective of history, Finney may seem a crude native variant of the early nineteenth-century revolt against the Enlightenment, exalting feeling and imagination above reasoning and demonstration. Actually he felt that he was preserving the intellect—"consciousness"—from corruptions that had been foisted upon it during the Protestant centuries by the schemes of emotional theologians. Curiously enough, his enemies at Princeton, whose massive tomes are to us the most unreadable of systematic logicalities, accused him of being the cold logician! The heart of his theology was his hatred for any form of the Protestant notion that Christian obedience is in any way "imputed" to believers, that without it and before it they are enslaved in the toils of inability. He was determined to put upon the unconverted the burden of responsibility, and brooked no opposition from metaphysicians. Early in the crusade a "doctor of divinity" told Finney that he felt more like weeping over sinners than blaming them: "I replied to him that I did not wonder, if he believed they had a sinful nature, and that sin was entailed upon them, and they could not help it." The message of Finney was wholly American: everybody *can* help it.

His methods, his style, his ideas all spring from this single conviction. His contention was that the historic doctrines of Protestant Christianity had been so erroneously translated into communal behavior that they were bound, in the actual human situation, to defeat their avowed aims. Ministers pray for a revival, beseeching God to pour down upon them His Spirit; the people try, but nothing happens —to Finney the obvious consequence. Theologians explain the absolute necessity for a radical change of heart through the Holy Ghost— but no hearts are changed. The clergy teach troubled souls that while they are praying for grace, they are resisting Christ—and consequently, with the best will in the world, they go on resisting. The churches joyfully hail those who are "under conviction," with the result that these misguided spirits settle down with a false hope and become petrified in self-righteousness. Theologians are wary about attempting to promote revivals by human means; they maintain that God will convert sinners in His own time. Not surprisingly, the time never comes. They exhort the people to persevere: the people persevere—in doing just what they have already been doing! Indeed, Finney's chapter on "False Comforts for Sinners" is so complete an uprooting of the historic conceptions of American Protestantism, so profound a reading of new meanings into the age of the Revival, that it is in effect a declaration of evangelical independence.

The root of the error in all the Protestant groups, said Finney (he included the "Arminian" Methodists), was not that they had yielded to infidelity or rationalism, but that they adhered to the dogma that, human nature being sinful in itself, sinners are entirely unable to become Christians, despite all desire, all sincere effort. Finney never denied predestination, never questioned original sin: he simply stood up and said, over and over, "all men may be saved if they will." All juries can decide a case if they understand it and have the will. Or, as he put it in one brief sentence: "Don't wait for feeling, DO IT."

There is, however, one sociological factor which must be connected with this extreme activism. The upstate New York in which Finney received his revelation and acquired his techniques was sparsely settled. In 1831 Tocqueville and Beaumont crossed it, reveling in their first encounter with the "wilderness." Yet they confessed their astonishment that whenever they came to a settlement, after traversing miles of virgin forest, they found a remarkable civilization. First of all there was the New England impress upon the land, but there was also a special character to the migration into York State. If we had only Cooper's *Home As Found* to judge from, we should say that the beautiful and sedate colonial order was being overwhelmed by a flood of riffraff. There were no doubt, especially after the Erie Canal was opened, rough and dissolute persons in the area, but the towns in which Finney won his victories were not hard-scrabble frontier outposts. One might almost call them "middle class," except that there was hardly enough of a class below them to count, and there was no class at all above them. Violent as Finney's revival may have seemed to Connecticut's Nettleton, in sober fact it was predominantly a movement among reputable citizens. In this respect, it was different from the tumultuous chaos with which Peter Cartwright had to contend in Illinois. The Finney pattern of the Revival, in time, came to supersede that of Cane Ridge even in Illinois and Kentucky, and thus to lend confirmation to the claim of "respectability" that had long been insisted upon even in the Kentucky mountains.

Finney was early told that he would never reach "educated" persons. He proudly relates, and insists upon it, that even from the beginning, "Judges, and lawyers, and educated men were converted by scores." At New Lebanon and for the rest of his life, he contended that his meetings were not crude orgies; they were conducted among "an intelligent, cultivated people." He was most successful "among the higher classes of society." He saw nothing surprising in his success with lawyers: "As a general thing, they take a more intelligent view of the whole plan of salvation, than any other class of men to whom I have preached." The legend in America had been that "professional men" were infidels at heart; but the fact was that ministers had "not grappled with mind, and *reasoned* so as to make that class of minds see the truth." He did admit that he was least successful in Boston, because there the orthodox, constantly exposed to the criticism of Unitarians, had become "over-cautious"; but even in Boston he could convert a young lady of manifest intelligence and education. "I could perceive that she belonged to cultivated society."

These phrases betray what the Revival aspired to. If we find there is everywhere a search for community, there is also at the heart of it a resolution to escape from the trammels of "inability." Finney proved, majestically, that these two desires need not involve an open rejection of Protestantism's basic persuasion about the sinfulness of man and the need for supernatural regeneration. By his oratory and his example, he brought the communities together and yet placed upon individuals responsibility for their own actions. He liberated and he invigorated. It would be false to say that in the second of his injunctions he was advocating what modern economic theory terms "individualism." With that he was not concerned. He was, rather, demonstrating a method by which all might participate in the mystery of communion, even to self-abasement before the eyes of the fellowship. Yet each person, out of his own resources and courage, might triumph because he achieved the progress to the anxious seat for and by himself.

CHAPTER TWO

Unity through Diversity

The government of God is the only government which will hold society, against depravity within and temptation without; and this it must do by the force of its own law written upon the heart. This is that unity of the Spirit and that bond of peace which alone can perpetuate national purity and tranquility—that law of universal and impartial love by which alone nations can be kept back from ruin. There is no safety for republics but in self-government, under the influence of a holy heart, swayed by the government of God.

— *The Spirit of the Pilgrims*, 1831

1.

SEPARATION OF CHURCH AND STATE

It was clear from the beginning of the American Revolution that the achievement of national independence would confirm the long colonial struggle for separation of church and state. The Virginia Ordinance of 1785 was revered by all churches as the codification of the victory and the First Amendment aroused no opposition. In Connecticut an established order was maintained until 1818, and in Massachusetts until 1833, but these were vestigial remains and eventually their abolition was greeted with full satisfaction by all parties.

A fact of great importance in the religious mentality of the early Republic is that nobody regarded this principle as having been violently or suddenly promulgated by the Revolution itself. Every denomination saw it as the logical culmination of native experience. American apologists were particularly annoyed by European notions that it had been embraced in a "revolutionary spirit." After his ten years in America, Philip Schaff returned to Germany to explain that the process had been one of natural growth. "Christianity proceeds in an altogether conservative spirit and with the tenderest regard for all existing institutions." Perhaps other groups might not put quite so much stress as Schaff upon the adjective "conservative," but there were few in Jacksonian America who saluted the First Amendment as a "radical" measure.

Nor would the religious allow Thomas Jefferson the credit he took unto himself. Jefferson may have boasted that his Ordinance reduced Christianity to the level of Mohammedanism or Hinduism, a bland pronouncement which "the arch-infidel" may well have uttered with a chuckle; but, insisted Robert Baird, the act itself "contains nothing to which a friend of full and equal liberty of conscience would perhaps object." As proof Baird quoted the act, with its preamble, "Whereas Almighty God hath created the mind free. . . ." Schaff was not convinced that separation was the perfect or final solution, but he much preferred the American way "to the territorial system and a police guardianship of the church." America proposed no such civil equality of atheism with Christianity as some members of the Frankfort Parliament advocated in 1848; for, as Justice Story explained in 1833, the object of the First Amendment is not to countenance or advance infidelity, but simply "to exclude all rivalry among Christian sects, and to prevent any national ecclesiastical establishment, which should give to a hierarchy the exclusive patronage of the national government." Though there were many in the country who disliked the tenor of Story's thinking, there was still universal agreement with his legalistic premise that the rights of conscience are beyond the just reach of any human power, and cannot "be encroached upon by human authority without a criminal disobedience of the precepts of natural as well as of revealed religion." The evangelical crusade to make and keep America Christian had to be conducted upon this explicit premise.

Those European theologians who listened skeptically to Schaff were invincibly persuaded that a state which officially declared itself neutral on ecclesiastical policy was *ipso facto* infidel, or at least non-Christian. Schaff and Baird stoutly fought this delusion. The Constitution, Baird patiently recounted, was intended for a people already Christian, and the fact that its authors enunciated nothing positive on the subject speaks "more loudly than if they had expressed themselves in the most solemn formulas on the existence of the Deity and the truth of Christianity." Such protestations, however, bespeak an inner uneasiness. In this period begins that silent conspiracy of ignoring the deistic propensities of the Founders and the legendary version of Washington's pietism. Baird admitted that he did regret that the Constitution had not specifically mentioned God and Christ; there were sporadic movements to get up a Christian amendment, but the more astute of the evangelicals gradually learned that the wisest policy, in terms of self-interest, was to leave well enough alone.

If they needed time to learn this lesson, the Jacksonian regime hastened their education. In the 1790's, while the churches were girding for the fight against French atheism, they could assume that the federal government was on their side because both Washington and Adams, following the example of the Continental Congress during the war, proclaimed days of thanksgiving or of fasting on emergent occasions, thus tacitly implying that the regime was sensible of standing in a Christian posture. But the need for serious thought as to just where they stood was thrust upon the pious in 1802 when President Jefferson, taking advantage of an awkward address from the Danbury Baptist Association (which minority in Connecticut was balking at being obliged to observe fasts appointed by the still-standing order), refused any longer to designate such holy festivals. In a much-quoted letter of 1808 he said that the federal government was strictly interdicted from meddling with religious institutions, and even to "recommend" a fast would be to assume religious authority. Many ministers might growl, but they were deterred from vehemence by the fact that a large number of the most devoted people (such as these same Connecticut Baptists) were grateful for Jefferson's restraint. Despite his sharing Jefferson's scruples, Madison did appoint a day of humiliation in 1812, but the effect was blunted because the Federalists denounced it as a ruse to force their support of his foreign policy. Monroe genially observed the custom, but in 1832 Henry Clay, in a misguided effort to embarrass Jackson, forced the issue to the floor of the Senate, and so compelled the conscience of the country to recognize, once and for all, that the state really was separated from all the churches.

In June of that year news of a cholera epidemic in Europe reached America, and fears that it would spread across the Atlantic amounted to panic. Revivalists, of course, improved the occasion, but the Synod of the Dutch Reformed Church requested Jackson to appoint a day of national humiliation, in the ancient manner. Jackson restated Jefferson's stand: he believed in the efficacy of prayer, but could not appoint such a day without disturbing "the security which religion now enjoys in this country in its complete separation from the political concerns of the General Government." Clay thought he saw his chance, and so introduced a resolution that Congress call upon the President to act. Betraying that this was a purely political, not to say cynical, maneuver, Clay confessed that he was not a church member, but that even so he had "a profound respect for christianity, the reli-

gion of my fathers, and for its rites, its usages, and its observances."
Carefully he guarded against seeming to violate the canons of Justice
Story by insisting that the Presidential recommendation "would be
obligatory upon none," that it would be grateful "to all pious and
moral men, whether members of religious communities or not."

Most Whigs supported Clay. Theodore Frelinghuysen recalled Madison's proclamation of 1812—an ineffectual gambit, since he had at
that time, along with his fellow-Federalists, sneered at Madison's
trickery. The Democrats, many of whom *were* church members,
affirmed the principles of Jackson's letter. Tazewell of Virginia flatly
declared that Congress has no power to make any resolutions concerning religious matters, and Davis of South Carolina effectively torpedoed the proposal by calling the custom of official fasts something
"derived from our English ancestors." Jackson was preparing to veto
the resolution, but the end came when so good a Whig, and also an ex-
Federalist, as Verplanck agreed with the Democrats (and with Story)
that pollution and degradation must be the result "of every attempt to
draw religion from her seat in the hearts and consciences of men, and
to associate her with power, or parade her before the world."

Jackson was at the same time arousing cries of anguish by insisting
that the mails be carried on Sundays. Whigs made what propaganda
they could by denouncing his administration as infidel, and in 1838
Frelinghuysen (he was generally supposed the author) painted pictures of ruin in *An Inquiry into the Moral and Religious Character of
the American Government* by solemnly asserting, "Without religion,
law ceases to be law, for it has no bond, and cannot hold society
together." There can be no doubt that many of the more articulate
Whig clergy denounced Jackson, even from their pulpits, and demanded that orthodox Christianity regulate legislation, virtually going
so far as to make a stand for some direct union, if not of church and
state, then of piety and politics.

But it is a mistake to suppose that all revivalists, or even a majority
of them, were opposed to Jackson, or that they were deceived by Whig
propaganda into misinterpreting the Jacksonian attitude toward the
fast. There was a vital thrust in the very heart of revivalism which
made it welcome the freedom to organize its own days of penance
within localities where the "work" was alive. Furthermore, a great
many "conservatives," of Verplanck's complexion, were satisfied to let
things be. The "Old School" of Princeton Presbyterianism positively
rejoiced in 1832 at being able to give up its "Utopian ideas" of a
great national church with perfect consistency of character. "Neither
the state of the country nor the temper of the age will admit of it.

Theological peculiarities, and sectional feeling call for separate institutions." And Philip Schaff, who out of his European experience
knew more thoroughly than his American colleagues what it was to be
really "conservative," startled his Prussian audience by informing
them that, with the blessings of separation of powers and full religious
liberty, there were two hundred and fifty well-attended churches,
"some of them quite costly and splendid," in New York, for a population of six hundred thousand, whereas in Berlin, a city of four
hundred and fifty thousand, there were only forty. He could safely,
and proudly, assert, "The United States are by far the most religious
and Christian country in the world; and that, just because religion is
there most free." Though he disapproved of revivalism, yet he had no
fears about freedom. No one of the present confessions can ever become exclusively dominant in America, he said, "but rather . . . out
of the mutual conflict of all something wholly new will gradually
arise." In this he spoke the evangelical hope—nay, the expectation—
which was a mainspring of the Revival. In 1800 the churches may have
thought that all their concern lay in repelling deism and saving souls,
but bit by bit, and by the 1830's entirely, they learned that they were
vindicating a radical thesis unprecedented in the history of Christendom: they were proving that a wild diversity of churches within a
single society could survive and prosper.

2.

THE VOLUNTARY PRINCIPLE

It is impossible to designate the precise moment at which the phrase
"voluntary principle" became the watchword of the American ecclesiastical system. Long before the reality received a theoretical benediction, various descriptive terms, more or less accurate, were employed,
but this conceptualization, when it did come, constitutes a major event
in the life of the American mind.

In 1788 Edward Livingston (of the Dutch Reformed) announced
that all the churches in America had in origin been appendages of
national churches in Europe, but "they now become national
Churches themselves in this new Empire." Here was truly a staggering
realization. Under the colonial arrangement, while the denominations
lived side by side, they thought of themselves, even in New England, as
emissaries of Europe. Suddenly these provincial bodies had, overnight,
to essay the majesty of maturity. The implications were bewildering,

40

their meaning undecipherable, and first responses to the challenge were awkward and fumbling. But by the 1820's, such revivalists as were inclined to speculation had come to at least two formulations: competition among the churches is healthy, and diversity encourages rather than hinders revivals. These, they could quickly perceive, were special American insights.

Would the churches be better off, asked George C. Cookman, bathed in a silent neutrality of quiescence? Not at all: in a motionless reservoir the waters of life stagnate. "Let them rather run and encounter the winds of opposition and the rocks of controversy, and they will clear, and purify, and sparkle." *The Christian Spectator* agreed, adding that these "peculiarities" of American society give every opportunity for "that success of the gospel which we call a revival of religion." The very fact that we have no religion defined by law means we must trust to one dwelling in the hearts of individuals.

Philip Schaff remembered enough of his European training to deplore the "sect system" in the abstract, because it contradicts that dogma of the unity of the church which theologians of the warring faiths had always put at the head of their Confessions. But when he descended from traditional concepts to the facts, he had to tell the still-incredulous Germans that the "voluntary principle, as it is called," promoted religious work out of the free-will offerings of the people. Maybe not always from the purest motives—sometimes only from a sense of honor or for selfish by-ends: "yet always from free impulses, without any outward coercion." Neither the Reformation nor the Medieval church had ever for a moment supposed this possible, and the minority sects of Europe had never had a chance to try it.

To Robert Baird, however, we must turn for the finest philosophical statement of the principle. Not that all or many of the revival leaders were capable of rising to the level of his analysis; and furthermore, Baird was fully conscious of the ferocity with which the churches often fought each other. Still, he propounded the principle to Europe as "the great alternative." Baird was so completely American that he hardly knew the existence of Schaff's scruples. "Upon what, then, must Religion rely? Only, under God, upon the efforts of its friends." While he tried to argue with Europe that success of the principle did not depend upon peculiar American conditions, he nevertheless linked it with the energy, self-reliance, of emigrants who have left the luxuries of civilization "for a life in the woods, amid wild beasts . . . pestilential marshes, and privations innumerable." Such a people learn to disregard trifling difficulties—such as state churches. So separation of church and state is not simply a negative device, it is a way of enabling religion to stand upon its own positive basis. It provides a chance, as Baird is certain no Old World society does, for the churches to act "*spontaneously,* if the word may be allowed." The key to his argument is this repeated word. The respect public men show to religion is the more interesting "as it can only flow from the spontaneous feelings of the heart." If Baird ever suspected that some public men put on a pious habit to gain votes, he lived on too lofty a plane to notice them. His discourse is the more important for the chronicler of the mind, though it may be less for the social or denominational historian, because it points toward the dynamic conception of religion which, not often so verbalized, had in fact arisen out of the Second Great Awakening. The voluntary principle is fluid, undogmatic, ever resourceful. It is a "vast versatility," a sort of evangelical Jack-of-all-trades. It extends itself in every direction, adapting itself to every circumstance, and so "acts wherever the Gospel is to be preached, wherever vice is to be attacked, and wherever suffering humanity is to be relieved."

It is hardly surprising that once the phrase "voluntary principle" achieved the dignity of such formulation, those who still attacked it were also those groups hostile to the Revival. Unitarians, for instance, said that full acceptance of it in theory made the minister entirely dependent upon the whim of his people, made them slaves of the vulgar. Instead of giving Europe a lesson, argued *The Christian Examiner,* the likelihood is we show "that the 'Voluntary System,' so called, as applied to the support of Religious Institutions, is a miserable failure." But Schaff, though he also condemned revivalism, was honest enough to deny that the Unitarian charge was valid. Americans expect a minister to do his duty, and so "they most esteem that one who fearlessly and impartially declares the whole counsel of God, and presents the depravity of man and the threatenings of the Divine Word as faithfully as he does the comforting promises." Isabella Bishop, as late as 1859, was astonished to find how little the ministers were intimidated, "as some persons in England suppose," by the rich and influential in their congregations. Surely in England she never had heard a preacher denounce the sins of every class and profession "and of professing Christians" with such boldness and plainness as in America.

The ecclesiastical historian may in rebuttal cite innumerable instances of acrimonious controversy between ministers and their people, of pastors ignominiously dismissed, or of secessions of those who despised this or that preacher. On the other hand, a careful checking of all the record might show these to be, however numerous, still exceptions. For our purposes, what is essential is that the populations making up the churches of the Revival—which is to say the majority of American Protestants—firmly believed that in the principle of voluntarism (not bothering their heads about the metaphysical subtleties of theological voluntarism) they had solved the historic dilemma of the Christian past. They had neither submitted the church to the civil authority nor called upon it to resist magistrates in the name of the Spirit. The whole problem was simply dissipated. And behold the magnificent result! Not only was the state relieved forever of the terrible duty of suppressing heresy and subduing dissent, but the churches so prospered that there was virtually no real heresy in the country, and dissent only strengthened Truth. And out of this dialectic, too complex for any mind to have devised in advance of the actual experience, through which they could have been led only by the hand of providence, they had found the soul of the nation. In this land beyond any other, modestly asserted Alpheus Packard in 1856, man recognizes a divine right, not for others to lord it over his conscience, but, without interfering with civil or religious liberty, to pay due reverence to divine ordinances and to exert freely his personal effort. What other, then, could be the lesson, but that "A peculiar principle, an essential feature of our religious institutions, the voluntary principle as it is termed, has tended, unquestionably, to foster the spirit of nationality."

3.

THE CONCORDANCE OF DISSENT

That other foe of the Revival, on the broad battlefield of the nation much more formidable than Boston's Unitarianism, was the Old School Presbyterianism, whose fortress was Princeton but whose armies marched with the frontier. It was not particularly opposed to the voluntary principle in the abstract, because it was confident that through synods and the General Assembly it could regiment its soldiers. While accepting as fully as the other groups separation of church and state—the General Assembly of 1789 had immediately revised the Westminster Confession so as to change the article on the Civil Magistrate to read that no preference should be shown any denomination—it still abhorred the very conception of "sectarianism." Like the Mercersburg Reformed, Presbyterianism was so rooted in the theology of the Reformation that it could not easily give up in theory, though it might in practice, its inherited ideal of THE Church. To accommodate to political reality was one thing; to confess apostasy was something else again. The schism of the Cumberland Presbytery in 1810, as a consequence of the Awakening, and the defection of Barton Stone's "Christians," eventually in 1832 to join with the Campbells' Disciples of Christ, further exacerbated Princeton's detestation of this baneful consequence of the voluntary principle.

By 1822 the orthodox Presbyterians were crying aloud that the American state of things was contrary to both the nature and precepts of Christianity, that it was a want of religion. "How different, in all probability, would be the result of spreading the gospel, if the energies and capabilities of Christendom were directed by one approved denomination, and concentrated in one grand system of operations!" But by 1832, as we have seen, Princeton accepted the inevitable and acknowledged that the hope of a national church in America was vain. It was the Seminary's opinion in that same surrender "that denominational lines are becoming more distinct, and sectarian divisions wider, notwithstanding all the cry of catholicism and union."

Yet the dream would not die, and it died harder at Andover Seminary than even at Princeton. In 1836 Leonard Woods looked out upon what seemed to him pandemonium, but he would not despair. God *must* be preparing a foundation. For there is in man a social instinct; he seeks community with another even in speculative beliefs. How much more, then, are feeling and emotions urgent in their demand for society? "The idea of *national churches* seems thus to be deeply founded in the very nature of religious development." If left to its own devices, Christian piety would inevitably lead "to the formation of Christian communities, at least as extensive as the civil bodies with which they are connected." Soaring into rapture, Woods conjectured that once there were everywhere established Christian governments, there might then follow a "general relationship."

We may find it implausible that such extravagances survived into Jacksonian America. In a sense, they are yardsticks to measure actuality, but in another they are more important as furnishing a clue to what men like Baird (who was a Presbyterian and had studied at Princeton) were after as, embracing enthusiastically the voluntary principle, they sought to make it a mechanism not of fragmentation but of national cohesion. That superlogical Presbyterian John C. Calhoun, fully concurring in Princeton's premise, drew the obvious conclusion that the disruption of churches between North and South showed that the people of the United States were incapable of thinking nationally. But the revivalists had another hope, another expectation, which, could they but make the populace comprehend it, would not only save the nation but bring the jarring sects into so magnificent a harmony as to render the problem of sectarianism as meaningless as that of a national church.

For again and again, in the full tide of a revival, sectarian differences *were* submerged. Cane Ridge was the mighty symbol of concordance, always to be cited as the model. There Presbyterians, Methodists, Baptists mingled as one Christian people, and fell in windrows before whichever sort of preacher could slay them. All groups were alike caught up in the Connecticut revival, and in 1818 (as disestablishment was being legislated), a Methodist magazine exulted in the united exertions which furnished in that state "a pleasing prospect of the extensive triumph of evangelical truth." But as the exemplar of interdenominational activity, Finney in his upstate revivals was supreme. In his protracted sessions, he mobilized all the clergy in the vicinity, and they participated without regard to their affiliation. It is indeed a fact that after his revivals subsided there were undignified struggles among the churches to garner the crop of converts, and Princeton might shake its gory locks at these. But Finney was above and beyond sectarianism (he did not regard Universalism as a sect, merely a dodge to escape facing facts), and for several decades the great camp meetings of the West reachieved, or almost reachieved, the comprehensiveness of Cane Ridge. Two Welsh Congregationalists who visited the churches in 1836 reported their admiration for the extraordinary unity of the revival movement. As compared with the compartmentalization of British religious life, America was an unbelievable exhibition of a "common footing."

If the evangelicals of America needed any further tuition beyond the co-operative Revival toward realizing how much they had in common, they received it with a rude jolt when in 1821, as a result (they assumed) of shrewd Massachusetts politicking, Jared Sparks, a Unitarian, was elected chaplain of the House of Representatives. He did not last more than a year, but that was long enough to let the outcry from the orthodox reach the pitch, according to a Unitarian magazine, of denouncing "an omen of the greatest national calamity." Ominously, the evangelicals united from every quarter of the union to confess that nobody doubted the moral character of Jared Sparks, and all admired his literary attainments, but "if his faith be wrong, all is wrong." In the over-all history of religious thought in America, Unitarianism looms large because so many of its spokesmen, like Sparks and Channing, were men of irreproachable integrity and of a literacy

45

beyond even that of a Baird. But what is seldom appreciated is the extent to which Unitarianism, by its very snobbishness, even when the masses were luxuriating in its national poets, such as Longfellow and Holmes, was an instrument for bringing the large denominations into an astonishing degree of collaboration.

Throughout the period there are lamentations, from other citadels than Princeton and Andover, about the divisive effects of party spirit, inflaming the denominations, according to *The Spirit of the Pilgrims* in 1831, "with jealousy and hatred, and paralysing their energy of action toward a common foe, and for the cause of their common Lord." As we might expect, these plaints became more numerous as the massive immigration of the 1830's and 1840's brought more and more Roman Catholics into the nation. But against these nervous confessions must always be placed the immense confidence of the Revival that, as a preacher in Tennessee said as early as 1817, "Christians of all denominations, countries and languages seem to be rising almost in a mass, to make a highway for their God throughout all the earth." Considering that European churchmen, Protestant even more than Catholic, supposed the United States to be an arena of sectarian chaos, it is astonishing to discover how much of the religious intellect was devoted, as for instance was Thomas Skinner's in *The Christian Spectator* of 1837, to proving that in the fellowship of the Revival "we find a principle of affinity, which, just in proportion as the wide-spread medium of spiritual emotion becomes purified, will draw all classes of true christians nearer and still nearer, until the practical ends even of external unity shall be fulfilled."

We return to Robert Baird's book of 1844 for the finest theoretical statement of that concept of unity amid diversity which sustained the majority of American Protestants, a statement which neither Unitarianism nor Old School Presbyterianism could shake, and against which such individualists as Emerson and Thoreau were ineffective. The several churches, Baird insisted, are the various corps of a single army. What unites them? The conviction of each concerning "the unlawfulness of any interference with its doctrine, discipline, and government, on the part of the civil magistrate." Thus negativism becomes positive assertion. The foreigner, like Alexis de Tocqueville, may see only disorganization, "yet all are in their proper places. . . . All is systematic order where the uninitiated sees nothing but confusion." Thomas Skinner would still insist in 1850 that the distinguishing traits of American society were, first, that it was antilatitudinarian, and, second, "that we are anti-sectarian."

46

A few European students, even on the eve of the Civil War, were able to get the point. James Dixon in 1849 marveled how all could unite on their common Christianity, "though differing in non-essential points," and Isabella Bishop in 1859 exclaimed about the harmonious action of the ministers "which exists irrespective of denomination differences." All this, naturally, makes the Civil War the more poignant, for it was fought, not by Puritans againt Cavaliers nor by republicans against royalists, but among the rank and file, all children of the Revival.

Early in the nineteenth century the evangelical churches of America could point to something more tangible than millennial oratory as evidence of their basic solidarity: the many "associations" in which they pooled their efforts, most notably for "home missions"—*i.e.,* the conversion of the wild and wanton frontier. A few of these were conducted under strictly denominational auspices, but the more spectacular managed to combine two or more communions in a common exertion—The American Education Society (1815), The American Bible Society (1816), The American Sunday-School Union (1824), The American Tract Society (1825), The American Home Missionary Society (1826), and The Society for Promotion of Collegiate and Theological Education in the West (1843). Baird adduced these as proofs of solidarity, "in which no particular denomination is represented as such." Their workings were possibly not always as harmonious as their apologists claimed, but they were effective, and above all they dramatized the ideal of unity. Eventually, predicted *The Christian Spectator* in 1832, the lines "of denominational demarcation will speedily grow indistinct, among such as agree in referring all things to the decision of that great standard, *the word of God interpreted by common sense.*"

We may well question whether men like Baird ever comprehended the sociological import of these associations. They persisted in seeing in them portents of some ecumenical union of Protestants, and in their enthusiasm underestimated the resolution of the churches to maintain their separate identities. They were distressed by the knowledge that among the member churches there was, especially in rural areas, outspoken hostility to the associations, particularly when these, from urban headquarters, sent out agents to raise money in the hinterlands. "Thus," cried one protester in 1837, "we have in our great Metropolitan centres overseers who are virtually lawgivers to the Church." We are not bound, said one true New Englander, "to look after all the world, and consult for the universal interests of all denominations at

47

home and abroad, and for all the heathen world." And among the Baptists, one group in the West became so annoyed at being worked upon that they seceded to become "Antimission."

Probably such ingrained provinciality among the congregations prevented the associations from ever becoming effective structures of unification. From Bangor, Maine, Enoch Pond pleaded that without the associations, our efforts "must be sectional, insulated, feeble, and ineffectual." Meanwhile, the associations seemed to prosper, providing occasion for much oratory about the glories of co-operation which still haunt the American Protestant imagination. Our Bible societies, declared George Cookman in 1828, are a line of forts along the enemy's frontiers; our Sabbath schools are military academies for young cadets, our tract societies are shot-houses for the manufacture of ammunition. Our Methodists are cavalry, Presbyterians are infantry, and the Dutch Reformed are heavy artillery. That the associations and churches never quite got themselves arrayed in so beautiful a military formation does not alter the fact that in the effort to combine them a vision of the American community took shape. As Gardiner Spring said in 1850, "Concentrated influence is powerful influence."

For the truth is that while the religious leaders were ostensibly talking about harmony among the churches, they were actually charting the way toward a homogeneous America. Association, said Spring, is entirely compatible with individuality; he then went happily on to announce that the last half-century had been one of astonishing progress because "It is an age of great associations, rather than great men." In a charming confusion of rhetoric, which by 1850 had become revivalism's bequest to the nation, he declared that we were living on the border of a spiritual harvest because "thought now travels by steam and on magnetic wires." If in the beginning there was pessimism about the human condition, and a fear of the Enlightenment, by mid-century the Revival could proudly assert, "More is now being done to elevate the intellectual, social, and moral condition of our race, than at any period since the Saviour was born." Thus inadvertently, the Revival ushered the country into modernity.

4.

THE REFLEX OF MISSIONS

"To elevate the moral condition of our race." The blaze of missionary passion in early nineteenth-century America, together with the voluntary principle, made this epoch something unprecedented in Christian history. "The spirit of evangelism is among the irrepressible energies of the age," said Skinner in 1850, ending his catalogue of its manifold expressions with, "Here is an altogether new style of procedure in the church." When the concept began to dawn upon the American church, said Eli Smith in 1833, the imagination staggered at the awful prospect of *six hundred millions* of human beings perishing for want of her assistance," and for a time she could do little but gaze in horror. But within only the last three decades, the mighty reaches have been broken up; impressions have become distinct and practical. "There is growing up a spirit of missionary enterprize, the effect of benevolence," which, according to Smith, pervades the churches just "as the spirit of commercial activity, the result of a desire for gain, is taking possession of the mercantile world." Mingled with the cries of the redeemed from camp meetings and tabernacles ascended a shout for the glory of missions, of which one example represents thousands:

Our own vast country is to be brought under the influence of the Gospel. The wide world is to be evangelized. The day of slumber is passed. The sacramental host of God's elect are marshalled in arms, and wait for ministers to lead them on to victory.

Of course there were repeated shouts of "Woe to those inhabitants of the earth who shall withstand all the overtures of the Redeemer's mercy, and be found at last among the incorrigible despisers of his grace!" Just how much of the national income was diverted to the cause is impossible to say, but in all likelihood it was as prodigious as the amount spent on cheap whiskey.

The connection may be obscure, but a primary assurance emerges that, for the contemporaneous consciousness, the fact of the Revival and the excitement over missions were joined. Looking back upon 1800, Heman Humphrey in 1859 pointed out that then there were no missionary societies of any sort: "At home it was deep spiritual apathy, abroad, over all the heathen lands, the calm of the Dead Sea—death,

49

death, nothing but death." But in so short a time, in a mere half-century, how altered had the scene become! "Those revivals stand connected, in the history of Redemption, with those aggressive agencies by which He is now turning our own moral wilderness into fruitful fields, and sending the gospel to all heathen lands." The two sentiments have a reciprocal action to invigorate each other, said Colton at the height of the ecstasy; in 1833 he ventured into the language which ever flowed spontaneously from the heart of the righteous before the mighty prospect: just in proportion as the spirit of domestic revival reigns, there comes the spirit of foreign missionary enterprise. And as the latter is "a sober, calculating, sublime spirit—a living principle, rather than a fitful flame—it imparts the same character to the former."

We may find the conjunction of the adjectives "calculating" and "sublime" bewildering, yet the Revival had no difficulty maintaining it. The influence of excitement is always transient, said a theorist of 1838, and all knew that revivals by their very nature were bound to subside. "Now in the missionary concern, we want something that can be *calculated* upon." In other words, while the missionary enthusiasm might be generated in a particular revival, because it required group organization and sustained endeavor, it became a mechanism for stabilizing and continuing the Revival. The preachers pounded hard on the admonition that a "person's religion would be greatly to be suspected, who, professing himself to have the spirit and enjoy the hopes of the gospel, should feel no promptings of earnest, benevolent desire to send others the blessings of the common salvation." For this reason, therefore, the several denominations could find a further bond of unity by joining together in wholesale denunciations of those churches which were lukewarm about missions, or, as were the Unitarians, actively hostile. That system, said Samuel Miller in 1821, which cannot be adapted to the capacities of the poor and the uneducated, which "takes away ALMOST THE WHOLE of the MOTIVES which the Orthodox feel for endeavouring to send the glad tidings of salvation to the ends of the earth" must assuredly be "false and rotten."

Meanwhile, there was an annoying embarrassment of history which reminded the armies of American Protestantism that their colonial forebears had not been "evangelical," at least in the sense which had become so peremptory by 1830. That is, the Congregationalists of New England, the Presbyterians, and the Baptists had carried to America the conception of the church as a stable center within a civilized community. Their "errand into the wilderness" was conceived as the conquest of an area—a township or a county—into cultivation, and then the erection within it of a church which would function in relation to the settled inhabitants just as a church in Norfolk or Holland functioned in relation to its parish. And even the Methodists, commencing their operations in America on the eve of the Revolution, still held John Wesley's notion that Methodism was a way of reaching the lower classes spiritually starved by the gentlemanly culture of an Established Church. Assuredly it was the Methodists, thanks to their organization and their orientation, who were most ready to undertake in the America of 1789 the mission to the frontier, but one can readily see in the memoirs of Francis Asbury, not to say of Peter Cartwright, that it took them some time to comprehend that circuit riders moving through Kentucky and Illinois were performing a different order of Christian exercise from that of the Wesleys preaching to neglected coal miners in Wales. As the other major groups joined in the effort to civilize the West, they all fell into a certain rude step. They all had to explain, even though sometimes at the cost of stifling or even suppressing their historical consciousness, that missionizing had in fact been a part of their original intention. Most of them had sufficient conscience not to plead the seventeenth-century profession of converting the Indians. If they knew anything, they knew that Protestant evangelists to the savages had nothing substantial to boast of as against the heroic record of Canadian Jesuits. What was required, coincident with the Great Revival of 1800, was some method for discounting the provincialism of the American past, a method which could combine callousness about the Indians with a passionate concern for the souls of white immigrants, and for organizing them into churches on the model of Northampton, Philadelphia, and Charleston.

Robert Baird strained his historical sense—which was rigorous—in the effort to present the colonial churches as having prepared the way for the efflorescence of missionizing. His arguments ring hollow. Though he spared his readers nothing concerning the theocracies of New England or the religious presumptions of royal governors, yet he spoke to his age rather than to historicity by summarizing the spiritual aspect of the settlements thus: the people left the Old World "not merely to find liberty of conscience in the forest of the New, but that they might extend the kingdom of Christ, by founding states where the Truth should not be impeded by the hindrances that opposed its progress elsewhere." Baird's proposition, in its belligerent assumption that Christians would of course extend the Kingdom of Christ if only they could find a society where Truth was not opposed, meant that Americans of his time, who above all peoples in the world *did* (as they believed) dwell in a state where Christianity was not impeded, had therefore a greater obligation than any other community to expend their hearts and pocketbooks in converting the heathen. If their colonial ancestors had been a bit lax, then all the more reason that the independent Republic should redress their shortcomings.

On the other hand, supposing that the American churches had learned, in the flush of national independence, methods for serving the Kingdom which neither Europe nor the colonies had dreamed of: would not this in itself be a vindication of the unique character of American existence? It is remarkable how increasingly, at least down to about 1850, the immense American missionary effort was presented as something basically *radical,* of a piece with the titanic entrance into the world of steam and electricity.

It is difficult to say just when and how the revivalists lent themselves to this argument; but that by 1830 they had surrendered their cause to the American motto of "Go Ahead" may be shown by a startling passage from *The Biblical Repertory:*

The spirit of the age is *ripe* for action, for it is a spirit of extraordinary enterprise. It is a *public* spirit also, and is ripe, if well directed, not only for action, but for *combined* action, on a scale of noble daring and sublime extent, hitherto unknown on earth. It is an age of revolution; and it is ripe not only for change, but for improvement too. [Italics *not* mine.]

In 1825, when "internal improvements" were still a novel and controversial issue, preachers might still insist that the moral and spiritual improvements of missions were more important than canals and railways, but by 1848 the mind had become so adjusted to the technological revolution that pious language was changed from contrast to analogy. The Almighty Himself, said James L. Batchelder in 1848, has constructed the railroad, and as Samuel Morse prophesied with the first telegraphic message from Baltimore to Washington, the purpose of his invention was not to convey the price of pork, but to ask, "What hath God wrought?" Over and over again, to the point of tedium, but never to satiety, orators identified missions with the industrial "scene of astonishing activity." Both together, asserted Skinner in 1850, are a sign from heaven "that the long-promised day is drawing nigh, when another scene will present itself—that of Christianity in its triumph— the world reclaimed and converted to Christ."

But in spite of what should have been a happy conjunction of religion and technology in a free society, America soon developed its peculiar mode of spawning flies in the ointment. In the Finney revivals, even in rural New York, the cry went up that no nation had ever before enjoyed greater advantages for wealth. But if this nation,

out of its prosperity, did not contribute to missions, would it not follow others into "wealth, luxury, extravagance, and vice . . ."? Avoid
the issue as they tried, missionizing preachers had to confront, even
though they would seldom give it a name, what the age defined as "the
course of empire." Yes, America was becoming an empire, faster than
patriots of the Revolutionary mentality had supposed possible. What,
then, was to keep it from going the way of Babylon and Rome? The
missionaries were the first in the field to warn against disaster, and to
propose a remedy. Of all the adversaries that have yet arrayed themselves, said George Cookman to the Methodist Church in 1830, the
most formidable have been, not Roman centurions, but "your cool,
prudent, calculating, common sense men, who would reduce the question to a mere sale of profit and loss." So we have the peculiarity,
more striking in America than anywhere else in Christendom, of a
continuous admonition to the merchant classes, who contributed the
finances for missionary endeavors, that they were at heart the secret
foes of the sacred enterprise. All during the decades before the nation
found itself confronted with the metaphysical issue of the Civil War,
the technological and commercial triumphs which promised Utopia
were constantly under indictment from missionary zeal. "Commerce
cannot be entrusted with the moral interests of mankind," said Joseph Thompson in 1857: "She has no principle that can withstand a
strong temptation to her insatiable cupidity." The fact that this was
said, and reverently received, should be for us a factor in our reading
of attacks upon the commercial community, not only by such writers
as have survived the oblivion inherited by the missionaries, but by
Thoreau, Emerson, Poe, and the Hawthorne of *The House of the
Seven Gables*. Not one of these, for all his pungence, said quite so
bluntly as did Thompson, "No social evil is so contagious as that of
luxury: none so surely saps the foundations of morality, the stability of
government and of society itself. *Mammonism* is as serious a foe to the
spiritual elevation of a community as infidelity or heathenism."

However, we should note that a religious thinker like Thompson
puts the emphasis upon "community." He is not a Thoreau, nor were
any of his ilk. Their denunciations of American commercialism were
never inspired by any Transcendental vision of the Self, but always by
the hope of forging a community out of a centrifugal society. Because
they were so deeply concerned with this aim—wherefore they could
accept Schaff's designation of conservative—they used the missionary
spirit to promote the ideal of a Christian millennium. Hitherto, as
they well knew, the millennial expectancy had been a radical engine,

calling down judgment upon existing society; they were instructed in the lawless working of the impulse during the seventeenth century. But they were convinced that in the special structure of American society, the ideal was at least realizable. "I cannot but view the Millennium," wrote Seth Williston in 1849, "as constituting a very *practical* subject." For the doctrine now seemed to have found its irresistible formulation. Give us in America the free operation of the principle of private property (even though we must berate merchants into doing their duty); then out of the wealth of America will flow the power which shall produce the conversion of the world. "To aim at this, is to fall in harmoniously with the course our Maker is pursuing, securing to ourselves a share in his success, and in the happiness it will occasion." What further need would there be, but in these universal terms, to define the purpose of American individuality?

Unfortunately, almost from the first conjunction of the Revival and the missionary passion, a problem arose. Should the main effort, or indeed the exclusive effort, be devoted to "home" or "foreign" missions? Possibly in the field of religion the issue never became quite so precisely formulated as in literary criticism, but for the masses of Americans the pietistic query was fundamental to their learning to know themselves. It made every difference to them whether their emotion and their money should be expended abroad or on their own continent. "That benevolence is ill-judged, if not spurious, that melts and burns for India or for China, while it turns a deaf ear to the moans of dying spirits in Iowa or Texas." For, notwithstanding Professor Hodge, there was something entirely *American;* while it could be argued that a function of Americanism was to spread the American spirit abroad, the primary consideration would seem to be the regeneration of the country. Those redeemed by the Revival had a stake in the matter.

It was a more divisive issue than any but a few of the revivalists admitted; those who realized its importance tried to play it down. But the pressure was so insistent that nobody in the religious communities could banish it from his consciousness. It appears that the Methodists were the most eloquent about universal conversion, though on the local scene they were more active than any other denomination. Toward all of these weird people, said Bishop McIlvaine in 1835, the Christian must feel an attachment, "whether of the church in Asia, or Africa, or Europe," more tender than any "arising from any local or political relations." But such pleas, although numerous, were overwhelmed by another sort of political evangelicism. As a characteristic orator proclaimed in 1842, a people whose institutions favor personal freedom, "who wield the energies of the steam-engine and the press," whose commerce covers three thousand miles of seacoast, "must exert a powerful influence on the destiny of less favored nations; and, consequently, the conversion of such a people is pre-eminently important."

Here was the crossroad of perplexity, where pious America found itself, in the midst of its majestic assertion, inwardly divided between dreams of cosmopolitan success and awareness of provinciality. For as Robert Baird kept reminding it, we have on our hands the "West." The thousands who go there risk losing all impressions they may have brought with them, "amid the engrossing cares and manifold temptations of their new circumstances; circumstances in which even the established Christian will find much need of redoubled vigilance and prayer." But some New Englanders, and these not Unitarians, put a spoke into the wheel of progress by claiming that true piety has ever flourished "among hills and sterile mountains, rather than on sunny plains and luxuriant meadows," and so refused to burden their consciences with the spiritual plight of Illinois.

In the face of this contradiction, a threat to the very ground of being for the Revival, one logical solution could alone arise: America has the divinely appointed task in history to become itself completely regenerated so that it may then legitimately convert the heathen world. Preachers of the era rang changes on the theme that westward the course of empire had always taken its way, and that westward, from the Holy Land, Christianity had moved; wherefore we must now transmit the heritage "to our friends and countrymen in the West, that they, in their turn, may bless the wide and benighted regions beyond." According to this reasoning, it was up to New England to salvage California, so that Californians could take on the responsibility for China.

One may easily ridicule this nineteenth-century rhetoric. Yet when one considers the twentieth-century role assumed by the United States he is bound to admit this same rhetoric contains the germ of that national disposition toward "heathen" communities which would have been incomprehensible to a Jefferson or a Washington. We absolutely must, said James Batchelder in 1848, evangelize our beloved country, that she may serve as "the hope of the world in a political and religious sense." The purpose of home missions must not be disguised: we are not merely saving the barbaric frontier for civilization, but by doing that, we reach the next phase: "that the American people, *as a missionary nation,* may be fully prepared, by the grace of God, to enter those three great Foreign Fields and reap the wasting harvest." When America's millions are all converted, and, says

Batchelder, "thoroughly disciplined," then we can exert our combined energies upon the world. What then can resist us? The religious argument, naturally, runs principally in terms of spiritual impact, but always there is tied to it an implication that we shall save the world not only in a religious sense but in a "political." "Our Heavenly Father," said William Williams in 1845, "has made us a national epistle to other lands." And all this, he added, because God has left us "unfettered by national endowments, and secular alliances."

There was, to be sure, another incentive for the revivalists to give a priority to home missions: by 1830 they began to be apprehensive concerning the immigrations of, as Baird put it, "those multitudes from the Continent of Europe who cannot understand or speak English," and consequently about the growth of the Catholic Church. Appeals for funds and recruits were repeatedly linked with the exhortation, "These United States are the bulwark of Protestantism." Lyman Beecher's famous *Plea for the West* in 1834 was a passionate challenge to American Protestants to prevent the Valley of the Mississippi from falling into the control of the Pope. He always denied that his utterance had anything to do with inciting the mob that destroyed the Ursuline Convent in Charleston, but, whether or not he was responsible, what with his preaching and the mob's action, fear of Catholicism became a morbid obsession of the Revival.

Gradually the motive which kept the missionary enthusiasm at so high a pitch became avowedly not so much the salvation of foreign lands as the excitation of the home congregations. As the Reverend Henry Mandeville said in one of the key works of the era, significantly entitled *Reflex of Missions,* the effort "electrifies the whole man," imparts energy to the intellect and tenderness to the heart:

In fact, it creates a difference between him and other Christians, as remarkable as that between an English operative, confined all his life to the manufacture of a pin head, and the inventive and enterprising American of all work, from trundling the wheelbarrow to guiding the ship of state.

How powerful, how precious must "that reflex influence" be! And most precious because through this "unity of spirit begetting union of effort, and union of effort reacting to strengthen the unity of spirit that gave it birth, the churches would arise in their strength." Missions thus became a means for assuaging the inner anxiety of American Protestants over their sectarian predicament. Under the power of this paramount object, Skinner announced in 1843, the different groups have "forgotten their party names and interests, and thus the evils of sectarianism have been gradually disappearing, and christian union advancing." A fusion of differences, out of which was generated the missionizing electricity, this, cried Skinner, constitutes a religious upsurge "scarcely inferior to those of the apostolic period," and assuredly beyond anything achieved by any other civilization since then. The great secret, said Samuel Cox in 1849, also discoursing on the "reflex influence," is that missions, foreign or domestic, work "on personal character, on national sentiment, as well as on national renown throughout the world, making us more the model nation, as well as the great republic."

We come to an inner, if not *the* central, mainspring of the missionary exertion as we recognize it as a form of romantic patriotism. As early as 1823, when the romances of Fenimore Cooper were commencing their fabulous vogue, Francis Wayland declared: "This very missionary cause combines within itself the elements of all that is sublime in human purpose, nay, combines them in loftier perfection than any other enterprise, which was ever linked with the destinies of man." In this age the "sublime" was a sanction not lightly invoked; just at the time when it was also becoming the banner of native genius in arts and sciences, Wayland offered it as the true signification of the massive exertion. By the 1840's it became the standardized yet compulsive image. The lines of prophecy are converging, announced George B. Cheever in 1841: "With every division and variety of its processes concentering to one sublime purpose, the plan of God moves forward to its completion." In 1848, Batchelder, in a book entitled *The United States as a Missionary Field*, sounded the war whoop of patriotic piety:

Its sublime mountain ranges—its capacious valleys—its majestic rivers—its inland seas—its productiveness of soil—immense mineral resources, and salubrity of climate, render it a most desirable habitation for man, and are all worthy of the sublime destiny which awaits it, as the *foster mother* of future billions, who will be the *governing* race of Man. That its *farther extension* will be stopped by no other barriers than those impassable ones, which limit a *continent;* is to some, an event to be feared; to others, one to be desired; to none, one of improbability.

This is not to say that hundreds who in the euphoria of the time received a call to go to China or Africa did not in all sincerity think their summons purely spiritual; nor is it to suppose that all those who came, singly or in bands, to rescue the ruffians of the border felt they were doing anything but the Lord's work in the wilderness. Not every missionary to the West saw the "sublime" prospect celebrated by Batchelder. Instead, said E. N. Kirk, "on all the face of this globe, I know no scene so dull and unpicturesque, so depressing to the spirit, as a country which, for miles, presents to the eye the endless repetition of tall, dead, branchless trunks, burnt logs and ragged roots scattered over hill and plain; offering no other variety than is furnished by the first rude encroachments of civilization on the wild homes of savage men and beasts." Yet the contrast between Kirk's realism and Batchelder's rhetoric is, in fact, the basic issue of American culture in the era, and about it the forces of piety, the Revival and home missionizing, were, often unwittingly, mobilized. But not always unconsciously, for the real thrust of their activity was grasped by the more astute. Edwards A. Park at Andover Seminary was a behemoth among the theologians, and when he lifted up his head and trumpeted, American Protestantism listened with rapture. God, said Professor Park, kept America hidden until both the art of printing and the Reformation were achieved; then He ushered it on stage, and only now, two centuries after the tentative settlements, can we see what God intended, for it has taken all the violence of the Revival and the urging of missions to make Americans realize their function:

So has he designed this land for the comprehensive and variegated activity of his church; and as he has mingled, so he will continue to mingle in it those diversified elements which coalesce in the richest and most durable character, and the result of which, under a liberal culture, will be a poetry, a philosophy, a theology more capacious, more profound, more soul-stirring than he has vouchsafed to any other people. A character gleaned thus from all nations, will be so versatile, so energetic, as to qualify us for mingling with them all and elevating their religious spirit.

The learned historian, Whitman the self-appointed bard, even the hermit of Walden Pond, would in their various fashions make substantially the same assertion. While their formulations are more memorable because expressed in the language of a literature which Professor Park scorned, they had less effect upon the mind of the democracy. Since dissidents had only two choices, either to hymn the rising glory of America or to criticize it for not living up to its opportunities, the mentality of the young Republic seemed precommitted to accepting the Revival's definition of itself and the missionary's terminology. What alternatives could counter the assertion of The American Home Missionary Society in 1842: *"Patriotism should constrain us to evangelize this nation"*?

5.

POWER IN THE PULPIT

The vast majority of the colonial people, said Robert Baird, "were simply Christians, who knew of no way by which men can be good or happy but that pointed out by God in his Word." By just such emphasis on the simple Christianity of the colonial churches, Baird was serving as accomplice to what might almost be called a conspiracy to obliterate the original dedication to a highly intellectual system of theology, a project in which, by the way, the historian Bancroft and the romancer Cooper joined. The great achievements of the provincial mind before the Revolutionary agitation were in systematic theology, and even the Quakers had their Barclay. After the Revolution, doctrinal theology continued to be stressed at Princeton and Andover, and out of New Haven came the theology of N. W. Taylor which, though a radical simplification of Jonathan Edwards, still paid lip service to the dignity of the intellect.

But as the Revival gathered momentum, the co-operating denominations found to their joy that they had a further bond in common in their repudiation of what they called "wire-drawn metaphysics." The glory of the combined operation of the Revival and the voluntary system, Baird boasted, is that it has steadily progressed "away from those philosophical and traditionary expositions of Christianity which it only embarrasses the preacher to deliver, and the hearer to receive." We have actually so made vivid the concept of God as moral governor that we have entirely suppressed that habit "so common to philosophers and philosophizing theologians—of contemplating God exclusively as the First Cause of all beings and events."

Baird was making a riposte to the many European theologians who were convinced that in America the queen of the sciences had been vulgarized out of existence. In their ultimate effects, revivalism and the voluntary principle may have had a deleterious effect on the masses. Yet it is still important to go back to the years under study and perceive precisely what sort of thinking provoked the mental revolution. For the astonishing truth is that in the early nineteenth century, the revolt against religious formalism constructed a rationale which the twentieth century hardly remembers.

The religious leaders, along with most other sorts of leaders, profoundly believed that theirs was an age abnormally cursed with the tendency to speculation. Emerson was speaking of more than budding Transcendentalists when later he said that in the 1830's "The young men were born with knives in their brain, a tendency to introversion, self-dissection, anatomizing of motives." Indeed, he pointed to what then was happening among the American churches and remembered how "It seemed a war between intellect and affection." Hitherto, said *The Biblical Repertory* in 1830, "God has employed intellectual power to reform the worst abuses in church and state, and to dissolve the unholy alliance of civil and ecclesiastical jurisdiction," but has not the time come when intellect must be put to the service of something far greater? The Revival was a romantic phenomenon, and nowhere better showed its inner nature, even while revivalists were denouncing almost all the imported literature of Romanticism, than by arraying the pious against their seventeenth- and eighteenth-century heritages.

Again, it would be tedious to trace the elementary stages of an evolution, but in this case we find it achieved by 1827, when Philip Lindsley delivered a Baccalaureate Address in Nashville, Tennessee. For centuries, he proclaimed, mankind has been disputing about heresies of a purely speculative character, while "practical truth has been comparatively overlooked. . . . Casuists, theologians, metaphysicians, may argue and speculate (in the same manner as they frequently have done) forever, without contributing one iota to human improvement and happiness." In no time at all, at least in Beecher's *The Spirit of the Pilgrims* of 1831, the renunciation of "CREEDS" becomes explicit. "While they remain, they are mere technical landmarks between truth and error—mounds against which the waves beat and are rolled back—and their existence in the letter only, without the spirit, killeth instead of giving life." Calvin Colton, before he reneged from the Revival, was certain that *any* theology which discourages revivals was automatically suspect. Princeton might still insist that Finney and the revivalists were caught in a metaphysical dilemma, but Skinner dismissed these relics of the Reformation with a barely polite wave of the hand: "There has also been an improvement in the science of theology, the result of its being pursued under practical influences, and in its relations to practical effect."

However, the revivalists, as they developed their criterion of practicality, soon learned to pay less attention to theology than to preaching, for it was in the pulpit that their "spontaneous" movement would have to be lost or won. By 1826 William Claiborne Walton was ready to explain in Baltimore how "that *natural, familiar, simple* method of illustrating and enforcing Divine truth" has proved most useful. "We

60

should endeavour," he said, "to make things so plain, that our hearers may *see them with their own eyes,* and that too, without much labor of mind." There we have, compactly, the theory of revivalistic preaching.

It is remarkable how little mention is made in the evangelical journals of the time of the technique of Finney. Clearly, his method was his own, always smelling, as he himself admitted, too much of the lawyer's brief. His colleagues were aiming at something else, something which they hoped might be more comprehensive and less particular, but equally effective with individuals. In the effort to formulate their attack, they had as much difficulty as did Coleridge in defining the Imagination, but in a sense they were working on an analogous problem. Finney might be too legalistic: their concern was to fill the minds of their listeners with compelling images. Out of the revolt against theology, and indeed against the academic disciplines of rhetoric and logic, the revivalists forged, and highly developed, a rhetoric of romantic communication.

Naturally the Methodists took the lead in this hermeneutical pragmatism. The first generations, Asbury and his paladins, and then even McIlvaine, were too busy doing to talk much about theory. They simply cut the Gordian knot of historic Protestantism with the scimitar of their unabashed Arminianism, and so turned to "practical" preaching with a zeal that required others to imitate them as rapidly as possible in the pulpit, the camp meeting, or on the hustings, and to catch up as lamely as they could with the theology. Actually, the most powerful impression the student can get of Methodist preaching at its peak is not in any contemporaneous documents but in later celebrations of the pioneers, those who like James Bradley Finley in his *Autobiography; or, Pioneer Life in the West* (1854) or Peter Cartwright in his *Autobiography* (1856) had the misfortune to survive into the days when even Methodists commenced to train ministers at seminaries and to teach them the rudiments of theology. "I was converted on a camp-ground," insisted Cartwright, and at the close of his days was sorry to say "that the Methodist Episcopal Church of late years, since they have become numerous and wealthy, have almost let camp meetings die out." But those like him who survived the horrors of the wilderness reinforced the legend which the martyrs consecrated, and did more by their reminiscences to fix the image of "practical" preaching than did those who, working their way out of Wesley's theology, perfected the form for American revivalism.

Of these backward glances, possibly the most monumental is Abel Stevens's *Preaching Required by the Times,* published in 1855.

Though it has not the salty colloquialism of Cartwright, it is for the historian a more penetrating account of what set the tone of early Methodist revivalistic oratory. "We heartily thank Brother Stevens," said Thomas Bond in the Introduction to this delicious volume, "for the scathing criticism" he has leveled against the sort of manuals which by 1855 were being furnished to young Methodist ministers and which, if followed, would "crystalize the earnestness of preaching into an iceberg."

Stevens made clear wherein the massive progression, from Asbury down to what he and Cartwright considered their degenerate decade, had been effective, and his adjectives are an eloquent commentary on the epoch. "The naturalness, the colloquial facility" of the great missionaries were the stuff of true oratory: "Introducing their discourses thus, our old preachers usually rose with the subject to higher strains, until the sublimest declamation was often reached, and the awe-struck people wept or groaned aloud." Once more we return, as we shall hereafter, to the "sublime."

Stevens and the old Methodist hands could thus bewail Methodist seminaries—in which, incredibly, students were given books on "homiletics." They stood to the end for the virtues of pure spontaneity. There are many sham arts in science, some in art; but what science is fuller of them than "that 'Dogmatic Theology,' (if we except the kindred one of Speculative Philosophy,) and what are more disfigured by them than 'Homiletics?'" These primitive Methodists, attacking the formalism into which they thought their church had subsided, were instrumental in engendering the last great American revival, that of 1857–58, which would assume a character they hardly understood. But meanwhile they summed up a convulsion which they had led and which the other Protestant denominations had been obliged to follow. There is vastly more genuine learning among theologians, declared Stevens, than ever before in Christian experience, but this shows itself in their sensible avoidance of the old dialectics, in their concentration upon "the *exposition* of *revealed* truth by learned research, rather than by original speculation." At the same time textbooks on homiletics do nothing but abuse "a simple and sublime subject." Effective preachers in any period are those who "by the impetuosity of their feelings, or the power of their genius, break over most of these professional habits." The greatest pulpit orator of modern ages, concluded Stevens, was Whitefield.

The Methodists, however, had no monopoly on the conception of "bold" elocution. Indeed, revivalists within the Presbyterian Church, to the disgust of Princeton Seminary, often went beyond even the greatest of the circuit riders, and because they were generally more learned could expound the theory more freely. Possibly the document most fascinating to us, or the most appalling, is the address, *Practical Preaching,* that Albert Barnes delivered in 1833 at Andover Seminary. Americans, he happily declared, do not worry about the process by which a result is to be achieved, and ministers must work on the same principle. The habits of contemplative ages will not answer today; the leaden rules of the older theology will not do. We must have a ministry apprized of the habits of action in these times:

It accords with the character of our people; the active, hardy, mighty enterprise of the nation. It is the manner in which all sentiments here spread, by deep, rapid, thorough excitement, and hasty revolution. A year may effect changes here, for good or bad, which an age might not produce on the comparatively leaden population of the old world. It accords with our history. It is the way, the grand, glorious, awful way in which God has appeared to establish his church in this land.

Barnes's very language shows him no ignorant ranter, as the primitive Methodists appeared to Schaff. His is a conscious doctrine, a deliberate rejection of the "profound, dry, technical, elaborate lucubrations" of historic Christian theology on the grounds of what seems to him a real revolution. As J. W. Adams asked in 1835, with equal precision, "What is the prominent feature by which the ministry of the present day is distinguished from other and less favored periods of the church?" and swept some nineteen hundred years of Christian declamation into the wastebasket by answering, "Not intellectual vigor, or mental furniture, but in the fire and unction of its eloquence."

Unitarians might still scoff at all this as mere frontier crudity and ignorance. However, their own pathetic effort, in the 1830's, to win a foothold in Cincinnati amply demonstrated how incapable they were of addressing the West. Princeton remained unperturbed, but the two-or-three-volume systems of doctrine turned out by her professors remained unreadable. Andover drilled its students in the metaphysics of Edwards, Bellamy, or Emmons, but those who went into the "field" thought only in terms of producing revivals. *The Christian Spectator* in 1834 fell into line by saluting George Whitefield as the greatest since the Apostles in urging "the plain simple truth of God upon the consciences of his hearers," and in 1835 took to task the Congregational parsons for not "throwing themselves upon their hearers by a bold, fervid, direct annunciation of the great facts." Men, said Gardiner Spring in 1849, "are creatures, not of thought only, but of feeling; they have susceptibilities to emotion; they are susceptibilities which seek to be gratified, and which ought to be turned to good account." By that date, though an extreme recalcitrant like Henry Thoreau might still object, there was virtually no voice in the Republic that would publicly object to so frank a prescription for working upon its religious emotionalism. Which in itself is a comment of resounding overtones when one thinks that it was made with casualness a little more than three generations after the Declaration of Independence.

"Ye *optimates* of the land," asked *The Christian Spectator* in 1825, naming specifically lawyers, legislators, and professors, do you suppose that religion is any longer a controversy of metaphysics? On the contrary, "it is a question of utility, and if any religion is necessary, it must be of the diffusive, controlling, energetic kind."

Where then was a Protestant culture, in an expanding economy, to find admonitions out of the historic past which might still control it? The fact was certain to *The Biblical Repository* of 1830 that "in this speculative age," more importance was attached to fashions, "and more temporizing policy in social intercourse and commercial transactions, than was common with our pious forefathers." Where was the formula for explanation to be found? Surely, no longer in the Puritan conception of a particular people in a specific covenant with Jehovah, for that could no longer fit the sprawling states of the Union. The answer arose not out of the traditions of theology, not even out of Calvinism, but out of the key words of the romantic movement. "Christians," concluded *The Biblical Repository,* "may employ their intellect as much on subjects of religion, but there is less of the heart put in requisition."

In the early days of Unitarianism, at a time when the "liberal" preachers were working their revolution not by denouncing Calvinism but by observing discreet silence upon its doctrines, they liked to argue, as did Jeremy Belknap in 1784, that talking about controverted points was not edifying, that "that preaching is generally the most successful, which is the most spiritual, the most practical," and so "we should aim directly at the heart." They evidently derived much instruction from their perusal of Dr. Hugh Blair's *Lectures on Rhetoric and Belles Lettres,* which was widely reprinted in America and in the 1780's became the standard text at Harvard. Blair advised strenuously against introducing abstruse questions into the pulpit and found the great secret of successful preaching "in bringing home all that is spoken to the hearts of Hearers." But as the Revival continued to sweep the country, and the hostility of Unitarianism to it was resented, evangelicals found themselves insisting that the undoctrinal methods of Boston were very far from addressing the heart. Though few of

them spent much thought on the matter, what they instinctively realized was that Belknap's and Blair's conception of the heart was entirely of the eighteenth century, and that what they meant was the
infinitely more palpitating organ being currently celebrated in romances and gift-book fiction. "A production which originates in the
head is, as such," wrote Calvin Pease in 1853, "artificial and arbitrary;
while one which originates in the heart, is spontaneous and vital." In
theology, as at Princeton, the heart has become absorbed and hardened
into abstract propositions "which suit the purposes of science," but
the glory of American Protestantism, as he saw it, was that out of a
half-century of experience, in our preaching "the brain . . . is held
in 'solution' by the heart, and thus made strictly subordinate and
tributary to the end of influencing the conduct and controlling the
will." By the 1850's the change in conception was so complete that
Stevens, in describing what was required by the times, brought the key
words into revealing conjunction: "Methodism is compatible with
large minds, as well as large hearts, and can employ them on the
sublimest scale of their powers."

The Sublime and the Heart! That they should, so to speak, find
each other out and become, in the passions of the Revival, partners—
this is a basic condition of the mass civilization of the nation. That the
religious, dedicated to the immediate tasks before them, did not see all
the implications in this union, which the Hudson River painters, Cooper, Melville, and Whitman later explored, simply underscores the
truism that these artists were as much children of the age as Charles
Finney. But what was apparent to revivalists, and what they constantly
talked about, was the happy consequence of this break with the eighteenth century for the underlying unity of the denominations. Speculative systems produce only dissension, said Eleazar Lord in 1835, but
the true evangelical method "addresses itself to the heart":

It aims to produce spiritual and practical religion. It is homogeneous wherever applied. With instruction it combines example and influence; and with
doctrine, mutual fellowship, prayers and good works; and lays the foundations of union in the affections, sympathies, and hopes.

Within the Revival, where the new power of the words "sublime" and
"heart" could work with a vengeance, the character of the American
intellect was emerging rapidly, showing the qualities it would retain
despite immense changes in technology and despite the strain of criticism from civilized Europeans. For, as The Spirit of the Pilgrims
roundly stated in 1831: "The cultivation of intellect has failed. Ages

the most distinguished for intellectual culture have been alike distinguished for voluptuousness, and all the elements of moral dissolution." Thomas Jefferson had died only five years before.

6.

THIS NATION, UNDER GOD

In 1811 there came on appeal from a lower court to Chancellor James Kent of New York the case of *The People* v. *Ruggles*. Ruggles, said The People, after partaking heavily in the local tavern, stood before its door and in a loud voice blasphemed God, Christ, and the Holy Spirit. The Chancellor upheld the stiff fine that had been levied upon him, and cited, lacking other precedent, Blackstone's statement that open blasphemy is an offense at Common Law. But Kent knew that many people in upstate New York stoutly insisted that no American citizen, even in his cups, was to be judged by English rules. So the Chancellor wrote one of his most carefully reasoned, and most widely cited, opinions.

"The people of this State, in common with the people of this country, profess the general doctrines of Christianity," so that publicly "to scandalize the author of these doctrines . . . is a gross violation of decency and good order." Of course, the Constitution of the state guarantees "the free, equal and undisturbed enjoyment of religious opinion, and the free and decent discussion on any religious subject," but to revile with contempt "the religion professed by almost the whole community" is to commit an offense "inconsistent with the peace or safety of the State." Though we have no establishments, still we may properly punish actions which "strike at the root of moral obligation and weaken the security of the social ties." To construe our religious liberty as breaking down Common Law protections of Christianity would, the Chancellor concluded, be a perversion of its meaning.

Besotted Ruggles vanished thereupon from history, and nobody then or since tried to make him a martyr, as Abner Kneeland became in Boston of 1838. But the evangelical forces of the country, which hardly ever noticed Kneeland, kept the Chancellor's verdict constantly in print as the supreme proof that this libertarian Republic, despite Jefferson, was fundamentally Christian. Baird told it to Europe, fortified it with facts about the observance of the Sabbath, the prevention of licentious books, and patiently mollified his critics (or tried to) by asserting, "The impression prevails among our statesmen that the Bible is emphatically the foundation of our hopes as a people."

It is not difficult to comprehend why European churchmen, or such observers as Tocqueville and Beaumont, who were worried about the portent of America, found all this confusing, not to say insane. From the vantage point of the twentieth century, wherein problems of church-state relations seem oddly to persist, we too may find ourselves bewildered by the official presentation which the dominant mentality —that is, the evangelical—then offered a skeptical world. "We are a christian people," said Henry Whiting Warner in 1853, "and we are free." This combination, inconceivable to a Europe in which organized Christianity and the apostles of freedom had been for more than a century in mortal combat, could be gaily accounted for: "Our political and civil institutions are all imbued with christianity in greater or less degree."

The student of the period is bound to stand amazed at how far, despite the fervent professions of devotion to the principle of separation, the mind of the country was from accepting the idea of a purely secular government, national or state. A few, like Edward Norris Kirk pleading in 1848 for home missions, could say that "republicanism," modified by Christianity, does exalt the individual soul, but only in his civil relations: "As a purely political system, it knows nothing of man's immortal nature, his relations to God and to eternity." But the majority of revivalists, including such an astute social theorist as Baird, insisted that notwithstanding the purely legalistic character of the constitutions, there was an indestructible link between the political institutions and the thrust of American religiosity.

For example, Heman Humphrey in 1831 acknowledged that the system of American government was not one of coercion, yet gloried that it was one of "influence." Moses and Aaron united in counsel for "the true American union, of which no Christian, and no patriot can ever be ashamed." It is a union of intelligence, public spirit, and moral principle: "that sort of union which makes every patriot a Christian, and every Christian a patriot." Albert Barnes, whose standard of rhetorical persuasion we have heard, found as evidence of this arrangement the stupendous unanimity merchants showed during the political campaign of 1840—their spontaneous rallying to "Tippecanoe and Tyler too"—"their hearts vibrating with a common emotion, from Bangor to New Orleans." By this example, he asked, "why there may not be as deep common feeling on the subject of religion?" Barnes conveniently overlooked the fact that even in 1840 a fair number of evangelicals must have voted for Van Buren, since Harrison's majority of the popular vote was not immense; still, from his point of view this sort of thinking did not so much circumvent the First Amendment as demonstrate, out of a profound sense of the community, that religious liberty opened the highway to a greater uniformity than the Church of Rome ever contemplated. Here, said George Bush in 1834, is an end to monasticism and asceticism, and good riddance to both of them! The Christian is "in a manner conformed to the genius of Christianity," to come directly into contact "with the temper, the pursuits, and the institutions of the world . . . he is to labour with the express, specific, definite purpose of promoting the temporal and secular well-being of mankind." So, reciting again and again the "sublime" prospect of the continent, men like Barnes boasted that this same prospect caused Americans to ask whether "the somewhat staid and leaden habits of the pulpit should not be broken up," whether the "active powers" should not be put to more use than the contemplative habits of "the fixed and Gothic" ages. We are striking out new modes of freedom, "We are forming a state of things, in this Republic, very much as if we had not the memorials of past ages." The supreme instrument of this conquest was not Roman legions, but the Revival. "*We* have nothing to conquer but the sturdy oaks of our mountains, and the obstructions of our streams, and the barriers to the free access to a soil given to us from the hand of God."

Hence we should not be astonished at, though we find it difficult to credit, the frankness with which revivalists announced their engine as a means of mobilizing what Colton called "*public opinion*." This, he exulted, does not have to present itself in palpable forms; it has ubiquity and a species of omniscience, "and there is no power on earth so stern in its character, so steady, so energetic, so irresistible in its sway." And only—God be thanked—in America has this power adopted Christianity, "and set itself up its advocate and defender, in the hands of an Almighty Providence." Even so gentle a spirit as Robert Baird was simply nauseated by Tocqueville's warnings against the tyranny of the majority, and roughly dismissed Tocqueville's book by asserting that in matters of religion and morals, the Protestant faith in America has so much influence as "to make public opinion, not only strong, but right, on all points on which it has been sufficiently informed."

However, behind these proclamations of conformity, which seem appalling to us in their smugness, there can be discerned an anxiety which all such pronouncements could not lay to rest and which constantly drove the Revival to more strenuous exertions. The reasons for this insecurity were summed up in a crucial article of *The Spirit of the*

Pilgrims for 1831, and chief among them, interestingly enough, was just that very sublimity of the American opportunity which, in other moods, even Beecher's magazine held forth as a major incentive. The dangers arise "from our vast extent of territory, our numerous and increasing population, from diversity of local interests, the power of selfishness, and the fury of sectional jealousy and hate." We have become prosperous, and thus full of voluptuousness and rash specula-tion. The intellect (with its attendant vice of "speculation") has got out of control. There are signs of an atheistic conspiracy which "would blot out the sun, suspend moral attraction, dissolve society, and turn out the whole family of human animals into one common field of unbridled appetite and lust." On steamboats, canals, railroads, the ungodly are gathering. Philosophy cannot stand against them, and even patriotism, though it may help, "cannot be relied on as a prin-ciple." What can save us? The title of the article was, "The Necessity of Revivals of Religion to the Perpetuity of our Civil and Religious Institutions."

The fascination of the piece is its stark avowal of what had become in the minds of revivalists the complete identification of the cause of the Revival with that of the Federal Union. "Unless some subduing, tranquilizing influence can be applied, superior to all which man can apply, our race as a nation is swift, and our destruction sure." But, as always, the evangelical resistance to "the course of empire" had its solution at hand. Revivals alone will turn the trick, because only they will "associate intellectual culture with holiness of heart." Education, even the most pious, will not avail: "Nothing but a phalanx of holy hearts around the Sabbath can save it." Gradualness will not protect us; conversion must be immediate, and only the interposition of God, "in great and general Revivals of Religion, to reform the hearts of this people, and make the nation good and happy." Without quite knowing how they had come to so remarkable a shift in their position, evangelicals of 1832 were saying, along with Ebenezer Porter, that revivals were the one hope "that the civil institutions of our country will be perpetuated."

By this time, a curious combination had been formed in the reli-gious mind, which almost defies analysis. Because the intellect and the "speculative" had become equated with the nonspiritual, then the intellect could be declared a threat to nationality, and so "un-prac-tible." Whereas the union of spirituality, symbolized by the heart, with the perpetuation of American institutions was the peculiar dis-covery of American Christianity. And somewhere in the 1840's the magic word *conservative* emerged to connote this assemblage of ideas.

Baird hit upon it when defending American preachers against European charges of vulgarity and ignorance:

To them the country owes much of its conservative character, for no men have inculcated more effectively those doctrines which promote obedience to law, respect for magistracy, and the maintenance of civil government; and never more than within the last year or two, during which they have had to resist the anarchical principles of self-styled reformers, both religious and political.

As measured against European experience, the full achievement of religious liberty in the United States was a triumph for radicalism. In the early nineteenth century, the problem of terminology was hardly solved by calling it also a vindication of liberalism, for there was still semantic confusion in distinguishing one from the other. Certainly the immense revivals of 1800, and the publication of the voluntary principle, seemed to the rest of Christendom an action which went beyond the polite limits of liberal thinking into the forests of radicalism. Europeans, from Captain Hall through Mrs. Trollope and Alexis de Tocqueville, could readily perceive that, though America might make a show of gentlemen, both in Boston and in Virginia, who expressed aristocratic scorn of the mobs who supported Jefferson and Jackson, there really was no interest in America which could be called "conservative" in the sense comprehended by restored Bourbons in Paris or High-Church Tories in London. Practically every American of a religious temperament, whether Episcopalian, Unitarian, or Old School Presbyterian, accepted as axiomatic the separation of church and state and the competitive disorder of sectarianism. Yet Schaff had the boldness to claim for this liberal anarchy the adjective "conservative"; Baird had preceded him, and there is a vast literature in the periodicals reinforcing the claim.

No clear definitions were ever established—which may be the tragedy of the period, but may also be its victory. But for revivalists, the issue was clear. What were they trying to conserve? Not a state church, not a uniform orthodoxy, but a pervasive spirit of communion which, they insisted, prospered rather than perished under a diversity of organizations. "I say," asserted E. H. Chapin in 1841, "that Christianity is the true conserving and developing power of a nation." He then called the roll, in the manner of all meditators upon the course of empire, of the great kingdoms which had perished—Chaldea, Egypt, Greece, Rome—but gave America the chance, unique in history, of escaping the treadmill to oblivion if it would only adhere to the conserving Christianity. In the same year, George Cheever, yielding him-

escape time

70

self to what had in literature and painting become, as we shall see, a strangely popular theme in the midst of American progress, told how he had stood beneath the walls of the Colosseum, of the Parthenon, of Karnak, and "read the proofs of God's veracity in the vestiges at once of such stupendous glory and such a stupendous overthrow." Clearly, God did not need to intervene in the course of events to demolish these nations by a supernatural bolt; he merely left them to perish by the natural consequences of luxury, avarice, pride, and injustice. If any find it difficult to believe that "the youthful vigor, the energy, the almost indestructible life of our own country" could come to a similar end, let him wander on the banks of the Nile and meditate on what must overtake even us if we lose the spirit of religion.

William Williams delivered in 1843 a discourse entitled "The Conservative Principle," and Charles White one in 1852 more specifically named "The Conservative Element in Christianity." These are merely examples of hundreds in the same vein, all calling attention to how previous empires had perished because they had relied entirely upon the intellect, upon "Political Economy," and upon "false liberalism." White gave full praise to the voluntary principle, but warned that it presented the danger of a combination which might become dictatorial, "while the conservative vitalities of the Christian Religion are undervalued and dispensed with." Wherefore, while hundreds of evangelicals were endeavoring to achieve unity amid diversity by associations and unions, they had always to contend with their own conviction, sometimes more explicit than at others, that, as White phrased it, "The Christian religion, fitted precisely by its conservative qualities to such exigencies, communicates a silent, tranquil power into the interior among all the disturbing elements."

In the end, the Revival had somehow to confess that though it first broke upon the world as an upheaval, a violent swell of passion, what it really wanted, and indeed always had wanted, was to preserve the union of the states, and that what it sought for were means of establishing the bond without relying upon the legal formulations of the intellect or of the law. As early as 1829 *The Christian Spectator* set what would until 1861 be the central problem of the religious conscience:

'What has religion to do with the State?' you ask. In the form of ecclesiastical alliances, nothing; but in its operation as a controlling, purifying power in the consciences of the people, we answer, it has every thing to do, it is the last hope of republics; and let it be remembered, if ever our ruin shall come, that the questions which agitate, the factions which distract, the convulsions which dissolve, will be but secondary causes: The true evil will lie back of these, in the moral debasement of the people; and no excellence of political institutions, no sagacity of human wisdom, which did not, like that of our Puritan fathers, begin and end with religion, could have averted the calamity.

The phrases are eloquent: "the last hope of republics," "our ruin," "calamity." In this era not only was America giving an exhibition of material advance beyond anything in recorded history, but the churches were resonantly asserting that they had solved the ecclesiastical conundrums of history and found a complicated method to achieve an indestructible national unity. We may therefore understand, and pity, the tempo of the revivalists' effort to proclaim, all through the 1850's, that religion and religion alone, in spite of Stephen A. Douglas or Barnwell Rhett, would hold the nation together. "True nationality," said a writer in *Bibliotheca Sacra* in 1856, "is an instinct of our being." Men have a feeling of unity with all associated with them under the same government and the same Christianity; this is not a mere fancy: "It is ordered so by our Creator; and, when we urge the cultivation of national feeling, we but carry out His designs." In its secret heart, the explosive Revival became a gallant effort, by insisting upon the purification of American hearts, to conserve the Republic.

CHAPTER THREE

Pentecost and Armageddon

We can trace, indeed, in the history of revivals, the influence of our progress
in association, since the days in which men were more massed and less
individualized, and as a consequence were more controlled by single minds
and less susceptible to the power of public and collective utterances, which
are in fact mighty and eloquent in proportion as they are the voice of enlarged
and strong individualities. Perhaps the day of the great preachers' revivals has
passed away with that of the mastery of single minds in general. We certainly
witness at present a revival of unprecedented power, in which *the people
are the preacher;* and this in beautiful harmony with the nature of modern
American existence. Democracy—under sin and infidelity the grimmest monster that ever made the earth to tremble—under CHRIST unites the intensity
of individual force with the majesty of multitude and the spirit of Eternal
Love.

> —WILLIAM C. CONANT, *Narratives of Conversions and Revivals,*
> 1858

1.

THE BANDS OF SLOTH

About 1835, or certainly by 1840, although revivals were still extending across the country at a staggering rate, revivalists felt that the
impulse was grinding to a stop. Bishop McIlvaine recollected, in the
confidence of 1858, how he had warned the faithful in 1836 that they
had ceased to preach Christ. In the 1840's, he said, the "world" could
finally boast its victory over the churches, and cited humiliating examples "of prominent professors of religion disgracing the Christian
name by grievous defections in pecuniary affairs."

Even before the financial crisis of 1837, the more sensitive of revivalists were aware that some mysterious hitch had occurred in the tri-
umphal procession. Nicholas Murray in 1836 published "The Causes

of Declension," which was a more drastic confession than most of his colleagues were prepared to make. What the "causes" were, "every lover of Zion should be anxious to know"; Murray and like-minded worriers could enumerate at least a few of them.

Murray's list, which was expanded monotonously during the next twenty years, constitutes an appraisal of American civilization within the perspective of the Revival. As early as 1836, and indeed for a decade before this, revivalists complained that the feelings of religious men had become so occupied with political issues that they could admit no religious consideration. Down to the actual rupture of war, this was to be the standard lament, South as well as North. If we leave aside, as I propose for the moment to do, the involvement of particular segments of Northern piety with abolitionism, we may note more specifically what evangelicals conceived to be the major distractions.

There is no way of judging how radically these evangelicals really intended to challenge the mercantile ethic. All one can say is that the rhetoric of the Revival conventionally accused the business spirit of having "done much to produce this lamented declension of vital piety." As might be expected—while foreign observers found it amazing that pastors dared so to preach to rich parishioners—ministers regularly denounced as the great source of iniquity among the people their *haste to be rich,* and inculcated Benjamin Franklin's method of "the steady, industrious, persevering course." "Go thou," said Hubbard Winslow in 1835, "and do likewise."

What bothered the Revival was that such warnings, which had driven pioneers of Kentucky and Illinois to distraction, seemed to have progressively less effect on merchants in New York and Cleveland. Preachers made what they could of the Panic of 1837, presenting it as a judgment upon the commercial spirit, but they enjoyed little success. Except for sporadic responses, ministerial indictments that Americans were experiencing in 1837 and 1838 God's visitation upon their mad haste to be rich left the people only momentarily chastened. No great surge of repentance followed.

Evangelicals solaced themselves with the reflection that the whole Revival, spread over time, was a pulsation. While it is true, said *The Christian Spectator* in 1838, that love must reign through all variations, still it needs times of revival and then times of "tranquillity." But they had to note that in periods of tranquillity the liturgical churches gained recruits. "Our forms are so simple and so few," said Joseph Dudley in 1849, "that when the spirit of them is gone, our religion is gone." For, Dudley admitted, there remains little to awe the mind: "Our system of worship has no power, no charm, if the

74

heart be not in it; and just in proportion as we are losing this, we are losing ground, and giving advantage to those systems which consist mainly of external grandeur." Considerations of this sort led Horace Bushnell at Hartford, student of Nathaniel Taylor and child of the Connecticut Revival, to break with the whole system, to denounce it in his *Discourse on Christian Nurture* of 1847. The furor against it caused its printers, the Massachusetts Sabbath School Society, to withdraw it from publication. But Princeton, which would later join the hue and cry against Bushnell's theological heresies, seized this occasion to endorse *Christian Nurture,* and so to make more explicit than it had hitherto dared its distrust of revival methods. Many consider these extraordinary systems, said Professor Charles Hodge, the only means of promoting religion: "They seem to regard this alternation of decline and revival as the normal condition of the church; as that which God intended and which we must look for; that the cause of Christ is to advance not by a growth analogous to the progress of spiritual life in the individual believer, but by sudden and violent paroxysms of exertion." Princeton could now speak out: "Life in no form is thus fitful." Excitation is unavoidably followed by a corresponding depression.

The Revival struggled within the toils of its own logic. While ecstasies such as that of 1800 or of the Mohawk Valley in the 1820's were ablaze, the gratifications were so engulfing that the idea of a depression was inconceivable. Yet even in the midst of them, anxieties arose; as the historian of the Oneida revivals said in 1827, *"The amount of holy feeling and effort ought never to diminish."* Ideally it should not, but the fact is that it did; so Finney and his fellow-incendiaries had to burn northern New York over and over.

Confronted with this problem, revivalists more and more gave thought not only to how to start a movement but how to keep it going, to prevent relapse. By the 1830's they developed two methods for forestalling declension: they published innumerable manuals on the approved conduct of a revival, so that it might be permanently effective; and they produced a class of professional, itinerant revivalists who, by perpetually moving from place to place, would either keep the fires from going out or would fan languishing embers.

Beecher and Skinner led the way in 1832 with *Hints to Aid Christians,* imparting such directions as: "Break, then, the bands of sloth; engage at once in the work; be courageous; be wise; turn many to righteousness, and you shall shine as the brightness of the firmament, and as the stars, forever and ever." Ebenezer Porter's *Letters on the Religious Revival* of the same year is a handbook for the novice, as circumstantial as a textbook on dentistry, telling how to answer questions, what texts to choose, how to emphasize topics. As in all these works, Porter, although he believed himself in the old Connecticut tradition and disliked the tumult of the West, elaborately argues that God does use "means" toward creating a revival and that the orthodox should have no theological scruples about doing God's work for Him: experience has shown at one and the same time "the indispensable necessity of means, and the sovereignty of divine grace." No law of nature is more invariable, said Skinner in 1838, "than that, in Revivals of religion, cause precedes effect, appropriate means are used to attain ends." God shows His power in them, but they are not miracles. By 1859, Heman Humphrey's *Revival Sketches and Manual* becomes just what the title indicates; there is no longer even a polite bow toward any theory of the Revival but only instructions on preaching, conservation of the preacher's energies, and the proper conduct of "inquiry meetings."

The drift toward formalizing the process became a tidal wave as the professionals began to eclipse the "settled" clergy. Connecticut had been proud in 1800 that its Awakening was conducted by the local ministry, except for the inoffensive itinerancy of Nettleton; the leaders at Cane Ridge attended as ambassadors from their churches; the Methodist circuit rider had his route laid out and was not free to heed a call from regions outside his jurisdiction. But Finney established, in this regard as in his methods, a precedent. He went where he was wanted or summoned, and never conceived of himself as fixed in one place, not even when he did for a few years hold forth regularly in the New York Tabernacle. Men like Jedediah Burchard (who relighted the fires in Finney's New York), Edward Norris Kirk (who revolted against his Princeton training), the two mighty Baptists Jabez Swan and Jacob Knapp were the most prominent among several. Methodists followed suit by assigning their most effective rousers, John Newland Maffit, James Caughty, John S. Inskip, to the nation at large. Of these, even those who had been schooled in Calvinism banished any memory of historic dependence upon the capricious overflowing of God's spirit; they openly "got up" revivals. Their techniques were susceptible of imitation.

But within a short time the vogue of these manuals and the achievements of the professionals created a perplexity more ominous than the one they were designed to solve. We have heard Baird and the early theorists insist that a revival was essentially "spontaneous." Finney and his generation revolted against the tyranny of the intellect, cast out "metaphysics," and identified religious expression with the heart.

How then could the Revival pretend that it was the same as in 1800 if it so palpably had, four decades later, to depend upon the set contrivances of the manuals, or on the standardized tricks of pious actors? John Woodbridge in 1841 attempted to forestall the question by admitting that perhaps "in the present state of the world we are not to expect revivals of the same character with those which existed forty years ago." It is indeed a problem to keep alive the same depth of conviction, solemnity, self-scrutiny, in "this age of sanguine hope, bustle, enterprise and revolution." No wonder that "new experiments" have to be tried. Yet no such plea could silence the objection of one of Finney's disciples that "*Lectures* upon Revivals are not the chief thing the Church needs. . . . You cannot, but at a frightful risk, lay down *rules* for Revivals of Religion. No rules will apply in all cases. This is a subject about which we cannot *legislate*." Finney himself growled against standardization; yet the irony of the situation was that he himself contributed to it by his most famous book, *Lectures on Revivals of Religion,* in 1835. If ever an author "legislated" on his subject, that was Finney.

Furthermore, while the itinerants were always represented in the religious press, or in the public press, as staging successful meetings, there was an augmenting hostility to them among the evangelical ministers and congregations. "To the credulous multitude," sneered Russell Streeter in 1835, "there is a *charm* in the very *names* of these men." He despised Burchard: "People experience unusual emotions in coming into their presence or their meetings, as the young and uninformed do, in coming before some celebrated *conjuror*." The suspicion grew that these stimulators were mountebanks. In 1842 R. W. Cushman, of the Bowdoin Square Church in Boston, a Baptist, denied to Elder Jacob Knapp the use of his pulpit; some of his congregation were outraged, but Cushman published *A Calm Review,* in which he excoriated such "improved machinery for the advancement of religion."

These hints of fissures in the foundation of American evangelism could momentarily be hidden by the gloss of professional unction, but they worried sincerely religious spirits. Meanwhile, a new set of internal tensions arose not so much within the foundation as in the wondrous superstructure which the Revival had erected to demonstrate its unity and through which it had mobilized its energies—the missionary organizations and the network of "agencies."

2.

THE PERILS OF BENEVOLENCE

The powerful interdenominational organizations formed in the second and third decades of the century were inspired by, and in turn reinforced, the ecumenical aspirations of the Revival. In those innocent years, it seemed not only plausible but a decided advantage to bless these associations with another weighty adjective. Robert Baird was firm in the conviction when in 1844 he said, in the course of defending the principle:

Men are so constituted as to derive happiness from the cultivation of an independent, energetic, and benevolent spirit, in being co-workers with God in promoting his glory, and the true welfare of their fellow-men.

The concept of the benevolent man—"the man of feeling"—figured largely in British literature of the late eighteenth century, and in the strain of moral philosophy which descended from Francis Hutcheson. It was raised to the status of a cult by the literature which historians call "Sentimentalism," all of which was reverently read in America. A man could no more safely, in America of 1820, publicly come out against benevolence, or announce that men were so constituted as to derive happiness not from benevolent dispositions as from the selfish calculations of Hobbes and Mandeville, than he could advocate sexual promiscuity. Alexander Hamilton had his reservations, but he expressed them obliquely by his financial policies. Jefferson would not profess orthodox Christianity, but that man in a state of nature, which was the state of most Americans, showed himself instinctively benevolent furnished the basis of his philosophy.

For the student of the American mind it is important to realize that the co-operative societies had ready to hand a sanction which seemed all the more reason for a common ground of all denominations: these bodies were manifestations of "Benevolence." This thesis accorded beautifully with the Revival's search for unanimity, with its enchantment before the "Sublime," and with its predicating the vitality of the movement upon the "Heart." Defining "The Character of the Present Age," *The Biblical Repository* in 1832 remarked, "The benevolent exertions, to promote the cause of Christ, and benefit man, which are the glory of our country, are awakened and sustained by high excitement." Sober calculations, it continued, acute reasonings, can accomplish nothing: "they must be combined with some strong impressive influence, which pervades the community." Or indeed, as *The Christian Spectator* had put it ten years earlier, "Benevolent exertions call into exercise all the graces of christians."

Wherefore it was too obvious to need argument, in the first decades of the Revival, that the energies of Christians were to be mobilized into societies and associations, not only the Sunday-School Union, but programs for the salvation of seamen, for prison reform, relief of the poor, asylums for the insane, the deaf and dumb, the blind. "Thus," predicted the *Spectator* in 1822, "piety grows by the operations of benevolence, and the operations of benevolence acquire new strength by the growth of piety." It was an unbeatable system—the capstone of America's freedom. And then the wonderful hope, the dazzling vision dawning upon American revivalism: might it be that by these exertions, both in home and foreign missions, with the power generated by the associations, America would in fact lead the way, without any Fifth-Monarchy nonsense, into the millennium?

One may fairly say that this grandiose ambition could not have been incorporated into the Revival merely by the ecumenical hunger, or even by nationalistic infatuation, had it not been also nourished by a universal homage to the ideal of benevolence. The crucial document is William Cogswell's *Harbinger of the Millennium*, in 1833. This secretary of The American Educational Society recited the, by then, astounding array of associations for benevolent purposes, and declared them "combined instruments in promoting the conversion of the world and the salvation of men." They are not rivals; they are companions in the cause both of Christ and of benevolence. Or, as Francis Wayland said in 1835, "The cause of benevolence is holy: it is the cause of God."

The indescribable advantage of conjoining to missions and reform the watchword of benevolence soon became apparent: a way could be opened for the activism of the American temperament. The combination would not require rejection of historic doctrines concerning original sin or moral inability. Methodist and Calvinist could meet on this program without having to waste time on abstractions. As *The Christian Spectator* happily announced in 1833, "The profound researches, the startling theories, the abstruse metaphysical niceties which were once almost alone expected in books, have given place to discussions that bear on duties, the responsibilities of men, their relations in society, their interests, or their pleasures, as a direct object, and commonly in an alluring, exciting form." In missions and in plans for reform the metaphysics of Edwards and Bellamy were "embodied in those practical effects, which truth clearly exhibited and influencing many minds in concert, has a direct tendency to produce." The title of this assertion was, significantly, "Moral Characteristics of the Nineteenth Century." There is no telling how much the author was conscious of the immensity of the revolution he meekly acclaimed.

Probably he was not aware. Throughout the literature, which mounts to an intoxication of joy that missions and millennium may at last be joined, there runs a confident assurance that the goal is attainable because it draws strength from an invincible urge toward benevolence. The emphasis, in Cogswell, Williston, and all the millennialists, upon the feasibility of reaching the millennium through missionary benevolence is so insistent that one concludes it had become a national obsession. "These questions," preached Charles Imbrie before the Presbyterian Synod of New Jersey in 1849, "cannot now at least be held as mere theories. The times make them eminently practical."

Curiously enough, as the conception of the benevolent gesture moved from its tentative beginnings into the dream of millennium, the accent upon practicability transforms it from an excitement into a job. In 1823 Francis Wayland saw, in the avenues awaiting American philanthropy, the lure of the "moral sublime." There was, to him, no room for criticism, for calculating chances:

To that enterprise alone has been awarded the meed of sublimity, of which the conception was vast, the execution arduous, and the means to be employed simple but efficient. Were not the object vast, it could not arrest our attention. Were not its accomplishment arduous, none of the nobler energies of man being tasked in execution, we should see nothing to admire. Were not the means to that accomplishment simple, our whole conception being vague, the impression would be feeble. Were they not efficient, the intensest exertion could only terminate in failure and disgrace.

Here, to begin with, was everything at once: sublimity and efficiency. Part of any explanation for the ferocity of this passion is that under the idea of universal benevolence the revivalists (escaping the clutch of Edwards and Hopkins) could launch themselves and their people upon a majestic ocean. "So the great objects of Christian benevolence, at this day," said Ebenezer Porter, also in 1823, "seem destined to swallow up the thousand minor objects of regard, to harmonize the views of hostile sects, and to combine by a common impulse, the efforts of princes, statesmen, and peasants, to promote the interests of the church." For years there seemed a glorious consistency to the operation, or, rather, within all the manifold operations, which was entirely centered upon the benevolent thesis. *The Spirit of the Pilgrims* in 1828 proudly asserted that "since the more general and extensive revival of pure religion, the spirit of benevolence has been excited, which is carrying into triumphant operation the numerous Christian and charitable institutions which illustrate and exalt the present age." That cause could become effect, and effect a cause—that there was a "reflex" action—made the triumph only more evident, justifying the discarding of metaphysical speculation. Revivals inspired zealous agents of the societies, and "these, in their turn, devote their newly inspired energies and zeal to the improvement and growth of the fostering institutions from which they first derived the light of life." This, at the high point of the Revival, appeared to be the vindication of three decades of endeavor. Who, Theodore Grimke rhetorically asked in 1829, would exchange for our benevolent institutions the seven wonders of the ancient world?

Who does not rejoice, when he beholds such institutions, with their simple, tranquil, charitable spirit, smiling through all our land, shedding their blessings on the social and domestic circle, scattering the treasures of their love at home and abroad, and sending up to heaven the never-failing incense of gratitude, supplication and praise?

Suppose we did yield these in order to gain the arts and sculptures of classical genius (to the revivalistic mind this was an either-or proposition): would we be the gainers? "*Those* would indeed make our country a theatre of wonders, to the eye of taste and science; but *these* have dedicated her to the service and glory of God."

In this mood, the Revival saw nothing arrogant or chimerical in Cogswell's prediction that the millennium was close at hand. He makes clear, said one reviewer, that the great era shall not be a day of sudden brightness but a time "when benevolent efforts will have been made to the utmost of the ability of the church, and crowned with Divine blessing." The moral is that the churches must live and act for the millennium, for nothing less, and pay no more heed to "the indolent and wretched spirit of many professors who, unlike the saints of old, make the divine predictions the pillows of their sloth, and every glorious promise a soporific drug." "Our field is the world," exclaimed *The Christian Spectator* in 1834; yet because we constitute a part of the world within ourselves, our action for good upon ourselves, "by a sort of solecism in language, may be called *benevolent* action." There is no cause for being ashamed of "propagandism." The spirit of it pervades literature, the pulpit. And look to experiment, whether it has not already demonstrated "the practicability of calling out in behalf of the world's conversion, the entire strength of the whole Christian community!"

Yet as we follow the literature through the 1830's, we are impressed by the gradations through which Wayland's vision of the sublimity of efficiency becomes transmuted into mere efficiency. By 1837 *The Christian Spectator* was contending that Christian sympathy is an emotion which spends itself, not in fruitless sighs and tears and passionate expressions, "but in prompt and vigorous action." And in 1843, Thomas Skinner, without awareness of how he was confessing that the glory had diminished, if not actually departed, delivered to the Commissioners for Foreign Missions a sermon blandly entitled *Progress, the Law of the Missionary Work*. He recounted the formation of this "system of benevolent agencies" which distinguished his age (in America) above all since the primitive triumphs of Christianity. He listed the "incidental benefits," chief of which had been the minimizing of sectarianism, and concluded that all could now perceive in the missionary enterprise, along with its kindred and "subservient" organizations, conclusive demonstration of the law of progress. Surely, of course, they had needed the blessing of God, but the way in which they had exercised their initiatives and co-operated in the work was a monumental exhibition of how God elects to work through means.

By the time Skinner thus smugly pointed out the inevitability of benevolent progress, a corroding doubt was at work within the machine. This was something more profound, more subtle, and potentially more destructive than a debate over the superior urgency of home as against foreign missions, more dangerous than the opposition of rural churches to visits from agents of the societies. It became a distrust of the principle of benevolence itself.

For the moment I am concerned with this skepticism only as it reared its head within the charmed circle of the Revival; there, as compared with the utterances of Emerson and Thoreau, it may seem fairly mild. But the revivalists were not affected by anything Transcendentalists said, and managed to conduct their intellectual life as though Emerson never existed. Wherefore, this creeping suspicion about benevolence as a slogan which had betrayed, or threatened to betray, the spirit of the Revival is, in the history of the American mind, a more arresting counteraction than Thoreau's announcing that he would not go into doing-good because the profession was overcrowded. Yet the existence of this anxiety in the community which surrounded the Transcendentalists, and the seriousness with which it was taken by the masses, gives poignance to Emerson's lifelong attempt to resist the demands of charity without himself becoming un-charitable.

As early as 1823, Ebenezer Porter coupled his praise of modern benevolence with the caution, recollected out of seventeenth-century casuistry, that the ardor of a man's heart may rise on purely benevo-lent principles, but he must take care lest it come from other sources: "The secret spring of his zeal may be, that the prosperity of this good cause, is honorable to his own efforts. The elevation of this good object, makes *himself* conspicuous." Porter was apprehensive about the multiplication of officers within the associations, and pointedly asked why, "in this boasted nineteenth century, this age of overflowing benevolence,—this dawn of the millennium," Christians needed to be flattered by votes of thanks from public meetings for doing the work of their Redeemer? Gospel union, Porter cautioned, is no doubt a de-lightful idea, "but we should not give up the *gospel* for the sake of union; nor be so civil to each other, as to forget the respect that is due to our Master."

This was the portent of a criticism which was basically theological, or at least moralistic, and which was quite different from the back-country grudge against urban societies. "Church members look far too much to ministers, and missionaries, and benevolent societies," abruptly declared the Reverend Nicholas Murray in 1836, "to the neglect of their own duty." With his article, in *The Literary and The-ological Review,* the lid blew off. "God is not about to convert the world by a committee," he snarled. At once the malcontents sprang to his side. Because the piety of former ages was cloistered in cells, said *The Christian Spectator,* we have exalted the idea that the action of mind upon objects outside itself is the sole stimulant of vital religion. "What commenced on principle, grows into a passion; until at length the excitement occasioned by external movement becomes the ele-ment of life." Hubbard Winslow told the pious, in language which came to most of them as a shock, that if they left the great work of spiritual regeneration and gave themselves up to every exciting sub-ject, such as missions or temperance, then "it demands no prophetic tongue to announce our doom."

By this time the Revival was confronted with a metaphysical antin-omy it had no equipment for resolving. The painful aspect of its dilemma was that the contradictions arose out of the Revival's own premises, those which it had defended against Unitarianism, Nevin, and Princeton. It had argued, and had proved, that out of revivalism are generated energies which can be channelized into benevolent associations, wherein the many sects will find a ground of union, and through which a religious nationalism can be enunciated, against which neither the animosities of sections, the barbarism of the frontier, nor the Philistinism of commerce may prevail. All this was clear, logical, beautifully symmetrical. But in 1837, the year of Emerson's "The American Scholar," R. W. Dickinson was lamenting that many whose hearts pant to do good "are prone to substitute their own projects for the humble use of scriptural means, while immediate success, that infallible criticism of wisdom to vulgar judgments, at once established in general estimation the utility of the scheme."

There had been only a decade before something magnificent, something sublimely defiant in Finney's curt rebuttal to his theological critics that they could, as far as he was concerned, literally go to hell, his warrant being that his results justified his methods. The very success of his methods—which were those of the Revival carried to logical extremes—created the societies. All had worked according to plan. But by 1836 *The Christian Spectator* was sagely attributing to this restless spirit, "which is at home only in scenes of bustling activity," the fact that too many of the redeemed suppose the "aggressive enterprises of the church" constitute the whole duty of man. Yes, it agreed, these projects "originated in the purest benevolence," but they have obliterated the duties of the closet. So fervent a revivalist as John Woodbridge in 1841 mourned that such activities implied no essential change in the heart of participants. The quest for nondoctrinal unity had come to the point where any "fervent vindication of evangelical truth, has been stigmatized as equivalent to indifference to the welfare of immortal souls and the cause of holiness." What we have, Woodbridge had the courage to assert, is an effort "to amalgamate the most discordant materials into a homogeneous mass of neutrality and insipidity." Real peace is not secured by affecting a union of feeling where there is no actual union. "Without such projects religion has been revived in former times; and it may be revived again." If it could not, then the best minds among the Revival comprehended that they were at an impasse: the Great Revival, having warded off, thrust aside, all opponents, threatened to defeat itself. Benevolence had undone it.

3.

THE MORALS OF THE CITY

When Robert W. Cushman explained to his Baptist congregation why he barred his pulpit to the foremost Baptist evangelist, Elder Knapp, he surprisingly argued (he was almost the first to say so) that a revival did no good in a city, that it was in fact an affliction. Whatever it may accomplish in agricultural areas, in a large town it only accelerates the "pleasure-party," which thereafter recoils from a fright proved to be groundless. If earnest revivalists were becoming worried about the inner contradictions of their movement, said Cushman, they had only to look at their failures in large towns. Boston had been subjected to its share of crusades, notably that of Lyman Beecher and of the Park Street Church, with the result that the morals of the city have been steadily deteriorating. "Even the temperance reform, which, up to that period, had been advancing, has since been manifestly on the decline."

Such blunt speaking gave a jolt to the whole benevolent wagon, because it brought the drivers up short before an obstacle they had hitherto pretended did not exist. Cushman was saying that the inveterate corruption of the city would resist the most generalized, the most undenominational of the Revival's benevolent enterprises. Even worse: the preaching of temperance in a city would only accelerate consumption.

There is no need here to retell the often-told story of the Temperance Societies, the Washingtonians, et cetera, which played a vigorous part in the social scene of the early nineteenth century. Had they not set in motion the impetus which carried through to the "great experiment" of the Eighteenth Amendment, they would be only curiosities. I need merely remark that within the framework of the Revival, temperance provided the platform on which the evangelical sects could most heartily come together. More than any other form of association, it was uncontroversial. As Charles Sprague said early in the movement, in 1827, we do not need laws, we speak only to "the unwritten majesty of Public Opinion." Here was the ideal issue on which the Revival could work with a minimum of internal friction, with a maximum of pious co-operation.

Political institutions, said Theodore Grimke in a moving address of 1833, supply no life-giving energy. We should rely solely on our societies, which are regenerating the country, "carrying it onward to a state of more beauty, grandeur, and felicity, of which the present generation can form but an imperfect estimate." Because the mass of temperance literature was, of course, devoted to the deleterious effects of alcohol upon physiology, we are apt to dismiss it as cranky. We thus lose sight of the central motive in the movement, which was, as Grimke explicitly declared, to discover a cause that was simultaneously Christian and American. In it "the principle of *individual responsibility* and *social influence* has ever been manifested." It makes every allowance for American individualism, but also holds persons responsible to the common stock. "The Temperance Reformation is peculiarly Christian, AMERICAN." If there was a "reflex" action of missions upon consolidating the religious community, how much more would temperance unite them! "We appeal only to experience to show the power of union for the sake of momentous truths and the influence of proclaimed principles of utility and virtue to temper the waywardness, and finally take captive the hearts of man." In essence, this is the program of the Revival, narrowed down to a single, a feasible issue. When we come to the innermost mechanism of the campaign, temperance reform was simply the most direct road toward the millennium. Intemperance, cried Albert Barnes in 1834, "stands in the way of revivals, and of the glories of the millennial morn. Every drunkard opposes the millennium; every dram-drinker stands in the way of it; every dram-seller stands in the way of it."

Interestingly enough, this passage comes from a volume which Barnes entitled *Intemperance in Cities*. Colton, the year before, in his authoritative treatment of the *History and Character of American Revivals of Religion*, pointed out that they flourished principally in communities where "every body knows every body," and Finney never made any bones about the effectiveness of a public spectacle in which all those present recognized at once the individual who surrendered to the anxious bench. By 1841, Barnes, in his equally authoritative *Sermons on Revivals*, was already speaking nostalgically. In country villages the infidel "usually stands alone." All men know their neighbors, and are accustomed to sympathize with them; there "the joy of conversion will strike a responsive chord throughout the community." But in New York or Philadelphia, alas, it often happens in a revival that one "stratum" of society is affected, but not the others. The combinations and alliances of sins are so complex that nothing can destroy them, not even the power of God in a revival. If this were really true—Barnes endeavored to show that nevertheless new methods might contend with the city—then the Revival was in danger of dis-

86

integration both from within and from without—from its internal confusions and its inability to cope with a growing challenge which neither Cane Ridge nor Connecticut had anticipated, the metropolis.

The tardiness of the evangelicals in realizing that the city presented an immovable obstacle to their irresistible force is, naturally, an index of the overwhelmingly agrarian character of their society. The mind of America was everywhere slow, or deliberately reluctant, to admit the fact of urbanization. The literary intelligence, as we shall see, was likewise hesitant; it is not, interestingly enough, until this same decade of the 1840's, when the revivalists confess their dilemma, that a group of New York writers endeavor to make capital out of the buzzing confusion, and betray by their bumblings that they have no technique for mastering it, though by this time all Americans, including most of the religious, were reading Charles Dickens, and wallowing in the sights and smells of London. Still, the notion that these burgeoning American cities were already such cesspools as that displayed in *Oliver Twist* was difficult to admit, even though every respectable citizen knew of the existence of the Five Points, and his New York hosts in 1842 arranged that Dickens should visit the noisome slum.

There had, of course, been premonitions both in literature and in the Revival. Finney came to Philadelphia and New York in 1830 determined to assault the Devil in his citadel. Early in the century there were infused into the American imagination forebodings about what ultimately their "empire" might become; both preachers and poets expressed their dread of its irresistible course, until the worry had become a staple of conversation and pictorial representation. But it took the evangelical mentality another decade or so fully to comprehend the danger. In 1853 (while Walt Whitman was composing *Leaves of Grass*) E. H. Chapin set it forth in a series of lectures, *Moral Aspects of City Life,* which in the realm of religion is as telling a recognition of the urban onslaught as was, in the theater, Benjamin Baker's *A Glance at New York* of 1848.

Though the Reverend Mr. Chapin would certainly object to having his book linked to so bawdy a play, still, just as the adventures of Mose the Fireman broke with the succession of romances which had dominated the stage and positively reveled in the vulgarity of New York, so Chapin discarded the literary convention that had dominated his age, according to which virtue dwelt in the country and cities were utterly vile. On the contrary, he said, "the interest of the city is as superior to that of the country, as humanity to nature; as the soul to the forms and forces of matter; as the great drama of existence is to the theatre in which it is enacted." However, by the time he has unrolled the panorama of New York, where conventionality stifles natural impulse, where men are driven by a passion for flaring wealth, where substantial citizens are heedless of their neighbors "in the Lower Depths," and where intemperance "dilates into the horribly sublime," we find that in spite of his obvious delight in the city he must declare eternal enmity between it and the Spirit of Christ. As more than one revivalist sadly admitted, while depravity is the same whether in the forests or in the city, still "in a metropolis, sin is more crowded and overt."

In the early 1850's evangelicals grew more and more gloomy. Perhaps the Methodists, who as Bishop Bangs said were "begotten, fostered, and grew up under the influence of the spirit of the revival," were the most apprehensive. The original Methodists had proclaimed their gospel with the sound of trumpets, said Abel Stevens in 1855, but what instruments have we that can be heard in the city? He proposed that circuit riders on the old model be concentrated in the cities, and that preaching deal more with actualities of urban life—gambling, business morality. But little or no progress was apparently made. "What remedy for these sad defects?" moaned J. T. Hendrick in 1857, and answered that obviously nothing but a true revival "can save the church from the fatal spell by which Satan now holds her bound under the delusive spirit of worldliness." The prospect was all the darker because "there never was a time, since the settlement of the country, when the churches have been in such danger from worldly prosperity." Religion had flowered resplendently among the gaunt hills of Kentucky, but amid the opulence of New York, what hope could there be for even its survival?

4.

THE EVENT OF THE CENTURY

And then, just when there seemed no alternative to despair, when "there was weeping in secret places over the general decline, and many prayers were offered for the return of the Spirit," the miracle was wrought. This event, beyond anything in the past, unanimously declared the clergy, was not the result of any human project, concerted arrangement, or prescribed plan. "No man pretends to have ever seen the like."

The Great Awakening of 1857 and 1858 was different from all previous revivals, first, in that it was concentrated in the cities, and second, in that it arose from below, among the laity, and the astonished ministers had to run fast to catch up with it.

It began, exulted Bishop McIlvaine, "just in that time of rebuke, and darkness, and apparent deep discouragement," and it sprang up "in our chief commercial centers, precisely where the credit of religion had been most impaired, and the tide against it was the strongest." The realization that this *could* happen was to leave an indelible impression on the Protestant mind. But even more startling and memorable, as another Episcopalian admirer declared, "it was begun by *the people,* and has been carried on by *the people,* almost entirely, without even the occasional aid of a minister, until within a fortnight or three weeks."

For a while the Awakening proceeded so quietly that few realized that any significant effort was under way. At first it took the form of spontaneously gathered prayer meetings of short duration, usually at noon during the lunch hour, and in the business districts. These seem to have commenced sporadically in Philadelphia in 1856, were being practiced in New York by the end of 1857, and from February to June of 1858 were observed with astounding zeal in almost all cities. They were marked by an entire absence of the old revivalistic noise; they were quiet, "no new revelation is made or pretended; no mighty machinery is set in motion." Most astonishingly, the groups caught up in the movement showed little interest in preaching: "they came together," marveled Alexander, "not to hear learned, elegant, or eloquent appeals, but to unite in prayer." A few of the clergy, like Heman Humphrey, worried lest the people hereafter "will rely too much upon the prayer offered up for them at the union meetings; and that they will think too lightly of ministers and their preaching," but the majority, after they recovered from their initial bewilderment, had the good sense to let the revival run the course it had itself selected.

Because the union prayer meeting was accommodated to the time schedule of commerce, "it was a revival of religion among business men, and in this it differs from all that preceded it." With their bosses attending, throngs of clerks and messenger boys also came. The sessions were "thronged," wrote a delighted William Conant, "by the men who have hitherto given their strength to the god of this world, and given to their country its preeminence in the daring, intense, and unexampled progress of worldly enterprise." While some wondered if the transactions of trade could ever really be brought under the rule of Christian principles, all had to confess that this work of God "seems to have had a marked relation to commerce, as though God intended to bring the influences of His Holy Spirit to bear upon this world-wide power." The assumption which for decades had been an axiom of American culture, that business and piety would not mix, was suddenly and effectively dissipated. A new vista opened before the churches, which they never afterward could forget.

Because the businessmen were in control, the meetings rapidly developed a legislation of their own devising, designed for maximum efficiency. A "five-minute rule" was imposed, limiting any speaker to that time, which the leader enforced by striking a bell. The singing was led by one person, and during the hour the use of tobacco was prohibited. All established one firm regulation: "No controverted points discussed or announcements of what denomination the brother may belong to must be made upon the floor." The natural consequence, as one admirer put it, was a warm spirit of Christian love, "a heartier union in all common and general efforts for the good of souls."

By the time the religious mind could grasp what was happening, it began to ask just what had caused the miracle. The obvious answer was the financial depression of 1857. No, no, answered Talbot W. Chambers, this movement—which far more than the opening of China, the Atlantic cable, or the reconquest of India is *the* event not only of the year but of the century—has been more like the Pentecost than any since then. Look at it as we will, the conclusion is unmistakable: "THIS IS THE FINGER OF GOD." Furthermore, it did not necessarily follow that a causal connection between the crisis and the revival subtracted from the glory of the event. "It would seem that the mighty crash was just what was wanted . . . to startle men from their golden dreams." This revival would not have commenced as it did, nor spread as it has, concluded Humphrey, "if the spell which held men in its embrace had not been broken by some sudden and violent convulsion." The charm of this interpretation was that it also accounted for what so far had been the mystery of the panic. Natural causes had been suggested—speculation, fires, and such—but the paradox remained that the commercial world had stood trembling in alarm and ruin, with its coffers full of gold. Now, concluded William Aikman, we know why: the means accomplished the end. The hardest head in Wall Street had been taught that God was as supreme in the world of finance as in other areas of His providence. "GOD IN COMMERCE, is the interpretation of the history of those years." This happy conclusion would also remain as a deposit in the Protestant memory, to be brought forth in strength when the religious conscience had again to contend with the vagaries of the business cycle.

On the other hand, a different but even more interesting method of interpreting the revival sprang up on every side, so that one can hardly say that any specific theologian invented it: this revival, being urban and businesslike, confirmed the union of the millennial expectation with applied science. The unanimity, which might at first sight seem wholly supernatural, was wrought by the telegraph and the press. These conveyed and published "the thrill of Christian sympathy, with the tidings of abounding grace, from multitudes to multitudes in every city simultaneously assembled, in effect almost bringing a nation together in one praying intercourse." Nor could it be only fortuitous that the movement should coincide with the Atlantic cable, for both were harbingers of that unity which is the forerunner of ultimate spiritual victory. "There can be little doubt that the millennial glory is to begin before many years." The Awakening of 1858 first made vivid for the American imagination a realizable program of a Christianized technology. Once rooted there, the conviction would die only under the heaviest bombardment of contradictory evidences.

What was saluted from almost every quarter of the nation, and with joy by the evangelical denominations, was the dramatic success of the union meetings in truly transcending sectarian limits. The rule so widely adopted that a speaker from the floor be forbidden to announce his membership was extravagantly praised by the churches themselves. "Arminians and Calvinists, Baptists and Pedo-Baptists, Episcopalians and Presbyterians, Congregationalists and Friends, sat side by side on the same benches, sang the same hymns, said Amen to the same prayers." In this Pentecost as at the first, what became evident to the followers of Jesus was not the things in which they differed but those upon which they agreed. J. W. Alexander, after a brief period of doubting the authenticity of the revival, beheld in the spectacle of sustained concert a source "from which we are to expect the sublime unity of a coming day." Methodist Bangs agreed: this makes men "for a moment forget their denominational peculiarities; it tears down their sectarian prejudices, and makes them feel all as one." That secret aspiration for unity which had long lain hidden in the Revival now came into the open; the hunger for cohesion could at last be sated. "Evangelical Christians of every name," sang Humphrey, "found they could come together and pray for the outpouring of the Spirit without any sacrifice of church order, and were astonished that they had not sooner found out 'how good and how pleasant it is for brethren to dwell together in unity' at the throne of grace." Two years before the election of Abraham Lincoln, the meetings sent up fervent prayers that Satan would no more get an advantage over this Republic "by rebuilding the walls which have so long kept us apart to our mutual discredit and loss." But scarcely anybody thought it strange that this display of concord should be achieved upon the explicit provision that no controverted points should ever be discussed, among them slavery.

Most remarkable was the benediction called down upon this manifestation even by those who hitherto had been lukewarm or even hostile to revivalism. Some High Churchmen in New York held out against the meetings; McIlvaine earnestly defended them, and an anonymous Episcopalian in New York read to his brethren the news that while formerly the churches were shut six days of the week, now they were all open for prayer "in the height of the work-day, and in the midst of the whirl and roar of the work-day world." Princeton, in the person of J. W. Alexander, capitulated. And even the Unitarians came round, with the conspicuous exception of Theodore Parker. Oddly enough, this most Transcendental of the ordained clergy in Boston held to the old Unitarian line that this revival, like every other, was "gotten up"; the means are as well known as those for getting up "a Mechanic's Fair, a country muster, a cattle show, or a political convention." In this case, there was a financial crisis; whereupon those responsible for it seized the chance to gain church members "and enforce belief in the ecclesiastical theology." All this machinery, Parker thundered, "is as well known as McCormick's reaper." But Parker spoke out of a forgotten, an obsolete radicalism. While he contended that the whole fanfarade was only a trick to keep ecclesiastical business "at the old stand," Unitarian churches in New York and Boston joined the weekly meetings; Frederic Dan Huntington at Harvard conducted Wednesday services, and Theodore Tebbetts, Richard Pike, and James Freeman Clarke scolded their fellow Unitarians for too much disregarding "the mysterious and spontaneous power of the union of hearts for the accomplishment of spiritual purposes."

Parker's criticism sounded pointless because this revival, in its beginnings, appeared to be as little gotten up as possible; it vindicated the spontaneous thesis. True, once it was moving, the ministers swung breathlessly into action. The professional revivalists organized union meetings, and Finney came out of the semiretirement of Oberlin to stump the nation. But in the calm delirium of this revival, the professionals banded together to hold "union" meetings which had no suggestion about them of a particular ecclesiastical interest. And in fact, out of this Awakening came the "Tent," to succeed in the city the camp meeting as the symbol of Christian fraternity. "In the tent are no distinctions: high and low, rich and poor, all stand on equal footing." Horace Greeley was so carried away that he predicted such a rebirth of conscience as would destroy slavery without a war.

A literature arose out of the Awakening which confirmed the nondenominational, noncontroversial character of this attainment of unity. It sold in vast quantities during the peak of its intensity: Henry Fish's *Primitive Piety Revived,* Newman Hall's *Come to Jesus,* and William E. Boardman's *The Higher Christian Life.* Their titles proclaim their content; they may be taken as the ultimate reaches of the Revival's long effort to elude the trammels of metaphysics, and serve as starting points for a new era in American pietism which, no longer concerned with doctrine, would seek a "practical Christianity" purely of the heart.

The great Awakening of 1858 had far-reaching effects. For the life of the mind they are all, as, for instance, the invigoration of the Y.M.C.A., symbolic of an urbanization of the Revival. Though the nation for a long time would remain predominantly rural, and the old pattern of revival persist in those areas (indeed, in the villages it sprang into new life during 1858), still within the city a new form had emerged out of the old; the way for Dwight Moody and Billy Sunday was prepared.

In relation to the national situation of 1858, the Revival is of immense importance, because into an urban context it carried the assertion of the unity of Christians and the expectation of an immediate attainment through a national religion of the millennium so long and so ardently sought in America. When our eyes behold such a work as this, asked Bishop McIlvaine (who was no reckless enthusiast), may we not see a "foretaste, in its diffusion, of what is to be, and must be, wider and wider, more and more wonderfully, till the whole promise is fulfilled, and the Spirit indeed is poured out on all mankind?" Neither was Princeton given to beholding visions, but after appreciating the vastness of the work, Alexander could not resist the persuasion that it was a work of preparation: "The Lord appears to be preparing his armaments and marshaling his hosts for new conquests."

Two years later, Governor William Gist proclaimed in South Carolina a fast day to implore the direction and blessing of Almighty God. In Charleston, Thomas Smyth delivered the sermon. What was the religion of the North? "Atheists, infidels, communists, free-lovers, rationalists, Bible haters, anti-christian levellers and anarchists." To you, the South, he said, "to you is given the high and holy keeping, above all other conservators, of the Bible, the whole Bible, and nothing but the Bible; and of that liberty of conscience, free from the doctrines and commandments of men." If the South builds her house on this rock, "the gates of hell shall not prevail against it."

American historians have not yet precisely defined the relation of the Awakening of 1858 to the Civil War. Assuming the long training in revivalism which the rank and file of both armies had undergone, beginning in 1800, the conflict was bound to have its religious aspects, and in certain phases, as among the regiments of Stonewall Jackson, it became at times more a revival of religion than a war. But since chroniclers are gifted with hindsight, they can hardly help perceiving that 1858 lifted the populace to its most grandiose conception of unity just before slavery sundered the country. As Timothy Smith observes, "The Awakening of 1858 appeared to contemporaries to deepen the national soul-searching and so pave the way to the election of Lincoln and the coming of the war." If there be truth in this divination, then one must also add that the special character of the excitement did something substantial toward reconciling the business community with the millennial hope. In it the Northern urban culture found a cohesion which for a decade before it had been losing—and which assuredly it could not recover through *Leaves of Grass*. The very means of communication—telegraph, railroad, press, cable—which the steaming cities felt were destroying their identities, received a religious sanction as bonds of solidarity. More important than any of these discoveries, perhaps, was the realization that in union meetings of the churches, in nondenominational prayer meetings, proof was manifested that a combination of the Revival with business could be managed without the loss of liberty—without businessmen having to submit to impracticable or utopian dictates of evangelists.

Most of these speculations concern the historical events with which this history of the mind is not obliged to deal. There is plenteous evidence that the ministers on both sides of the battle lines preached their cause as a holy crusade. Only after Southern defeat, however, could the evangelical spirit of the North take stock of the disaster, and try to extract from the suffering what had been promised in 1858. In 1868 Jesse T. Peck brought out his *History of the Great Republic*, which proved popular and which may be taken as the finest effort to salvage the prewar Revival. His thesis was simply that God "formed this Great Republic; and that religion is the only life-force and organizing power of liberty." We are now at a point where we can summarily dispose "of the *feeling* of difference, always stronger than the reality." With the war, "the intellect and heart and enterprise of the American Church" have been released from restraints once imposed "by a powerful internal despotism." His meaning emerges as confidence that with slavery no longer the divisive issue, the church will become "broader and freer in its out-spoken veracity, its gushing sympathies, and aggressive labor, than heretofore."

After 1860, American Protestantism was called upon to confront the forces of a new age—of industrialism, urbanization, economic conflict. To begin with, it had only the armory of weapons with which it had been equipped by the Great Revival—concepts of sublimity, of the heart, of benevolence, of the millennium. But above all it was committed to the absolute conviction that, amid a multitude of forms, revivalistic piety was the primary force in maintaining "the grand unity of national strength." This was the evangelical heritage.

THE LEGAL MENTALITY

CHAPTER ONE

The Rise of a Profession

"Why then do you venture in a place where none but the strong should come?" he demanded. "Did you not know that when you crossed the big river you left a friend behind you that is always bound to look to the young and feeble like yourself."

"Of whom do you speak?"

"The law—'tis bad to have it, but I sometimes think it is worse to be entirely without it. Age and weakness has brought me to feel such weakness at times. Yes—yes, the law is needed when such as have not the gifts of strength and wisdom are to be taken care of."

—NATTY BUMPPO, in *The Prairie*, 1827

1.

NATURE VERSUS LAW

In 1823, by creating in *The Pioneers* the aged scout Natty Bumppo, James Fenimore Cooper gave America its first universally accepted folk symbol. Cooper seems to have worked more by instinct than by design, and only subsequently realized the majesty of the figure he had created. Because the public enthusiastically adopted him, Cooper was moved to fill out his biography in four more volumes, so that by 1841 the figure had been variously unfolded as the Deerslayer, Hawkeye, Leatherstocking, and the Pathfinder. In these several incarnations he appeared heroic, a man of action and decision, a dead shot, intuitively chivalrous and naturally pious, a very colossus, who keened elegiacally over the despoiling march of civilization through the beauty of the American landscape. But even in the first volume, old and decrepit as he was presented, he won the hearts of Americans because the central action of the novel brought him into conflict with the law.

Natty has a squatter's hut on land which, when he had first known it, was as free as the air. Now this land, a great territory around an exquisite lake, has been secured by grant to Judge Marmaduke Temple. American readers, well aware that Judge Temple was a sketch of the author's own father, a judge who became the patroon of Cooperstown, therefore took even greater delight in the book from their appreciation of the ambivalence of Cooper's own attitude, his sympathy with Natty's untutored protest against the imposition of law on the wilderness, his inability except by this indirection to challenge his father. *The Pioneers,* with a sure insight that must have been something deeper than mere calculation, struck into the very center of what by 1823 had become a tormenting American dilemma.

Judge Temple imposes game laws, but Natty, who has always hunted for just the amount he needs and no more, kills a deer out of season. Although on this very morning Natty has saved the Judge's daughter from the attack of a "painter," the Judge, declaring his determination to see the law executed, issues a search warrant. Natty resists, pointing his rifle at a constable, so that the Judge must order his arrest. The formal hero of the novel, who ultimately will marry the daughter, pleads for mercy to the old man. Marmaduke Temple is aware of Natty's patriotic record and of his own debt to the scout's heroism, but judgment must be whatever the law demands. "Would any society be tolerable, young man, where the ministers of justice are to be opposed by men armed with rifles? Is it for this that I have tamed the wilderness?"

To this argument the hero, although a man of cultivation, gives the American answer on behalf of the natural Bumppo:

He is simple, unlettered, even ignorant; prejudiced, perhaps, though I feel that his opinion of the world is too true; but he has a heart, Judge Temple, that would atone for a thousand faults; he knows his friends, and never deserts them, even if it be his dog.

So the great issue of the nineteenth century, the never-ending case of Heart versus Head, was wonderfully, though at tedious length, dramatized by the son of William Cooper. Natty is arraigned according to the forms of the Common Law; though he clearly has resisted an officer, he is still as untamed as once had been the wilderness Judge Temple undertook to discipline:

I may say not guilty with a clean conscience, for there's no guilt in doing what's right; and I'd rather died on the spot, than had him put foot in the hut at that moment.

Wherefore the Judge delivers his charge to the jury: "Living as we do, gentlemen, on the skirts of society, it becomes doubly necessary to protect the ministers of the law." When sentenced to a fine and a month in prison, the avatar of American freedom wails over the wickedness of shutting up an old man "that has spent his days, as one may say, where he could always look into the windows of heaven." This was enlisting still another recruit to the cause of the Heart. The Judge tries again to say that he must be governed by the law. "Talk not to me of law, Marmaduke Temple," answers the Leatherstocking. "Did the beast of the forest mind your laws, when it was thirsty and hungering for the blood of your own child!" Temple must play out the part, his private feelings must not be considered. Then, declares the man of the people, listen to reason:

I've travelled these mountains when you was no judge, but an infant in your mother's arms; and I feel as if I had a right and a privilege to travel them ag'in afore I die.

Natty Bumppo's long confrontation with the law did not weary Cooper's public, for in the American imagination of 1823 the time when judges and lawyers were only infants in their mothers' arms, and the energy of the people could freely be exercised through the pathless wilderness, was only the day before yesterday. That public more or less knew that nearly half of the signers of the Declaration of Independence and of the drafters of the Constitution had been "lawyers," but the profession in the Revolutionary era had so recently come into being, and the training of men like John Adams and Alexander Hamilton had seemed so rudimentary, that as an organized phalanx they did not then loom as rivals to the clergy or even to the merchants.

By the 1820's the social landscape was greatly altered, and the American intellect was barely beginning to comprehend a revolution more far-reaching than the military resistance to Great Britain. Here again Cooper knew, out of his experience on the frontier and out of his acidulous observation of his father, wherein the controversy lay. The legalist Marmaduke Temple, who had secured his grants by somewhat devious means, looked into the future: where others saw nothing but a wilderness in central New York, the Judge was envisioning "towns, manufactories, bridges, canals, mines, and all the other resources of an old country." He, in short, was positively, aggressively, on the side of the "Course of Empire." He shed no tears over the forlorn, defeated end of Natty Bumppo, forced by the march of civilization to flee to the far side of the Mississippi. And the philosophy by which Temple subdued the wilderness was terrifyingly simple. When his daughter, who although a creature of civilization retains a feminine sensitiveness to Nature, pleads with her father against humiliating the Leatherstocking, he says she talks of what she does not understand, because "Society cannot exist without wholesome restraints." No judge can hesitate to inflict these restraints out of any promptings of his own heart. And it was precisely out of such convictions that Judge Cooper erected his metropolis in the wilderness, his methods those of "wholesome restraints," where the heart should be checked by the intellect, "Nature" by the "Law."

The mass of the people in rural or frontier regions cherished around 1800 an ingrained hostility to the law as a profession. Interestingly enough, this aversion did not spring exclusively from those who were caught up in the Revival or from that minority which still remembered Tom Paine: the majority simply hated the law as an artificial imposition on their native intelligence and judges as agents of constraint. Hence the astonishing popularity, in the country as in the city, of *The Pioneers*. By 1831 the central character of the "Autobiography" of David Crockett, "the original humorist and irrepressible backwoodsman," was a more synthetic product than Natty Bumppo, since he was manufactured not by a creative artist but by Whig politicians to demonstrate that some children of the wilderness opposed Andrew Jackson. Crockett blithely explained that he served as justice of the peace "only a little distance in the purchase, and no order had been established there." But he made out all right: the people didn't "fix" any laws because they supposed everybody would know enough law for ordinary purposes, and Crockett boasted his own judgments were never repealed by higher courts, "as I gave my decisions on the principles of common justice and honesty between man and man, and relied on natural born sense, and not on law learning to guide me." As he proudly affirmed, while the nation applauded, "I had never read a page in a law book in all my life."

There was, naturally, somewhat greater difficulty in getting into formal expression, outside such fictional devices as Natty Bumppo and the still more fictitious Crockett, the basic American distrust of law in all its forms. It was not that the American people were positively resolved on becoming lawless, in the manner of cinema badmen, but they did profoundly believe that the mystery of the law was a gigantic conspiracy of the learned against their helpless integrity. In literature and poetry the lament of Leatherstocking became a staple of the 1820's, and was declaimed with no greater enthusiasm than by some of the jurists. But when the opposition arose among men trained in the law, or at least professing it, then the fraternity rallied; its counterattack carried the ideal of law to a triumph which Hamilton had barely imagined and which the aging Jefferson could only vainly lament.

Out of all this spontaneous literature, which Leatherstocking and Crockett exemplify, perhaps the most trenchant document is P. W. Grayson's *Vice Unmasked*, of 1830. It is all the more poignant as it comes after its cause was already lost, when even the sprawling frontier had been taught that in the wake of the Revival came the Courts.

There can be no worse falsification of American history than to suppose that this antilegalism of the early nineteenth century was merely "Jacksonian," merely the expression of a party. True, Whig propaganda did so clever a job at presenting him not only as the arch anti-intellectual but as the enemy of all legality that the image persists, even though recent re-evaluations have shown that many ardent Jacksonians were legal scholars. When the General entered the field, ran a characteristic blast in 1835, all power was centered in his person: "the law of nations, the civil law, nay, the law of nature, were at once annihilated, and the bayonet, the prison or exile, rendered the legislator, the judge and the citizen, obedient to his will, or removed them from his path." The ludicrous hyperbole of such a passage shows that the hysteria was excited not merely by the specter of "King Andrew." Instead, as the effectiveness of Cooper and Crockett demonstrated, the mood was something more pervasive than either of the parties could control, something deep, atavistic, persistent in the community. This was the opinion to which Grayson gave utterance. These eulogists of the law, he said, suppose always that there is something in it "far too subtle, pure, intricate, and profound for the apprehensions of vulgar intellects." On the part of these self-acknowledged "vulgar intellects," Grayson condemned the law in general—at least, the law as practiced. Lawyers assume it to be "our part to be content that all its precious mysteries, its wondrous depths and beautiful harmony, should be unfolded; and to them alone, the gifted receptacles and conductors of the light of justice, it were becoming in us to rejoice that we were privileged to receive it." Surely, said Grayson, voicing the obstinate American conviction, all this is "despisable trash and superstitious jargon."

As Grayson developed his case, there emerged his picture of what American society might become if only it were exempted from the tyranny of law:

How simple would such a government be! How simple, too, would man himself be! Freed from the tortures of endless prescriptions—the maddening harassments and insolence of authority, and secure in all that is dear to him, his nature, for the first time on earth, would begin to unfold its beauties and exert its energies.

Surely, in America, "this unfettered, unpolluted creature" would find the true sources of his happiness. The task for the lawyers was to find a

method, not for obstructing Utopia, but for making the historic wisdom of the law serve this uniquely American opportunity.

It was not that the mind of the early Republic wished to withhold
admiration for the lawyers who had pleaded the colonial case against
Great Britain, for Patrick Henry and James Otis, but the problem was
how to prevent this veneration from beguiling the nation through
some scholastic mystique, against which its native genius and the
genius of its Revival were antipathetic. It is fair to say that into the
post-Revolutionary period survived something of the old Puritan hostility to lawyers as being men sworn to advocate any case regardless of
its merits. But by 1790 or 1800, as Grayson expressed it, the distrust
had become basically suspicion of the law as by its very nature sophisticated, whereas the American people are natural, reasonable, equitable. A last echo of this legal pietism persisted as late as 1846 in the
claim that the Gospel forbids brother to sue brother; "therefore all
matters of difference in a professedly religious community should be
settled by moral law." While this possibility, though it occasionally
had support in the Revival, became daily less and less tenable, James
Fenimore Cooper could return to Natty Bumppo in *The Pathfinder* of
1840, and, perhaps because of his own melancholy experience with the
courts in cases of libel, hold up anew, and to general American exulta-
tion, the concept of a man who knows justice not by law but by
instinct:

The most striking feature about the moral organization of Pathfinder, was
his beautiful and unerring sense of justice. . . . In short, it was said of the
Pathfinder, by one accustomed to study his fellows, that he was a fair example
of what a just-minded and pure man might be, while untempted by unruly
or ambitious desires, and left to follow the bias of his feelings, amid the
solitary grandeur and ennobling influences of a sublime nature; neither led
aside by the inducements which influence all to do evil amid the incentives
of civilization, nor forgetful of the Almighty Being whose spirit pervades the
wilderness as well as the towns.

The romancer was still instinctively at variance with the judges—although many on the New York bench were his friends. He could still
embarrass them by keeping alive the image of a human being, uninstructed in an academic discipline, who, by following the bias of his
natural feelings, would maintain the dignity of sublime Nature against
the constricting efforts of the intellect and of intellect's vice-regent,
the law.

2.

LAW VERSUS THE COMMON LAW

Almost as soon as the lawyers of the young Republic began to mobilize the forces of the Head against the anarchic impulses of the American Heart, they found themselves further embarrassed by a hostility, even more deeply ingrained in the American mentality, to any and every use of the English Common Law. This antagonism was basically an inheritance from colonial experience; it had been strengthened by the patriotic hatred of everything British. And further, just as the battle lines were forming over what might have been a merely learned dispute, they became inflamed by the anger of Jeffersonian Republicans against the Federalists' merging of their political program with an appeal to the Common Law.

It was not too difficult for such great law teachers as David Hoffman at the University of Maryland to dismiss the *"phobia causidicorum,"* even though lawyers remained objects of popular jeers and of ridicule in the drama, since Hoffman by 1837 could point out that they had become "the most entrusted, the most honoured, and withal, the most efficient and useful body of men" in the country. Large segments of the community would, even though reluctantly, be brought up short by Francis Lieber's argument that popular declamations against law and lawyers actually contained the same principle on which absolute monarchies functioned: "They wish for a paternal government, a monarch who may rule, untrammeled by fundamental laws, according to the fatherly desire of his heart." A quite different sort of controversy began when Federalist judges and congressmen supported the Alien and Sedition Acts, the prosecution of pro-French privateers, and the suppression of combinations of laborers in New York, by pleading:

What other law can be contemplated but Common Law; what sort of equity but the legal discretion which has been exercised in England from time immemorial, and is to be learnt from the books and reports of that country?

Jefferson wrote Edmund Randolph in August of 1799, "Of all the doctrines which have ever been broached by the Federal government this novel one, of the Common Law being in force and cognizable as an existing law in their courts, is to me most formidable." Thus encouraged, his partisans pressed the attack. The Common Law, said Jesse Root in the first volume of Connecticut *Reports,* comes from "a people grown old in the habits of vice." "Can the monarchical and aristocratical institutions of England be consistent with the republican principles of our Constitution?" demanded Benjamin Austin: "We may as well adopt the law of the Medes and Persians." In 1800 the Virginia Assembly instructed its representatives unalterably to oppose the principle "that the Common Law of England, is in force under the government of the United States." One of the earliest books printed in Ohio, at Steubenville, was Milton Goodnow's *Historical Sketches* (1819), which demonstrated the inadequacy of English law for the frontier, while in New Hampshire a judge announced common sense a much better guide: "It is our duty to do justice between parties; not by any quirk out of Coke and Blackstone—books that I never read and never will." In the flush times of Mississippi, Joseph Baldwin was to recollect, the "iron rules" of English law were denounced as being unsuited to the genius of American institutions: "There was nothing technical in this, certainly."

Again, however, we should note, at least parenthetically, that distrust of the Common Law existed also among Federalists, especially those in rural areas. As with Jeffersonians, the target of this hostility was Blackstone. Daniel Chipman, several times Chief Justice of Vermont and in all other respects an ardent Hamiltonian, declared in a fascinating booklet of 1793 that Blackstone was enamored with the British forms of government and "blazoned" them with his rhetoric. Unhappily the *Commentaries* are the only general treatise to which the American student as yet has access; he must therefore carefully learn to distinguish the principles and reasonings found therein which are dictated by a corrupt society:

He ought to know, that they are not universal; that in a democratic republic, they are wholly inadmissible. This is not enough. He should be led through a system of laws applicable to our governments, and a train of reasoning congenial to their principles. Such a system we yet want. Surely genius is not wanting in America. Can none be found equal to the arduous, the important task?

The "nativist" spirit in the realm of law was by no means limited to the "isolationist" circles of Jeffersonian Republicanism. The spirit of the Revolution remained alive, a fact which helps to explain the formidable difficulties faced by the writers of commentaries in the ensuing decades who strove to create in the United States a "system" which should be cosmopolitan enough to be intellectually respectable and at the same time a triumph of American "genius."

The most scholarly, and probably the most effective because the most restrained, discussion of the issue came as a learned appendix by St. George Tucker, successor to George Wythe as Professor of Law at William and Mary, in his monumental edition of Blackstone's *Commentaries* in 1803. Carefully reviewing everything that then could be ascertained about colonial law, Tucker noted how few states had ever explicitly adopted the Common Law; he expounded the Constitution in the light of this fact, denied that there could be among the states any uniform rule, and concluded that there was no authorization whatsoever for the federal government to declare the laws or statutes of England or of any other nation to be the law of this land. William Duane, editor of the Philadelphia *Aurora,* was less temperate; in 1805, while Jefferson's abortive attack on the Supreme Court was still under way, he printed *Sampson Against the Philistines,* wherein he accused the entire legal profession of obfuscating the simple rules of ordinary justice, of having "as effectually kept the *law books* out of the hands of *non-lawyers,* as the clergy formerly kept the *bible* out of the hands of the laymen."

Jefferson's failure to oust Judge Chase, along with his own conviction that Marshall's acquittal of Aaron Burr was a foul trick of the Common Law, is properly interpreted as meaning that no power thereafter could quench the zeal of the lawyers for incorporating that law into the body of American doctrine. Yet even after the violent passions of 1800 were diminished, other passions—sometimes political, but often purely conceptual—continued to inspire assaults on the Common Law. Charles Ingersoll's address at Philadelphia, in 1823, *A Discourse Concerning the Influence of America on the Mind,* called for rejection of "the brutal, ferocious and inhuman law of the feudalists" as a necessary prerequisite to the achievement of cultural independence, though he was optimistically persuaded that this "colonial acquiescence" was passing away. In that same year, however, the rambunctious William Sampson, exiled Irish patriot, hater of all things English, in a discourse to the New-York Historical Society, where he faced friends of James Kent, exhorted the nation to stop treading "the degrading paths of Norman subtleties," to forget "models of Saxon barbarity," and instead "to resolve every argument into principles of natural reason, universal justice, and present convenience." The Common Law, said Sampson, is like the Dalai Lama, evermore sitting cross-legged upon its antique altar, "for no use or purpose, but to be praised and worshipped by ignorant and superstitious votaries." The time is near at hand, he cried, when the rigid forms of English law will be made to bend to the requirements of American society; when "it will be separated from the rubbish and decay of time, and stripped of the parasitical growths that darken and disfigure it."

The time to succeed where Jefferson had failed seemed indeed to have arrived with the election of Andrew Jackson. Democratic lawyers were certain that now we could rid ourselves of feudal barbarity, customs "contained in ten thousand different books so intricate, so ambiguous, so contradictory, that no man ever yet understood them, and which it is the height of hypocrisy to pretend to understand." We have Americanized every public interest, our industry and useful arts, declared John P. Tarbell on July 4, 1839, in, of all places, Groton, Massachusetts; we have thrown off allegiance to every foreign influence in legislation and political economy, and in literature (Ralph Waldo Emerson should take note!). But the judiciary is still in colonial vassalage; if a judge can find no American statute, he goes back to the "old Blackstone Moorings," selects from the ocean of English jurisprudence "a principle upon which he convicts, condemns and imprisons an American citizen, holding in this manner the absolute power of a despot over the lives, liberties and property of the citizens." To repeat, the depths from which such cries emerged were not vats of hostility to all law in general but to what seemed to the democracy a retention by the courts of a perverted, foreign, unjust and above all un-American method of decision.

The greatest of these last-ditch enemies of the Common Law was undoubtedly Robert Rantoul, of Massachusetts, whose heart and energies were expended in every "liberal" cause of the effervescent period —temperance, free trade, antislavery, abolition of capital punishment —and who fought hard to make the General Court indemnify the proprietors of the Ursuline Convent gutted by anti-Catholic rioters and who yet championed the right of atheists to have their oaths in court respected. In an oration at Scituate on July 4, 1836, Rantoul summed up America's indictment of the Common Law. It sprang from the dark ages, had its origin in folly, barbarism, feudalism; to apply it in advancing, changing America, where every day new cases require fresh decisions, is "subversive of the fundamental principles of a free government." Rantoul fought this fight to his premature death in 1852, and may figure as the last spokesman of that primitive hatred of the Common Law which was generated in the Revolution, and against which the imposing, the erudite jurists of the age had to contend, an awareness of which is a tacit major premise of all their writings and pleadings. But if Rantoul went down to defeat, he had sometime before his death been granted a second vision; he perished in the confidence that eventually the law as upheld by his enemies would have to bow its arrogant neck to the yoke of "Codification."

3.

"THE HIGHEST POLITICAL CLASS AND THE MOST CULTIVATED PORTION OF SOCIETY"

A phenomenon of fundamental importance for both the social and intellectual history of America is the amazing rise, within three or four decades, of the legal profession from its chaotic condition of around 1790 to a position of political and intellectual domination. Had this triumph been achieved merely as a professional advance in prestige and wealth, it would deserve only our passing notice; but it was expressed through a massive philosophical formulation, culminating in the voluminous commentaries of Hoffman, Kent, and Story. Progressively unfolded in the wide-ranging opinions of such judges as Marshall and Shaw, hammered out before the bench in the classic arguments of famous lawyers who to the people were figures as majestic as Finney or Beecher, the formation of American law in this era embraces a mental adventure of heroic proportions.

It was the more remarkable for being accomplished in the face of the widespread hostility of ordinary Americans to the very concept of law and more specifically their bitter antagonism to the Common Law. As the lawyers looked back from their later eminence to the situation of 1790, they could only marvel that the profession had survived at all. Kent says that when he went on the bench in 1798 there were no reports or state precedents; we seemed to have no law of our own, nobody knew what the law was, and all the time he was Chief Justice, no counsel could quote to him opinions of his predecessors. There were no American lawbooks, and of those imported from England there were so few copies that not all courts could consult them. It was a desperate moment, indeed, recollected Chief Justice Parker of Massachusetts, when we had to enlarge old rules, to infuse the system with a vital equity; we needed somebody the equal of Lord Mansfield "to breathe into our common law an energy, suited to the wants, the commercial interests, and the enterprise of the age." But what hope was there that a Lord Mansfield could be evoked out of the wilderness?

The law schools—Tapping Reeve's at Litchfield from 1784 to 1833, the lectures of James Wilson, already famed as statesman and jurist, at Philadelphia in 1790, the tentative beginnings under Kent at Columbia in 1793, plus the tuition of Wythe and Tucker at William and Mary, the professorship at Transylvania in 1798, the Harvard Law School in 1817, and the Yale School in 1843—commenced to bring order out of chaos. We confidently expect, said a reviewer of Kent in 1827, that these institutions will result in "a bar more generally erudite and profound than heretofore, and a gradual retirement of ignorant and impudent pretenders, to their merited obscurity and insignificance." Yet we should note that the law schools made their way against widespread popular suspicion, similar, as we shall see, to that aroused against the early medical schools. Charles Follen, for example, took occasion as late as 1833 to insist that the apprentice in a law office could never gain "that fundamental and comprehensive knowledge of the law, without which the most consummate practical discernment still retains the character of a sort of instinct." The populace in general, however, were strongly of the opinion that if there were to be lawyers at all, those who worked by instinct were the most tolerable. They were seldom moved to enthusiasm by such distinctions as Follen made between the scientific lawyer and the empiric: the former "never rests until he has entered into the inmost nature of the law, as well as the general character of the cases to which it is applicable, and on this account is never at a loss to discern, in any case, the accidental accompaniments and the essentials; and to distinguish between those circumstances which afford ground for argument, and those which predetermine the decision." For the generality this kind of talk was highly unpalatable and resolutely ignored, but it could not be hushed up or its long-range effectiveness muzzled.

Until, however, this effect could be realized, there was a legend to inspire the profession: the one man who pointed toward the glorious fulfillment was Alexander Hamilton. A modern student may be puzzled as to just how much law Hamilton did learn in his apprenticeship of 1783, but though in some six months of study he may not quite have made himself master of all that Chief Justice Mansfield knew, his pleadings remained the lodestar of subsequent aspirants. Hoffman declared him the greatest genius of which the country could yet boast; Kent, leaving aside Hamilton's other achievements, said he would merit this encomium had he been nothing but the lawyer. Our jurisprudence was a "blank" until Hamilton began to pour light and learning upon it:

His arguments on commercial, as well as on legal questions, were remarkable for freedom and energy; and he was eminently distinguished for completely exhausting every subject which he discussed, and leaving no argument or objection on the adverse side unnoticed and unanswered. He traced doctrines to their source, or probed them to their foundations, and at the same time paid the highest deference and respect to sound authority. . . . We may truly apply to the efforts of his mind . . . that "principles were stated, reasoned upon, enlarged, and explained, until those who heard him were lost in admiration at the strength and stretch of the human understanding."

Kent's language reveals what the followers of Hamilton set up for themselves as the ideal of the great lawyer, what they imparted to their students and apprentices. Yet there is also implicit in the passage Kent's awareness that unless the lawyers could live up to this standard, both of erudition and of force, they would never make headway against the sullen resentment of the democracy. Their only weapon was the intellect, which Hamilton showed them how to wield. In 1836, when Jackson was President and Kent had delivered another of his panegyrics on Hamilton, Story wrote, "I always believed that his title to renown was as great as you have portrayed it."

As the lawyers began to feel their power, they also began to utter on ceremonial occasions larger claims for the part played by the bar in producing and guiding the Revolution—claims which in the 1790's only the clergy had dared make for themselves. Though William Sullivan, addressing the Bar of Suffolk County in 1824, confessed that the majority of Massachusetts barristers and attorneys had proved Tory or at least neutral, yet he could chant, "Whoever examines the history of this country to know, by whom the most bold and effectual measures *in the cause of freedom* were suggested, and carried into effect, will feel, at least, some respect for *Lawyers*." Occasionally lawyers would grant that "some other order of men" might have opened the drama, but, as Job Tyson demanded, "Who but lawyers could have roused the country to the vindication of rights merely speculative and theoretical —rights affecting abstract principle, and wholly unfelt in curtailing the happiness and enjoyments of the people?" A constant reiteration of this thesis had by the 1830's so carried the day that it colored the writing of history, even that of Bancroft, and what had been the decisive work of the ministry in mobilizing patriots waited to be rediscovered by twentieth-century research. And with every implication, along with this rehabilitation of the profession, went the lesson that the lawyers of the Revolution and the Constitution had been nurtured on the Common Law, even though within the fraternity it was common knowledge that their knowledge of that science had been fairly rudimentary.

As a matter of history, one may say that the mania "for going to

law" which European travelers noted as a veritable disease among
this law-hating people would inevitably have encouraged an increase
in the number of practitioners, but that sort of business might have
produced, as in great measure it did, only pettifoggers. On a higher
level, the augmenting dignity of the profession is to be attributed to
the legal intelligences which almost miraculously emerged, and secon-
darily to the fact that these luminaries had none of the clergy's modesty
about impressing their dignity upon the public. In *The North American Review* of 1817, Joseph Story marveled that there were lawyers yet
living who could attest the low state of the calling a few years previously, and had to wonder at the change:

It at once became fashionable; and this circumstance, combining with the
nature of our political institutions, (which make a legal education, if not a
prerequisite, at least a very important qualification, for political distinction
and public office,) has contributed in a very high degree to that great increase
of the bar, and that ascendency in society, which distinguish the profession,
in this, more than in any other country.

But even as Joseph Story, who by 1817 was learning to moderate his
youthful rhetorical raptures, wrote thus judiciously, more popular en-
comiums of the profession were pointing the way to a grandiloquent
vein which was to pulsate with mounting intensity in the following
decades. *Port-Folio* for December, 1815, had already opened the
floodgates:

Greece and Rome were many centuries before they produced, the one a
Demosthenes, the other a Cicero: and we should think more humbly than
we do of the destinies of our country, did we not believe that it will be her
lot hereafter to dazzle the world with a similar luminary; an event which
has not yet occurred to shed lustre on her annals. The pre-eminence of the
continent of America over every other quarter of the globe in the magnificence of its outline and the grandeur of its features—unequalled lakes and
rivers, forests and mountains—with the excellence of its climates, the fertility
of its soil, and the inexhaustibility of its mines of the precious metals—these
considerations conjoined furnish a foundation of belief, by no means
chimerical, that it is also destined to exhibit, in time, a decided superiority
over other regions, in the intellect of its inhabitants. . . . Mind is very
peculiarly the result of surrounding circumstances: and we feel assured that,
with the lapse of years, circumstances will not fail to arise calculated to
elevate even the "law mind" of America to a higher pitch than it has hitherto
attained.

With such a passage we commence the transition from the conception
of the law as a symmetrical science in the framework of a Newtonian
universe, such as John Adams entertained, to the histrionic style culti-

vated by great "romantic" pleaders like William Wirt and Daniel Webster. Something of this new manner would affect even those jurists who, like Kent, Binney, and Story, openly endeavored to resist it. Even they could not entirely escape the influence because they too were patriots. Through the expansive sense of a nationalism in law, the American profession found ways to reconcile their fellow-citizens to their methods—and to their fees.

Perhaps the first comprehensive statement of the full majesty of the calling came in David Hoffman's lectures, beginning at Baltimore in 1817. The importance of these has been slighted among historians because of the greater reputations of Kent and Story, although both of them paid Hoffman tribute. In all ages, said Hoffman (conveniently forgetting whole segments of Western history), lawyers have been esteemed the most transcendent benefactors of the race, not only because they promote tranquillity, but because they cultivate a clear discernment of cause and effect. In America, however, they take even more exalted rank because by their perspicacious talent they are "led to the recognition of these general principles,—to use them in the interpretation of old, and in the framing of new enactments; or that steady, and liberal understanding by which general consequences are regarded instead of particular, and general justice is distributed, without reference to private or partial inconvenience."

It is important to note that this blowing of trumpets for the glory of the law was not in America confined to Whig or, as some modern misinterpreters like to say, "conservative" practitioners. When it came to these mighty phrases, Rantoul's attacks on the Common Law and his pioneer advocacy of codification are merely minor divisions within a society of mutual admiration. When he, for instance, defended partisans of Dorr in the Rhode Island "rebellion," he displayed a scholarship in the Common Law equal to Story's in order to prove that his clients could not be tried in another jurisdiction than their own. The more vehement William Sampson asserted that our law is justly dear to us "because it is the law of a free people"; all he was objecting to was "the complication of these stinted usages." And going further back, St. George Tucker, although in his famous appendix he did argue that the Common Law was not the uniform rule of the land, still felt it reward enough to spend his energy on making Blackstone become in America an essential part of legal education. It is as easy to cull from the Democratic lawyers as from Whigs statements which constantly kept the law before the people's gaze as that which served all parties with equity and justice: "The strength of the law laughs fortresses to scorn, and spurns the intrenchments of iniquity. The power of the law crushes the power of men, and strips wealth of every unrighteous immunity. It is the thread of Daedalus to guide us through the labyrinths of cunning," et cetera, et cetera.

Because Alexis de Tocqueville found lawyers so everywhere enthroned, he wrote his often-quoted conclusion about the legal profession serving as a "counterpoise" to democracy. By the time he printed these pages, in 1835, he had diligently sought for every conceivable ideological position which might check the march of what most concerned him, absolute and brute equality. True, he had consorted in New York and Boston largely with Whig lawyers who filled him with horror stories about Andrew Jackson. Not at all grasping the principle of judicial review, and only vaguely aware of the Common Law, Tocqueville decided that while the lawyers did not actively scheme to overthrow the democracy, "they constantly endeavor to turn it away from its real direction by means that are foreign to its nature." He somewhat dazedly admitted that the people seemed no longer to mistrust the profession, and that the lawyers had adapted themselves to all movements of the social body, but he still listed them as in the covert opposition, because they "form the highest political class and the most cultivated portion of society."

There was as much scorn in America for Tocqueville's fantasy about the lawyers as there was for his notions about the evangelical regimentation of thought. Indeed, had Tocqueville studied the professions more closely, he might have detected the inner tension between the clergy and the lawyers which by 1835, although latent, was real. "While the law deserves reverence," ran a typical clerical warning of 1838, "not every one that writes himself her minister need be respected. Let him prove himself worthy of his calling, and the dignity of that calling will descend upon him; but if unworthy, like the immoral clergyman, he will be the more degraded the higher he has assumed to aim."

Though an occasional commentator like Thomas Clerke in 1840 might say that lawyers were the aristocracy of the land, he hastened to note that they enjoyed no hereditary rule, no exclusive privileges, and were largely elected by the people to offices of power because they were the best educated, the most competent. B. B. Minor, in *The Southern Literary Messenger* of 1847, would allow not even this much. Lawyers, even the most brilliant, sprang from the people, and were prevented from any consistency of purpose "by the fluctuations in their ranks, the diversity of individual interests and their necessary dependence upon those over whom they would be supposed desirous to tyrannize, or elevate themselves," from ever becoming any sort of "aristocracy" at all. We may safely take this as the ultimate opinion of democratic America; if in some frontier areas the law was still unwelcome, the tremendous achievement of the lawyers and the perseverance of judges had very nearly eliminated the colonial antagonism.

What, however, does become a striking aspect of this voluminous literature against the law and the Common Law, with the still more voluminous vindication of both, is the virtual absence from it of the sort of anxiety Natty Bumppo had enunciated in 1823. A good Jeffersonian, later a Jacksonian, Richard Rush, son of the great Dr. Benjamin Rush, published a prophetic little book in Philadelphia called *American Jurisprudence* (1815). On the surface it is an early effort to convert the democracy to a respect for, even a veneration for, law. Rush appealed to the nation's pride by pointing out that only in this department of the intellect does "the United States probably approach . . . nearer to a par with the old nations than in any other that could be named." Our manufactures are crude, our poets provincial, our painters inexpert, but the fact is that by 1775, as Burke had declared, more copies of Blackstone's *Commentaries* had been sold in America than in all England. From that day, we have moved toward a vaster and vaster prospect, the true sublime, and the consequences are not to be dreaded but to be rejoiced in:

As our lonely territory continues to be overspread with cultivated fields, and to glitter with the spires of villages and cities, we shall, to be sure, witness a corresponding increase in the professors of this science.

Upon this assumption, the expanding profession operated, taking for granted everything that Judge Temple preached to Natty. Why tame this wilderness? Cooper, both sensitive and masculine, followed his picture of Natty amid the beginnings of civilization with a tragic depiction of him after his escape to the Great Plains, far beyond the reach of the law. There Natty finds the true despoiler of Nature, not the loyal, decent scout that he had been, but the brutalized, rapacious, neolithic tribe of Ishmael Bush. "I own the land I stand on," cries the villain: "Can you tell me, stranger, where the law or the reason is to be found, which says that one man shall have a section, or a town, or perhaps a county to his use, and another have to beg for earth to make his grave in?" Natty himself—even the intuitive Leatherstocking—is caught in the American dilemma. "I cannot say that you are wrong," he mourns, "and I have often thought and said as much, when and where I believed my voice could be heard." The victory of the formative period was a steady dwindling in the power and effectiveness of Natty's voice. When the crisis finally came, the principal agent in preserving the unity of the nation so that it could resume its imperial course was a creature emerging from the wilderness, originally as untutored and almost as unlettered as Natty Bumppo (his opponents would long insist he never was any better), who had disciplined the instincts of his heart by the study of Blackstone, and who would insist on waging the Civil War—regardless of what the clergy might declaim —not as an evangelical crusade but strictly as a vindication of the Common Law thesis that no party to a compact solemnly entered into can thereafter wantonly withdraw from it.

CHAPTER TWO

Intellectual Elegance

Indeed we may say of the Law in this country, that whether we regard the immense extent of our judicial system, the number and variety of its tribunals, the number and character of their decisions, the multitude of reports, the number of original treatises upon various departments and heads of the law, the number of eminent men who have enriched its learning and given form and force to its principles, no similar example of the same rapidity and strength of growth can be adduced from either ancient or modern experience.
—M. RUSSELL THAYER, *The Law, Considered as a Progressive Science,* 1870

1.

THE CRITERION OF REASON

James Kent in person witnessed Alexander Hamilton's spectacular performances of the 1780's before the New York Bar. He remembered them as might some passionate devotee of the theater treasure into the dull nineteenth century his recollection of Mrs. Siddons as Lady Macbeth. For our comprehension of the legal aspect of the American mind during the next half-century, we must consider that the usual accounts tell how Hamilton crushed his opponents by the sheer vehemence of his attack, how also James Kent in his first lecture at Columbia in 1794 insisted that legal study had become the equal of classical scholarship, because in this country the law was not a mystery: here the science of civil government had been "stripped of its delusive refinements, and restored to the plain Principles of Reason." This Yale graduate, class of 1781, lived long enough to sneer at the vogue of Carlyle: "a disciple of the Platonic School of Philosophy, beyond the reach of man's understanding." Because Kent was the pre-eminent expounder of American law, towering even above such giants as Tucker, Hoffman, Story,

he more than any other person carried a solid remnant of the Enlightenment into the romantic ebullience of his country. Because he
and his fellow-jurists lifted themselves to a position of excellence
which, in spite of Jefferson and Jackson, governed the polity of the
nation—and more importantly because they expressed their conception
of the universe not merely in *ad hoc* decisions but in systematic com-
pendiums—they guaranteed that the mind of the Republic would
never be swept wholly into the enthusiasms of revivalism or Transcendentalism. From their point of view, they preserved sanity throughout an insane era.

This was a delicate, a difficult operation, not only because of the
external pressures of native hostility to legalism, but still more because
of tensions within their own philosophy. If, on the one hand, they
were dedicated to domesticating the Common Law in this raw community, on the other they had to admit that colonial precedents were of
little worth, and that therefore we had no such venerable body of
antique wisdom as gave the Common Law in England its sacerdotal
power. The history of our bar, lamented Joseph Willard in 1829, lacks
that indistinctness of origin, that combination of fact and fancy,
"where the light of truth and the uncertainty of tradition are insepa-
rable; where the inception may almost shadow out a present deity,
reflecting back the rich colorings of romance." Henry St. George
Tucker, inheritor of the Jeffersonian mantle, did not doubt that Nature has implanted in the human heart an intuitive sense of right and
wrong, but by 1844 had to insist that the original Jeffersonians were
wrong in trusting too much to its automatic functioning. "The true
mode of ascertaining what is morally right is to inquire what the
reason, the *cultivated reason* of mankind must necessarily pronounce
on the matter in question." The Jeffersonians, however, by their veneration for "reason," had long before this played into the hands of
James Kent; Hugh Henry Brackenridge in 1812, arguing that a merely
mechanical decision in terms of precedent could not be considered law
if it were against reason, declared, "*I know nothing but the mind that
is to judge.*" This sort of pleading would prove no hindrance to the
advancing legions of the lawyers; as Horace Binney said in his 1827
eulogy on Justice Tilghman of Pennsylvania, few, if any, decisions are
"mechanical." A judge has to compare, discriminate, adopt, reject—
"in fine to bring into exercise his whole understanding."

It soon became evident that the rationalism of the lawyer was a
different business from the widely advertised Law of Nature or the
purely philosophical Rationalism of the eighteenth century, though it
might indeed be a lineal descendent from both. As Timothy Walker

said in his textbook of 1837, to discover the criteria of law, you cannot, as in natural science, apply the principles of mathematical demonstration: "Nor can you as in ethics, appeal to the monitor within." Conscience may mislead you. The achievement of the lawyers after the Revolution, the speed with which they vindicated the thesis that a body of legal precepts, such as in 1790 hardly existed, should become declarations of legal reason—this was a truly impressive performance. Story greeted Hoffman's *A Course of Legal Study* with the rejoicing of one who had fought his way through Coke on Littleton to the tune of such anguish as had caused him to weep. Already, Story happily declared, instead of the sparse and scattered maxims with which we commenced, "we have regular systems, built up with symmetry of parts; and the necessary investigations in new and difficult cases are conducted with more safety, because they are founded on inductions from rules better established and more exactly limited." In the pride with which Story records this attainment (in which, we note, there is an admission that not all compartments of Reason are yet fully defined), we perceive the aspiration which drove these men: in the only terms available to them, they were saving civilization in America by creating a rationality for the law.

An indication of the tone which became explicit in the tuition of law professors and sounded in memorials of distinguished jurists was, in the language of Job Tyson, the injunction to keep one's "temper" calm and unruffled. In an age when crucial cases became gladiatorial combats, the prevailing ideal was that which Horace Binney found incarnated in Jared Ingersoll, in whose office he had studied law: his mind, says Binney, was constantly excited, but not in the manner of the poetical imagination that takes flights into the ether, but in that of actively considering the relations of life and the concerns of men. Or, as David Brown characterized William Rawle, though Rawle's temper was naturally enthusiastic, "to him, as to Socrates, divine philosophy had imparted such self possession and control, that amid scenes the most turbulent and tempestuous, he never for a single moment lost his serenity and composure." Brown held up this model in the same year in which Emerson published *Nature*!

In maintaining against the irrationality of democracy and of millennialism an imperative of control of temper by logic, lawyers could argue that because America does have written constitutions, that because here the basic law does not grow by chance but is explicitly formulated, then throughout our municipal law "Reason is the great authority upon constitutional questions, and the faculty of reasoning is the only instrument by which it can be exercised." The figure of

John Marshall loomed as the paragon of reason, as vivid a symbol to the American imagination as Natty Bumppo. John H. Bryan in an oration of 1830 at Chapel Hill made the often-repeated point that in Marshall's decisions the position taken may to many be unacceptable but that everybody must respect his vindication of man's logical prowess: politicians do not always acquiesce in his conclusions, but the most recalcitrant Jacksonian cannot doubt the strength and depth and clearness of his mind. He has solved the most embarrassing questions "by his gifted intellect, as by intuition; and the arguments by which his decisions have been sustained, while they are intelligible to the meanest capacity, are such as to reflect honour on the highest intellect." Bryan's choice of terms by which to command respect for Marshall's mind despite the political tendencies of his pronouncements is exquisite. Even more adroit were those employed by Horace Binney in 1835, especially because his doctrinal agreement with Marshall was so much a matter of public record that he needed not even to mention it. In Marshall, said Binney, the work of reason was perfect—"in simplicity, perspicuity, connection and strength." Marshall never, insisted Binney, made "analogy" the principal support of his arguments. In defiance of the vogue of romantic poetry, Marshall commenced his great decisions with "it is admitted." Joseph Story rejoiced in his association with a mind of whom it could be said, "once admit his premises and you are forced to his conclusions," and chuckled that counselors tried to encourage each other by crying, "deny every thing he says."

These lawyers could not live in ignorance of the fashionable terminology of their age; they might be reluctant to admit that the rhetorical modes of a particular time pertained to their profession, but by 1829 even Hoffman would have to explain to his students that man is endowed with both heart and intellect. For all their professions of devotion to Socrates, the lawyer had to come to some sort of accommodation with the speech of Leatherstocking. "It is the unenvied province of the Court," said Mr. Justice Johnson, "to be directed by the head, and not the heart." In the law, "no latitude is left for the exercise of feeling." Timothy Walker went so far in defiance of the age, knowing that his colleagues supported him even though few would dare be so candid, as to tell his students that the highest conception they could form of a judge would be a pure intelligence, utterly divested of passion or sympathy:

If a statue could be imagined to have a mind, but no heart; an intellect, but no feeling; in a word, to be endowed with the single capacity of deciding unerringly what the law is, in every case; it would be a perfect chancellor, as well as judge; for just in proportion as this icy standard is approached, both become faultless ministers of justice in their respective departments.

Here, in as naked phraseology as the times could produce, was the basic challenge of the law to an explosive, dynamic democracy. Tocqueville was unable to specify just wherein the legal profession was a "counterpoise" to the tyranny of the majority. It was only peripherally inspired by any such motive. While in great part its record, especially in the Supreme Court, may be read as an effort to restrict the surge of democracy, the lawyers' real controversy with their society was that they stood for the Head against the Heart. Pathetically enough, humanitarian lawyers, supporters of Jackson—such as Rantoul—tacitly accepted this limitation of the arena, and staged their opposition within the confines which the profession persuaded a reluctant America to accept.

2.

THE REASONABLENESS OF IRRATIONALITY

The Common Law, said Mr. Justice Story in 1829, is "that collection of principles, which constitutes the basis of the administration of justice in England." This definition naturally lent support to the arguments of such Jeffersonians as Sampson or Jacksonians like Rantoul that an independent, democratic America should have nothing to do with it. The esprit of the legal corps and the lawyers' claim to a monopoly of the faculty of reason armored the profession against such complaints. Yet the more they fortified their redoubt, the more they had to confront the danger that, in building it upon the Common Law, they might discover the foundation dissolving beneath them. For the Common Law was not a construction of systematic reason: it was a haphazard accumulation of precedents, quirks, obscurities, which some of its English champions, most conspicuously Burke, publicly and positively boasted was wholly a matter of prescription, fundamentally irrational by its inherent nature.

Within the very sanctum of the Common Law, in 1842, before the bench on which Joseph Story still sat, in the crucial case of *Swift* v. *Tyson* Richard H. Dana (who was no Jacksonian insurgent) stated the issue upon which the lawyers were in danger of tearing the guild apart. Indeed, as Story insisted, when we come to trial by jury, to *habeas corpus,* we must resort to the Common Law for interpretation of terms. But, asked Dana, because we use some of the terms, are we therefore become subject to this entire body of foreign legality? We borrow terms in science and the arts "without being pledged to the principles to which they may have been applied." The physician uses the nomenclature of the Greeks without being controlled by Greek notions of therapy. Dana had the spirit to focus the issue where it really lay, though few of his contemporaries could fully comprehend what he said. "Our law idiom is essentially of common law origin," he pleaded, "yet not foreign." Of course, he could point out, to the discomfort of Story, our federal and state constitutions have erected by statute a system of American law, and within these enactments everybody agrees that we pay no attention to the Common Law. But the overriding concern is: can the courts, without the aid of a statute, call in the Common Law to support their verdicts?

Story, Kent, and the luminaries of the profession answered, in effect, yes. This, if I may so term it, intramural contest among the lawyers would prove of more enduring import to the Republic than the more publicized hostility to law itself among the strident democracy. The lawyers were gaining control of the society through their skill in guiding it into their theoretical version of the Common Law. Yet all the time they were at odds among themselves as to what the Common Law meant. John Pickering in 1829 might say he was merely amused by the vehemence on the one side of those who exhausted their "lilliputian artillery in trying to batter down the venerable fabric," but on the other side he was apprehensive about the adversaries "who with about the same justice have poured out their idolatry to their supposed native English law."

Even so staunch a Jeffersonian as Brackenridge, though prefacing a few qualifications, would assert, "THE COMMON LAW OF ENGLAND, may be justly styled THE FOUNTAIN OF AMERICAN RIGHTS." Peter Du Ponceau in his *Dissertation on the Nature and Extent of the Jurisdiction of the Courts of the United States* of 1824 made a gallant effort to explain why a body of English law could also be American. Viewed from without, the Common Law does present "a rude and misshapen mass, *rudis indigestaque moles,*" and so demands that its separate parts be dwelt upon for some time before its beauties can be appreciated. But he who perceives the beauty also sees why up to the moment of independence the Common Law was claimed as the birthright of American citizens: it was then synonymous with the British constitution, from which they claimed their liberties. Of course, with the Revolution we have an altered situation; our institutions no longer depend on traditions but on the solid foundation of express and written compact. Yet, granted that the Common Law is no longer the *"source"* of political power, still it has been steadily improved, especially in America, so that any serious student, Du Ponceau concluded, must revere it. The argument that colonial ancestors brought the Common Law with them was indeed advanced by a hundred apologists, though there was always a slight implication that no one could precisely affirm just how much of it had been effectually transported.

The French Du Ponceau, bred in the civil law, was still able to perceive why in America the Common Law had its "warm enthusiasts" as well as its violent enemies without wholly condemning the latter, but there was a vigorous band who in the 1820's decided no longer to tolerate dissent. As Binney said of the decisions of Tilghman, they displayed an absolute devotion to the Common Law; since Tilghman dreaded, "as an implication of his conscience," the slightest hint of judicial legislation, he inquired of the oracles of the law, and having learned from them, though he might not personally agree, he applied the precedents. "He acted upon the sentiment of Lord Bacon, that it is the foulest injustice to remove landmarks, and that to corrupt the law, is to poison the very fountain of justice." Actually, when the lawyers spoke thus, they were echoing not so much Bacon as Coke in his famous rebuke to King James, that cases "are not to be decided by natural reason but by artificial reason and judgment of the law." Perhaps they were hesitant to speak thus bluntly in a society where an assumption of every man's immediate access to the principle of natural reason had become sacrosanct.

In New York, for a variety of local considerations, the battle for the Common Law, both within the profession and outside it, was especially violent. At the Constitutional Convention of 1821, Ogden Edwards momentarily saved the cause by orating, "When our ancestors came to this country, although they fled from the persecutions they experienced in their native land, yet such was their attachment to the common law, that they brought it along with them, and subjected their conduct to its regulation." As a result, while other states have sunk into the confusion of experiments, New York's judicial establishments have remained firm and stable, "revered by the people." Illumined by this "blaze of experience"—American experience—the convention was persuaded to endorse the Common Law.

In New York, however, the blaze of experience was shed primarily from the refulgent mind of James Kent. As Chief Justice from 1804 to 1814, and as Chancellor from 1814 to 1823, he was so deferential to "the generous oracles of the common law," to which he would "listen with delight and instruction," that he frankly acknowledged he would apply them even where he thought them unjust. His reasoning was a bit more complicated than Tilghman's. The English law, Kent would say, "has fostered the soundest and most rational principles of civil liberty"; English courts have "protected right to a degree never before witnessed in the history of civil society." Such a defense would make it doubly difficult for assailants outside the walls to penetrate, and also would keep discipline within the garrison.

Kent took full command of the operation as he published the four volumes of his *Commentaries* between 1826 and 1830. They seemed the most towering achievement the mind had yet wrought in America; their demonstrations of how the Common Law had become the law of America made the jibes of Sampson seem childish. The Judiciary Acts of 1789 and 1793, and indeed the Constitution itself, Kent never tired of insisting, prescribe remedies, not according to the miscellaneous practices of state courts, "but according to the principles of common law and equity as distinguished and defined in that country from which we derived our knowledge of those principles." He took satisfaction in emphasizing those areas of American jurisprudence—maritime captures, for instance—where courts in the United States are obliged to follow the English; here there are no alternatives in domestic sources, "and there is scarcely a decision in the English prize courts at Westminster, on any general question of public right, that has not received the express approbation and sanction of our national courts."

Kent did not for a moment suppose he was discouraging the progress of his country by thus construing the native situation. On the contrary, he believed that he was supplying America with the instrument it most needed, a coherent legal rationality. In this work he was assisted by Joseph Story, from 1811 to his death in 1845 an associate justice of the Supreme Court, combining that arduous work after 1829 with serving as Dane Professor of Law at Harvard, and, on top of these occupations, composing during the 1830's and early 1840's his array of commentaries. Though they do not make such good reading as Kent's, they were of incalculable importance in providing a frame of rationality for American jurisprudence. In 1818 he reported far and wide that John Adams himself had said, "if he had ever imagined that the common law had not by the Revolution become the law of the United States under its new government, *he never would have drawn his sword in the contest.*" Back in 1774 or 1775, John Adams may not have been so emphatic, but Story was pleased to believe the account so that he, Story, could enact into American precedent as much of the Common Law as possible, and otherwise disseminate it by teaching and publishing. He delighted to write, as an American, to an English judge in 1840:

What nobler triumph has England achieved, or can she achieve, than the proud fact that her Common Law exerts a universal sway over this country, by the free suffrage of all its citizens? That every lawyer feels that Westminster Hall is in some sort his own?

Again, Story would say this as the most patriotic of Americans, and sincerely believe that he was exhibiting an admirable and natural progress. When this point of view was backed by the mountainous learning of his commentaries, it surely seemed that the naïve naturalism of a Davy Crockett would quickly be banished from the legal forum.

However, on every side, and even among those most devoted to the Common Law, there had to be an admission, even though reluctant, that it could not be brought entire to this country, that there were segments of it which had no relation to American circumstances. Daniel Webster began his career as legal philosopher in 1807 by confessing that precedents are not statutes, that they operate only in cases which statutes do not reach. The great point about precedents is that, once they have been mobilized, they give the lawyer a full view of his subject, and so enable him to arrive at the very same conclusion "to which, probably, his own mind would in time have conducted him by a slow and painful process of ratiocination." A murmur arose that maybe the American lawyer, like the American poet or landscape painter, ought to trust his own "genius," even though more slow and painful, rather than to appropriate European methods. Du Ponceau endeavored to silence uneasiness by pointing out that since we now have explicit constitutions, the Common Law, for all its majesty, is "a SYSTEM OF JURISPRUDENCE and nothing more." That is, it is not a source of power, "but the *means* or instrument through which it is exercised." Kent was happy to agree. Indeed, he found the solution for an annoying metaphysical puzzle in Du Ponceau's doctrine, and so could serenely grant that courts get no right to act from the Common Law; however, when constitutions and legislatures do give them jurisdiction, "*the rules of action* under that jurisdiction, if not prescribed by statute, may, and must be taken from the common law, when they are applicable, because they are necessary to give effect to the jurisdiction." This may not have gained all that partisans of the Common Law wished, but it made the least possible concession to legislation, and kept free a wide area in which, if only legislatures could be restrained and juries made docile to instructions from the bench, the Common Law would determine the character of the nation. And then, as Kent charmingly suggested, even in those fields where it was no longer relevant, as in real estate, still it continued, "like other venerable remains of the Gothic system, to be objects of examination and study, not only to the professed antiquarian, but to every inquisitive lawyer, who, according to the advice of Lord Bacon, is desirous 'to visit and strengthen the roots and foundation of the science.' " These magisterial observations ought surely to be sufficient to force upon blatant American denouncers of the Common Law an awareness of their pitiful ignorance.

Because recent histories tend to label Kent a "conservative," and thus bury with him the vast range of his thinking, it should be noted that in his first lecture at Columbia, in 1794, he asserted that legal education should be drawn from America's own history and constitutions. For him it was important that lawyers imbibe the principles of republican government from pure fountains, that they not receive improper impressions "from the artificial distinctions, the oppressive establishments, or the wild innovations which at present distinguish the Trans-Atlantic World." Though this may sound as though Kent was more concerned with defending the country against the French rather than the English infection, one may also argue that he was striving for an American independence from either. Many Jeffersonians, such as Brackenridge, once they stopped denouncing Judge Chase, showed themselves as little sympathetic with Davy Crockett's philosophy as was Kent. Precisely because, said Brackenridge, the Common Law is not in every particular applicable in America, then to determine what parts are and what are not "requires scientific investigation, the leisure of opulence, persevering application, and even professional skill." Hence the mass of society, those whom this "liberal" was satirizing in *Modern Chivalry*, should "resign these advantages to men of erudition and distinction."

To make reassurance the stronger, Kent said that the Common Law, when cultivated in subordination to the jurisprudence of America, had nothing in it of the slavish maxims of Justinian; on the contrary, in its improved condition "under the benign influence of an expanded commerce, of enlightened justice, of republican principles, and of sound philosophy, the common law has become a code of matured ethics, and enlarged civil wisdom, admirably adapted to promote and secure the freedom and happiness of social life." Here he was utilizing an argument that Hoffman, Du Ponceau, and others of his predecessors had diffidently worked out, that the historical, evolutionary character of the Common Law makes it especially appropriate to America, because it can develop along with a rapidly changing society. Possibly the tardiness of the lawyers in perfecting this justification is a sign of their slowness in recognizing the immense economic, and subsequently legal, reorientation wrought by the War of 1812—the new importance of admiralty law, the beginnings of manufactures, and the sudden need of policies for patents, for the development of canals and turnpikes, and soon thereafter for railroads. In great part, however, it was rather their difficulty in shifting from a philosophy of law which was primarily contractual in character to one that was conscious of history—which is another way of saying that, like other active minds, they had the problem of getting out of the eighteenth century and into the nineteenth.

David Hoffman here, as in so many departments, led the way in 1817, glorifying the doctrine that the law of England was *not* a fabric begun and completed by a single legislator or council, that it embodied "the history of the manners and opinions of a people advancing from barbarity . . . to a high degree of civil and political liberty, of physical and intellectual improvement." Therefore he could tell his students that both political and legal wisdom "will be found to be the offspring of experience, not of theory," and so to assert the innermost rationality of the apparently irrational chronicle of the Common Law. Joseph Story welcomed Hoffman in *The North American Review,* chiming in that the Common Law has pre-eminently proved its power of enlarging itself: "The narrow maxims of one age have not been permitted to present insurmountable obstacles to the improvements of another." In his inaugural address at the Harvard Law School, Story celebrated the human mind for its power to "hold out forever an unapproached degree of excellence" toward which "it moves onward in the path toward perfection." But even more than Story, Chief Justice Lemuel Shaw of Massachusetts (whom some historians also label a "conservative"), in the railroad cases of the 1850's, presented the Common Law as no series of detailed practical rules but as "a few broad and comprehensive principles, founded on reason, natural justice, and enlightened public policy, modified and adapted to the circumstances of all the particular cases which fall within it." Thus, though steamboats and railroads were "but of yesterday," the Common Law provides a deep foundation for determining the rights and duties of carriers.

The happy consequence for those who did the mighty work of adapting the Common Law to American conditions was that they could universally agree, in a country founded on explicit constitutions and bills of rights, and governed by statute, that there was no need for any disquisition on the metaphysics of law. Our law, said Silas Jones in a book significantly entitled an *Introduction to Legal Science*, is eminently historical, and requires of us such researches as "possess all the interest that the traveller feels in lingering about the ruins of ancient cities, monuments of exquisite taste and skill in the arts." Or, as *DeBow's Review* put it in 1846, "Our own system, sometimes erroneously supposed to have been dug out of our peculiar form of institutions, is but ancient ore, dug in other countries, and passed through the furnace of men's minds for centuries." This by implication explained why lawyers had become the intellectual masters of the Republic. So into the 1850's, as the country struggled within itself to maintain identity, lawyers would continue to propose the only hope of preservation their wisdom permitted, that the Common Law was not an episode in our life, it was the very life of the nation: "It is stable, because its principles are founded upon truth; it is capable of amelioration, because that is of the nature of humanity."

Here we should observe that the nationalistic obsession of American jurists prevented even the most clear-thinking of them from taking advantage of the divinely given opportunity then offered them. Unlike the judges of England, the Americans were not bound to ancient precedents, since they could arbitrarily decide which of them had relevance to America. Unlike Continental judges, they were not restricted by any codes except the loose ones of the state and national constitutions. In short, they, and they alone in the Western culture, had the chance to apply to their emerging jurisprudence the laws of historical development, of the relativity of temporal standards. They were obliged to resort to some such considerations when they reviewed the history of the Common Law so as to exempt the United States from those portions of it which did not apply to the Republic. In the process of discriminating, an inspired few sometimes reached momentarily the conception that all laws evolve out of circumstances. But even the most relativistically inclined were precluded from any radically "pragmatist" notion by both the rationalistic universals of the age they were leaving behind and by the romantic generalities of the period they were entering. And they were even more inhibited by their patriotic and dogmatic adherence to the thesis that the adaptation of English Common Law to the American order solved the legal problem of merging particular decisions with the universal rule of right and of eternal wisdom.

It is indeed fascinating to see how near they often hovered on the very edge of an evolutionary philosophy, how nearly they approached an insight into the organic. A report in *The North American Review* for October, 1836, said that legal science is not abstract, that it depends on the state of society and improves in proportion to the improvements of civilization. So, "he, who, in our days, should govern himself in this science by the rules of Lycurgus or the Decemvirs, would not be more wise than a countryman of Arkwright or Laplace, who should calculate the motions of the stars like the astrologers of Chaldea, or weave our garments on such looms as were used by the fair-haired matrons of Troy." An article in *The Southern Quarterly Review* declared flatly that "History is the best, and, we may say the only school in which the reason of the law can be learned," but only because laws have been a natural result of civil combinations of men. At the close of our period the sense of development was becoming more profound. At Columbia University in 1858, a year before Darwin's masterpiece, Theodore Dwight said that even statute as well as the Common Law must be studied historically:

While, then, the student is mastering the present law, he must descend through all the strata of centuries, hammer in hand, till he comes to the hard granite of the feudal system. It would in general be useless to seek to get any lower, or to chip away much of its substance.

We hold our breath for a moment of suspense before passages of this tenor, but further analysis reveals that the motive behind them was never a real concern for historical growth but a nervous resolve to demonstrate that the Common Law was not an artificial invention of man but wholly "natural." Hence it could legitimately be transplanted to the American landscape and be permitted to grow according to its inherent disposition amid flora of the new world. Law and the administration of justice have grown up noiselessly, said *The Western Law Journal* in 1851, no one knowing how. "Hence"—and here is the happy conclusion concerning the Common Law—"whoever would ignore the past, sets up his own weak reason against the instincts of society; instincts as unerring as those which guide the wild fowls in their annual migrations, and teaches the little wren, the swallow, and robin, how and when to build their nests." (William Cullen Bryant had already assured the American public through the most popular of native lyrics that the power which guided the flight of the waterfowl would guide aright the steps of man; this was the same power that guided the flight of the Common Law from England to the American wilderness!) Nature, said a *Southern Review* essay on Kent's *Commentaries* in 1828, is everywhere the same, so that (by a logic which Emerson would soon shatter in his gentle wrath) our literature and science will never exhibit any strictly national peculiarities. But our juridical institutions are quite other:

In this respect, our founders could not, if they would, be mere imitators. They could bring with them from the mother country, only the general principles of government and jurisprudence—the great outlines of a free constitution, and the invaluable maxims of the common law. But its institutions were more or less inapplicable to their present circumstances, and their civil polity had to be recast and built up anew from the very foundation.

In short, the historical character of the Common Law should assure patriots that it was no foreign scheme being foisted on them by cunning lawyers. In 1859 Emory Washburn took pride in the advances that had been made in American jurisprudence during the last generation. But, he said, if we contemplate this period in contrast with the life of the Common Law, it dwindles to a moment's space: the origin of that mighty system is so distant that the long vista of ages "blends in its perspective the hues of truth and error, like the melting of the dim outline of the blue ocean with the bluer sky, when we look out upon its waters, as they sleep in the stillness of a summer's twilight." Americans, then, of all the peoples on earth should accept the Common Law, for, as Story said in his Inaugural, under its aegis, the struggle in the courts is a contest fit "for men of strong sinew, and deep thoughts."

The lawyers had all the more reason to cohere as a professional elite and, down to the last moment, cling to the assurance that the inherent reasonableness of the Common Law would save both them and the nation, because they were all brought up on Sir William Blackstone. Even such a rebel as Rantoul served his apprenticeship to Blackstone and could hardly repudiate the tuition even when trying to escape from what he considered the coils of Blackstone's serpents. For Blackstone taught them, authoritatively, what the great jurists of England affirmed, "that the law is the perfection of reason, that it always intends to conform thereto, and that what is not reason is not law." Modern critics, employing techniques for legal and psychological analysis which the early Americans did not possess, now discover contradictory premises at the base of Blackstone's façade. Indeed, even in the early years of the Republic the American subservience to him was not everywhere as abject as usually is reported. Hoffman in 1823 said that his was only a "bird's eye view" of a complicated science, and Story, always saluting him as the greatest of the moderns, drove his own students far beyond the *Commentaries*. Yet when St. George Tucker edited the classic in 1803, even though, as we have seen, he followed his leader Jefferson in denying that the Common Law was an inherent part of American federal jurisprudence, he still devoted himself to this endeavor because Blackstone's *Commentaries* transformed the rude chaos of English laws into "the semblance of a regular system." Hence there could be no better model for Americans to observe. Tucker made a gallant effort to supplement Blackstone, to require the student to learn American municipal law along with the English, but he in effect reinforced the general proclamation which arose from courts and law schools that Blackstone was the magician who stretched his scientific wand over the illimitable ocean and brought from it, in the words of Josiah Quincy,

a well-proportioned, well-cemented fabric, pleasing to the sight, satisfactory to the taste, approved by the judgment, its architectural principles just, its parts orderly and harmonious, in which justice was found consorting with reason, and controversy guided by the spirit of truth, and not by the spirit of victory.

By 1841, Henry St. George Tucker, son of the Jeffersonian editor, pushed aside his father's scruples and hailed Blackstone as the Linnaeus of the law. The student of botany or natural history, Tucker said, may be ushered into a disordered magazine wherein the treasures of knowledge are thrown together like heaps of lumber; but just as the great scientists are enabling the neophyte to enter instead a beautifully arranged museum where he can command at once a general view of the various compartments and different classes, so by coming into the law through Blackstone he possesses from the beginning a coherent plan. Blackstone "placed the study of the law in the rank of the sciences, by system and classification." This proposition became for the profession, in the time of its glory, an article of faith so axiomatic that he who questioned it might in that America be more easily denounced as a heretic than one who, like Abner Kneeland, denied the existence of God.

Because America had conned what Blackstone had wrought, the profession could early turn defense of the Common Law into an attack upon its American enemies by presenting as virtues the very characteristics that had been most suspect. These detractors wanted the Republic to restrict its legality to statute law, and in cases of perplexity to trust entirely to the "reason" of judge and jury. "For heaven's sake," cried Joseph Hopkinson of Philadelphia in 1809, in a vigorous assault upon Jefferson, "do not let us, in a search after certainty, throw down the permanent rules of the Common Law," to erect in their place the caprices of juries. For the supreme quality of the Common Law is precisely that amid its complexities it sustains order, supplies certainty. It is not because it is English that we should receive it, continued Hopkinson, "but because it is the law of *reason* and *justice*." It should bind us to the extent that we ourselves are reasonable. If from this premise the Jeffersonians conclude that reason will best be exercised by dealing with matters "expressed in black and white," they show themselves ignorant of the nature of reason. Consider the dictionary: "scarcely a word in our language has a single, fixed, determinate meaning." Mere language is no means for stabilizing ideas; what to the ignorant seems a floating mass of imprecision actually is the most precise engine ever devised by man: within it are included not only the rules of reason and nature but the tested accretions. "You cannot separate the law from the construction of the law." Brute statutes are liable to misconception until weighed in a series of decisions, "which in fact is common law." While the average citizen, who assumed that of course what was reasonable could be made into law and then be applied, blinked in amazement at this curious logic, the lawyers pressed their point all the harder, especially as Andrew Jackson was inaugurated in 1829. The democratic reasonableness found itself accused by Joseph Willard in that year of becoming an "ocean of universal skepticism" which threatened to inundate "that venerable pile, the common law." The folly of the insurgence can be refuted by the slightest consideration of the nature of this pile: particular decisions, not necessarily connected to begin with, have in the process of time been grouped into general principles, and so the Common Law has become a science.

In short, then, we cannot, whatever demagogues promise, escape from it. "It becomes," concluded Willard, "our sustaining peace and happiness, dwelling with us at all times, encircling our persons, our characters, and estates, restraining the army of violence, and preserving us in the enjoyment of our rights." Du Ponceau publicized a phrase which Kent gratefully took up, that the Common Law is the very atmosphere we breathe. Kent improved upon the idea: "we meet with it when we wake and when we lay down to sleep, when we travel and when we stay at home; it is interwoven with every idiom that we speak; and we cannot learn another system of laws, without learning, at the same time, another language." This wisdom without dogmatism, said *The American Jurist* in 1829, alone "is adequate to securing the great ends of government, the protection and happiness of its citizens."

At this point historians may perceive the inner tendency of the movement for domesticating the Common Law, though many advocates were never fully conscious of what they were doing and the resistants never altogether comprehended why they objected. The lawyers' aim was exactly the opposite of that of the revivalists. Instead of dreaming of creating on the continent a distinct, unique millennial utopia, they were striving to subject the society to a rule of universality. Even as they argued that the Common Law could and should be adapted to America, they in reality were contending that, leaving out the portions which pertained only to a feudal and royal order, the national spirit, as Du Ponceau phrased it, should be so conformed to the Common Law that it has "an undoubted ascendancy through the whole or a great majority of the States." Because, said Charles Jackson in the crucial year of 1829, the system of action established by the Common Law "needed only to be known, to be universally approved," the lawyers could finally contend that the very idea of a unique, exceptional America is nonsense. The thesis took shape with such writers as Hopkinson: a young country, he said, must use the experience of others. Du Ponceau, Hoffman, Kent, Story, Parsons hammered it into shape. By 1851, for instance, a writer on legal education in *The United States Monthly Law Magazine* proclaimed that should our law students be confined to the peculiarities amid which they were born, if they never inquired beyond the limits of their county courts, if they never had any larger prospect "of the realms of universal jurisprudence" than the reports of their native states, we may remain fellow-citizens, but we shall be strangers to one another. The law may stretch its network over the expanding circles of business, but it will never become, as through glorious centuries the Common Law did become in England, "a living product sympathizing with the national mind, inwrought with the ripest lessons of experience and the soundest deductions of philosophy, to rule by the attractive simplicity of its provisions, and the commanding justice of its requirements."

There is nothing in all this literature to permit any suspicion that these apologists were not as nationalistic as Charles Grandison Finney. But they, in contrast to (and, as we shall see, sometimes in open conflict with) the religionists, were the first to work out a philosophy of national personality within a frame of cosmopolitan reference. Under the form of accommodating English law to the United States, they were asserting the universal against the particular, the comprehensive rationality of traditional wisdom against the fiat of individual statute, the heritage of civilization against provincial barbarism. Their quest for inherent rationality within the Common Law rapidly became a very different concern from what had occupied Blackstone or still occupied English jurists. The English had only to continue discovering, if they could, deeper ranges for that reasonableness; Americans had to assert the rationality, assume it perfect, and impose, by force of argument and judicial rule, this sophistication upon a recalcitrant people. Jeffersonians sensed the nature of the plot in such an apparently innocuous statement by John Marshall as this:

I understand by the law mentioned in the statutes of the United States, those general principles and those general usages which are to be found not in the legislative acts of any particular State, but in that generally recognized and long established law, which forms the substratum of the laws of every State.

The democracy was the more apt to discern a purpose in this sentence because Marshall voiced it in the Burr trial. Perceived in that context it reveals the often inarticulate premise of the lawyers' endeavor, that on the basis of this ubiquitous Common Law they might hold the nation together and guide it to prosperity. If they should fail, the national federation would disintegrate.

3.

SCHOLARSHIP

As early as 1815, Richard Rush, aware that in literature, painting, architecture the boasts of the Republic had not yet been vindicated, sought consolation in asserting that amid these various "excitements of mind" only in the field of jurisprudence did the United States approach the old nations. The lawyers took care to make this point frequently, for they were acutely uncomfortable with the recollection that, measured by the standard of professional skill they were rapidly acquiring, American practice down to the Revolution had been frightfully crude. A majority of the colonial judges had never been trained as lawyers, and as for arguments in court, said Wilkins Updike in 1842, they had consisted mostly of appeals to passion based on the characters of the contestants. Only in the 1790's did the publication of reports commence. The student at the turn of the century had Blackstone to begin with, and was then, as Story remembered, plunged into Coke on Littleton, where he was long bewildered.

In two short decades the situation was completely changed. We now have, said Story to the Suffolk County Bar in 1821, over a hundred and fifty volumes of reports, and our happy danger now is not that we shall want but be overwhelmed. Even in Rhode Island, where from 1819 to

1826 a farmer served as Chief Justice, the "ameliorating progress," said Updike, was working so admirably that the epoch had come "when the cause and its merits, and not the character of the parties, will be the only legitimate subjects of trial." At a bound, one might say at a single bound, the profession emerged from a condition in which it had to rely on "uncertain or obscure traditionary information" into what seemed a dazzling wealth of documentation.

As their arsenals thus became stocked, the lawyers began to stress the argument that precisely because in America there had grown up, in the shapeless colonial jurisprudence, no separation of functions, the American lawyer was entitled to all the greater respect because he had to be a Jack-of-all-trades. We already have, said Rush in 1815, courts of common law, chancery, admiralty, criminal, registery, orphans, and so on, but here the profession "is not subdivided . . . in the ways that it is in England," so that the American lawyer is called upon at various times to plead within each of these areas. Story made so much of this consideration that we wonder how any simple citizen had the temerity to question his massive accomplishment; the English acquire perhaps a technical skill by their specialization, but that is of little moment, Story moralized, compared with what the American learns by surveying the whole structure: he is led "to large and elevated views, to brilliant and successful illustrations, to reasonings from various contrasts and analogies of the law, and to those generalizations which invigorate eloquence, and shadow out the finer forms of thought." There were many in Story's lifetime to tell him to his face that he thus modestly described himself, and so both by precept and example he set the ideal. For, as Matthew Henry Webster observed in 1837, the fact that the American lawyer has to practice in all the courts may mean that while he has not the specific accomplishments of an English barrister, yet he has something infinitely better—an enlarged and comprehensive intellectual power which prepares him not only to do his duty toward clients but "to assume any of the numerous public stations which our institutions require, and to perform its functions with credit to himself and advantages to the commonwealth."

As leaders of the bar repeatedly voice this contention it becomes clear that they are fighting two enemies. One is the still-lingering hostility of the public to legal necromancy. Joseph Willard at Worcester, Massachusetts, in 1829 frankly advocated frequent meetings of local bar associations because these will incite the profession "to those intellectual efforts that will secure the favorable public sentiment." The other foe was that body of ill-educated "pettifoggers" who could qualify under the lax requirements of most Western states and so bring the craft into contempt by their avarice and incompetence. The associations, continued Willard, must suppress those who try to be lawyers without the proper notions and who will ever retain, notwithstanding their later efforts, the "deficiencies arising from defect of early mental discipline."

Joseph Story was the most vigorous in beating down the surge of vulgarity within the guild, and for this reason was cordially hated by the majority of practitioners. In 1821, even while congratulating the country on the immense progress already made, he denounced the prevailing ignorance of general principles, the looseness of our declarations and pleadings, our aberrations from a settled and technical phraseology, "and a neglect of appropriate averments, which not only deprive our pleadings of just pretension to elegance and symmetry, but subject them to the coarser imputation of slovenliness." We must not, he kept insisting, "rest satisfied with mediocrity, when excellence is within our reach." Yet Story was not alone in his insistence upon scholarship. Edward Ingraham, for instance, in Philadelphia in 1828 excoriated those dolts who seek in the law a resting place, "however unacquainted with the proper preparatory studies, or even a common English education." *The Carolina Law Journal* in 1830 pointed out that since the legislature now required a thorough schooling for physicians, so "it should be equally rigid in exacting proper qualifications on the part of the gentlemen of the bar."

Again and again the lawyers impressed upon the democracy the idea that to attain distinction at the bar required so severe an intellectual discipline that few could even hope to measure up to it. They devised a litany in which the awesome terms were regularly flung out. The law "demands the energies of the most powerful minds, and exhausts all the stores of learning." The profession is allied to every department of human knowledge: it must with the metaphysician explore the mysterious powers of the mind, with the logician it must master the rules of evidence, with the moral philosopher ascertain the duties and obligations of men, with the artisan it must learn methods and processes. In short, said Warren Dutton, "it calls to its aid all that the wisdom and experience of past times has recorded, and, in its highest exercises, becomes a model of all that is powerful or captivating in eloquence." Nor was the discipline any less strenuous in Virginia by the time Henry St. George Tucker set forth the requirements: the lawyer has to be acquainted with science, be versed in history, know the precedents, have a mind acute enough to perceive subtle distinctions but so tempered as not to be misled by metaphysical ingenuity. "He must moreover be blessed with an analytical mind, which can draw order out of chaos, and arrange his numerous materials so that they will illustrate each other, instead of producing embarrassment and confusion." In their own conclaves of self-congratulation the lawyers so rapidly fell in love with themselves that in 1828 Joseph Willard summarized their infatuation by announcing that only the law affords the grand exercise of human reasoning powers—"the process of comparing, combining, separating, and searching, that gives strength and readiness to the powers of the mind."

Indeed, the very loftiness of the lawyers' conception of their class as alone privileged to extract particular applications from universal rationality betrayed them into a certain embarrassment when one of their luminaries could be accused of declension, under the stress of political passion, from these noble pretensions. Against Daniel Webster, especially after March of 1850, the charge was levied that by stooping to compromise he betrayed not so much humanity as the integrity of the calling, that while he was possibly great in understanding, in mastery of statutes and strategy, he was woefully deficient in "large reason." Rufus Choate, in one of his many eulogies of Webster, tried to answer this criticism in language which, however effective as apology for Webster, shows how the legal mind strove to reconcile its worship of erudition with its general profession of fidelity to moral principle. Of course, said Choate, Webster spoke habitually in the language of the Constitution, not of philosophy; he confined himself, deliberately, to historical maxims, "because it was America— our America—he sought to preserve," rather than any abstract conception of humanity. Within these self-imposed limits, he combined ideas instead of fastening on one only; "is it therefore inferred that he had not the larger form of intellectual power?"

By the 1850's there was an increasing doubt in many quarters that even the most ample intellectual power in the law would prove adequate to the complexities of the Union, but Choate could still celebrate its triumphs because the lawyers had very nearly subdued the nation. The work of Joseph Story was not to be negated even by the Civil War. His impress upon the Republic was further reinforced by his steady adulation of James Kent, so that it may be argued that quite apart from Kent's immediate contribution to the picture of legal erudition, Story did as much by making Kent the hero of American law. "In truth," Story wrote him in 1819, "nothing is more difficult than to preserve in the profession a steady spirit of original investigation, and to unite a deep respect for authorities with an habitual inquiry into their consonance with principles." In his review of Kent's chancery decisions, in *The North American Review* for July, 1820—which was to be widely quoted—Story portrayed the ideal legal intelligence in words which could never thereafter be forgotten:

... such a mind, at once liberal, comprehensive, exact, and methodical; always reverencing authorities, and bound by decisions; true to the spirit, yet more true to the letter of the law; pursuing principles with a severe and scrupulous logic, yet blending with them the most persuasive equity.

However, there is one interesting quirk to be observed in all this literature of judicial complacency; in neither their theoretical statements nor their eulogies of each other are the lawyers disposed to salute "genius" in the law. They came near to admitting it in the person of John Marshall. Story confessed that when he himself examined a question, he went from headland to headland, but that "Marshall has a compass, puts out to sea, and goes directly to the result." But even when, after his death in 1835, they orated upon Marshall, they stressed his gigantic industry, his patient study, his ability to take into view all the bearings of a complicated subject, rather than any flair for instinctive perception. All the textbooks and most of the memorials on departed lawyers emphasize, as did John Gorham Palfrey about Chief Justice Parker of Massachusetts in 1830, that a great judge, on unexpected emergencies, draws "from the stores of a patiently acquired learning." They are not poets, but men capable of addressing themselves "to the solution of intricate questions." They often reminded themselves that Blackstone had given up poetry; likewise, Joseph Story, "following out the precepts of Blackstone," abandoned the muse and "plunged at once into the dark labyrinth of the ancient learning of the law."

On every possible occasion Story admonished that the "most diligent study and practice of a long life" are scarcely sufficient to keep one abreast of American legal developments. Until we become absolutely perfect in our actions, "there will remain immeasurable uncertainties in the law, which will call for the exercise of professional talents," and he made it quite clear that he really had no interest in "Utopian dreams," much preferring the endless arena of talent. "We must serve in the hard school of discipline; we must invigorate our powers by the studies of other times." His admiration for Kent emphasized not Kent's originality but his learning, research, diligence; in 1829, giving his inaugural address as Dane Professor at the Harvard Law School, Story reached the ultimate in his celebration of the law as, beyond anything otherwise conceivable in America, the citadel of erudition. Mere genius, he said, can hardly keep pace with the incessant demands of the Common Law; it requires laborious study. "There is no royal road to guide us through its labyrinths." Whereupon he proceeded to demonstrate, at voluminous length, that by not trusting to genius the young jurist could avoid not only the mistakes of genius but also its bad manners. A reviewer of his *Law of Bailments* paid it the high compliment of being written "in a simple and unpretending but pure style." The style enabled him to combine theoretical fullness with practical illustrations by cases:

It is in this way only that legal commentaries, by combining the two modes, can be rendered interesting to the general scholar and man of literary taste, out of the walks of the profession. The dry and somewhat technical features of the common law would thus be divested of some of its terrors, and philosophy would enlarge its boundaries and its power.

As the massive *Commentaries* rolled off the press, and the world wondered that one head could possibly carry all Story knew, even he had to explain, as at the end of *Equity Jurisprudence* in 1839, that while the grandeur of these subjects staggered the imagination, still the youthful jurist should be informed that if he gives his days and nights to the perusal of the great masters, "he may hereafter entitle himself to a high place in the ministrations at the altars of the sanctuary of justice." And what higher place, was Story's implicit query, could any young American dream of? Compared with it, to be a mere President in the manner of Andrew Jackson was nothing.

New England, of course, had its deeply rooted tradition of a learned clergy, and we should not be surprised that there the conception migrated from the clerical to the legal calling, though it is somewhat astonishing to see how far the lawyers by about 1830 were outdistancing the ministers in demanding the most athletic ideals of study. There might in the South flourish a freer expression of admiration for inspiration in the courtroom, but, even so, the call for accurate and encyclopedic knowledge was just as insistent. St. George Tucker, as we have noted, cushioned his edition of Blackstone with an appendix denying that the Common Law is automatically a part of federal law, but otherwise delighted in his labor because Blackstone was a model of legal perspicuity: "a work in which the author has united the various talents of the philosopher, the antiquarian, the historian, the jurist, the logician, and the classic." Hence his tomes should be in the library of every "gentleman," whether or not he be a lawyer, for they are a major bulwark against ignorance, which is invariably the parent of error, and "where it is blended with a turbulent and unquiet temper, it infallibly produces licentiousness, the most terrible enemy to liberty, except despotism." Joseph Baldwin, in *The Flush Times of Alabama and Mississippi,* gave a lively description of the bar in the wide-open Southwest, but insisted that the great figures, however erratic or melodramatic their personal and political lives, were serious scholars. The picturesque Sergeant S. Prentiss on the hustings was a spread-eagle orator, but in court showed that he "was a laborious man, even in the tapestring sense." There he depended not at all upon forensic flourish but upon "knowing and being able to show to others what was the law." His statements were clear and compact, his language simple and sententious, though in his literary tastes he reveled in Scott and often reminded Baldwin of Byron. J. F. Jackson in *The Southern Quarterly Review* would not quite exempt even Byron from the category of methodical application: "Brougham and Byron were both hard workers—one by unintermitted exertion, the other by *regular* spasms." And of course from South Carolina came John C. Calhoun, whom his age regarded as the embodiment of hard, ruthless logic, while out of New England came Webster, who, though his powers of concentration were tremendous and though he arrayed a massive amount of evidence in his arguments, put on infinitely greater displays of "inspired" eloquence before the judges than Calhoun would have thought fitting.

The formulators of this intellectual standard, once they had employed it to beat down native opposition to the Common Law, went on to contend that even those areas of that law which did not apply to the United States, or which had become obsolete, should be studied if the candidate were to be anything more than an ignorant "empiric." Hoffman in the 1820's was sternly declaring that in difficult problems the lawyer will have to find explanations "by research into the antient foundations of the law," while at Harvard Theophilus Parsons the younger, writing in 1852 on Kent, said that the sound lawyer will learn the old rules even if these have lost their positive authority: "and he who learns them may never perhaps find them in his hands as the instrument of practice."

Along with this concerted endeavor to impress upon the disorderly American mind the claims of professional antiquarianism, the leaders also called for a stiff education in the classics. Here again Story was highly vocal, but other teachers, such as Job Tyson, argued with passion, "The law is not only a learned, but a *liberal* profession." He who does not bring to it the perspective of Seneca, Cicero, and Plato does injury even to the "practical tendency" of the science. There is a great danger, warned George Sharswood in 1854, that an exclusive reading of the law will cramp the mind, "shackle it to the technicalities with which it has become so familiar, and disable it from taking enlarged and comprehensive views even of topics falling within its compass as well as of those lying beyond its legitimate domain." On the eve of the Civil War there were increasing lamentations, arising from both South and North, that the cultural quality of younger lawyers was deteriorating; yet the great lawyers of the preceding age gave so magnificent an exhibition of mastery not only of technical law but of what Story called "general literature" that their memory still plagues the profession.

Joseph Story put still another heavy obligation upon the neophyte: not only must he know the ancient and now useless chapters of the Common Law, and the Greek and Latin classics, but he must also keep himself fully informed of the English decisions pronounced since the American Revolution, even though these were no longer binding on this country. Indeed, through Story's decisions and his writings the names of Mansfield, Hardwicke, Brougham, Erskin, Lyndhurst, Eldon, Ellenborough, Stowell parade so frequently that even John Quincy Adams, let alone certain Jacksonians, was moved to protest. When Story quoted Mansfield and Stowell in his 1829 inaugural as though they were archangels, Adams jolted him by calling Mansfield a "Scottish Jacobite, with the principles of Sir Robert Filmer," and adding that Stowell was utterly unconcerned about "the inextinguishable rights of human kind." Story replied that he spoke of them only in their legal character, not in their political, and so continued to treat them with punctilious respect. Nothing ever more gladdened Story's heart than learning that his commentaries were praised by the English judges.

The commentaries of Kent and Story, and such systematic institutes as Hoffman's, were the principal instruments by which the scholars forced their philosophy upon the country. The *Lectures on Law* which James Wilson delivered in Philadelphia in 1790 were published after his death in 1804. They are eminently readable surveys of the Enlightenment, devoting considerable space, for instance, to refuting Berkley and Hume and defending the common-sensical realism of Reid; but when it comes to information about American law, they reflect the vacant state of scholarship in that year. With David Hoffman's lectures, the first being *A Course of Legal Study* in 1817, we enter into a different world, where the grand outlines are traced; but they include the warning that "to hope from them particular and definite knowledge on any of its various doctrines, were a like folly with expecting an accurate draught of St. Peter's in a map of Italy."

This was a spirit Story could share and admire when he reviewed Hoffman and exhorted that even one year at the new Harvard Law School would lay a foundation of learning "upon which our ingenuous and ambitious youth might confidently hope to build a fabric of professional fame." When he joined to the crushing burden of his work on the Supreme Court and on the circuit the labor of teaching at Harvard, his prestige made the Law School a national institution. From this point on may be dated the rapid growth, one might even say the efflorescence, of law schools, so that by mid-century the time when a youth could set up as a lawyer merely by reading Blackstone in the office of the local practitioner was fast becoming a thing of what seemed a distant past (even though the custom did not entirely disappear until the late 1880's).

The histories of these schools have been written, and need not here detain us. What the great teachers like Hoffman inculcated was not so much legal erudition as a veritable ecstasy of scholarship. In one year at Harvard, plus another year with William Wirt, Rufus Choate, who was to become the most successful pleader of his day, succumbed to this ecstasy, and for years recited it with a fervor as great as Story's:

Is there not something in the study and administrative enjoyment of an elaborate, rational, and ancient jurisprudence, which tends to raise the law itself, in the professional and in the general idea, almost up to the nature of an independent, superior reason, in one sense out of the people, in one sense above them,—out of and above, and independent of, and collateral to, the people of any given day?

But even as this vision of triumphant coherence had reached the stage of intoxicating eloquence, a cloud no bigger than a man's hand began to form on the legal horizon. Benjamin F. Butler indirectly acknowledged its existence in 1835 when preparing a *Plan* for the law school at New York University: "The great principle of division of labor, adopted with so much success in other departments of industry and science, is equally applicable to a Law School." The science has now become so complex, and contains so many subjects which have little connection with each other, and the whole business has become so difficult, that to hope to turn out universal scholars of the law is to condemn the students to years and years of "laborious research." It would be much better, mused Butler, to submit the law to "as minute a subdivision of labor as Theology or Medicine." By 1852 Theophilus Parsons had sadly to note that there were now shaping up two opinions within the American bar: one held that its various departments were so extended that each scholar must specialize, the other held to the position which had been won against prejudice, that the law, like all true sciences, springs from a few simple principles which can readily be acquired. Parsons supported the latter conception, but there is a sort of melancholy admission in his article that he sees the future failing him. The behemoths of legal scholarship had overreached themselves. They had created so massive an engine of rational erudition that the intellects of ordinary American students could not keep up with it.

Yet it would take time before the colossal achievement could be torn asunder. In 1853 Massachusetts called a convention to revise the state constitution, and there were present advocates for the popular election of judges. Rufus Choate made what may, in the perspective of history, be called the last stand of the vernal period of American law. In this day, he asked, which boasts of its advances in science and education, "will any one disgrace himself by doubting the necessity of deep and continued studies, and various and thorough attainments, to the bench?" A judge is to know not merely the law of statute and constitution, but that other, that boundless Common Law, "that old code of freedom which we brought with us in the Mayflower and Arabella, but which in the progress of centuries we have ameliorated and enriched, and adapted wisely to the necessities of a busy, prosperous, and wealthy community." And where does a judge find it? In volumes which now must be counted by thousands, exacting long labors—"such labors as produced the wisdom and won the fame of Parsons and Marshall, and Kent and Story, and Holt and Mansfield." Choate therefore concluded that secure tenure must be given the judges, so that they may have a lifetime to learn the whole intricate subject. But actually he was arguing a much larger cause, one which he feared was lost. By 1868 George W. Brown would lament, "It is a great misfortune that the brightest ornaments of the bar have, in the public councils, given place to time-serving politicians." Yet even then, few were able to appreciate what in fact had become the issue, which simply was whether this "busy, prosperous, and wealthy community" could any longer afford such ornaments of scholarship as James Kent and Joseph Story.

4.

STYLE

In recommending that a copy of Blackstone's *Commentaries* should be in the library not only of every lawyer but of every gentleman, St. George Tucker was echoing Blackstone's own recommendation that a knowledge of law is "the proper accomplishment of every gentleman and scholar; an highly useful, I had almost said essential, part of liberal and polite education." Blackstone did not need to hesitate over that "almost." From the inception of his lectures, he addressed himself not so much to professional lawyers as to "our gentlemen of independent estates and fortune, the most useful as a considerable body of men in the nation." James Wilson commenced his lectures in 1790 for an audience that included the cultivated ladies of Philadelphia and President Washington. In 1826 Kent's preface hoped that his work would be helpful to "gentlemen in every pursuit," and as late as 1852 Theophilus Parsons approved of this "liberal" disposition.

To us it is clear that Blackstone tailored his masterpiece to the needs of an eighteenth-century England, wherein the gentry still ruled as justices of the peace, with the House of Commons as their club. St. George Tucker found nothing incongruous in addressing his edition of Blackstone to Virginia planters, since even in Jeffersonian circles they figured as gentlemen. Only the few resolute opponents of the Common Law *in toto* ventured to attack Blackstone's aristocratic assumptions, but even they acknowledged themselves at a disadvantage because in Blackstone they had to deal with what Tucker called a model both of legal perspicuity and of "methodical elegance." No advocate, said William Sampson in 1824, ever pleaded his cause with more "Eloquence and grace," though not even Blackstone, according to Sampson, could make a science out of the muddle: "the more he brought it into light, the more the sunny rays of his bright genius fell upon it, the more its grotesque forms became defined, the more they proved to be the wild result of chance and rude convulsions." Had Blackstone lived to contemplate the forms of this Republic, he surely would have been obliged to contrast them "with the decayed and vicious institutions which he has so extolled." Meanwhile, Sampson would caution American youth not to be misled by Blackstone's "fascinating eloquence" into accepting his myriad "sophistries dangerous to the principles which every citizen ought, and every professor of our laws is sworn, to maintain."

Surprisingly few such admonitions found their way into print, though we may suspect they reflect a more prevalent attitude than the documents indicate. John Anthon of Philadelphia published *An Analytical Abridgement* in 1832 with a preliminary warning that a student born and educated under free institutions should not be weaned from them "by seductive language and elegant panegyric." There was no getting around Blackstone, but we should cultivate a becoming circumspection, "especially when engaged in training up the future ministers at our civic altars." What clearly made these critiques of Blackstone halfhearted at best was the pre-eminence as a stylist with which Blackstone dazzled the provincial culture. Americans could argue substantively that hundreds of pages in Blackstone had no meaning whatsoever in a democratic republic, but they bowed in abject admiration before what the English editor in 1796 called his "beautiful and lucid arrangement, the purity of the language, the classic elegance of the quotations and allusions, the clear and intelligible explanation of each subject." Because Blackstone had indeed addressed himself to the lay intelligence rather than to professional technicalities, his work became all the more effective in America. By his tone rather than by his content Blackstone exerted an irresistible appeal to a profession coming to a precocious maturity, which for several decades would have to maintain its prestige by standing before the society as a guild both of scholarship and of cultivation. Blackstone, said Parsons in 1852, speaks of law "as a scholar and a gentleman would wish to speak of all things."

Kent and Story, naturally, were foremost in this imitation of Blackstone's manner. Kent was lost in reverence for Blackstone's "perspicuous and elegant, and we may truly add, masterly disquisitions on the feudal law," which made it of no matter that America had no need for feudal law. Story seized every opportunity to celebrate Blackstone's luminous method, his research, but even more his purity of diction, comprehensive brevity, richness in classical allusions, "whether introduced for illustration, or ornament, or instruction," so that it was not too much for Story to say that Blackstone "stands unrivalled in our, and perhaps, in every other language."

Upon this adoration of Blackstone's style, Kent and Story grafted an immense veneration for the literary charms of later English decisions, however much extreme nationalists like John Quincy Adams might frown. The judgments of the High Court of Admiralty, said Kent, render "certain and staple" many loose general principles, and in addition "are pre-eminently distinguished for sagacity, wisdom, and learning, as well as for the chaste and classical beauties of their composition." Story could overlook Lord Stowell's part in precipitating the War of 1812 because of the simplicity of principles, "the classical beauty of his diction," his discriminating but indulgent eye, through which he wastes nothing upon empty speculation, "whose origin is enthusiasm, and whose end is uncertainty or mischief."

So we should not find it surprising, though in the modern perspective the endeavor may appear quaint, that the learned jurists of America promoted each other into positions equal, by American standards, to those of Blackstone, Mansfield, or Stowell. Story in 1834 dedicated his *Conflict of Laws* (his most erudite publication) to Kent, in terms wherein the basic ambition of both these polymaths was proclaimed:

You have done for America, what Mr. Justice Blackstone in his invaluable Commentaries has done for England. You have embodied the principles of our law in pages as attractive by the persuasive elegance of their style, as they are instructive by the fulness and accuracy of their learning.

Though Story was leader of the chorus which sang the praises of James Kent's elegance, other leaders of the profession chimed in. Kent, said John Anthon, followed the method of Blackstone, yet "his elegant and classical mind will be found to have added new beauties to a picture on which all the embellishments of art seemed already to have been exhausted"; he has molded the *disjecta membra* of American law into a system "with a power and energy by no means inferior to his great prototype." In 1836 the veteran Hoffman could only repeat tributes to Kent's deep research, "the classical embellishments, the apt illustrations, and the clear and manly style," which by then were too well known to need mention.

James Kent was never one to withhold praise of others who exemplified the traits for which he was saluted, especially when they wrote about himself. He told Joseph Story, upon reading Story's review of his chancery decisions, that he was not insensible "to the easy and elegant manner in which you display your various learning and cultivated taste," and congratulated Story for living in New England, where society was "equally distinguished for intellectual vigor, exalted morals, classical erudition, and refined taste." In 1826 he pronounced Story's *Phi Beta Kappa Discourse* superlative "for just thought, varied information, refined taste, brilliant imagination, and elegant and eloquent language."

On this matter of style, whether in pleadings or decisions, the masters could further accentuate their demand that lawyers know the classics. Only a familiarity with Greek and Latin, said Story, can furnish such a polish as to impart "that subtile elegance and grace which color the thoughts with almost transparent hues." Anthon went further: only a familiarity with the authors of antiquity can impart to the lawyer's intellect that "generous liberality," that "lofty bearing and magnanimous courtesy," which must be the foundation of legal eminence. Where, asked James Richardson of the Norfolk Bar in 1834, among contemners of ancient learning can we find the immortal poet or orator? Obviously, not here. Only the lawyer steeped in this literature will exhibit in his pleadings "that combination of intellectual power, brilliant but chaste imagination, pure language, calm self-possession, graceful and modest bearing, indicative of a spirit chastened, enriched and adorned," which would win for the profession cultural hegemony within the Republic.

This distinction in style was, as Story frequently moaned, difficult to achieve in the law because much of the technical doctrine, "drawn from remote antiquity, and expanding itself over the business of many ages," has an inherent tendency "to chill that enthusiasm, which lends encouragement to every enterprise, and to obscure those finer forms of thought, which give to literature its lovelier, I may say, its inexpressible graces." But the problem of clothing learned jurisprudence in graceful language thus became all the more urgent: unless the profession could charm as well as instruct, it could not hold the attention of an impulsive democracy. The great lawyer *must* be a great orator, Story insisted, because while aiming to convince the understanding he will have to mingle "with the close logic of the law those bewitching graces which soothe prejudice, disarm resentment, or fix attention." As these gentlemen conceived their situation, their function, in the new society, they realized that they could not protect the mystery against attacks on the Common Law or on the independence of the judiciary if the best showing they could make before the populace was dry-as-dust pedantry.

Hence it is interesting to note the adjectives they habitually employed in extolling the prose of Blackstone or of each other: the three that figure most often are "perspicuous," "elegant," and "liberal." These terms had acquired prestige in the literary discourse of the English eighteenth century, indeed had been precisely, though often variously, defined in aesthetic theory. Almost to a man, the mentors of these legalists were Pope, Addison, Swift, and Samuel Johnson: Story thought himsef daringly modern in admiring "the unconscious moral grandeur of Crabbe and Cowper," and could enjoy Scott; but as for the new literature of the "Romantic Movement" he could only express an aversion toward something which threatened the very foundations of the intellectual edifice he and his fellows had patiently constructed. The most recent poetry, he said in his *Phi Beta Kappa Discourse,* ten years before Emerson's *The American Scholar,* insists too much on extravagant events, seeks to be wild and fiery, and portrays "natural scenery, as if it were always in violent commotion," describes human emotion "as if man were always in ecstasies or horrors." This was the opposite of elegance, for that classical conception teaches that he who paints nature "will rarely depart from the general character of repose impressed upon her scenery," will prefer "truth" instead of "ideal sketches of the imagination." When James Kent eulogized a departed jurist who had exemplified the aesthetic of the profession, he effectually defined its sense of the elegant: "In his calm, chaste, methodical and logical arguments at the bar, he was free from all loose and declamatory expansion, and his speeches were a steady flow of sound principles, supported by sound authority, and bearing strongly on the point in discussion."

These unrepentant holdovers from neoclassicism still took their cue from Johnson's *Dictionary*, in which elegance was defined as "rather soothing than striking; beauty without grandeur." Also, most of them were familiar with Burke's terming the elegant a minor variation of the beautiful, and so opposed to the "sublime." And they had certainly read in Sir Joshua Reynolds how Burke's distinction between the beautiful and the sublime was false, but how the elegant, being paired with taste and fancy, could stand firm against the genius and imagination of the sublime. American lawyers were not literary metaphysicians and paid small attention to quibbles between Burke and Reynolds, but, being assured by a whole century of exposition that the elegant was the archenemy of the sublime, they inscribed that emblem upon their banner. It may be that simply by education and temperament they found congenial an aesthetic which strengthened their suspicion of "genius" in the courtroom, though on the other hand their advocacy of elegance may well have furnished them with a professional antipathy to the undemocratic quality, whether in politics, literature (as they understood it), or in the law.

At any rate, we may pause for a moment to note how the notion of genius struck two great American lawyers. In January, 1838, when Abraham Lincoln delivered an address to the Young Men's Lyceum of Springfield, he was not a great lawyer (as, in the technical sense, he never would be), yet he was a child of the discipline, even though self-taught. He lamented the outbreaks of mob violence pervading the country from New England to Louisiana, and warned that such confusion offered an invitation to "genius." For Lincoln, on the Illinois frontier, genius was synonymous with Caesar or Napoleon; one has little need of the prophetic spirit to tremble upon reading his words of 1838, knowing what his brief instruction had wrought:

Is it unreasonable then to expect, that some man possessed of the loftiest genius, coupled with ambition sufficient to push it to its utmost stretch, will at some time, spring up among us? And when such a one does, it will require the people to be united with each other, attached to the government and laws, and generally intelligent, to successfully frustrate his designs.

One element in the mysterious compound of Abraham Lincoln is that the potential Caesar of the prairies learned from the ethic of American law how to check the impulses of genius, so that his countrymen should learn somehow, without benefit of genius, to be united each to other.

But there was another aspect of this problem of genius in the law, of which Lincoln in 1838 was only vaguely aware. Then he was concerned only with warding off the man on horseback, though subsequently he was to show that he fully understood the issue. This other side appears in a conversation which William Wirt records himself as conducting with John C. Calhoun in 1824, when Calhoun (Secretary of War) advises Wirt (Attorney General) "to study less and trust more to genius." This notation is all the more striking because in his arguments before the Supreme Court, as we shall observe, Wirt figured for his times as the epitome of genius in the law. But in 1824, and presumably for the rest of his forensic performance, Wirt concluded that genius had best be avoided in the courtroom: "A lawyer must understand the particular facts and questions which arise in his cause, before genius has any materials to work upon; and in that preparatory examination consists the labor of the profession." Said Abraham Lincoln in 1838, "Reason, cold, calculating, unimpassioned reason, must furnish all the materials for our future support and defence." This was no abstract hostility to the sublime, nor was it, in any modern sense, opposition to the romantic: it was merely what the legal profession had preserved and were determined to defend in America, although often, as with Wirt and even with Lincoln, by an eloquence which romantics could hardly equal. The curious point about them, and about the mind of America, is that both Wirt and Lincoln assumed they were opposing the cold circumspection of legal rationality to the fantastic exercises of romantic genius. That both should be remembered as geniuses—Wirt less spectacularly than Lincoln—only underlines the irony of the whole stylistic endeavor of the American legal profession.

Likewise in their constant use of the word "liberal" the juristic gentlemen (who like Sergeant Prentiss and Abraham Lincoln held firmly to the civilized standards of the profession amid the roughest tumble of the frontier) intended a fluency of manner and speech which they opposed to the barbarity of popular clamor and to what seemed to them the hysteria of self-appointed geniuses. To the extent that they lived up to their conception, the powerful jurists of the period would be bewildered to find themselves classified in modern histories as conservatives and opposed to liberalism merely because most of them were Whigs. In part, their connotation for "liberal" was the traditional academic one, of the Liberal Arts. More specifically, however, the term conveyed that liberation from pedantry, that respect for erudition but yet easy employment of it, which in their opinion made them the truly free spirits on the continent. Kent complimented the District Court of Pennsylvania for its pioneer work in maritime law because "in a spirit of free and liberal inquiry" it had discussed the claims of mariners "under the influence of a keen sense of justice, a strong feeling of humanity and an elevated tone of moral sentiment." He fought for a public-school system in New York so that there might be "a liberal and efficient provision for the universal diffusion of common and useful instruction." Story's reviews of Kent always praised a mind "at once liberal, comprehensive, exact, and methodical"; in 1820 Story assured Kent that he would die content if his own researches should eventually prove of use "in assisting in the foundation of liberal principles of national law and constitutional law." Story died in 1845, his last years troubled by his belief that the federal courts were being manned by men of illiberal qualifications. He is often interpreted to have meant Democratic judges; but in justice to him the historian must report that he was more concerned about the code of the profession than about politics. At any rate, among his colleagues his demise was an occasion for reasserting the virtues he had publicly exemplified. He had, said Greenleaf, given up poetry, as did Blackstone, but his gravest decisions were "finished with the highest ornaments of intellectual affluence"; while never unmindful of the severer demands of the law, he made his work within it a part of "elegant literature." Robert Waterston took satisfaction in saying that Story's greatness did not consist in the disproportionate development of any one of his varied powers so much as in the balancing of them. "There was nothing exaggerated about him. There was with him no morbid activity, but a calm and clear self-possession, and a symmetrical beauty of proportion."

However, when we come down from the high level of theory and lofty compliment to the figure the lawyers actually cut in the society, we find fascinating contradictions. Tocqueville would say of them that, since they served as arbiters among the citizens, their habit of directing the blind passions of the mob inspired them with contempt for the judgment of the multitude. Story's *Phi Beta Kappa Discourse* expressed his scorn for what was becoming the literary appetite of the multitude, a denunciation of which Kent approved and which was applauded by Lemuel Shaw, whose daughter would marry Herman Melville. The old models of fine writing, said Story, are disregarded;

on the one hand we have a new cult of naturalness and simplicity (he meant Wordsworth) which in practice has become loose, artificial, "feeble and drivelling," while on the other those who have no aptitude for polished perfection or accuracy go in for hurried tones, glowing and irregular sentences, intensity of phrase, abrupt transitions, forcible expressions. In these latter, "Excitement is produced, and taste may slumber."

Yet through all these decades, while the mentors of the bench were inculcating a chaste and elegant liberality, in the state courts and especially in the Supreme Court of the United States, counsels were putting on exhibitions of forensic melodrama which rivaled the splendiferous performances of the theater, exhibitions widely reported across the country, and attended by as large crowds as could squeeze into the narrow chambers, always on featured days including numbers of "the fair sex." On these occasions the performers played shamelessly to the galleries, and were hailed, like an Edwin Forrest or a Junius Brutus Booth, as geniuses.

Story, both as observer on the Supreme Court and as a justice, was profuse in comment upon the style as well as upon the content of those who addressed it, and was frequently happy to report of someone, as of William Rawle, that "he argues with a very pleasant voice, and has great neatness, perspicacity, and even elegance." Still, there was a vivid recollection among the American pleaders (albeit they had heard of the pyrotechnics only by report) of the stunning exhibitions of Fox, Burke, and Sheridan during the impeachment of Warren Hastings in 1786. Probably John Randolph's attempt to exemplify all three of those parts in his bizarre personality helped to effect the miscarriage of Jefferson's attack on Judge Chase in 1804. Randolph's debacle did not inhibit other counsels, when they had the glory of pleading one of the well-advertised cases, from emulating the oratory of English legend. Though they had to parade their eloquence before John Marshall—whose language, said Story, was "chaste, but hardly elegant"—many of them promoted themselves into the character of inspired geniuses rather than placid liberals, and so played into the forces which Kent and Story reprehended, but to which these judges could not refuse to pay tribute when they were displayed before their benches.

There was, for instance, William Pinkney of Maryland, who had learned in London the manners of the dandy—acquired, said William Ticknor, in the cockpit—who, according to no less an authority than Story, was "vehement, rapid, and alternately delights the fancy and seizes on the understanding." Pinkney could be close in logic, but also step aside at will and strew the flowers of rhetoric about the court. Beyond any man he had ever heard, Story acknowledged in 1819, Pinkney possessed "the power of elegant and illustrative amplification." Audiences would be transfixed to their places, "and taking a long-drawn breath, they would say, almost involuntarily, 'how beautiful!'" Then there was the Irishman Thomas Addis Emmet, who, with his brother Robert Emmet, had agitated rebellion against England, and fled to New York in 1803; he was "bold and free in his language," and extremely persuasive. There was also William Wirt, who while Attorney General wrote a life of Patrick Henry and who argued his cases before the court in what he conceived to be the style of his hero, to the enchantment even of Joseph Story. The reporter for *The Richmond Enquirer* said of Wirt's argument in *Gibbons* v. *Ogden* in 1824 that it was nothing less than the "finest effort of human genius ever exhibited in a Court of Justice"—which was in effect to say that he transcended the professional restraints. "Every face was filled with the fine transport and prophetic fury of the orator, and all united in applauding the peroration, as affording for matter, diction, manner, happy applications and striking effect the most powerful display of real oratory that they ever witnessed."

Wirt's writings show that, at least in print, he never cast loose from the late eighteenth-century rhetoric of Jeffersonian Virginia, and even his fictional re-creations of Patrick Henry's bursts of eloquence keep the "forest-born Demosthenes" within the patterns of Pitt and Fox. Even so, he presented Henry as a genius rather than a man of cultivated perspicuity, and he himself, though ostensibly educated, invited the dangerous compliment of speaking as a genius. In 1848 a bill to relieve justices of the Supreme Court from circuit duties passed the Senate but was defeated in the House; during the debate spokesmen for the democracy attacked the "spectacle" aspect of the Supreme Court and asked why ladies should be invited "to witness the displays of elocution; and that too, in a case, which if rightly argued upon the plain, stern principles of the law, could afford no kind of amusement." If the court was overburdened, they argued, why does it not limit the duration of counsel's arguments, so that it be not regaled by interminable "dissertations or scholastic essays" on axiomatic topics?

For years all such attempts at reform were lost (though in 1848 some limitation was imposed on counsel) precisely because the nation did enjoy if only vicariously through reports in newspapers the tournament of the court. And in these joustings far above Pinkney, Emmet, or even Wirt, towered the majestic figure of Daniel Webster. Modern students are so concerned with the senatorial career and with

Webster's politics that they slight the tremendous impression he made by his legal forensics. Not the least element in the impression of genius he imparted—along with his great brow, his dark complexion, his burning eyes—was that he moved freely from long debates in Congress to learned argument in the court, so that on some days the Congressional galleries would be emptied as the crowd, including John Quincy Adams, followed him into the basement where Marshall or Taney presided. Webster established a goal at which he was ever afterward to shoot by his emotional appeal in the Dartmouth College Case of 1817. The stenographic reports of that hearing are not complete, and it may be that Rufus Choate, after Webster's death, fabricated the version that still rings in American ears, just as Wirt perfected the unrecorded legends of Patrick Henry, but the impression Webster then made upon the country only grew with retelling. In 1819, with *M'Cullock* v. *Maryland,* and then in 1824, in *Gibbons* v. *Ogden,* wherein he was fully reported, he vindicated his title to being not only the epitome of legal erudition but the veritable demon of judicial eloquence. He kept up this reputation with staggering vitality, through the Charles River Bridge Case of 1837, *Smith* v. *Richards* in 1839, or even when losing the Girard Will Case of 1844, wherein he brought the crowded audience to enthusiastic applause.

In the memory of those who attended all these spectacles, *Gibbons* v. *Ogden* remained the stellar show. There Webster and Wirt played against T. J. Oakley and Emmet. Not until Barrett and Booth were to act on alternate nights as either Othello or Iago was anything comparable to be seen in America. Over two decades later, Daniel Lord said it was the "culmination of professional eminence," and still wondered how any court felt itself competent to arbitrate among such brilliant arguments. Mr. Justice Story, however, had no difficulty: though Wirt might be a genius by Virginia standards, Story beheld in Webster all that he had dreamed of:

. . . his clearness and downright simplicity of statement, his vast comprehensiveness of topics, his fertility in illustrations drawn from practical sources; his keen analysis, and suggestion of difficulties; his power of disentangling a complicated proposition, and resolving it in elements so plain as to reach the most common minds; his vigor in generalizations, planting his own arguments behind the whole battery of his opponents; his wariness and caution not to betray himself by heat into untenable positions, or to spread his forces over useless ground.

Here, at last, was the proof of perspicuity, elegance, and liberality. "Remark his style," said Rufus Choate in a memorial eulogy of 1852.

Webster kept separate the eloquence of politics from that of the bar, and never so far merged the political genius with the legal as to forget that in the courtroom he must be cogent as well as eloquent. Whereupon Choate could conclude, in terms which make for confusion today, that especially as a lawyer Webster set the pace for American law by demonstrating himself "uniformly and liberally conservative."

Allowing for the language which the American lawyers had taught themselves, Choate's characterization of Webster as "liberally conservative" may not be quite the contradiction in terms it appears to the twentieth century. It is remarkable that he used this semantic tension to keep from calling Webster, whom he admired unto idolatry, a genius. Story said of Webster's colossal argument that he utilized legal strategy and came out with resolutions which should commend themselves to common minds. That was always the jurists' concern, that they should never get out of touch with the commonalty, though they knew themselves possessed of an erudition which the masses could hardly comprehend—making them, as Tocqueville to their embarrassment bluntly said, "a sort of privileged body in the scale of intellect." Supposing this so, and supposing that the lawyers knew it, there was still an overriding consideration, which Tocqueville blunderingly recognized, that the people should not "mistrust" the profession. Jurists might stage their mighty battles of Webster against Emmet, and there might be a disturbing sense that behind these rhetorical combats more sinister issues were lurking; but if the profession could keep from bringing into the courts any such irresponsible genius as Rantoul threatened to be—if they could keep the practitioners from fancying themselves as geniuses, chartered to rail and name the beasts anew—then they could preserve the precarious society.

Even so, they had sometimes to give the game away. Not by becoming geniuses, but by their love of the profession. David Hoffman extolled the impressive commentaries, and in 1825 marveled at "the beautiful, extensive, useful, and ingenious structure" which successive ages have created. The next year, as he continued his lectures, he said he had imposed upon himself an ordinance of restraint so as not to present themes "sublime."

There was a logic in the events, though the learned and liberal lawyers fought it to the end of their strength, and though ultimately it circumvented them. They kept genius out of the courtrooms while they luxuriated in the genius of Webster, Wirt, and Choate. But when it came to controversies between the states, after the Supreme Court in 1846 settled a minor boundary dispute between Massachusetts and Rhode Island, and after it arbitrated one between Missouri and Iowa in 1849, the younger lawyers were swept up into an exaltation of eloquence of which Kent and Story might well have been wary. For these cases exemplified something new, something unique to the Republic. Edward Everett proclaimed in 1851 that while he had seen the Courts of Westminster and of the Palais de Justice, with much deeper emotions did he enter the chambers of the Supreme Court: "Not that I have there heard strains of forensic eloquence, rarely equalled, never surpassed, from the Wirts, the Pinkneys, and the Websters; but because I have seen a bright display of the moral sublime in human affairs." Here, from the lips of a venerable magistrate, came the voice of equity, preventing what in Europe "all but brought a million men into deadly conflict with one another." And likewise Lewis Cass in the Senate, on January 17, 1855: the Supreme Court is an impressive spectacle, "almost a sublime one," determining questions which in Europe are adjudicated by bayonets and cannon, marked with ruin and devastation.

This should have been the ultimate triumph of the lawyers. There was nothing in their rhetoric to suggest that it could be otherwise. On Friday, March 6, 1857, the Supreme Court delivered its opinion on *Dred Scott* v. *Sandford*. There were, in substance, only two dissents against the sublime seven. The profession had, by an obiter dictum in which Taney's rhetoric only created confusion, let itself in to a dispute which no liberal, perspicacious elegance could placate. *The North American Review* said in October that for the country the greatest calamity of the decision would be a total loss of confidence "in the sound juridical integrity and strictly legal character of their tribunals." In the considered opinion of the legal veterans who either had themselves witnessed or whose fathers had described to them in their youth the "almost sublime" displays of language in the various courts of the nation between the Dartmouth College Case and the Girard Will Case, it was the vulgarization of discourse that triumphed with *Dred Scott*, which was the primary reason why at last the United States, like Europe, had to appeal to an arbitration by bayonets and cannon.

The Science of the Law

The object in some measure peculiar to my plan of instruction, is to teach the law—the *common* law, especially—not as a collection of *insulated positive rules*, as from the exhibition of it, in most of our books, it would appear to be; but as a *system of connected, rational principles:* for, such the common law unquestionably is, not only in its fundamental and more comprehensive doctrines; but also, generally speaking, in its subordinate, and more artificial provisions. In this view of the common law, I regard our books, in general, as extremely defective. They treat it, rather as a code of arbitrary, but authoritative rules and dogmas, than as a *science*. They are conversant, too exclusively, about *doctrines*, to the neglect of *principles*. They deal much in *rules*, and little in *reasons*. In other words, they teach us *what* the rule is; but seldom, *why* it is.

—JAMES GOULD, "The Law School at Litchfield,"
United States Law Journal, 1822

1.

INDUCTION OR DEDUCTION?

A Western lawyer, striving to exonerate his client by the simple laws of his state, was thrown into such a rage by the judge's constant quoting from Kent and Story that he demanded point-blank whether the commentaries of these Eastern gentlemen had ever been authorized by statute. History records not what the judge answered, but there can be no doubt that the accumulated weight of these tomes (which now gather dust on the shelves of law-school libraries) rolled through the decades before the Civil War like a juggernaut. Hoffman's lectures and the volumes of Kent and Story were reinforced by other classics of what Roscoe Pound calls "doctrinal writings": Reeve's *Baron and Feme* (1816), Gould's *Pleading* (1832), Greenleaf's *Evidence* (1842–

1843), Parsons's *Contracts* (1853–1855), Washburn's *Real Property* (1860–1862), to mention only the most ponderous. Against the whimpering protests of beginners who felt that all they need know was American statute, such overpowering figures as Thomas Sergeant of Philadelphia patiently explained that these treatises were indispensable. Maybe they are not always finished, nor need they always serve as authorities, Sergeant said in 1838, but by connecting scattered principles and cases, they shed upon the law a light of order "without which no science can easily be taught or understood."

As the law schools increased in prestige, they carried this light of order deeper and deeper into the regions of Natty Bumppo. Repeatedly honoring those whom they acclaimed as the true pioneers of the American intellect—not Natty Bumppo and not (in their estimation) Jefferson, but James Wilson, Nathaniel Chipman, St. George Tucker, H. N. Brackenridge, David Hoffman—they beheld the culmination of their effort, the vindication of their being, in Kent's *Commentaries*. Not only at Columbia and Harvard was this conviction maintained, but also at Transylvania, in Lexington, Kentucky, which since 1798 defended an outpost of legal civilization in the wilderness. Opening there in 1837 his course on equity, Professor George Robertson assured his unhappy students that law must be expounded like any other science, "with a system, an interest, and a patience, corresponding with its magnitude, utility, and destiny," which cannot be done except in schools, "where system and science prevail."

As American law, by means of reports, commentaries, and schools, began to achieve solid form, patriots of both parties were moved to salute a recognizable triumph. Story in 1819 threw modesty to the winds by declaring that Johnson's *Reports* for New York "will bear comparison with those of an equal period in the best age of the English law"—for him an American extravagance beyond any that Walt Whitman would later reach. In 1827 Democrat George Bancroft greeted Kent's *Commentaries* with the cry that they proved the American science would now shortly by its own force—*vi propria*—expel from our shelves the masses of foreign lore, "and perhaps (the idea is not at all wild or extravagant) . . . we venture to say, make the works of our writers on jurisprudence the ornaments of the libraries of foreign jurists." One must never forget the peculiarly nativist thrust in the work of these jurists, even among those most obsequious toward English decisions.

The authors of textbooks and the burgeoning law schools had the advantage, of which they made the most, that they could plead that they were merely making it possible for students to achieve legal competence much more expeditiously than under the apprentice system. Horace Binney in 1827 said of Chief Justice Tilghman of Pennsylvania that he achieved his distinction by commencing with "a methodical study of the general system of law," pursuing its "derivative branches in logical succession"—a method "by which the student acquires a knowledge of principles that rule in all departments of the science," and so learns to *feel* as much as to know what is in harmony with the system.

Apprentices in law offices faced a hard task in their attempt to think otherwise: they were all presented with the implacable Blackstone. Sir Matthew Hale, said Nathaniel Chipman in his epochal *Reports and Dissertations* of 1793, was the first who conceived that the law of England could be reduced to a system, but his aim of "scientific analysis" was only truly realized by Blackstone. That author won the hearts of Protestant America by insisting that only the Papacy had prevented English universities from the study of what he called the science which distinguishes the criteria of right and wrong, which employs the noblest faculties of the soul, which is accommodated to each community and which yet comprehends the whole. Josiah Quincy said at the dedication of the Dane Chair at Harvard, in 1832, that Blackstone had abolished foreign jargon, that he had "introduced the science of the English law to men of general science." From his day forth, which included the days of America, men were no longer to be repelled by the barbarism of legal terminology: "By the labors of Blackstone the rough scene was changed." Or, as Story gladly exclaimed in 1817, during the reign of George III more was done to give a "scientific cast" to legal doctrines than in all preceding ages.

Again the erudite lawyers of independent America were calling upon citizens to recognize the "scientific arrangement and harmony of principles," the "spirit of scientific research" displayed by the opinions of post-Revolutionary judges in England, even though these were reprehended in the States. Mansfield's judgments on trusts, last will, contingent remainders, said Story, "are reduced to a very high degree of exactness and consistency, and followed out into their regular results with a truly logical conformity to principles," which we do not have in our own annals, and which therefore we should respect.

Story made these observations in reviewing David Hoffman's volume of 1817; to Hoffman belongs the honor of first advancing the claims of the "science" to be pre-eminent among the ambitions of mankind. As the law relates to human conduct, it is of "sublimity"; as it respects moral action, it is infinitely varied, and as it concerns man's rights and obligation to God, country, or himself, "it must necessarily be a science of vast extent." In later editions, Hoffman improved the last phrase to read that the seat of the law is indeed "the bosom of God, and whose voice is the harmony of the world." It may be, as some contemporaries whispered, Hoffman did little more in his surveys than concoct a crude digest of miscellaneous enactments; if so, he has justifiably been forgotten where Kent and Story are remembered, but to him must go the credit for solidly propounding the large conception of American law as a science rather than a mere accretion.

It is, however, an interesting aspect of Hoffman's mind that he declared legal science unsusceptible of "the experimental demonstrations of physicks." In particular, he had the courage to continue, municipal law responds to unforeseen emergencies of public policy, must necessarily vary with the temper of the ages, and so to the untaught observer presents "an intricate and impervious mass of unintelligible combinations." If the internal law of a country gains solidity, then this must come "in the course of experiment."

Whereupon a gulf opened at the feet of American jurists which for the rest of our period they tried either to disregard or to overleap. They could easily assert that an inherent rationality ran through the epochs of the Common Law, but once they announced to the Republic that the body of law which they administered was a science, they had to avow—not so much to their critics as to themselves—whether they constructed their wisdom by induction out of particulars into generalities or by deduction from basic principles into specific instances. They were victims of their age and situation, and proved incapable of resolving their dilemma.

For many of them the magic name became Francis Bacon—whose mind, said Hoffman, "united in the most eminent degree, the comprehensive and the minute." All the most articulate lawyers were wont to say, along with Judge Peter Thacher of Boston, that Bacon had showed the way, which Blackstone pursued, toward the liberation of law from systems founded in fancy "rather than on a patient deduction of truth from actual experiment and mathematical demonstration."

But was Thacher not playing too freely with the word "deduction"? In 1824, for example, Peter Du Ponceau claimed for the law that like medicine it had abandoned nostrums and formulas, had fixed itself firmly on fact and experiment. At Harvard, Simon Greenleaf, in his introductory lecture of 1838, said that adjudicated cases are to the legal student what facts are to the natural scientist, that they are data from which "by the process of induction, his mind ascends to the higher regions of the science," through which he advances to leading principles. Thomas Sergeant betrayed the strife within the thinking of the profession by endeavoring in 1843 to exonerate their master Blackstone: indeed, wrote Sergeant, Blackstone composed his *Commentaries* on the basis of pure reason, but afterward he hunted out in Lord Coke the authorization of precedent. Would this method not prove that precedents derive their authority, not from having been pronounced, "but from being the results of the deep research and meditation of various minds, matured by common deliberation and discussion"? Why, therefore, should an induced science not also be deduced?

In other words, as American lawyers realized that at last they were entering into their inheritance, they commenced to ask themselves whether they did not have a ready-made body of principle which, though it might have grown in England through induction from particulars, now came to them as so systematic an order of the mind that they, and they alone, could work from generalities down to cases instead of upward from miscellaneous data to universals. They preached a wariness by which we are tempted to say they sought to conceal their confusions. No doubt, said Horace Binney, in such scientific works as Newton's or Franklin's, the character of the researcher pervades the whole, but the law is a "practical" wisdom which must from day to day retain the same shape. "A speculative, inventive, imaginative Judge is a paradox." A good judge, such as Tilghman, does not exhibit the "magnificent variety" of the ocean, at one moment serene and the next tempestuous, but is, rather, like the equal current of a river that "safely bears upon its bosom the riches of the land." Yet if a river is to maintain an "unvarying surface"—this was Binney's implication—it may have to be restrained by dikes and other devices for flood control. Hoffman would say, going beyond the cautious Binney, that these confines must be formulated not simply by courts but by the laws of human nature. "Such is the intimate relation between *mind* and *matter* as to render it impossible to proceed far in the philosophy of natural and political jurisprudence, without some acquaintance even with the phenomena of mental philosophy." Lawyers would need more than collections of reports in order to define their terms, to untie the combinations of fancy. To some extent they would have to be metaphysicians. Not, Hoffman quickly added, learned in the jargon of Kant and Fichte, but fully possessed of the philosophy of Reid, Locke, Stewart, and Brown.

Yet, though these philosophers opposed the a priori, what else did they bequeath to the American jurist but an assemblage of concepts out of which they could argue for their clients? By 1851 *The United States Monthly Law Magazine* could set forth the American idea as a demonstration of how a science that had grown in Europe through induction could be presented to this country as deductive:

Like other sciences, it is supposed to be pervaded by general rules, shaping its structure, solving its intricacies, explaining its apparent contradictions. Like other sciences, it is supposed to have first or fundamental principles, never modified, and the immovable basis on which the whole structure reposes; and also a series of dependent principles and rules, modified and subordinated by reason and circumstances, extending outward in unbroken connection to the remotest applications of law.

The article further contended that such was now the attested method of the Harvard Law School, wherein the student commences with general studies in order to advance to the more intricate and particular. Professor Greenleaf in 1838 had revealed, a bit inadvertently, why this ideal prospered in Cambridge: because, he said, by observing it, the lawyer learns to ascertain the public will not as expressed through executive functionaries—*i.e.*, Democratic Presidents—"but as it is heard in the harmonious system of a liberal science, permanent in its principles." As strains upon the union increased, many lawyers became increasingly declarative, until in 1858 Theodore Dwight at Columbia would leave far behind the Common Law scruples of Hoffman and flatly declare that the science of astronomy is none the less scientific because in some cases astronomers have a problem of applying right principles to the intricacies of the stars. So there is a vulgar notion that law is not science, that it is mere haphazard and chance. If it does appear so, then this false impression is the result of maladministration. In truth, "no science known among men is more strictly deductive than the science of a true Jurisprudence."

The obvious lesson, continued Dwight, is that lawyers need more education, not in order to memorize the mountainous library of reports (for those can always be consulted through their indices) but in order to achieve the subtle and difficult balance between induction and deduction. James Walker chided American lawyers for their inability to descend from general to particular, "the ordinary mode of imparting scientific information," rather than to ascend from particulars to generals, "the ordinary method of discovering truth." But in the practice of the truly competent, both methods were employed simultaneously, and thus law "deserves to rank as a science almost in the same class with geometry." Clearly, as James Campbell insisted at the opening of the University of Michigan Law School, "the task of studying out this system of jurisprudence, and harmonizing with it our numerous statutes, can not safely be entrusted to ignorance or inexperience."

There was the more need for exquisite skill in the handling because while the law could be hailed as a science, the lawyers were always careful to admit that it seldom became identified with ideal justice. It must always be subject to some uncertainty, said Story, not at all from the obscurity of decisions, "as the vulgar erroneously suppose, but from the endless complexity of human actions." John Pickering discussed this dilemma before the Boston Society for the Diffusion of Useful Knowledge in 1834, and showed in language which unwittingly anticipated W. S. Gilbert's just where there could be no possible, probable shadow of doubt. The science itself, he maintained, is as certain as sciences in general, but when applied to the innumerable objects about us, it, like mathematics, encounters uncertainty. Nobody doubts, likewise, that Scripture contains the perfect system of divinity; but behold, how divided are Christians about interpretations! The predominant cause of uncertainty in the law is an ambiguity of language which, to some extent, is unavoidable, especially in a community where every man has an equal right to decide the construction; there is therefore only one way to bring the law closer to solid and unvarying justice, which is to argue cases before the judicial authority, arriving at certainty "only by the positive decision of a tribunal, which gives to doubtful words a determinate signification." So the vulgar charge of fluctuation and contradiction levied against the courts should, upon proper comprehension of the intellectual situation, be transformed into an affection, nay even a veneration, for "those institutions and laws which are to govern our conduct through life, and which therefore will so far affect our permanent happiness." In this large and extended view of jurisprudence "we may well overlook those comparatively rare and unimportant cases which happen occasionally in the system at large," even though these do at times "appear to be in violation of its general harmony of action."

After we have gone through even some thousand of the pages lawyers devoted to this theme, we realize that the volume and intensity have a purpose which is seldom made explicit. As Horace Binney said, the War of 1812 wrought destruction to American commerce, but thereby brought prosperity to the American bar. This in great part explains why after 1815, in addition to the old colonial wariness against skulduggery, the public more ferociously expressed its suspicion of the courts. Hence these celebrants of legal "science" are always aware that the people regard "with a strange sort of jealousy and distrust" a body of men who arrive at eminence only by subordinating their avarice and ambition to the rules of their material. The revivalists could present their operation as inspired by the precisely opposite flow of energies. Occasionally a legal apologist became exasperated, as did Job Tyson in defining the "integrity" of the judicial character, over the fact that "while the study of the law is highly esteemed as an elevated science, there are, perhaps, few objects against which popular prejudice has been so unsparingly directed, as the legal profession." Tyson was chagrined to observe his colleagues furnishing themes of jest and reproach, for he was thereby forced to acknowledge, reluctantly, that in Philadelphia, where the bar had every reason to compliment itself on its distinction, antilegal sentiment was peculiarly venomous. As a result there had already emerged into common discourse the scathingly pejorative phrase, "a Philadelphia lawyer."

A few of the spokesmen never stooped to argue, but trusted to beating down opposition by the sheer force of magisterial dignity. Du Ponceau concluded his address to the Philadelphia Law Academy in 1821 with the sort of summons lawyers in the next four decades never tired of proclaiming or hearing:

Be not deterred by the fears of the weak or timid, but persevere with steady courage in the work that you have begun, and may the Great Legislator of the universe bless and direct our endeavours to promote a science which, under the revelations of his divine will, is the surest guide to lead mankind into the ways of justice and righteousness.

While professors from the flourishing law schools grew bolder in advertising that the logic of the courts was far more severe and exalted than common principles, they inquired of beginning students what science could be more lofty: "He who cannot feel the glory, which a just understanding of his profession inspires, has not a mind to be elevated by any contemplation." By the same token, "he, who will not, or dares not defend it, when it is unjustly assailed, deserves at least none of the honors or rewards which it can bestow"—a confession that it was still being assailed.

Even so, the profession did prosper, both in wealth and in prestige. There were orators in the 1850's, as for example one at the University of North Carolina, who would boast that the days in which lawyers were deemed a company of mere technicians had passed:

The profession is no longer obnoxious to the reproach of attaching undue importance to the technicalities and subtleties of the science. Lawyers now strive to become eminent as expounders of the law, according to its reason and spirit, seeking to climb up to the vantage ground—as Lord Bacon calls it—of science, rather than to become experts in the art of perverting and defeating the ends of justice. . . . The result is, that the law is now what it was always designed to be, THE SCIENCE OF JUSTICE.

To this euphoria of self-satisfaction lawyers had brought themselves by two generations of intellectual effort. As they compared 1850 with 1790 they could honestly feel that they had every reason to enjoy their achievement, not to be modest about calling attention to it. Just when they were most certain of themselves, at what seemed the moment of their greatest security, they felt the tremors of crumbling ground beneath them.

2.

THE CIVIL LAW

William Blackstone was a man of his century and therefore constructed his organization of the Common Law upon a premise which his age took so much for granted that he hardly needed to state it: all positive law is an endeavor to enact universal natural law. As to precisely how the Common Law, in its heterogeneity, managed to incarnate the homogeneous law of nature has been, for students of Blackstone, a subject of debate. For readers in America, however, he seemed entirely straightforward, and simply confirmed their own uncomplicated axiom. This law of nature, Blackstone gracefully observed, is coeval with mankind, is dictated by God Himself, and so is superior in obligation to any other. "It is binding over all the globe in all countries, and at all times; no human laws are of any validity, if contrary to this." Having professed this orthodoxy, Blackstone could devote his four volumes to the peculiarities of the Common Law, which on the surface might seem a defiance of both nature and reason, confidently exhorting the student to form his style by perusal of the purest classical writers, to learn to reason with precision, to heed the example of experimental philosophy, and to impress upon his mind "the sound maxims of the law of nature, the best and most authentic foundation of human laws."

All this was, inevitably, welcome doctrine in the United States, if only because these states appealed to mankind in the name of nature and nature's God. They could have made this appeal without requiring help from Blackstone (though they were grateful to him for the assistance he did give), because the concept of a law of nature was deeply imbedded in their intellectual inheritance. It came down to the patriots from scholastic formulations, transmitted through the several forms of Protestantism, especially Anglican and Calvinist, and it had been strengthened by their reading in Stoic authors. They also knew

Locke and the popularizers of Newton. Every influence that played upon their minds in the eighteenth century confirmed the reality and power of this idea. Those who had any doubts kept their skepticism to themselves, and the Revolutionary divines combined the law of nature with the tuition of the Old Testament in order to encourage resistance to the house of Hanover.

Hence it was in order that the first efforts to manufacture a doctrine of American law after the Revolution should devote long sections to the law of nature, particularly because in 1790, when James Wilson delivered his lectures, there was so little accurate information about what constituted law in America. The law of nature, Wilson said, is immutable and universal because it has its foundations in the nature, constitution, and mutual relations "of men and things." Thus it is divine, and is one with the law of revelation. Our instincts, if unperverted, and our conscience lead us unerringly to it; it is the basis of all our enactments.

Nathaniel Chipman's pioneer *Dissertation* in Vermont was equally confident that every law made under the Constitution "is ultimately derived from the laws of nature, and carries with it the force of moral obligation." He also identified natural law with intuitive moral perception: the foundation of civil society is not, as Hobbes and even Hamilton would say, in the wants and fears of individuals but "in the adaptation of man to the social and civil state by that nature, which is the constitution ordained by creative wisdom and goodness."

Both Wilson and Chipman exhibit a tendency almost everywhere characteristic, in the post-Revolutionary decades, among the jurists to attribute a quite baffling comprehensiveness to the law of nature: it was not only the law of physical objects, it was also the moral law promulgated by the Bible, the innermost prompting of natural conscience, a bald calculation of the benefits of ordered social intercourse, and in addition—within cautious limits—a vision of perfection to which this society might uniquely aspire. Professor D. T. Blake at Columbia University in 1810 delivered an exhortation to young lawyers at a moment when the eighteenth-century wisdom was in process of transformation into an instrument of American expansion:

The science of the Law is, of all others, the most sublime and comprehensive, and in its general signification, comprises all things, human and divine. The heavens, the earth, and all creation, are governed by laws, universal, eternal, immutable, and fixed. In whatever relation we view them, they are important to man, to society, and to nations; they comprise in them the sublime precepts of revealed truths; they point out those rules, which are to regulate him in society, and lay down those fundamental principles, which govern the affairs of states, countries, and nations.

For the next forty years—and even indeed into the decade of the 1850's, though by then mechanically and without often communicating much conviction—an immense amount of legal eloquence was devoted to similar exclamations. It is painfully evident that those who so indulged themselves were relieved to find a method by which lawyers could claim their share, along with evangelical ministers and with scientists or inventors, of the supreme sanction of the "sublime." Despite their noble endeavors to make the Common Law appear a systematic wisdom, to invest it with the halo of Blackstone, they could never quite fumigate it of the smell of the grubby. It *had* grown up by accident, out of low contention. To shed upon it the light of the sublime was a tricky enterprise. But once the Common Law could be caught up into the superior effulgence of natural law, of the law of nations, then it also could be covered by the canopy of Christianity. By this maneuver, the profession could evade the charge of hardheartedness. In 1843, G. B. Emerson combined the sources of law in Massachusetts into a pattern of sublimity which critics of the system could hardly deny: "Such is the system which had its origin in Saxon love of right, which grew up under Saxon intelligence and love of liberty, has been improved by Greek and Roman jurisprudence, and perfected by Christian philanthropy."

Unhappily, American theorists were driven both by the nation's predicament in the world of commerce and by their efforts to achieve independence of the English courts into the fantastic effort—which may seem to us an excercise in lack of reason—of translating the universal law of nature into the "law of nations." James Kent began his immense *Commentaries* with the basic question: if there does exist an international law, is it one with the law of nature, or is it merely "positive"? In all candor, he had to reply that, in so far as it exists at all, it has come about by specific agreements. Yet, even so, it does derive from natural jurisprudence. Its fundamental principles "are founded in the maxims of eternal truth, in the immutable law of moral obligation," and so it maintains "a steady influence, notwithstanding occasional violence." Its great protector is public opinion, wherefore no nation can violate public law without being subjected to the penal consequences of reproach, "to be inflicted in open and solemn war by the injured party."

Joseph Story's devotion to this concept went beyond Kent's, to become almost fanatical. As Webster said after Story's death, his range of mind enabled him to compare the codes of nations, to allow for differences of origin, climate, religion, and thus to exhibit "their concurrence in those great principles, upon which the system of civilization rests." From the beginning of his career Story was fascinated with the prospect not so much of the dictates of natural law as of their application "to the intercourse, and duties, and contentions of independent nations." This beyond any influences of "a dry and hardening practice" would exalt and purify the mind, show that the science of jurisprudence was indeed "the pride of the human intellect."

Story's eloquence about the law of nations, which he would turn on at any provocation, reveals the driving force in the profession's constant echo of him. It was not so much a philosophy of international comity as a method for subduing America to the ideal of "civilization." Here again, as in their fight for the Common Law, legalists were contending for what they meant by the "large and liberal spirit." Their aim was something that might be called a social aesthetic rather than a league of nations. Wherefore Story, reviewing Sir James Mackintosh's *Lectures on the Law of Nations* in 1826, disregarded Byron and declared that nothing like it had come from England, "so just and beautiful, so accurate and profound, so captivating and enlightening, so enriched with the refinements of modern learning, and the simple grandeur of ancient principles." In Cincinnati, in 1837, Timothy Walker told the sons of pioneers that with this subject they would come face to face with high moral grandeur: "Next to religion, I know not that the human mind can employ itself in contemplations more interesting or sublime; and if the law of nations be not as practical, as the branches which follow, it certainly makes up in grandeur, what it lacks in every day utility." Such oblique confessions that the investigation would not help the practitioner in his daily business inevitably suggested to the youth intent on making money that his professors were taking him down the garden path, for which reason the professors redoubled their efforts to convince the student that he must entertain sublimity. While Timothy Walker did rank the law of nations as next only to religion in moral exhilaration, with him as with Story we may justifiably suspect that this was a concession to the mores. Actually both were intent upon redeeming not so much the world as America by impressing upon it the superior obligations of an international ethic.

Inevitably this reaching out from provinciality to the law of nations put into the hands of American aspirants the works of European "civilians." To some extent these studies had begun before the Revolution: John Adams read Justinian in 1760, and Wilson's *Lectures* show him at home with Pufendorf, Grotius, and Vattel. The great impetus came after the Revolution, particularly in New York, where a body of law had to be hastily devised to suit the needs of commerce. For this reason Story admired Mansfield and Stowell: they created commercial law, and did it by drawing not merely on the law of England but upon "the law of the world—the results of human reason and human learning, acting on human concerns, with reference to principles absolutely universal in their justice and convenience of application." Early in his public statements Story insisted that no country on earth had more to gain from a knowledge of foreign jurisprudence than the young America; he hailed Kent's first volume because the author had not stopped with "the mere Gothic structures of the law," but had examined the beautiful systems of Rome and the Continent. For three decades the propaganda for Civil Law was so intense that it gives the impression of an organized campaign. The tenor of it may be represented by *The Pennsylvania Law Journal* of 1846: American commercial relations and the peculiar relations of the states to each other make it necessary for us to study "every modern system," not overlooking Roman law, "its healthful influence" too often forgotten. All these we are able to profit from because we have none of "that prejudice against foreign systems of law, merely because they are foreign, which is all-powerful in England."

All this time, we remember, these molders of opinion, especially the Anglophile Story, were waging their fight for the Common Law. Story's colleague on the court, Henry Baldwin, could never see any reason for going outside the Common Law: only a system "unshackled by the casuistry of schoolmen" is the true one "for a free and young country." There were other mutterings that under the code of Continental Europe justice might be snatched by the hand of power. These objections seemed to be overborne by Hoffman's assertion that the Civil Law originated "in times of the highest civilization, the offspring of philosophy and science," and that no eulogium could do justice to it. "Should it longer be neglected by the American student?" Enthusiasm for it was particularly vocal in the South. Hugh Swinton Légaré and James M. Walker in Charleston sang its praises and Jesse Bledsoe at Nashville in 1827 said that the Roman code, that "code of written reason," having become "attempered by American soil," was purged of everything foreign and uncongenial.

We are hardly astonished that Francis Lieber and Charles Follen, educated in Europe, should argue the superiority of their training over the Common Law. Lieber would admit that Americans might find some features of the codes repugnant, but insisted that "they will always furnish us with ample matter for fruitful reflection." Charles Follen made no concessions. In a review of Hoffman in *The North American Review* of 1833 Follen held that the Roman jurists supported equal rights and the sovereignty of the people. The Common Law is the rule of feudalism, whereas the Justinian code is more pertinent to American conditions.

Such convictions on the part of two cultivated immigrants might be expected, but it is a bit puzzling that this Boston magazine began as early as 1820 to print pieces in praise of the Civil Law. Caleb Cushing declared that nothing more checks improvement "than a jealous or contemptuous rejection of foreign wisdom"; the Common Law is defective on many subjects, especially on property and commerce, and some of it is "so palpably ridiculous and unjust, that our ancestors repealed it among the first acts after their emigration." Story never waxed quite so passionate, and Kent observed moderation, but they both were on record as admiring the great civilians.

Here we are obliged to ask: what were they trying to gain by ruggedly defending the Common Law on the one hand and on the other seeming to rank it lower than the Civil? I think we find the answer in Hoffman's urging that students of this country "will perceive the propriety of seeking for the depths, the refinements, and the last polish of their legal knowledge in the abundant wisdom of the corpus juris civilis." While the lawyers had indeed to resort to it because there were whole areas of practice for which their inherited Common Law was inadequate, they also took pleasure in so doing because a knowledge of it became a badge of cultivation. They could dazzle clients and juries merely by reciting the esoteric names of Domat, Valin, Pothier, Emérigon, Straccha, Roccus, Huberus, et cetera, et cetera. Thus they could further express their contempt for those who did not follow the law "as a liberal and scientific study." One such could be identified by the fury with which he countered a citation from the Civil Law: "he feels all the patriotic indignation that inflamed the bosom of his ancestors, when they declared that the bastards of England should not sit in the barons' halls."

In practice the courts and the writers of textbooks did not make such extensive use of the Civil Law as the learned advocates pretended. Story's method assumed the pre-eminence of the Common Law. His object, he wrote in *The Conflict of Laws*, was "to present the leading principles upon some of the more important topics, and to use the works of the civilians, to illustrate, confirm, and expand the doctrines of the common law, so far at least, as the latter have assumed a settled form." Gulian Verplanck in 1825 admitted that American laws of contract needed reform and that we would have to resort to the Civil Law; but he warned that we should not import its Stoic morality which, though it contained some stern and grand truths, "is not in unison with the true nature of man." In a short time the magic word for the process came to be "eclecticism," which Reselious said in 1854 was the method of Story, Kent, and Mansfield. What it demands is an end to "the narrow-minded and petty bickerings about the superiority of one system over the other," for "sectarianism can find no permanent place in the science of jurisprudence."

By the 1850's spokesmen began to play down the idea of America's owing much to the Civil Law. The intermixture has ameliorated some of the asperities of the Common Law, said *DeBow's Review* in 1847, but as they have become intermingled a body of native rule is emerging which is neither one nor the other; the time is not far distant "when the universal . . . principles of justice, to be found in either, shall have been blended and combined into one—and when a code of law more just and perfect than any separate system shall have been formed by a combination of all that is admirable in either."

It is difficult to say how serious was this nineteenth-century love affair between American lawyers and the Civil Law. Some accounts attribute the vogue for French and Dutch juristic writings to a surviving hostility to England and to a Jeffersonian dislike of the Common Law. The story is not that simple. Those who most proclaimed the charms of the civil wisdom were also most vigorous in defense of the Common Law against such attackers as Sampson and Rantoul. Possibly there never was a real danger that men like Joseph Story would be seduced. As he went on to say at the beginning of *The Conflict of Laws*, a large part of the works of civilians of Europe "abound with theoretical distinctions, which serve little other purpose than to provoke idle discussions, and with metaphysical subtilties, which perplex, if they do not confound, the inquirer." The decades in which Story and his colleagues flourished these foreign names served the function of elevating the legal profession to such eminence that no mob could tear it down. The distinction between lawyers of liberal and scientific culture and the miserable journeyman was complete. The lawyers had not abandoned the essential heart of American law, but they had, they could tell themselves, served America well. William Wetmore Story found it the highest praise he could speak of his father: "As America takes to itself and naturalizes the people of all nations, who seek its protection, thereby creating a composite people, so he thought it should be cosmopolitan in its jurisprudence, and embody into its law all good rules and principles, whatever might be their birthplace."

3.

EQUITY

In 1760 Lord Kames presented to Benjamin Franklin his *The Principles of Equity*. Franklin answered that he would send copies to the Americas, not only to those which had courts of chancery but to those which, "having no such courts, are obliged to mix equity with the Common Law." The book would be of service in either sort, since few of the colonial judges "have been bred to the law."

In the colonies, such controversies as in mid-eighteenth-century England were finding their way to Chancery usually had to be adjudicated, if at all, by the legislatures. Their jurisprudence, Story would charitably relate, was "lax." Hence the new nation had no viable precedents. It got little help from its favorite textbook: Blackstone said so little about equity as to make it sound unattractive. The liberty of considering cases in an equitable light, he said, should not be indulged very far, "lest therefore we destroy all law." Though Common Law without equity might appear hard and disagreeable, the public good would less be served by equity without law. Pure equity, Blackstone warned, "would make every judge a legislator, and introduce the most infinite confusion."

Wherefore, when the American profession, acting upon Franklin's insight, advocated a system of equity, it found itself with still another, and this time extremely bitter, fight on its hands. Hostility was particularly virulent in Massachusetts. There, Erastus Worthington commented in 1810 how only a few years before the people had imagined the Common Law to be a terror, but now, twenty years after that debate, their veneration for it had become so fanatical that they rejected proposals for equity by shouting, "Touch not with unhallowed hand a single particle of this mighty fabric." In 1829, said *The American Jurist*, equity was still being presented to the populace "as a shapeless monster that would destroy the law; and the court of chancery has been described as a sort of bottomless pit where thousands of suitors are engulfed in ruin." Another legal journal placed the blame, as did all apologists, upon politicians who, in order to promote selfish interests, made equity diabolical. A pamphlet which circulated through Albany during the Constitutional Convention of 1821, signed by "Hamilton," attacked everything for which the lawyers believed

Alexander Hamilton had stood, especially accusing the property interests of trying to thwart republican institutions through the tyrannical establishment of Chancery.

Nor should we assume that opposition to equity arose only out of the ignorant backwoods. In 1826 Anthony Laussat published in Philadelphia *An Essay on Equity in Pennsylvania* which almost persuaded John Marshall that the two kinds of courts should not be separated—but not quite. Laussat drove home his point by repeating the pleas of the lawyers that the "malleability" of the Common Law is such that —if the judiciary shows a proper disposition—all the ends of equity can be accomplished under ordinary forms. Instead of fabricating a distinct code, he said, we should remodel the Common Law to meet our emergencies—as we in America are free to do. Champions of equity had to consider their position carefully when Gulian Verplanck in New York said that collisions between equity and law in matters of contract would show that in equity there exist no uniform principles. The argument over equity versus Common Law cannot easily be resolved into a debate between Democrat and Whig; on the contrary, it cut across party alignments, to the confusion of the multitude, though a fair number of the populace were persuaded that equity meant only one more legalistic scheme to curtail their liberties.

Popular distrust of equity arose first of all from the fact that it dispensed with juries. This became the central issue, but in the early decades the democracy was even more outraged because in equity witnesses were put under oath and were directly interrogated by a judge. Joseph Story braved the wrath of America by explaining that courts of equity, in proceeding without juries,

address themselves to the conscience of the defendant, and require him to answer upon his oath the matters of fact stated in the bill, if they are within his knowledge; and he is compellable to give a full account of all such facts, with all their circumstances, without evasion, or equivocation.

No wonder that Tom and Dick, let alone Laussat and Verplanck, bethought themselves of their fathers' protests against the Star Chamber or High Commission, and dug in their heels. While in one mood the people had complained about the expense of special pleading, in another, when demanded thus to stand and deliver, they found protection in the skill of a clever lawyer.

Beyond even these objections, the mass of the nation worried over the prospect that a judge in Chancery, unchecked by a jury, could deliver his opinions at random, according to his subjective notions of right and wrong. They did not trust such wisdom. The Chancellor, said "Hamilton," sits *"in foro conscientiae,* surrounded by frail mortals, and he a frail mortal like themselves." Such an arrangement, surmised the populace, could produce justice—provided that all participants were angels. But, "whatever the friends of such an institution may say of the obligatory force of precedent and law in controlling the opinions of the chancellor; rely upon it, it all resolves itself into his gracious will." By the nature of the plot, he will appoint himself keeper of the conscience of the people. He alone will determine questions of fraud, misfortune, accidents, trust. Would it not be better for the people to keep their own consciences instead of surrendering them to a James Kent, who "Hamilton" said was convinced of his own infallibility? In Massachusetts, the Constitution of 1821 did allow for a court of Chancery, but in spite of the urging of Story and other judges, "the terrors of the court"—which to the public were "terrors of the unknown"—restrained the General Court from establishing Chancery until 1877.

Kent and Story did not win the multitude by their admission that in equity the courts would have to depend even more upon post-Revolutionary English decisions than in law. We have nothing domestic to guide us, Kent reasoned: "We *must* resort for information to the courts of that nation from which our jurisprudence, as well as the best of our institutions are derived, and we can do it with uncommon advantage." On these topics Story repeated his admiration for Mansfield, Hardwicke, and above all for Lord Eldon—who has given dignity "as well as finish, to that curious moral machinery, which, dealing in an artificial system, yet contrives to administer the most perfect of human inventions, the doctrines of conscience *ex aequo et bono."*

If Story entertained doubts as to whether in America equity could be made into a "science," he was assured by his reading of Kent's career as Chancellor. Kent brought American equity to maturity, and his work showed that America should be grateful that "the beautiful and varied principles of Equity" were tardily developed here, because otherwise we might have on the benches men "inadequate to the duties of their stations, from their want of learning." Kent remedied all that. In delivering the bar's epitaph on Kent in 1848 John Duer compared his opinions as Chief Justice with those he gave as Chancellor, characterizing the latter so that all the world could see, if it would, how Kent had brought equity to a point of scientific perfection:

They deal more in the investigation of principles; they are more discursive and argumentative; more scientific and lucid in arrangement; more sustained, dignified and impressive in style—they embrace a far larger variety of topics, and these topics are not narrow and technical, but are drawn from the general principles of our nature, and reach to all the relations and interests of civil society—and the learning that he employs to adorn, illustrate, or enforce his views, is more various and recondite, and more elevated and classical in its tone and character.

This summarizes the ideal of the profession, and by implication says that if the ideal could be thus realized in Chancery, then Chancery was part of legal science. By this time the pseudonymous "Hamilton" was forgotten.

The great volume of the literature shows how long it took the lawyers to persuade the American people to tolerate suits in chancery. Worthington in 1810 pleaded that chancellors will be as much bound by reports as judges in Common Law, that equity in civil cases will "ameliorate the severity" of the law, that it will not trespass upon cases which require a jury, that it will cut down special pleading, that it is "more consonant to sound and unfettered reason," that it is "liberal and unembarrassed with forms." A circumspect public, which only recently heard the lawyers extolling the virtues of the Common Law, suddenly heard it accused, as compared with equity, of the very vices American common sense had raised against it. They listened in amazement to Worthington's peroration that equity "has established a system of rules which by sound and exquisite logic nicely defines the rights of men and cautiously obliges them to observe those rights."

Story took up his championship of the cause with a review of Johnson's *Reports* on Kent in *The North American Review* of 1820, a piece that was discussed throughout the nation, but his greatest service to the cause was contained in two immense volumes of *Equity Jurisprudence* of 1835. He contended that there are cases, and in modern society an increasing number of cases, where a simple judgment for either party will not do equal justice to both sides. Yet courts of Common Law have no rituals of remedy; they can give a general judgment only in the prescribed forms. Equity does not merely fill in vacuums of the law, it is a distinct science. The great advantage of equity courts is that they "can adapt their decrees to all the varieties of circumstances, which may arise, and adjust them to all the peculiar rights of all the parties in interest." Should we continue striving to dispose of these problems under the Common Law, we shall shake "venerable foundations."

And what constitutes the new kinds of issues, the simple-minded kept asking. What requires this "refined and elevated system"? Worthington attempted to spell them out: he started, mildly enough, with paupers, bankrupts, ecclesiastical polity, paternal and guardian authority, and the property rights of married women. He then disclosed where the drive for equity originated by enumerating contracts, trustees and trusts, probate, mortgages, bailments, and injunctions. It would not tax a rural member of the General Court to perceive that these were matters arising out of the world of business, that the advocates of equity were looking toward a society in which such transactions would become central. Yes, the Common Law, with its great adaptability, was capable of growing along with the economic changes, but equity was still more responsive. You ask, is equity important? "Is it important," answered Story, "to administer substantial justice, to suppress frauds, to relieve against inevitable casualties, to succour the injured, to interpose preventive checks against malice and oppression, or mistaken claims of right?"

One point, we note in passing, Story took pains to drive home. If people supposed that a chancery judge simply lolled at his ease and delivered his opinion out of untutored instinct, let them know that in this field the scholarly requirements were even more exacting than in the Common Law.

James Kent made the classic argument in 1821 before the New York Convention—we wonder whether the level on which he spoke meant much to the rabble. It would, he said, be contrary to the cautious policy of a free government to concentrate the two powers in a single system—all the while, his opponents supposing that by maintaining separate systems he was undermining *their* cautious system. Instead, Kent so bewildered them by warning against the hazard "of having equity so intermixed with law, and law so intermixed with equity, as to lose the certainty and distinct character of each" that they could respond only by such a furious discharge as the anonymous "Hamilton's."

Story admitted in 1820 that in states where the concept of equity prevailed there was a tendency to make it "a sort of arbitration-law, or to decide cases upon their peculiar circumstances, without reference to any general principles." Nothing could be further from his ideal of equity, and nothing more harmful to the profession and to the nation. He contended that no longer even in England was equity "the length of my Lord Chancellor's foot." The freedom of equity provided an opportunity to confirm and illustrate old doctrines "by unfolding new analogies, and expounding the nature and limits of principles, in a manner full of instruction and interest." The public could not be more mistaken in supposing that equity consists of "discretionary justice." In reality, there is no department "more completely fenced in by principle, or that is better limited by considerations of public convenience." However, because it is "an intricate, but an exquisitely finished system wrought up with infinite care," administration of it requires a corresponding skill and erudition. It was a business for professionals.

The insistence of the lawyers that the best of them, even though a precious few, succeeded in the delicate feat of balancing law against equity sounds like a sign of nervousness. Both Binney and Du Ponceau in their eulogies of Tilghman asserted that his equity was as scientific as his law. By equity, Tilghman never meant, "as some have affected to understand that word," the fluctuating emotions of a judge, "but those eternal principles of right and wrong," a science reduced to a regular system so rational that its superiority was admitted even by practitioners of the Common Law. The same contention was affirmed throughout the next decades; to survey the literature today is to grow weary of the repetition, yet also to marvel at the necessity for keeping it up. Equity *is* justice, George Robertson was typically declaring at Transylvania in 1837; it is not variable like the changing sentiments of the multitude, but is "as constant as the fixed and rational principles of civil right and civil law." In that year Timothy Walker's textbook conceded that the "early definition"—he does not say just how early —may have countenanced the notion that equity consists in the application of moral principles to human transactions, but that we had so far come of age in America that we could categorically say, "conscience is now no more the guide of the chancellor than of the judge." Indeed, such a concept of discretion "would not be tolerated in any magistrate, under a free government."

On these grounds the lawyers made their plea—that equity be regarded in nascent America as a distinct, but scientific system of jurisprudence. Let us grant, argued James Holcombe, that the early Chancellors of England arrogated a "wide latitude of authority" to themselves, "and partly from the use of the word" in a sense more enlarged from that permitted by the civilians; still in England, and hence in America, equity has been limited to remedial justice of a sort which the Common Law simply cannot administer. Progressively forgetting what their progenitors had said, commentators like Henry St. George Tucker explained that "the rules of the common law are too strict and rigid to adapt themselves to the various wants of men, to the necessities of justice, and to the important alterations which are continually occurring in the changeful character of human affairs."

Whereupon Tucker perilously went on to admit what his own father would not have allowed, that the boundaries of the two systems might sometimes overlap. To this objection he answered that the suitor was better off if presented with alternatives. The wise David Hoffman, however, posited a warning as early as 1825 which would trouble not only the American public but the lawyers themselves. Distinctions between equity and Common Law, he said, often seem "nice and metaphysical"; in fact they are matters of expediency. Should we try to abolish equity, our whole legal system would need to be remodeled. But if, on the other hand, we force upon Common Law tribunals the task of administering both jurisdictions, we shall produce "a hybridous, and unseemly monster of the law," which would have "the comeliness and virtues of neither parent."

The lawyers thus put a spoke in their own wheel. Story argued that the two should be separate but co-ordinate jurisdictions, their judgments, if at variance, to be reviewed by still a third organization. He could foresee the horrible consequence wherein all clear distinctions of right and wrong would be confounded, wherein lawyers would be betrayed into "unfrequented labyrinths." He appealed to the ingrained American belief in checks and balances, and he appealed in vain.

Though some states, notably New York under Kent, enacted separate systems, the lawyers undid themselves by their already registered boast that in America both counsel and judge were prepared, unlike the English, to work both sides of the legal street. Even in New York, where in 1843 Murray Hoffman in a two-volume manifesto defended the Court of Chancery, it had to be admitted, somehow, that though no "scientific compilations of modern knowledge, exhibit a system of such pure morality, so consistent with the dictates of a sound unbiased reason," still delay and expense had marred the beauty of equity even from the very birth of the court.

From the point of view of such theorists as Kent and Story, their failure to impose upon the United States a precise differentiation was a defeat. But they were resourceful men, and quickly learned how to plead the enumerated classes of cases upon equity assumptions rather than upon those of the Common Law. One illustration out of a hundred may suffice: the security of patents.

Here, above all, was the category of dispute in which an appeal to a jury would be unfortunate. A man's right to his invention could be sustained only by the untrammeled wisdom of a particular judge, skilled in the techniques and learned in knowledge of the craft. On this point, the law was called upon to resist the democracy's contention that useful devices serving the general public were the natural possessions of those they most benefited. Today we find it hard to suppose that in the Republic there could arise such a contention, such a readiness to profit by the inventions of genius without regard to the genius; the fact is that such an attitude did exist. The lawyers were powerless to refute it under proceedings in Common Law. They ventured into equity, and there they succeeded.

In this crucial area the connection between the campaign for equity and the technological transformation of the society is most obvious. Thomas Fessenden published in Boston in 1810 a pioneer defense of patent rights, the tone of which is still eighteenth-century: he argues grandly, in the manner of a Franklin, that authors of useful improvements in the arts deserve reward, because to them "mankind are indebted not only for the comforts, ornaments, and luxuries of life, but even for those necessaries, the want of which would convert the human race into hordes of wandering, naked, and houseless savages, much more miserable and defenceless than the brute inhabitants of the wilderness." After 1815, as the industrial revolution proceeded in New England at a pace which then seemed dizzy, Joseph Story would indulge himself less in neoclassical rhetoric and simply insist that in order to improve factories the law of patents should be developed through a "liberal construction," and that this was possible only in equity. By the middle of the century, however, a new rhetoric was devised for the enhancement of patents; not surprisingly, Daniel Webster brought it to full flowering in his last appearance in court, as attorney for Charles Goodyear in 1852. Interestingly enough, Webster's opponent was Rufus Choate, which indicates that even at this date the self-advertised "conservatives" could not entirely agree about patents. Webster argued his cause with a burst of the old Websterian power. He ridiculed the superstition that the right of an inventor to his invention is a monopoly, and grandly assumed that by now the American people had become so intelligent that as few of them would "pick a flaw" in an inventor's title as would question their neighbor's title deed. Yet what carried the argument, with the court and with the public, was Webster's portrait of the solitary, self-reliant, suffering pioneer of technology. Having ignored his years of lonely endeavor, those who had laughed at Goodyear opened their eyes in astonishment:

They then saw what they had been treating with ridicule, was sublime; that what they had made the subject of reproach, was the exercise of great inventive genius; that what they had laughed at, the perseverance of a man of talent with great perceptive faculties, with indomitable perseverance and intellect.

It dawned on them, Webster concluded, as though another sun had risen in the hemisphere. Thus it was that in equity lawyers who were bound by the Common Law to distrust genius could escape from the trammels of their profession and could join, at least rhetorically, with their clerical rivals in saluting the "sublime."

From the beginning of this legal crusade, however, one point was clear, that the doctrine of patents would prove to be, as Story predicted in 1818, "the metaphysics of the law." Here, if anywhere, we have to depend not on general principles but on "the minute and subtle distinctions which occasionally arise in the application of those principles." In 1849 George Ticknor Curtis put together a textbook on patents which frankly declared that in this administration precedents counted for less than the nice discrimination of decision under varying circumstances of fact. John Kane in the same year drew the obvious moral that decisions in this area could not be left to "those whose minds have undergone no special training in science—for whom there are no axioms, no starting points in argument, no definitions, no vocabulary, no alphabet even!" Which was to say that in patent law the necessity of getting rid of juries was especially apparent.

Throughout the debate, juries were the issue. Lawyers might persuade a grumbling populace that equity had its precedents, but they could not conceal their eagerness to extend the categories of cases to be tried in equity in order to prevent citizens from meddling. At the beginning of the controversy Brackenridge warned that America had an advantage over England: without distinct courts of Chancery "we have the assistance of a *jury* to whom the *facts* may be referred upon which constitutes the exception, and upon which the *equity* arises." Forty years later Lysander Spooner published in Boston *An Essay on Trial by Jury*, which was a last short blast against Chancery. Government, he mourned, must be formed only by voluntary association, of which a jury is the most precious; juries should be allowed to decide both law and fact. The scheme of equity is a cheat, perpetrated by those who imagine themselves to have a more exquisite sense of justice than the people:

They cannot claim or expect that the whole people shall practise the folly of taking on trust their pretended superior knowledge, and of committing blindly into their hands all their won interests, liberties, and rights, to be disposed of on principles, the justness of which the people themselves cannot comprehend.

Because they knew that the people would not bow before this fancied superiority, they deceived them by inventing Chancery.

Joseph Story insisted that he and his sort had no intention of eliminating juries from trials in which they played a legitimate part—in criminal actions, for instance. Yet William Duane's attack on the "Philistines" in 1807 predicted that if property disputes were to be settled without the aid of the people, then the democracy would be undone. By 1815 Story was delighted to find that the merchants of Boston preferred equity in admiralty cases: "They declare that in mercantile causes, they are not fond of juries." Yet for obvious reasons, the lawyers exercised restraint in admitting that they often found juries a nuisance. Chief Justice Durfee of Rhode Island in 1840 exposed the tensions which soon erupted in Dorr's Rebellion by baldly stating that all law is so complicated and artificial that, though it does begin with natural reason, it simply cannot be understood by any except those who have studied it carefully. Only these can move amid its "adventitious and invented forms and modes of proceeding," whereof most juries are incompetent.

Granted that such open utterances are rare, still the nagging attacks on Chancery show that there persisted an apprehension that educated lawyers were plotting to eradicate juries of the uneducated. Eventually it was not a lawyer who brought the accusation into the open, but a member of that landed oligarchy, who was a friend of Kent's but also a sometime idol of the American democracy, the "national novelist," James Fenimore Cooper. His last effort in fiction, published in 1850, was *The Ways of the Hour*. As a story, it is a pathetic book; but under the circumstances—considering his fame as creator of Leatherstocking, his feud with the American public, and his own conduct of libel suits in the New York courts—this labored, wooden book received immense attention. It was an assault upon the vulgarity, ignorance, emotionalism, the utter incapacity of the American jury when it came to judging either law or fact.

Cooper's central figure, a civilized New York lawyer whom he calls Thomas Dunscomb, is a copy of the recently departed James Kent. He is called on to defend an innocent woman before a country jury. Cooper announces his theme in his preface, that the institution of juries may be admirable in a monarchy, but is unsuited to a democracy. The very principle which makes it an engine against royal presumption "renders it unsafe in a state of society in which few have sufficient resolution to attempt even to resist popular impulses." Dramatizing his thesis at tiresome length, he indicted the jury system as irresponsible, vague, and unprincipled, in a society where men are not urged by outside pressures to perform the right, where they "are left to the perverse and free workings of a very evil nature."

Cooper's novel aroused more of that patriotic execration which had been heaped in 1838 upon *Home As Found,* but editors, especially in New York, had to be circumspect because of the suits he had conducted against them in the previous decade. Hundreds of lawyers were secretly delighted, but few came into the open. A few years later Horace Binney informed Sir J. T. Coleride that the prejudice against trial by jury had been steadily growing in America, though in ordinary esteem it remained the ark of the covenant. Interestingly enough, only in *The Western Law Journal,* published in Cincinnati, was Cooper's book favorably reviewed. "To select an ignorant farmer (whose talk is of bullocks)," said the anonymous commentator, "to determine the sanity of a testator, or the principles of a steam engine, would seem the height of folly—a folly which men do not commit, who voluntarily select arbitrators for the amicable adjustment of such disputes."

Significantly, the Cincinnati writer selected as illustrations two classes of cases for which Kent and Story had created equity—testaments and patents. In this sort of business, he informed the democracy, "jurors are men of little intelligence, ignorant of the sciences, and unaccustomed to intellectual efforts." When the contest over equity is reduced to this degree of explicit admission, we may say that at last the object which all along had been the aim of the lawyers stands revealed. Yet it is easy to become so gifted with hindsight as to forget what had for men like Tilghman, Kent, Story been a larger comprehension of the purposes of equity. Indeed, they disliked the tumult of a clownish jury, and were eager to expedite the business of a commercial community. It is also true that in equity as in the Civil Law they saw their sort of vision. Story's son, paraphrasing the father, said that in the broad doctrines and "liberal" spirit of Chancery, the great Justice delighted:

Its free, flexible, and yet distinct and practical principles, comported better with the character of his mind, in which the love of Justice and Freedom was native, than the narrow and more technical doctrines of the common law. Equity, in his mind, was a central sun, raying out its principles into every department of the law, and animating all the systems around it, from the nearer system of Commerical and Natural Law, to the distant system of Real Law.

The victory that these campaigners won, though it was not as complete as they desired, was substantial. When the Constitution of the United States had made the distinction, "in law or equity," the nation hardly knew from its own experience what this signified. By 1850 the separation had become a part of the national consciousness. In a manner of speaking, this achievement was as important for the attainment of an American mentality as any in other areas of struggle.

4.

PRACTICALITY

Midway through his career at the Philadelphia Bar, Horace Binney, in a mood of candor, declared that the practice of law added nothing to the lawyer's intellect. He is concerned to win, but win or lose, he forgets the case as soon as he has been paid. The physician learns new facts, increases his knowledge from every patient, "but the lawyer's facts are unproductive of all benefits, except to the fortunate client." All of this, conceded the sage, justifies the "sneer which is commonly directed against the mere lawyer."

During the years in which Hoffman, Du Ponceau, Kent, Story were creating the rational science, reading the civilians, devising an American equity, there were circulating among the populace such handbooks as, to mention only one, John M'Dougal's *The Farmer's Assistant* (third edition, Chillicothe, Ohio, 1815), which eloquently was subtitled *Every Man his own Lawyer*. Herein, boasted the author, the tradesman, farmer, mechanic or manufacturer may perceive a correct table of forms and precedents adapted to his concerns, so that he may transact his business without the assistance of lawyers. The sale of works of this nature suggests that hundreds were not fully persuaded by the rhetoric of the great jurists.

David Hoffman addressed himself against this anti-intellectualism more than did Kent or Story. In 1836, he pleaded that a liberal mind must discover its zeal by collecting from the range of science and art whatever may embellish it. In his last valiant appeal, his *Circular* of 1844, he stood at Thermopylae: he would have naught to do with the notion that law students are to be merely mechanical artisans. No attorney could be "a good and lasting one" who was not versed in the reasons of the law.

I therefore cannot acquiesce in, and never will yield to the vulgar error of putting *practice* before and above theory—it is an unnatural *inversion* of the established order of nature—an ignorant and slovenly way of urging young men on to attempts far beyond the powers of the human mind.

Hoffman knew the enemy, if only because he, the veteran instructor of young attorneys, lacked the judicial immunity of Kent and Story.

The American Jurist for 1830 saluted Hoffman's service to legal education, but objected to his prologues on the nature of man and of society. The student, said this critic, has no need to study the properties of the sea anemone or the metaphysical theories of Descartes, much less to be confounded by theological preliminaries about moral liberty and free agency.

These grumblings became thunder before the storm when Benjamin F. Butler issued his *Plan for the Organization of a Law Faculty* for the University of the City of New York, at the request of the Council, in 1835. Here was voiced anew that intractable concern with practical results which, since the days of pioneer justice, had looked askance upon the towers of intellect the lawyers were erecting. The ordinary "scientific" course, said Butler, commences with the law of nature, goes through the law of nations and constitutional law, before condescending to the municipal law, which comprises the only body of jurisprudence with which students must actually deal. This may be a "philosophical order," but nothing can be more useless for training a practitioner. The first two volumes of Blackstone and the whole of Kent's *Commentaries*—Butler dared to assault the throne—"are at this time almost equally inappropriate, because they have little or no connection with the practical business of the office, which will therefore be utterly unintelligible." Butler was not quite so radical as he sometimes sounded: he merely proposed to "invert" the standard order of study, so as to devote the first year to practice and pleading, and to transfer the law of nature and of nations to the "General Course." But what he meant was that young men could go forth with some basic instruction in pleading, and leave the law of nature to their senile meditations. Butler scored heavily against the theorists by insisting that the method he proposed was natural, that it would be similar to the instruction followed "in the mechanical and other arts," where the learning of practice preceded the acquisition of principles.

Had Butler been an isolated phenomenon, he might have been dismissed as a Jacksonian vulgarian, even though the spokesman of a university. But in 1835 Francis Hilliard issued *The Elements of Law*, which he advertised as a comprehensive survey of all an American lawyer needed to know. The basic principles, Hilliard said, are so few and simple that a child can grasp them. Subtleties and nice distinctions can quickly be demolished. "Municipal rules are founded upon the basis of equity, reason, and right." The Common Law is, in American courts, reduced to the rule of common sense. The science of matter has been deprived of mystery, and so likewise has been the science of mind. "In the new spirit, no less just than liberal, that now prevails, all knowledge is held to be *practical*." Hilliard insisted that the law should be brought into rapport with the mentality of the century.

Men of the majestic era of John Marshall—for whom Hoffman spoke—were simply bewildered at this rising insistence upon practicality. They never held that lawyers should not test their learning in the courts, that they should not seek to win decisions. But that, with their erudition in the Common Law, in civil law and in equity, they should ever conceive of themselves as mere technicians—this notion they repudiated. So, in 1846, those who survived were the more dismayed by William A. Porter's address to the Law Academy of Philadelphia, printed in so reputable a vehicle as *The Pennsylvania Law Journal*, which frankly declared that theory without practice is valuable only as an amusement, and that in the law, as in the case of any machine, well-informed persons "will infinitely sooner entrust business to mere men of practice, of whose learning they know nothing, than to those whom they have every reason to believe most firmly grounded in the principles of their professions, but of whose practical ability they have no good evidence." As the historian moves into the 1850's he is struck with how plaintive become the laments of the periodicals that the profession has been subverted by lawyers who regard the law as a mere aggregation of arbitrary provisions. Such are never to be admitted, said *The United States Monthly Law Magazine* in 1851, "into a comprehension of the great principles, the wide, extending analogies, which are everywhere pervading and everywhere giving a reason and consistency to the law." But increasingly thenceforth, up to the disputations of the war, laments of this sort became mere whistling into the wind. As catastrophe loomed, Theodore Sedgwick in 1857 ridiculed the logic-chopping of the textbooks—meaning those of Kent and Story—by declaring that the lawyer's science was entirely practical:

It is only by an intimate acquaintance with its application to the affairs of life, as they actually occur, that we can acquire that sagacity requisite to decide new and doubtful cases. Arbitrary formulae, metaphysical subtleties, fanciful hypotheses, aid us but little in our work.

In more senses than Sedgwick understood, he marked the end of an era, just as the revivalists of 1858 comprehended little of how effectively they closed a period in the religious excitement. The "pragmatists" in both piety and in legalism believed that they drew upon native inspiration; though they paid a formal respect to what the mind had wrought, they sought, after long years of exasperation and recent years of political frustration, to get on with a commonsensical notion of their function. This resolution seemed deceptively feasible in the euphoric world of the Revival. In the realm of the law, simplification was oddly enough more difficult because lawyers more than the ministers found themselves tangled in the contradictions of their morality.

CHAPTER FOUR

Law and Morality

Indeed, the judges are the organs, or conduits, through which the chief blessings of a free government must be derived. . . . An able and upright judge does, among men, perform the office of God's viceregent. The ministers of religion, as is their duty, may shew the divine anathema pointed against crime and unrighteousness; but it is the sword of the law, wielded by the judge, which, from its nearness and immediate effect, operates most strongly to deter from their commission.

—JESSE BLEDSOE, *Introductory Lecture on Law,*
Nashville, Tennessee, 1827

1.

LEGAL BENEVOLENCE

As many have remarked, democratic Americans were preternaturally ready to sue each other in courts of law, especially in the primitive turmoil of settlement across the Alleghenies. They had constantly to employ lawyers, and often they made folk heroes out of those champions who, like Sergeant Prentiss in Alabama, could turn the courtroom into a circus. It was the legend of Lincoln's wily resourcefulness before a jury that helped to earn him the title of "Honest" Abe. To be sure, the widely advertised dignity of Marshall, Story, Kent, Pinkney, Wirt, and a hundred other nationally famous paladins of the law went far to quiet native prejudice, and to convince—or half convince —the populace that the profession, at least on their exalted levels, were at heart dedicated not only to winning cases but to disinterested justice. Then too, the massive doctrinal works of Hoffman, Du Ponceau, Kent, and Story reinforced this lofty image and served in some measure to overcome the lingering distrust of legal chicanery.

Nevertheless, distrust persisted. Farmers and shopkeepers might drink with the circuit rider in the tavern at night, and be delighted (as they were with Lincoln) at his witticisms, but the next day when he appeared in court, they calculated that he had cards up his sleeve. In their inarticulate fashion, they suspected, what Tocqueville had concluded, that the American lawyer "resembles the hierophants of Egypt, for like them he is the sole interpreter of an occult science."

As Hoffman and Kent forced upon the reluctant nation an admission that the law was more than a mere bag of tricks, residual cynicism assumed a more sophisticated form. In a society where revivalist morality permeated the multitude, including even those who had not undergone conversion, an inevitable accusation arose: lawyers may not be agents of tyranny, but by the very nature of their calling they are dishonest. They are committed to vindicating their client regardless of the merits of his cause, to making the worse appear the better case.

This renewed assault, by those whom jurists often labeled "the infallible mob," portrayed the successful lawyer as nothing better than a sort of licensed knave, a minister of Satan. In the mob's view, "To conceal truth, to pervert evidence, to mislead juries and brow-beat judges, are supposed to be the grand attainments of legal ambition." In the early days of the lawyers' struggle for prestige, and indeed for years thereafter in Western communities, jurists combated these charges by insisting that jurisprudence consisted in administering the Second Table of the Ten Commandments. Washington Van Hamm in *The Western Law Journal* of 1849 offered the challenge: if our statutes or decisions can be proved violations of divine principles, "then we will cheerfully admit that our laws should be so altered as to conform to this great code of Divine Law."

Defenses in this vein—of which there are thousands—had the effect only of augmenting suspicion. A more persuasive argument was devised by William Williamson in 1843: because the two professions, clerical and legal, do not contend for power as they did in medieval England, we dwell in a happy era wherein "the reciprocity of our ministers and men of the law, in sentiment, and in coordinate efforts for the public good, have originated resemblances between them."

All this, however, could be dismissed by the pious—some of whom were lawyers—with a sweeping observation that the legal methodology was now so complicated that its relation to moral integrity could not readily be perceived. The more the lawyers protested that their justice was identical with that of the Golden Rule, the more the righteous mob accused them of perverting abstract concepts to the manipulation of technicalities. It is very easy, said a South Carolina professor in 1838, to bring in the basic axioms of moral philosophy, but as for the law itself, that "is now so technical and artificial in its character, that its relations and connections with [the moral] cannot be well compre- hended or expounded by one not professionally learned in the law." Midway in the rise of the legal profession, the threat arose that its progress might be checked, nay, even destroyed, unless it could decide within its own cohorts where its own dedication, its own highest obli- gations, lay. Throughout the Constitutional debates of the 1840's and 1850's, down to the fatal actions of 1861, this was the issue that drove them, that haunted them, that led many to reminiscent falsifications of their careers. The inability of the best-trained minds to comprehend what they had to deal with, their often pathetic efforts to preserve their reputation for consistency, amount both to the glory and the tragedy of the era.

In terms of immediacy, the problem for the lawyers around 1840 was to dispose of the accusation that by becoming increasingly technical they betrayed morality. This charge is difficult to document because, while we know it was everywhere half articulated before the Revolu- tion, it makes its way stealthily into the record only thirty years thereafter. The accusers are vague, but the defendants show by their responses that they felt the sting. In 1822 Henry Dwight Sedgwick, in an attack upon applications of English Common Law to American situations, said with mischievous irony that the faith of a lawyer is much akin to that of a theologian. Both are trained to reverence the wisdom of their ancestors, and so the lawyer identifies justice with particular forms and rituals:

Any interference with these he considers as endangering the existence of all law and justice, in the same way in which many pious Christians sincerely believe the particular rites and dogmas of their own sect to be the very body and soul of religion, and that whatever affects the one must endanger the other.

Thus both evangelical and Unitarian piety reacted against the eleva- tion of law into an intricate system of reason by insinuating that lawyers, like the overintellectualized theologians of New Haven, sepa- rated substance from form, spirit from letter, and sacrificed justice to technicality.

The most obvious riposte the lawyers could make, and one which they resorted to interminably, was to argue that there is nothing inher- ently wicked in formal rules. J. F. Jackson, in the popular *Knicker- bocker*, recognized that many regard the law as a mere mechanism, "words destitute alike of philosophy and meaning"; but in order to demonstrate that the practice of the advocate could be consistent with personal integrity he pointed out that every science has its forms, that grammar and mathematics have rules and figures of demonstration, and so "it is only through the technicalities of the law that its spirit can be imparted and the understanding reached." Some apologists, however, were more aggressive. Employing the lawyers' distrust of "genius," they sought to prove to a populace already jealous of whatever surpassed the norm that the training of a lawyer excited the normal affections of the heart. Genius alone, said William Barry at Transylvania, can accomplish much, "but it acquires additional force and derives its principal charm from virtue." By this logic it followed that a profession which demanded of its neophytes knowledge of the greatest number of facts also excited the "amiable affections of the heart" which "impart lustre to the utility of learning."

Barry in 1821 was plagiarizing from David Hoffman's first volume of 1817. His words may seem puzzling to a modern reader unfamiliar with the devious paths through which America made its way out of the eighteenth century into the nineteenth. One thing, however, is clear about them: though Hoffman and Barry do not venture to say that jurisprudence *is* Christian, they strive to assert the morality of the law by mingling within the heart of the lawyer amiability and utility. We get, I believe, a hint of what is going on behind the scenes from a lecture by James Kent at Columbia in 1824:

No man can preserve in his own breast a constant and lively sense of justice, without being insensibly led to cherish the benevolent affections. Those affections sharpen the perceptions of the moral sense, and give energy and a proper direction to all the noble powers of the understanding. The observation I have somewhere met with, is no less profound than striking, that wisdom is as much the offspring of the heart as of the head.

This reveals the strategy: when pressed with a frontal attack upon their fortress of erudition the jurists make a sally by the flank and confound their opponents by a demonstration that the real source of legal technicality is a heart as much imbued with benevolence as that of any revivalist.

Obviously they drew upon their inheritance from the "benevolent" eighteenth century, but they also invoked the newer vogue of the concept which had been spread in America by the theology of Edwards and Hopkins. Further, they allied themselves with the sentimental version of benevolence that by the 1820's was becoming the staple of gift books and annuals. Yet at the same time the lawyers were employing a masterful subtlety. For the idea of benevolence, either in its eighteenth-century meanings or in the altered connotations of the nineteenth, always carries an implication of doing good for one's fellow men. The virtue upon which the structure of the law is erected, said Hoffman—he called it "sublime"—"is that of Happiness, or (its other name) Utility." Josiah Quincy, speaking in 1822 about applications of the laws of Massachusetts to poverty and vice, was fully in possession of this legal moralism which absolved the laws themselves from the jurisdiction of moralists. The moral and religious attributes of man, he began, are the most elevating; of all the means "within the command of society" for disseminating moral and religious influences among the masses, none can be compared with the administration of justice. Wherefore Quincy concluded with the question which needed no answer: "Indeed, truly considered, what is justice itself, but the essence of all that religion teaches, and all that morality suggests, abstracted and adapted by human wisdom, to the exigencies of man in society?" Using the same sequence of propositions at Transylvania, and in the same year—thus showing that legal conscientiousness was no monopoly of New England's—Jesse Bledsoe assured Kentuckians: "The Great Author of nature is here the only legislator, and reason, aided by those manifestations of his will which he has been pleased to make by revelation, the only interpreter of these laws." So what to the mob might from the outside seem to be an occult science imposed by pagan hierophants turned out to be, when seen from within, a translation into technicalities of Almighty Wisdom—and thus became the instrument of social prosperity. Or, as Samuel Chapin said in 1829, the instructor in jurisprudence teaches his pupils not merely rules of procedure but the basic principle that civil society is an ordinance of heaven, that it is as truly designed to aid man in securing the end of his being as is the church. "It is not a combination simply for the protection of life and property; but it is an association for moral improvement."

The end result was, to the confusion of citizens who ventured to complain about the delays and expense of the courts, that despite appearances the whole fraternity was sanctified, not because all of them were professing Christians, but because their religion was social. Daniel Webster characteristically summarized the dialectic in his eulogy upon Joseph Story:

And whoever labors on this edifice, with usefulness and distinction, whoever clears its foundations, strengthens its pillars, adorns its entablatures, or contributes to raise its august dome still higher in the skies, connects himself, in name, in fame, and character, with that which is and must be as durable as the frame of human society.

Faced with this conception of the legal function, how could a society concerned with social progress object to the "technicalities" of the law? How could they call in question the moral integrity of the profession? It was indeed true, said Archibald D. Murphey of North Carolina in 1830, the courts cannot form principles into a general system; they can only contribute to particular branches of ethics, such as contracts. It is the business of philosophers to construct codes of morals, but there was no need to conclude from the unsystematic nature of the Common Law that administration of it was remote from the great principles of ethics; on the contrary, the chancellors and a few of the Common Law judges of England ("having Lord Mansfield at their head"), the American Supreme Court, "chancellor Kent of New York, Judge Cooper, and a few others, have contributed more to the development and illustration of the principles of ethics, and their proper application to the business and affairs of life, than all the other learned men of the world." Their principles, thus spread before the people at last, "are gradually weakening the force of precedent and adding new beauties to our system of jurisprudence."

There was more to come. Social happiness, sought for by benevolent lawyers, might mean just any society—England, France, or China. But in America, the frame of society was unique. So it followed that the benevolent heart of the lawyers and their amiable disposition, which was one with their devotion to utility, were also identical with their selfless, disinterested patriotism. Leaving aside lawyers who go into politics, said Rufus Choate, the ordinary practitioner "performs a function of peculiar and vast usefulness in the American Commonwealth." In this respect he is more serviceable than any other professional or business man, for upon him supremely rests the responsibility "to preserve our organic forms, our civil and social order, our constitutions of government,—even the Union itself." Once patriotism and rectitude were thus combined, it was obvious that the profession operated under a religious sanction, even when engaged in the most hairsplitting disputation. "Such is the spirit of active interchangeable beneficence diffused by them [the lawyers] through our Christian community," said William Williamson, "that has contributed, in no small degree, to found and foster our free institutions, and distinguish us in the grade of nations." Even in the backwoods, lawyers were variously aware—thanks mainly to the teachings of Story—that the forms of law in America were not native, that Americans had lessons to learn from the Common Law, from nineteenth-century developments in England, and from Continental civil law. But when they countered the charge of legalistic chicanery, they, along with the revivalists, appealed to the peculiar purity of this society, which they identified with the purity of its institutions, and which they dedicated, whether in the South or the North, to the preservation of the national Union.

2.

THE CHRISTIAN FORUM

Despite all these invincible demonstrations, a basic problem was still unresolved. Granted that, although at times the law appears a mere logomachy, it is essentially rational and in that sense moral, that it is fed from the springs of benevolence, and that it is passionately devoted to the Union: the question remained, was it specifically Christian? No matter how upstanding and honest the lawyers might be, if their rectitude was no more than that of the best of the heathens, no more than the virtue of a Seneca or a Cicero, then was there not something in their trade inherently antagonistic to the faith of Americans? Were not the founders of New England correct in their hostility to lawyers? And should not a nation recalled to Christianity by the Revival properly regard the legal profession as a conspiracy against its very life?

These anxieties were stirred anew in 1829 by the publication of an inquiry Thomas Jefferson had written, probably about 1764, as to "Whether Christianity is a Part of the Common Law." He denied Blackstone's assertion that "Christianity is part of the laws of England," and, denouncing the union of church and state, found in such establishment the explanation of why the judges had for centuries been accomplices in the "frauds" of the clergy. Furthermore, Story contributed to the unrest by depending heavily in his expositions of equity upon the opinions of Lord Stowell; not only was Stowell abominated by American patriots for his part in enforcing the Orders that roused America to fight in 1812, but his assertion that Christianity was an integral part of the laws of England displayed a fanatical devotion to the Tory ideal of an Established Church, coupled with a disposition to oppose any and every movement toward softening the lot of Dissenters. The majority of Americans, being the sort who in England would have found themselves opposed to the church, drew the natural conclusion that a judge could enforce Christian precepts only where such an establishment existed. Did it follow that in a democracy which had completely separated the church from the state, and where such a diversity had arisen among the churches that no single statement of Christian theology could any longer pretend to official orthodoxy, the courts could justifiably invoke the concept of a *Christian* ethic?

Many lawyers were troubled by these questions, and resorted to various devices in order to demonstrate that, far from there being any opposition between them and the clergy, both were partners in a common enterprise. One such device was for them to occupy their leisure composing briefs to prove, on purely *legal* principles, the reliability of Biblical narratives, and especially of the miracles and the resurrection of Christ. Story asserted that to establish Christianity upon the basis of rational evidence was an infinitely better method than by "appealing to the result of unknown powers, supposed to be innate in the mind, which may be disputed, and have ever been in dispute." This was his way of warning the clergy against leaving the sure ground of legality for any supposed charms of Transcendental intuition; the mass of orthodox revivalists, though they played upon emotions in a manner Story found vulgar, would to a man have agreed with his philosophy of Biblical plausibility. Story was often heard to say, said Simon Greenleaf, that "the great facts of the gospel history were attested by a mass of evidence, which, in any court of law, would be perfectly satisfactory and conclusive." How then could Story as a judge have ruled in any case except by the lights of Christianity?

Undoubtedly more energy was devoted to this enterprise by New England Unitarians than by any other group, since the Revival held them not to be Christians at all and Princeton Seminary accused them of having spawned Transcendentalism and all its horrors. In 1831 Peter Thacher paid tribute to Samuel Dexter by remarking that he too had made an objective inquiry into the facts and concluded that the Christian religion was manifestly divine. Wherefore he exhorted the Suffolk Bar to an examination of their faith; though he assured them they need not enter into the mazes of theological controversy, they were encouraged to ponder the evidences of Christianity in order to refine their taste, strengthen their judgment, and "purify" their affections. The masterpiece of this literature was Greenleaf's *An Examination of the Four Evangelists*, published in 1846, which rigorously adhered to the rules of evidence administered in courts of justice. He felt called upon, amid his many duties, to compose this work because the influence "of the legal profession upon the community is unquestionably great." Needless to say, after cross-examining the Evangelists "by the rules of evidence applied in human tribunals," he found them fully entitled to a "conviction of their integrity, ability and truth." By exonerating them in court he also exonerated his profession.

But did this really answer Jefferson? Not directly, perhaps, but surely by implication. Indeed, Story made this explicit in his inaugural speech as Dane Professor by naming Jefferson aloud. "There never has been a period, in which the Common Law did not recognize Christianity as lying at its foundations." The only error it ever committed was to tolerate only the Christianity of an Established Church, which did indeed debase religion by calling in the aid of secular authority; this mistake, poisoning the inherent Christianity of the law, was merely a superficial blemish, which, according to Story, our republican institutions have entirely washed away. Yet it was Kent who most energetically asserted that the Common Law of the nation, notwithstanding the separation of churches from the state, was based not alone upon the universal rules of natural morality but specifically upon the truth of Christianity. A toper in upstate New York, being ejected from a tavern, stood in the street and shouted that Jesus Christ was a bastard and Mary a whore; this Ruggles was tried before Kent and severely punished. At the Constitutional Convention of 1821 Kent defended his action:

It was not because Christianity was established by law, but because Christianity was in fact the religion of the country, the rule of our faith and practice, and the basis of public morals. Such blasphemy was an outrage upon public decorum, and if sanctioned by our tribunals would shock the moral sense of the country, and degrade our character as a Christian people.

The authors of the Constitution, Kent continued, never meant to extirpate Christianity any more than public decency, and his court was preserving not merely morals but morals founded on Christianity. Surely we are a Christian people. "Do not the ninety-nine hundredths of our fellow citizens hold the general truths of the Bible to be dear and sacred?" Therefore, though we have complete .religious liberty, any attack upon these truths is an attack upon the order of society, to the correction of which the Common Law is sworn.

The union of Christianity and the law was asserted most comprehensively by Chief Justice Shaw in 1838 when passing sentence upon Abner Kneeland. This case had for five years been intently followed by all the religious in the nation. The story has often been told, and has its comic as well as sinister aspects. Abner Kneeland, a home-grown, self-educated, and belated provincial incarnation of eighteenth-century rationalism, delivered lectures in a Boston theater to large audiences and published a periodical, *The Investigator*, which had a circulation among the "mechanics" of the city. Operating under an act of 1782 against blasphemy, the Commonwealth indicted Kneeland in 1833 for having wickedly published a "scandalous, impious, obscene, blasphemous and profane libel" on the existence of God. Kneeland, in the tortuous course of argument and appeal, stood five trials. The charges delivered by the several judges to their juries, especially one by Thacher of the Municipal Court, show that "liberal Unitarians" could wax as frenetic as any revivalist in maintaining Story's thesis against Jefferson. In one of the hearings the public prosecutor sneered at Jefferson as a "Virginian Voltaire" and contended, successfully, that Christianity was part and parcel of the constitution of Massachusetts. Kneeland argued his own case in the last of these trials, invoking the Massachusetts Declaration of Rights, with its guarantee of freedom of worship. "I stand on a ground as broad as space," he summed up, "and as firm as the rock of ages; to wit, on the right of conscience, together with the privilege of the freedom of speech and the liberty of the press." Thus Kneeland brought into open juxtaposition, exposing their basic incompatibility, the logical definition of rights which the lawyers had carried over from Blackstone, from the Common Law, and from the civilians, and the conception implanted throughout the society by the Awakening of 1800 that it was creating a Christian unity more solid than any official establishment by marshaling the sects into the Revival.

Lemuel Shaw, a Unitarian, imposed the final sentence on Kneeland, who ultimately served sixty days in jail. Shaw took two years to think about the problem before announcing his decision—which certainly indicates the complexities of the issue—but in the end concluded that Kneeland was guilty of willfully denying God "with an intent and purpose to impair and destroy the reverence due to him," and that Kneeland was guilty at Common Law because Christianity is incorporated therein. A petition by one hundred and sixty-seven Massachusetts intellectuals—including Channing, Parker, Emerson, Ripley, Garrison, Alcott—could not persuade Governor Edward Everett to pardon Kneeland, but in a sense their opposition marks the high tide of the democracy's effort to heal its schizophrenia by pretending that its Common Law was the same as its Christian piety. The irony is that this last gesture of futility should have been made not by an evangelical judge in Illinois but by a Unitarian in Boston.

For in the first three or four decades of the century enough of the eighteenth-century, even of the Jeffersonian, persuasion endured so that a considerable reluctance to follow Story, Kent, and Shaw on this particular proposition remained among jurists who otherwise virtually worshipped these pundits. In 1812 Thomas Cooper published a commentary on Justinian (which Story found respectable), in which he agreed that Ruggles deserved the sentence Kent pronounced upon him, but only for disturbing the peace, not for the reasons Kent derived from the offense. Kent's doctrine "may be carried to a length, that would authorize any species of ecclesiastical tyranny"; nor, added Cooper, is the doctrine strengthened by citing cases (he meant those of Eldon and Stowell) "from the jurisprudence of a country where there is a religion by law established." No, Cooper insisted, the more the public is accustomed to "dissonance of opinion" on religious subjects, the more it will comprehend that performance of the duties of a good citizen is all that, in legal propriety, society can require.

Furthermore, even in polite New England, while the best people applauded Shaw's painful decision, there are indications that the legal mind felt some annoyance with the religious. This restrained irritation came out most revealingly when lawyers, proud of their region, had to mention the Salem witchcraft disgrace of 1692—particularly since Southerners never let them ignore it. These "wretched butcheries," as Story bluntly termed them, were the consequences of a religious zeal ignorant of, and so unchecked by, any knowledge of law. Here, mourned Emory Washburn in 1840, every rule of evidence was abrogated, the court was left untrammeled by the "quibbles of the law," and see what happened. It may be that human nature has so changed that a judge equally unacquainted with the rules of procedure "might stand against a strong popular delusion or excitement, should such an occasion again occur, but he must disregard the light of experience who could hope to be safe under its administration." In this period the standard reprehension of Cotton Mather takes form in New England historiography—"the sanctified leader of this diabolical frenzy." But at the same time a notion appears, which not even Judge Shaw can dispel, that the petitioners for Abner Kneeland may not have been protecting blasphemy but protesting against a new form of religious persecution.

In other quarters the problem of atheism and legal procedure seems strangely to have worried the courts. Strangely, I say, because the historian can find practically no avowed atheism, hardly even agnosticism, in the period. In 1827 Chancellor De Saussure of South Carolina boldly ruled that a witness who did not believe in future punishments could still take an oath because a belief in present correction would bind his conscience, but the Chancellor dreaded that a time might come when he would have to decide whether a witness should be rejected because of disbelief in God. In 1830 a writer in *The American Jurist* (published in Boston) dared contend that an atheist, though obviously suffering from an aberration of the mind, could speak truth and so should be heard under oath. But the segment of Boston society for which Shaw spoke could not permit such heresy. Simon Greenleaf, already at work upon his *Examination,* came in 1839 to Shaw's defense by asking upon what grounds could any suppose "that the man who, in a christian country, in this day of light and knowledge, still disbelieves the existence, the moral government, and the retributive justice of the Supreme Being, will be governed by any other motives than his interest, his prejudices, or his passions." One might as well require the formality of an oath from the elegant Gibbon or the disgusting Paine; this would surely be a mockery of justice. "What," he resonantly concluded, "was the state of veracity in revolutionary France?"

As far as legal rhetoric goes, here the doctrine of the atheistical witness appears to have rested until well after the Civil War. That there should have been a flurry about it, however brief, in the 1830's shows perhaps how the lawyers, confronted with novel and disturbing ideas in the community, had only the inherited wisdom to rely upon. In Boston and Cambridge, the Reverend Andrews Norton—as staunch a Unitarian as Shaw—was calling the "Transcendental" effusions of Emerson, Brownson, Parker a form of "infidelity," and English law in the eighteenth century had focused the controversy between Christianity and infidelity on the single question of whether the oath of an atheist could be received. So, at the slightest suggestion of a disseverance of law from religion, lawyers brought up the traditional rejection of the atheist's testimony—even though poor Abner Kneeland insisted he was not an atheist but a pantheist!

It rapidly became evident that men like Greenleaf were lashing the empty air. The tension between law and Christianity in America was not to arise out of the confrontation of atheism and dogma: it was to become something unknown to European experience, something so bewildering as to be for a long time (and possibly even to the present writing) a puzzle to the American intellect.

Timothy Walker commenced a course of lectures in Cincinnati in 1837 with a statement which may express his liberation from New England. They are in error, he said, who suppose jurisprudence based on the expectation of immortality; it begins and ends with this world, it regards men only as members of society. "Its proper scope would have been the same that it now is, had no voice from Heaven, or from the depths of the human soul, proclaimed another world beyond the present." Now, this was not atheism. Nor was it a defiant venture into rationalism, in the manner of Jefferson, to expel Christianity. It was simply a quiet, undemonstrative statement that law in a utilitarian

United States need not bother about the afterlife. In its very matter-of-factness, Walker's definition of the legal function was a more devastating severance of the law from the Christian concern than any atheistic or deistic attack would have been. And the awful import of this intellectual revolution was brought home to the mind of the nation only with the spectacular trial in the Supreme Court of the Girard Will Case in 1844.

3.

A DIFFERENT FORUM

It was about the most gaudy of all the stellar exhibitions enacted in the cramped quarters of the Supreme Court. On every one of the ten days of argument, the room was crowded to suffocation: "You can scarcely get a case knife in edgewise," reported the New York *Herald*. As usual on these superdramatic occasions, the presence of "ladies" is noted, and they are invariably pretty. The *Herald*'s correspondent was impressed by the sight of these creatures "seated and filling up the spaces between the chairs of the Judges, so as to look like a second and a female Bench of beautiful Judges." The *Herald* sold out extra editions in the general rush by "parsons, clergymen, saints, the elect of all sects, including sinners," to buy verbatim reports of the argument of the Godlike Webster.

Webster put on a stupendous histrionic show, surpassing in everybody's estimation his already legendary performances in the Dartmouth College Case or in the reply to Hayne. Associated with him was General Walter Jones, then regarded as a magnificent legal orator. Opposed to Webster were two great luminaries of the Philadelphia Bar, John Sergeant and Horace Binney. This array was in itself enough to make the contest gladiatorial. An added attraction was the fact that Webster had just resigned as Secretary of State and was confidently expecting to be nominated four months later as the Whig candidate for President. But more arresting than the display of genius and the political implications was the fact that the question at issue was whether a trust could legally survive in opposition to the Christian religion. In this case, law and religion came to that parting of ways which both lawyers and evangelists had long feared, which they had striven to postpone, and which for the next three decades they both pretended had not taken place in February of 1844. The irony of the story—or, rather, the pathos—was accentuated because Chief Justice Taney was too ill to preside and so Joseph Story sat in his place; all the world knew how thoroughly—many said how abjectly—he had previously declared his agreement with Blackstone and his detestation of Jefferson.

There were several issues confusedly bound up in the Girard Case— officially entitled *Vidal et al.* v. *Philadelphia*—such as the competence of a city to act as trustee and the jurisdiction of Chancery, but the central question, as the populace knew and as Webster made unmistakably plain, was that of the religiosity of the law. Stephen Girard, a French immigrant who had prospered fantastically in Philadelphia's commerce, died on December 6, 1831, leaving seven million dollars to found a college for poor white male orphans. In 1831 seven million was an astronomical sum. His relatives were naturally disappointed, and filed a bill in the Circuit Court to have the will set aside. Soon it became apparent that all their legalistic contentions were subordinate to their primary objection, that Girard's will explicitly enjoined "that no ecclesiastic, missionary, or minister of any sect whatsoever, shall ever hold or exercise any station or duty whatever in the said college; nor shall any such person ever be admitted for any purpose, or as a visitor, within the premises appropriated to the purposes of the said college." Girard said he cast no reflection on the clergy, but that since in America there was such a multitude of sects, he wanted his wards to be protected against "clashing doctrines," in order that they might be taught "the purest principles of morality" and so go into active life ready to "evince benevolence towards their fellow creatures" and eventually to embrace such religious principles as their "matured reason" would enable them to accept. Here, of course, was the real tangle: in the name of this universally honored ideal of benevolence, to which revivalists and lawyers alike paid homage, Girard used his seven million dollars to prevent ministers from so much as setting foot within the confines of his charity. The mass of American Protestants, the whole Revival and also—for once—the Unitarians, could construe this provision as nothing less than a calculated insult. An orator at Randolph-Macon College, for instance, in 1834 spoke for the outraged piety of the Republic: "this generation has not given birth to another absurdity so monstrous as that which would exclude from our seminaries of learning the open and vigorous inculcation of the religious faith which is acknowledged by our whole population, and which pervades every one of our free institutions." So piety again united with patriotism turned to the law, confidently expecting that a profession guided by Kent and Story would now make good its professions that Christianity, being a part, the fundamental part, of the Common Law, and therefore the basis of the American system, would promptly decree that such a contrivance of "French atheism" must not be tolerated in a free republic.

Webster did not disappoint them—"that wonderful man," as the *Herald* called him. He brushed aside Girard's notions of rational benevolence, for three days propounded the thesis that Christianity is basic to the Common Law and thus fundamental to the law of Pennsylvania. Since religion is to be taught only by the clergy, by excluding them, Girard manifestly intended to ridicule them, and so to send his hapless youths into the world with only deism or atheism as their guide, "equally in defiance of Heaven, and in scorn of the law." The Common Law has never sanctioned such a scheme, "and the law of Pennsylvania, of which Christianity is a part, must disown and reject it." Girard's project could not be considered charity, either in a Christian sense or in the sense of jurisprudence. As Webster worked up to his ultimate paroxysm of eloquence, he wept, the ladies wept, the Judges wept. All the founders of America, he intoned, Puritans, Quakers, Presbyterians brought with them the principle that Christianity inheres in the law of the land:

And where there is any religious sentiment amongst men at all, this sentiment incorporates itself with the law. *Every thing declares it.* The massive cathedral of the Catholic; the Episcopalian church, with its lofty spire pointing heavenward; the plain temple of the Quaker; the log church of the hardy pioneer of the wilderness; the mementoes and memorials around and about us; the consecrated graveyards, their tombstones and epitaphs, their silent vaults, their mouldering contents; all attest it. *The dead prove it as well as the living.* The generations that are gone before speak to it, and pronounce it from the tomb. We feel it. All, all, proclaim that Christianity, general, tolerant Christianity, Christianity independent of sects and parties, that Christianity to which the sword and the fagot are unknown, general, tolerant Christianity, is the law of the land.

Here, in the inspired words of the greatest lawyer of the age, was the legal formulation of what the Revival had all along been groping toward: a tolerant uniformity (note that Webster took care to include Catholicism!) which, reveling in multiplicity and virtuously abjuring the sword and fagot, would readily find methods for not tolerating the will of Stephen Girard.

When Webster, the audience, and the Judges wept, Horace Binney did not. He let Sergeant argue the equity aspects of Girard's benevolence, with his own acumen concentrated upon maintaining that law is one thing while religion is another. The question before the court, he insisted, "is and must be altogether a question of law, for the Court considers and decides no questions but questions of law." The Judges have no warrant to ask whether Girard's directions are expedient or disrespectful to the clergy. Girard was a respectable citizen, not even by remotest analogy an Abner Kneeland—whom surely Binney would contemn. Binney was a Philadelphia lawyer, a breed peculiarly dedicated to clarity, and he made hash of Webster's specious pietism. Whether he entirely apprehended what his argument meant may be doubted, and whether Story appreciated its import may be even more queried, but Horace Binney struck the blow from which the Protestant apparatus could never recover when he softly said:

I have no pleasure in a public investigation of even points of law, that require me to speak upon the subject of religion. . . . I desire, therefore, if possible, to raise myself above these dangers, by treating this question as I have a right to treat it, as a question of law, to be submitted by the court under the responsibility of my professional character, and not under the guarantee of my religious opinions. I do not mean to make any profession of them, or to speak of them. I will not suffer my own conscience or my conscientious belief to be even named by me. My remarks will be addressed to the judicial conscience of the court, and if I satisfy that, I can easily satisfy myself that the rest belongs to a different forum.

In the measured phrases of Binney's argument—by no means a reassertion of Gibbon, Paine, or even of Jefferson—there stood forth a nineteenth-century concept of legalism which demanded that the particular case be examined on its merits. "After eloquence has done its best and its worst," Binney said, counsel must ask whether pains have been taken to discover Girard's design, or only to fulminate ignorantly against what Webster supposes it to have been. "The cold question," as Binney aptly called it, is whether any of Webster's elocution has for a single moment fairly interpreted the will of Stephen Girard.

Story's decision (in which his colleagues concurred without altering a word) was defeat for Webster. He upheld the will. That reverse may have helped bring about the nomination of Clay instead of Webster the following June. Story refused even to consider Webster's argument, and resorted to legal "technicality." For this the great man was excoriated in the churches, though possibly his stratagem in the Girard Case is his claim to our gratitude. The court, he said, has no right to interfere with the policy of a state unless it be demonstrably contrary to the federal Constitution. Behind this negativism he partially concealed his denial of Webster's absolutism. He wrote to his wife, in distress of spirit, that he had always been a defender of religious freedom, and so "took no small pains to answer Mr. Webster's argument on this point, which went to cut down that freedom to a very narrow range."

Even so, he who had denounced Jefferson could not let the controversy rest entirely upon mere technicality. Story invoked the concept of "benevolence," upon which both revivalists and lawyers would be forced, in view of their voluminous protestations, to agree. There was nothing in Girard's plan for inculcating this virtue which ought to be construed as anti-Christian. Girard had not been malevolent. As long as society agreed that benevolence was, as it must be, the supreme manifestation of Christian culture, there was no reason to accuse his school of atheism. Apprehensive for the future, it was "unnecessary," he insisted, for anyone to fear what might be, at some later date, "the legal effect of a devise" for a school or college, in Pennsylvania or in any state, "for the propagation of Judaism or Deism, or any other form of Infidelity." Such a case, Story affirmed, was not to be presumed possible in a Christian country, and such remote inferences, such "speculative tendencies" were not to be applied to the case in hand. By thus identifying Girard's use of the term "benevolence" with a residual Christian spirit, Story emerged as the champion of a secularism which need not be accused of infidelity "in a country composed of such a variety of religious sects as our country." He could remain consistent, so it seemed, with the assertion of his address of 1819, that Christianity is incorporated within the fundamental law.

We may wonder whether, had Girard called upon the city of Philadelphia to act as trustee for an out-and-out anti-Christian endowment, Sergeant and Binney would have defended the bequest. Fortunately, Girard defined his intent as "benevolence." With that sanction behind him, Binney was able to plead, and Story able to support him, that the wealth of the nation could be used for something other than the promotion of the kingdom of God. Girard offended the morality of the community, but the law stepped in between its moral indignation and the "cold question" of a man's right to do what he wills with his own. Story's decision, by its ingenious equating of benevolence with a vaguely Christian purpose, avoided the basic issue, and left to the future to decide whether in this pious nation a purely secular, not to say unreligious, institution could hold its own. That interesting question remained for the future to determine. What Binney wrought, whether or not this was what he aimed at, was a fatal dislodgement of Webster's thesis, appropriated from Blackstone, that Christianity in any theological definition must be deemed a part and parcel of American law.

4.

TREPIDATION

The implications of the Girard decision, the cold reasoning of Horace Binney, were only gradually comprehended by either the profession or the public, and even where appreciated were countered by an obstinate response that the law still remained Christian. Or, if not too specifically Christian, then at least moral. But after the agitation over Girard's will, a transformation occurs in American discussion of legal ethics. While the case was still pending, in 1838, Noah Webster wrote to David McClure (who was projecting a curriculum for Girard's college) firmly asserting that every civilized code must be founded on Christian preachments, not only the rules concerning theft and murder, but those of insurance and charity. "Every wise code of laws," pontificated old Noah, "must embrace the main principles of the religion of Christ."

If anybody could speak for the primitive American conviction, Puritanical to the core though liberated in dogma, it was Noah Webster. Yet after the Girard Case, Noah Webster's exhortation quickly became as irrelevant as Daniel Webster's declamation before the Supreme Court. The question of moral responsibility suddenly narrowed down to the relatively minor query of whether a lawyer is required to do all he can for the exoneration of a client whom he inwardly believes to be guilty.

This was, of course, an old problem in the history of the law. Because the Puritans were convinced that lawyers would defend a bad case as long as they were paid, the colonies tried to suppress the profession. In the 1830's Henry Brougham's declaration—and he, as contrasted with Bentham, was esteemed in America—that for an advocate the will of his client was an absolute obligation, seemed downright shocking. Wherefore, though the quandary had bothered moralists for centuries, it is remarkable that coincident with the Girard Case a reinvigorated discussion should commence in America, and that the debate should be opened in *The Democratic Review* by a reformer already destined to become the advocate of "codification," David Dudley Field. Is it truly lawful, Field asked in 1844, to pervert noble faculties, to abuse the immense learning of a Kent and a Story, in order to make false reasons seem true, to cover up weak points, to vilify an adversary? Indeed, Field would admit, a lawyer may undertake the defense of a man he knows to be guilty, but only if he endeavors to prove extenuating circumstances. Likewise, in civil cases, he may legitimately invoke laws of whose principles he disapproves. With the accumulation of years Field was to be more and more distracted by the moral concern, and to insist upon it so stridently that for three decades he virtually appointed himself the conscience of the profession. Later, when he assumed the defense of Boss Tweed—acting by his own twisted standards of consistency—he precipitated a crisis of introspection which still bedevils the profession; but in the 1850's he was the mighty voice proclaiming that advocacy of particular claims could and should always be guided by an overriding devotion to abstract justice.

The more David Field insisted that a lawyer's duty to his client did not swallow up his duties as a citizen—the more he asserted that "to assent to the bad scheme of an unjust client, is to become equally guilty with him"—the more the evangelical conscience winced. Not, of course, because the American conscience approved of legal technicalities being used to sustain a bad cause, but because the American intellect had gradually, and especially after the Girard decision, been forced to recognize that the "self-styled *conscientious lawyers*" were bound to try their cases in their own chambers. The result, said *The Law Reporter* in 1846, is that "they insist upon the wrong with the same pertinacity, earnestness, and personal feeling, that they do upon the right." It took some courage to say it, but this writer had the welcome bluntness: Yes, he said, lawyers may select causes and refuse retainers, "yet the sober truth is, that the more mercenary our profession is, the more it will deserve respect." In 1850 *The United States Monthly Law Magazine* with equal courage asked what was disgraceful in bringing before the judicial mind all that can fairly be urged on either side of a doubtful question? Throughout the next decade the effort to vindicate the ethical conduct of lawyers takes on a concerted vigor, as though to show that while the political situation was deteriorating the lawyers needed some renewed assurances that they were respectable. Joel Parker, for instance, praised Daniel Webster as a jurist (a portion of his career about which there circulated whispers of sharp practices, to say the least) by insisting that practically all American lawyers recognize the overruling providence of God and the duty, founded upon His law, of justice and equity. True, the advocate is required at times to maintain that the rules of the law applicable to a case furnish the equity which must decide it; yet even so, "the conscientious lawyer, in a statement of facts which tend to impeach the justice of the dealings of his client, does not attempt to shield him by a weakening of the bonds of moral obligation or an undermining of religious faith." George Sharswood told his students in Philadelphia that no profession, including the sacred ministry, more demanded "a high-toned morality," but he along with all these apologists protested that this morality is entirely compatible with arguing any and every case. The advocate is not a moral censor, and it does not matter what his private conviction may be. "The judge is there to adjudicate the law, and the jury to determine the facts. His share in the proceedings consists in endeavoring, if possible, by all fair means, to obtain a favorable decision from both. There is nothing immoral in this."

One who surveys this literature is bound to feel that the reiteration of the plea should be linked with the deepening spiritual unrest that protestations, North and South, that American law is fundamentally Christian, despite Horace Binney, points toward the same climax. And much of this compulsive declamation betrays the reason for its prominence. If evangelical Christianity, said Henry Boardman in 1849, were enthroned in our halls of justice, "It would moderate the spirit of faction—the bane of all republics." From this pious wish it was only a step to pretending that it was actually fulfilled, that Christianity did pervade the courts and that therefore faction was bound to disappear. "In proportion as a community is possessed of a deep sense of the sacred nature of justice, it is possessed of a correspondingly profound sense of the solemn nature of religion." This age, exulted *The Democratic Review* in 1851, or the next following age, "is to introduce that great political economy, the morality of the Bible." Closing his eyes resolutely to the Compromise of 1850 and the Fugitive Slave Law, this Democrat bravely continued in 1851: "Christianity, by whose aid jurisprudence has arisen to its present stature of beauty, and governments been purged of their crafts and policies, of knaves and demagogues, and politics been enlarged by more comprehensive measures, shall baptize them with her mystic waters, and incorporate them into a common sisterhood with the majesty of her truth."

Expressions in this vein reach a veritable paroxysm coincident with the Revival. *The Southern Literary Messenger* proclaimed in 1858 that so far as human laws are written or have been expounded in the American courts, "the principles which underlie and regulate them are found to be, are designed to be modelled after and built upon the principles of Divine truth." This essay was reprinted as a pamphlet by the Baptists of Baltimore, and all anxiety should have been allayed by its flatly saying that the Christian lawyer who defends a client he knows to be a culprit obeys "the cardinal rule of love to his neighbour,

laid down specifically by the Saviour." Geology, said a Georgia jurist
in 1859, may confuse the mind, but the noble science of the law causes
no such embarrassments:

On the contrary, it is relieved from all such difficulties, for it accepts the
Divine account as a matter of Faith; in other words, it recognizes the imper-
fection of all human knowledge. It is a simple fact, that from a Law Library
may be arranged as complete a Code of Morals, and as perfect a Creed of
Christian Faith, as would be satisfactory to the most exacting Professor of
Religion, or the most orthodox Christian Church; therefore no Lawyer
properly imbued with the teachings of his Profession, *can* be an Infidel or a
Skeptic.

To the extent that this sort of emotion was widely shared—and by
1860 it seems to have been almost universal—the general intellectual
temper of the Republic had come a long way from its deep distrust of
law, of lawyers, and of the ethics of advocacy which signalized it
around 1790. The lawyers who wrote the Constitution would have
been astounded could they have been brought back to hear lawyers
saying that in the Common Law were reflected "the principles of Divine Law, as promulgated by Moses and as expounded by Christ."
But they would surely have perceived, as we also must perceive, that
these acts of homage to the law spring not from a true conversion to
the scientific creed of the profession, but from an anguished hope that
by thus announcing its Christian character it could somehow save the
nation. By this time the mighty tomes of Kent and Story seemed the
creations of a far-off era, when the mind had had free play. By 1860
what was being produced were either guidebooks to courtroom techniques or demonstrations that such techniques constituted a manifestation of evangelical piety. Behind this nervous activity lay the desperate
hope that the law might somehow prevent the bloodletting. When it
became clear that it could not, an era in the history of American law,
as well as an era in the history of the American mind, was brought to
an abrupt and violent conclusion.

CHAPTER FIVE

Definition by Negation

The lawyer has entrusted to him the social life of man. This is his function, to preserve the social life in security and soundness; and by his preservative care secure its full and complete development. For it is worthy of remark here that the professions, all alike, partake rather of a negative than of a positive character. They all bear on the side of infirmity and disease, as curative, sanative, rather than on the positive as directly invigorative and formative. Providence has given to all these forms of life a power of self-development of their own, inherent in their own nature; and human art is called in rather as corrective, remedial, and protective.

—HENRY N. DAY, *The Professions*, Hudson, Ohio, 1849

1.

TELEOLOGY

Probably every interpreter of the law, from Hammurabi to Blackstone and even Bentham, would not quarrel with the assertion that the major function of any system is to specify those actions which people should not perform and the punishments to be imposed upon those who nevertheless do them. There would, however, be disagreement among them—in fact there has been—were they asked whether this definition fully describes the purpose of the law. Is it solely an instrument for restraint, for inhibition, for compelling to conformity? Or does it, can it, play any part in activating the energies of the community?

Because the central element of such legal wisdom as the new nation found itself possessed of—or possessed by—was the Common Law of England (even though it had hastily to find out exactly what that law comprised), it inherited a body of statute which had mainly been devised through centuries of struggle against a monarch. The great achievements of the lawyers—*habeas corpus,* for instance—had been victories for confinement, not for freedom. That they had implications for liberty could be celebrated, but technically they were impositions upon a theoretically unlimited power. The English experience could be summarized in the brief compass of the first ten amendments to the Constitution, and so these historic delimitations of royal prerogative were imposed upon a republic where there no longer existed even the shadow of a king.

Still, because the American conception of law had perforce developed in opposition to England, and because, as the Declaration of Independence adroitly pretended, all these controversies had been with the Crown, the "Bill of Rights" carried the antimonarchical emphasis into the affairs of a democracy, and in effect challenged the federal government to dare to fill the vacuum left by the deposition of George III. In a sense, even though few (if any) really intended that this federal authority should advance such pretensions, the nation could hardly help accepting the challenge. In spite of itself, it steadily augmented its power, from the first National Bank through the Louisiana Purchase to Lincoln's call for volunteers in 1861. Yet all this is relative as viewed in the perspective of world history, or even of British history. Hamilton's plans for strengthening the central government would in England have seemed dangerously liberal to a Wellington or an Ellenborough. As a result American jurists of the early nineteenth century were caught in a dilemma which was not of their devising and from which they constantly struggled to be liberated: on the one hand they were required to administer a legal method premised upon the assumption that all government was a constant threat to the liberties of the citizen, and on the other to adapt this method to the official proposition that in this nation no such threat existed. Possibly the burden of this antinomy explains, in part, why so many of them sought surcease in the Civil Law, wherein they did not always have to assume the pose of striking down despotism. *"Sic semper tyrannis"* could become a tedious, not to say an enervating, rule of action.

We sense that an urge toward some more aggressive philosophy than that of the Bill of Rights had emerged by the third decade of the new century. It seems remarkable, for instance, that in 1829 Joseph Willard would tell the Worcester Bar how no other profession "so winds itself around, and penetrates society in its innumerable operations, and exercises so controlling an influence in its sphere of action." In succeeding years a set of rhetorical phrases become so stereotyped that they appear in almost every forensic discourse: the law is (this from

Story) the "great elastic power which pervades and embraces every human relation"; it is the minister to man's social necessities and the guardian of his social virtues; it is the "bond" or "cement" of society; or, most frequently, it is the "ligament." These terms, reaching blindly toward a concept of dynamic function, abraded the obligatory assumption of a contractual origin of society, but even that inconvenience could be circumvented when, comparing the law with gravity in the solar system, it could be saluted as the "soul" of the "Machine"!

Yet even as some theorists were taking the first hesitant steps toward a more organic idea than Blackstone might have permitted, the profession was forced back upon the philosophy of restriction by its increasing awareness that another power than the political despot threatened the stability of this "Machine." Lawyers called it variously "faction," "party," a "spirit of insubordination," "mobocracy," or most succinctly "anarchy." William Rawle, for instance, voiced at Lafayette College the sort of gloom which, in this ebullient epoch, was becoming virtually the staple refrain of the lawyers. The heart of the philanthropic patriot sinks, he said, at the sight of the dark and portentous cloud which hangs over "this sublime and magnificent landscape"—a cloud compacted of riots, lynchings, license. If the law cannot vindicate itself against this "self-destroying principle," then life and liberty will be of uncertain tenure, and the slave who bends under the yoke of Russian tyranny "is safer, happier, and more free, than he who boasts the proud name of an American citizen."

Apprehension of this sort increased in severity during the year 1829 for the basic reason we have already noted, and came to a climax in the much-publicized trial of Judge James H. Peck in the United States Senate. As a judge of the District Court in Missouri he had rendered a decision against the clients of a lawyer symbolically named Lawless; he had then published in a newspaper the reasons for his action, which Lawless held were unsound. In 1826 Lawless endeavored to file a bill of impeachment with the Judiciary Committee of the House; that committee refused to heed it, but Lawless persisted, and in March, 1830, a new committee, with James Buchanan as chairman, passed a resolution of impeachment and the House voted that Peck be charged with high misdemeanors in office. The case tells much about the legal dilemma in America, for Lawless was accusing Peck of exceeding the limits of judicial self-restraint. Counsel for the judge adroitly turned the argument into a contention that Lawless, by intruding into the sphere of judicial independence, was the one who had crossed the barrier of legal propriety. The most eloquent of Peck's attorneys was William Wirt, who in January, 1831, delivered one of his greatest speeches, which not only won acquittal for Judge Peck but furnished the classic statement for that age of the American philosophy of government by negation. Wirt declared that after studying the case minutely he could find no evidence of the horrors which the prosecutors had poured forth in torrents; he was forced to conclude that these existed only in the imagination of Mr. Lawless. From this he moved skillfully to his great point: "there is no good that does exist or can exist, unless guarded by restraint." What chance had either Lawless, or any advocate of something more positive in the law, against Wirt's barrage:

Sir, this principle of restraint has the sanction of Almighty wisdom itself, for it is impressed on every part of the physical as well as the moral world. The planets are kept in their orbits by the restraint of attraction; but for this law, the whole system would rush into inextricable confusion and ruin. Does it detract from the simplicity, the beauty, the grandeur of this system to say that one of the laws which upholds it is the law of restraint?

After a succession of these purely rhetorical questions, wherein language is so manipulated that the mere holding of things in check becomes merged with the sublime, Wirt then proceeds to his summation: "Look where you will, then, Sir, above you, around you, below you, you see that the great conservative principle is restraint." Men like Lawless—who emerges from Wirt's denunciation as obviously a pettifogger—were simply assaulting the authority of Peck's tribunal.

Simon Greenleaf, in his inaugural at Harvard, took an even more troubled look at the "desolating flood of wild misrule" which threatened the nation, but consoled his audience by assuring it that as long as the tribunals were filled "by men of extensive learning, of minds capacious and highly gifted, of unblenching courage and uncompromising integrity," the storms of party may beat outside the walls of the temple, but all will be peace, security, and confidence within. Yet as events followed in what seemed a chaotic rush, with not only such outbursts of violence as the Astor Place riot but the subjection of the bench to popular elections, thereby depriving the administration of such men as Greenleaf described, the legal tone grew more and more pessimistic. By 1857 Theodore Sedgwick illustrated the vein of whistling to keep their courage up which by then had become the universal tune of the lawyers: the law of nature, the moral law, the municipal law, and the law of nations, he said, form a system of "restraints" before which the most consummate genius, the most vehement will, the angriest passions, are compelled to bend, "and the pressure of which the individual is forced to acknowledge his incapacity to resist." By the time the renewed emphasis upon restraint had reached this intensity, the best legal minds had forgotten how earlier in the century they had, for a brief moment, in their happier employment of terms like "soul" and "ligament," contemplated a definition of municipal law which might have nourished a purposive vision.

Americans had a difficult intellectual problem if only because they owed so much to Blackstone. He had indeed told them that the vindicatory part of the law is more important than the declaratory, the directory, or the remedial, because "dread of evil is a much more forcible principle of human actions than the prospect of good." But his conception of vindication was moderated through the consideration that invidious ambition will always be restrained by the superior power of a free monarchy, "from whom all honour is derived." In the American Republic, there was no such source of honor. John Jay, in his charge to the First Circuit Court of New York in 1790, tried to adjust Blackstone's teachings to the unprecedented situation by saying that civil liberty consists not in the right of every man to do as he pleases but in the equal right of all to do whatever the constitutional laws of the country admit to be consistent with the public good. Behind Jay's statement is the tacit assumption that all sorts and conditions of men will automatically recognize the public good. By 1821 Samuel Knapp, introducing his portraits of leading lawyers, had to point out that amid our vacillating population, members of the American bar had the peculiar mission of preserving such a judicial neutrality as was unknown to English jurisprudence. "They spring from all ranks, without the peculiar feelings of any one." So, if they keep the aristocracy (who are they?) from exercising oppression, they also prevent "democracy from sweeping away every thing, by wild uproar and confusion."

It is against this background of anxiety that decisions of the courts concerning early labor unions must be interpreted. Inevitably, in the light of what the unions have become in American society, these first pronouncements, which imposed upon American societies the rules of the English Anti-Combination Act of 1800, have been represented as Whig-Conservative efforts at suppression. Beginning with the Philadelphia Shoemakers' Case in 1806, down to Lemuel Shaw's ruling of 1842 in *Commonwealth* v. *Hunt,* the judges had regularly found unions an incipient form of democratic conspiracy against the stability of society, and condemned them as uproar and confusion. These convictions have acquired infamy with posterity, and have generally been denounced as politically inspired. Because in the Massachusetts case the journeymen shoemakers were defended by Robert Rantoul, an enthusiastic Jacksonian, and the charges delivered against them by Judge Peter O. Thacher in 1832, 1837, and 1840 were patently Whig expressions, historians have found it easy to identify the cause of labor with the Jacksonian party.

Actually both Thacher and Shaw, before whom the case ultimately arrived, were Whigs, and so, to the extent the term applies in America, were "conservatives." But to the charge of criminal conspiracy, Shaw declared that the journeymen committed no crime in banding together: "Such a purpose is not unlawful." The difference between them points up the confusion in legal thinking as to just how and where the principle of restriction should be applied so that it might somehow also be a constructive principle. The operations of society, said Thacher, cannot proceed unless the law, "which like the air, is over every thing, and pervades every thing, and is the life of every thing, protect, in full extent, the principle of equal and fair competition." Hence he concluded that when individuals combined together to gain an advantage over others, they violated this principle. But Shaw discovered that the purpose of the journeymen's combinations was not pernicious; on the premise that the law pervaded all society, adjudicating peaceful disputes by incessant pressure, he found it not criminal "for men to agree together to exercise their own acknowledged rights, in such a manner as best to subserve their own interests." Shaw's opinion had, as hardly need be remarked, immense effect on the subsequent history of labor relations, but he himself was unconscious of what he wrought. He was simply adhering to the one rule which the philosophy of American law left to him, that the ligament of society is a neutral umpire within the machine. "It is through competition," he said, "that the best interests of trade and industry are promoted." He was willing that a union compete with a corporation. We pervert the logic of the period when we read too glibly into juridical differences connotations which arose only after decades of industrialization.

In 1845, speaking at the opening of a new courthouse in Worcester, Lemuel Shaw made clear that he had no recollection of having wrought any major innovation in *Commonwealth* v. *Hunt*. The function of jurisprudence, he then said—and not even Rantoul would contradict him—is to restrain the exercise of unlicensed authority, to impose "restraining power" upon every individual, "however elevated in social and political condition." Indeed, with the genius for succinct statement that enshrined his image in the memory of Justice Holmes, Shaw hit exactly the point which his generation hoped would outlast the storm: although all have a deep and abiding interest in the law, yet "it commands little popular applause, it cometh not with observation, and is perhaps best known rather by its terrors, than by its beneficence."

All this should, perhaps, serve to caution us to be wary of what attributes we attach to the term "conservative" in this revolutionary period. The most obvious is that it meant people with incomes, with well-furnished houses. Few of them seemingly realized the rate at which they were traveling, the rate at which the society was being transformed. American capitalism of 1830 to 1860 was a riot of extravagance. Hundreds of those who glistened in New York and Boston in the 1840's are forgotten. A few families—Lowells, Biddles—managed to maintain continuity, but they were few. The number who went down to ruin invited a chronicler equal to Dickens. However important may be the fact that certain fortunes created in the Jacksonian period—one thinks of Astor and Vanderbilt—survived as fortunes, the persisting names contributed nothing whatsoever to the life of the American mind. Rather, we must turn to lawyers such as Rufus Choate for exposition of the proposition that America could be conservative in the midst of economic convulsion.

Choate is the most interesting of the lot, in this respect more so than Kent or Story, because in 1845 he ventured to use the word "conservative" in something like a modern sense, and to set up the law as a conservative bulwark against the evolution of the country. Choate was perpetually dismayed by what he witnessed. The very idea of a "State" was "held to be no more than an encampment of tents on the great prairie, pitched at sundown, and struck to the sharp crack of the rifle next morning," instead of—what Choate dreamed the law should mean—"a structure, stately and eternal, in which the generations may come, one after another, to the great gift of this social life." Though Dickens and Thackeray were demonstrating to thousands of Americans, who read these chroniclers rather than Melville or Whitman, that even in England estates decayed, that neither Deadlocks nor Esmonds could survive, American lawyers still dreamed that without entering into the labyrinths of English Chancery they might preserve on this frontier the eternal verities of consistency.

American lawyers were—if the language be not too strong—hoodwinked into contending that in this country ancient law could be embraced without a tincture of its feudal connotations. We commence, said Choate, with all the reforms still contested in England already achieved. "With us the age of this mode and this degree of reform is over; its work is done. The passage of the sea, the occupation and culture of a new world, the conquest of independence,—these were

our eras, these our agency, of reform." It therefore seemed to follow—
and it is memorable that Choate put the phrase in quotes—that the
"organic forms" of our law are shields against acts of legislatures or
even against judgments of courts. Choate encouraged himself to say, in
his most extravagant declaration, that law conceived as negation
would not be the creation of any will, majority or minority, but of the
pure "justice of the State, enlightened by the perfect reason of the
State." Starting from an initial denial that the state had any intent
beyond the punishment of disobedience, the lawyers of America strove
by might and main to extract from it some concept of absolute reason.
No wonder that so astute a critic as Theodore Sedgwick in 1857
warned that American lawyers had overworked the concept of limitation. By seeking protection through multiplication of "precise texts of
written law," Sedgwick prophesied, we invoke not the protection of
principle but merely one of authority. "And the exercise of authority
always, and eminently with us, excites jealousy and provokes resistance." So the states drove on into violence, and once again the lawyers had to take stock, as few were prepared to do, as to how much
they had precipitated the war they had fervently striven to prevent.

2.

INHERENT DEPRAVITY

A large number—probably a majority—of the lawyers in early America found in the study of law a liberation from the theological restrictions of their youth. They did not always need to be summoned like
Joseph Story into Unitarianism, or like Horace Binney to acquire an
Episcopalian latitudinarianism; they could merely learn to think for
themselves, as did Henry Clay and Abraham Lincoln.

The result, judging by their statements concerning themselves, was
that they were of all men the most disillusioned about human nature.
There is a "romance" in the law, said L. J. Bigelow, but the principal
effect on the practitioner is a loss of faith in humanity. "He is too apt
to believe the depravity of man innate and natural, allowing of no
cure, and beyond the reach of reform." No matter how sympathetic he
may be with ordinary frailties, he soon learns not to concern himself
with removing them "so much as to keep them restrained within the
decent proprieties of life and rules of law."

Consequently, while throughout this period revivalists took for
granted the fall of man but in their invitations to regeneration still

held forth a boisterously happy prospect, if one wishes to find real excoriations of human vileness he must go to the dignified lawyers. They, as Story never tired of repeating, are sentinels on the wall and at the gates; their job is to "triumph by arresting the progress of error and the march of power, and drive back the torrent that threatens destruction equally to public liberty and to private property, to all that delights us in private life, and all that gives grace and authority in public office." In their doctrinal writings, Hoffman, Kent, and Story pronounce the word "mischief" with such unction—they linger so lovingly upon it—that they appear to get immense satisfaction in contemplating the universal human propensity to indulge in it. They were acutely aware that the great empires of the past had followed a course of growth, and then decay and death. "Such," wrote Story (and Marshall approved), "are the melancholy lessons of the past history of republics down to our own." The only chance America had of escaping the cyclical fate was the law, which alone could restrain mischief and confine anarchy; yet the lawyers often relished the thought that even they could not stave off the inevitable. The example of ancient states made clear to Hoffman that "the best have been unable to save the community, when the springs of the machine were weakened by vice, and impeded by corruption."

It must be noted that the lawyers on the whole were impartial in their denunciations and did not let their interest in the expansion of commerce interfere with declaring, "Our commercial community seem to make a common cause with every delinquent trader, and to treat the most criminal extravagance, the most thoughtless indiscretion, the most daring and desperate speculations, with the lenity due to accident and misfortune." By 1836 Chancellor Kent could fairly exult in a picture of the society as irrevocably depraved with all the gusto of a seventeenth-century preacher of social jeremiads—and with more vigor than any of his ministerial contemporaries brought to the work. He listed the evils:

The rapidly increasing appetite for wealth; the inordinate taste for luxury which it engenders; the vehement spirit of speculation, and the selfish emulation which it creates; the contempt for slow and moderate gains; the ardent thirst for pleasure and amusement; the diminishing reverence for the wisdom of the past; the disregard of the lessons of experience, the authority of magistrates, and the venerable institutions of ancestral policy.

In the legal perspective, then, much more than in the evangelical, this hard-working, pushing society appeared headed for catastrophe, and jurists fancied themselves the only guardians who could sound the tocsin. Judge Parker felt it highly probable that we would fail to maintain the "institutions of civil liberty . . . the happiness of the private hearth—and the privilege of the public altar—"; that all these blessings would be swept away and no vestiges remain "except upon the page of the historian who relates that such things were." So not the least fascinating of the paradoxes which make up the pattern of the American mind in this epoch is the fact that the lawyers rose so rapidly to social and financial eminence to the tune of a keening despair over the future of the nation.

They seldom had a more congenial occupation than when expounding the American constitutional system as a triumphant playing off of depravity against depravity. The authors of that document made as fair a bid for the preservation of their work as any men in history because, said Hoffman, in their machinery of checks and balances they so combined simple forms "that the besetting vice of each may be counteracted by some opposite quality of that with which it is combined." On ceremonial occasions oratorical lawyers would cry that the composition of this government "presents a novel and sublime spectacle in political history," but when they resolved this sublimity into its components, they found that it consisted chiefly in enabling all citizens, to use the language of Story, to "watch the exercise of power in every department of government; and ascertain, whether it is within the prescribed limits of the constitution." His and Kent's massive treatises on constitutional law often become merely repetitions *ad nauseam* of the glories of delimitation. A Bill of Rights, said Kent, is even more to be desired in a republic than in a monarchy, because the immunities are then "constantly placed before the eyes of the people, accompanied with the imposing force and solemnity of a constitutional sanction." In similar vein Kent expatiated on the majestic wisdom shown in the creation of a Senate, which is perfectly designed "to destroy the evil effects of sudden and strong excitement, and of precipitate measures springing from passion, caprice, prejudice, personal influence, and party intrigue." The Senate is not a House of Lords, and since it comes equally from the people, the people need not resent it, wherefore it the more effectively functions "as a check upon the intemperance of the more popular department."

Historians of the Constitution insist that the principle of judicial review is fully contained, or at least implied, in the document. Without, however, entering into these arcana, I think it fair to say that the tremendous concern of the legal generation of 1820 to 1850 for the imposition of negatives upon the emerging society is largely responsible for the great esteeem the principle has subsequently enjoyed.

In 1794, before it had been publicly phrased, let alone really applied, Kent said in his introductory lecture at Columbia, "I consider then the Courts of Justice, as the proper and intended Guardians of our limited Constitutions, against the factions and encroachments of the Legislative Body." Kent—who came from Connecticut—was confronted as a legalist with a problem similar to that which had plagued his Puritan ancestors: he had to posit somewhere in the universe an absolute, irresponsible power, and then devise ways for caging it. He was not concerned, as was Thomas Hooker, with the Creator of the universe; he was an American citizen, and so Jehovah was less of a problem to him than the American democracy. His method of dealing with his demon was, oddly enough, precisely that which the founders of Connecticut had used: Kent acknowledged the irresistible power of the whole people, just as Hooker bowed before the sovereign might of God, but then he hastened to remind irresponsibility that it too had agreed to the terms of a covenant, and so was henceforth liable to trial by jury. The Puritan covenant had been that of God with his elect; the American covenant was an act of the people, "speaking in their original character," as a result of which "every act of the legislative power, contrary to the true intent and meaning of the constitution, is absolutely null and void." Had Kent paid more attention to the theology of his region—which bored him—he might have remembered that the religious fraternity had already been shattered by its inability to certify just how either a God or a people spoke in an original character, or to designate what voice was authoritatively to say that a particular enactment was contrary to the intent of the covenant.

Of course, when Kent wrote his *Commentaries,* he had adequate grounds for asserting that the Supreme Court was, in this secular covenant, the final adjudicator. Lower courts would naturally resist the force of passion or the temptations of interest to sacrifice constitutional rights, but eventually, if the case required, the Supreme Court alone could interpret the paramount law—which thus became "the highest evidence of the will of the people." This was to imply—though Kent would have been horrified to hear it said—that by the legal metaphysics into which he led his cohorts, the Supreme Court was becoming, or should become, the representative of God on earth, because in it was manifested that ligament which held the social universe together. As a eulogist of Mr. Justice Washington blandly said in 1830, the Supreme Court "is the regulating power of the complicated machine of our government; without it every part would be speedily thrown into disorder, and run wildly into confusion and ruin." Confusion and ruin, I may remark, are the badges of innate depravity.

At this point the wheel comes round again, and the lawyer finds himself shorn of that social anxiety in which he has luxuriated. The revivalist was always threatened with the dismal prospect that success would deprive him of his occupation; the lawyer had to recognize that if the Supreme Court ever did, to the satisfaction of all, interpret the Constitution to its utmost implication, and impose its will upon all anarchic legislatures, the law would become, as Samuel Chipman hoped it never would become, an arena only for compromise, and no time would "be left for action." Practitioners and teachers were only occasionally visited by glimpses of their dilemma, but often enough to be driven to some remarkable exercises in rhetorical confusion. For instance, Timothy Walker in his textbook on American law of 1837 found the balance between the Constitution (expounded by the court) and the liberty of the citizen almost but not quite beyond the power of words to convey:

I cannot use language too strong on this subject. From the commencement of civilization, the grand problem in politics has been, to attain the exact medium between anarchy on the one hand, and despotism on the other. . . . Of course the fair conclusion is, that we enjoy that golden mean so long looked for, but never before discovered. . . . The stately machine continues to move on, though its parts be undergoing repairs.

The hope of the profession, as of the clergy, had to remain that repairs would continue to be needed. The decade of 1850 did not disappoint them.

3.

MARSHALL, STORY, AND TANEY

The history of the Supreme Court up to the Civil War has been recounted in such detail that I need not review it. The court served in these decades as a forum for what Americans fondly supposed were their greatest exhibitions of intellectual maturity, though often, as I have mentioned, it seemed to take on the aspect of a plebeian version of a Roman holiday. Examining the record for what it has to say about the activity of mind, we are bound to confess that it is a sorry spectacle. Rules were laid down and procedures established without the benefit of precedents, and these achievements remain for American lawyers important landmarks. But as for the major issue so lengthily debated, it comes down to that of whose ox was being gored by the horn of delimitation—whether the cattle of the states or the sacred cow of the central government. The student of economic enterprise, and especially the historian of technological progress, may well conclude that this legal sideshow, in which restraint was alternately imposed now on the states, now on the nation, was a providential blessing to the young Republic, because between the opposing positions a steady forward thrust continued. Just as an implicit concurrence among revivalists, even while the denominations fought for supremacy, released energies for common action, so the incessant effort of the courts to confine activities to the stated limitations kept open a wide gateway for commercial and inventive enterprise.

Jefferson, we know, constantly denounced John Marshall's court for "driving us into consolidation." Oddly enough, all Marshall's great decisions were aimed at striking something down, whether a state or the administration. Whatever may have been his inward dreams of empire, what he most notably did as a jurist was to prevent people from acting. No doubt this was due in large part to the predicament in which, thanks to the peculiar Constitution of the United States, he found himself. No doubt he did, by asserting the power of the court to test legislation against the document, enhance the authority of Washington against the states. But in a sense that aggrandizement of federal power, much as it has been celebrated by legalists, was less important than the fact that in every important case he imposed a specific restraint upon somebody.

Actually it is difficult to find in the writings of Marshall or of his allies much that amounts, in modern terms, to a program of "nationalism." Joseph Story did indeed permit himself, in the euphoria of 1815, a hope that with peace the national authority might be extended to the full extent of the power granted by the Constitution, and enumerated military and naval schools, national banks, systems of bankruptcy, navigation acts, national justices of the peace, as goals for the new nation. These would have seemed to Jefferson and John Taylor schemes for creating centralized "despotism," and excited in them fears of a Caesar, but Story's ambition was more circumscribed: "By such enlarged and liberal institutions, the Government of the United States will be endeared to the people, and the factions of the great States will be rendered harmless." Story's use of the word "liberal" warns us anew against employing in this American context the European meanings of "liberal" and "conservative." It further reminds us that these opponents of Jefferson were not so much concerned with building a superstate as with checking the depravity of local factionalism. They were thinking, even at their most aggressive, in terms still negative. It was always Marshall's fundamental belief, said Story, that this republic was in no danger of perishing by the power of the central government, "but by the resisting and counteracting power of the state sovereignties . . . that in our government the centrifugal force is far greater than the centripetal."

So while Story held to his conviction that the government of the United States was too weak for anybody to worry about, "that the danger always is much greater of anarchy in the parts, than of tyranny in the head," he and his associates resented the charge that they were consolidating central power when what they were actually doing was imposing restrictions on the states. In their eyes the greatest blow they ever struck was the Dartmouth College Case, which enjoined upon the states the obligation to respect a contract. This more than any other act, said Kent, threw "an impregnable barrier around all rights and franchises derived from the grant of government," gave "solidity and inviolability to the literary, charitable, religious and commercial institutions of our country."

It has been remarked that constitutional disputes up to the Civil War were apt to find parties aligned according to party or sectional interest. As a Richmond newspaper noted in 1809, the Federalists of 1799 protested against the interposition of the state legislatures and clung to the federal courts as the only tribunal for trying the constitutionality of a law, but now "they seem to be flying from these Courts to those very Legislatures against whose jurisdiction they have so solemnly entered their protests." In South Carolina a Jeffersonian judge had to call Mr. Jefferson's embargo an act of despotism and invoke the concept of restraint against officers of the United States. While great economic concerns were at stake in the party battles, and somehow the nation did thrive and expand, the only constitutional principle it had to work with was that of negation. The never-ending uncertainty was whether the courts, and inevitably the Supreme Court, would restrict the Congress or the states. Binney was sad to see Webster go in 1852, and could find only one consolation: "My fixed faith, after forty years' observation, is that the most that a pure and wise party can do for the country is to become a check and counterpoise."

In the opinion of these legal gentlemen the conduct of Andrew Jackson was neither pure nor wise; during his reign their insistence upon the function of the law as the inhibiter of action became a strident clamor which was interrupted only by the wail, "This government is becoming daily more and more corrupt; and the decline and fall of the American Republic will not be less a matter of history in an age or two at farthest." Another of the charming ironies of the epoch is the fact that those who, like Kent and Story, considered themselves the heirs of Alexander Hamilton became entirely negativistic in their thinking, even though at the same time Robert Rantoul, whom they held to be a demagogue, was stoutly insisting that the federal government "should be restricted within the narrowest constitutional limits, and where any power is doubtful, it should not be exercised."

Upon the death of Marshall in 1835, Democrats hoped and Whigs profoundly feared that Jackson would create a Chief Justice who would enable his party to carry forward its more constructive, nationalistic program. In Roger Taney many were sure that Jackson had found the man, especially when he delivered the decision in the Charles River Bridge Case in 1837. Kent thereupon lost all confidence in the guardianship of the Supreme Court, and wrote Story, "I had now rather read the more humble labors of Circuit and State Courts." To him Taney's opinion destroyed the Dartmouth College bulwark, and so led toward anarchy. It took the mind of the profession some time, and of the country even longer, to realize that Taney was merely imposing another restraint on the Commonwealth of Massachusetts, to keep it from preventing the progress of railroads and canals, that he was in effect following the philosophy of negation even further than had Marshall. Historians of the court always have some difficulty with the subsequent history of Taney's thought, because it soon becomes difficult to make any sharp distinctions, or any that seem important today, between his processes and those of Marshall. When, for example, in 1847 he rendered his great affirmation of the right of eminent domain against the arguments of Webster, he did not theorize about positive exertions of governmental authority, but saw in this action still another negation. All contracts are made in subordination to certain conditions "superinduced by the pre-existing and higher authority of the laws of nature, of nations, or of the community to which the parties belong . . . conditions inherent and paramount wherever a necessity for their execution shall occur." While many Democrats exulted that this ruling was a blow for free men against corporations, the more astute could perceive that Taney was still arguing for the sovereign right of restraint. In 1843, in the case of *Bronson* v. *Kinzie*, holding that an Illinois statute changing the mortgage law of the state impaired the obligation of contracts, he reinforced the Dartmouth College doctrine with an argument that would have amazed Marshall and did delight Story. And when he came to the act of his judicial career by which his name will be known to fame or infamy, the case of Dred Scott, Taney beautifully believed that he was adhering to the native American tradition, that he was making no affirmative determination, that he was merely denying to Congress any power to exclude slavery from the territories.

There is both a charm and a pathos to the history of Constitutional thinking in these decades, though both of these qualities are lost in modern accounts. The bogyman was "usurpation." But which was usurping, the national government or the states? While each strove to keep the other in chains, the national energy flowed into inventions, explorations, and wars. Often the student of the Supreme Court grows weary of dire predictions, so often made by opposing counsel, that unless this or that case is decided aright, the nation will fall apart, regress into the "anarchy" of the Confederation. After a while he realizes that, no matter how eloquently this awful alternative was presaged, it was a rhetorical gambit which ministered to psychological needs rather than to precise legal definition. There never was a serious possibility of reverting to the Confederacy of the 1780's. The only live option was a civil war. The lawyers and the judges cherished the bogy because they were afraid of the other, more terrible prospect. The Marshall court and the Taney court thus kept their purpose fixed upon the idea of restriction, because, perhaps, if nothing were permitted, no violence would result. The party differences within the profession become, in the larger perspective, of minor importance. Whether they always knew what they were doing—and despite their acumen it seems all too often that they did not know—they were striving to clear a highway to the future by negating *something*. They no doubt had in the back of their minds, or at the bottom of their hearts, a conception of American destiny. What they variously said, in fact, was that by imposing restriction, here, there, or everywhere, this destiny might of itself be fulfilled.

CHAPTER SIX

The Hinge of Negation

Some governments may chiefly seek to guard against the turbulence of the poorer classes; some to repress the oligarchical insolence of a privileged class; some to prevent the union of the powers of the Church and of the State; some to check the authority of the sovereign. These points were certainly not overlooked by the founders of our government,—the heroes and leaders of a popular revolution; but it will hardly be denied that with us as a practical question, the legislative power is the most formidable, nor that our system chiefly aims to guard the citizen against the legislature,—to protect him against the power of a majority taking the shape of unjust law. And it is to be observed, also, that the unjust action of government with us is most likely to take the shape of attacks upon rights of property. All government, indeed, resolves itself into the protection of life, liberty, property. Life and liberty in our fortunate condition are, however, little likely to be injuriously affected by the action of the body politic. Property is very differently situated. It is therefore of the highest moment, if possible, to obtain a clear idea as to the nature and extent of the protections which guard our rights of property from attack under color of law,—to determine, in other words, what is a *vested right*.

—THEODORE SEDGWICK, *A Treatise on the Rules which Govern the Interpretation and Application of Statutory and Constitutional Law*, 1857

1.

BLACKSTONE AMERICANIZED

It is a truism that the long struggle of English lawyers against Crown and church was not only for rights of assembly, free discussion, religious liberty, but chiefly for the sanctity of the citizen's private possessions. Americans assumed that they had entered into this heritage. Laws as to personal property were crude in the Middle Ages, said

Kent, "until the revival of trade and manufactures, the decline of the feudal tenures, and the increase of industry, wealth, and refinement, had contributed to fix the affections upon personal property, and to render the acquisition of it an object of growing solicitude." More than any other nation, England proved that by learning to respect property rights it could attain unprecedented worldly prosperity while fully enjoying "enlightened civil liberty."

In the inspired phrasing of the Declaration of Independence the conventional trilogy of the English eighteenth century—"life, liberty, and property"—was changed into "life, liberty, and the pursuit of happiness." Thomas Jefferson left to posterity a conundrum, but the mass of American lawyers never doubted that his happiness was a polite genteelism for the acquisition of wealth. In the agrarian days of 1790 this would have been too obvious to need stressing, but with the dizzy rush of the economy after 1815 an apprehension arose lest Jefferson's words might become a real threat. The lawyers rallied once more to the figure who had so often provided their strength and conso- lation: Blackstone. Here he was of tremendous help, for he freed them from allegiance to the notion that property rights derived from the Lockean social compact or that they were in any sense dependent on the society's recognition that the owner had made something his own by mixing his labor in it. Not at all, said Blackstone: the concept of property exists even before there is any society at all; to protect the individual in the enjoyment of this absolute right, vested in him by the immutable law of nature, governments are created. The law "will not authorize the least violation of it; no, not even for the general good of the whole community." Blackstone would not even admit the validity of eminent domain, so that American Whigs could congratu- late themselves upon their "liberal" mentality, in the legalistic con- notation, when they learned to consent to this principle. Above all, said Samuel Chipman, Blackstone exploded the errors of Locke, Gro- tius, and Pufendorf by demonstrating that property is a law which "nature herself has written upon the hearts of mankind: that the no- tion of property is universal, and is suggested to the mind of man by reason and nature, prior to all civil institutions." Thus the absolute right of property was prior to the Constitution of the United States, to the constitutions of the states, to all enumerated bills of rights, to Jefferson's dangerous verbiage, but above all prior to and supreme over any of the political trickeries associated with the name of Andrew Jackson. True, acknowledged Chipman, society may rule here and there about the modes of acquisition, but let it never dream that property is "an artificial system." Blackstone has shown us: "The right of property . . . is founded in the law of nature, and is antecedent to all civil regulations."

The work of James Kent may be said to be that he improved Blackstone into an explicit denial of the contractual idea upon which the American society was supposedly founded. Gingerly he mentioned the names of Hobbes and Machiavelli, who he knew were in ill repute among the righteous, but he took immense (and obvious) satisfaction in saying that the notion of a state of nature preceding the existence of separate property was the most extravagant of human fantasies. Here he spoke not only as the New Yorker, but even more as the Connecticut Calvinist—he having shed his Calvinism. "It has been truly observed," he said with conscious irony, "that the first man who was born into the world, killed the second; and when did the times of simplicity begin?" Kent, whose leisure was relieved with copious readings in Latin, had his fun at the expense of Ovid and Virgil. They dreamed foolish visions, by which America should not be distracted:

The sense of property is inherent in the human breast, and the gradual enlargement and cultivation of that sense, from feeble force in the savage state, to its full vigour and maturity among polished nations, forms a very instructive portion of the history of civil society.

America must never permit itself to be seduced by classical mirages of the Golden Age, or ever suppose that its own colonial primitivism was not a fiercely contested struggle for property. By obedience to this law of acquisition, man "is enabled to display the various and exalted powers of the human mind."

Precisely here, however, the problem of property in a democracy became worrisome, for as Kent constantly said, "A state of equality as to property is impossible to be maintained." Constant insistence that the function of the law was to respect property by checking attacks upon it meant the positive assertion of inequality. This made for no metaphysical difficulties in England, where a hierarchy of classes was the premise of the whole society, but it had to be stated more cautiously in a democracy. One possibility was the dressing of economic differences in the garb of morality, as did Story when saying that the basic problem in government "must always be a question of the highest moment, how the property-holding part of the community may be sustained against the inroads of poverty and vice." Yet there seemed something more than a little incongruous for lawyers in America to turn poverty into a moral rebuke. The clergy could improve economic status into the evidence of a man's spiritual condition, yet even they had to be careful. The more circumspect jurists had the sound instinct not to confuse disciplines, but to insist simply upon property as a legal right and let the consequences follow naturally. Thus Theophilus Parsons, delivering the Phi Beta Kappa address at Harvard in 1835 (two years before Emerson!), gravely argued that the way to avert the horrors of anarchy was not by police, parties, or ballots, "but by bringing home to the minds and hearts of the people, the indisputable principles, the clear and simple truths, on which the rights of property rest." If these truths were infused throughout the whole society, then "the two contending classes," those who have wealth and those who covet it, could meet on a common basis: "Then would property be safe, for who would dare assail it, when the whole would rise up to defend it, for the reason that it lay in the hands of its possessor, and was known to be there, for the benefit of the whole." The beautiful advantage of this pleading was that it offered no gratuitous insult to the morality or intelligence of the propertyless, and yet appeared to enlist them of their own volition in the work of imposing restraint upon themselves.

There was a further advantage in this way of presenting the case, that the onus for anarchical tendencies could be laid, not upon ordinary yeomen, but upon the political scoundrels whom they, in their innocence, were beguiled into electing. Story built this appeal into a clever rhetorical question. What, he asked, is personal liberty if it does not include the right to enjoy the fruits of one's industry? "What is the privilege of a vote, if the majority of the hour may sweep away the earnings of our whole lives, to gratify the rapacity of the indolent, the cunning, or the profligate, who are borne into power upon the tide of a temporary popularity?" In public speech, as contrasted with their private lamentations, the great of the age endeavored to excuse the democracy for the vulgarity of its leaders, and were wont to conclude with every show of confidence, as did Story in his inaugural of 1829, "that a knowledge of the law and a devotion to its principles are vital to a republic, and lie at the very foundation of its strength." This conclusion emerged, however, at the end of an eloquent paragraph which commenced with the proposition "There can be no freedom, where there is no safety to property." In his private talk, Story lived in a cloud of augmenting gloom about the national future, a darkness which he enjoyed and which never dampened his spirits. A year before his end, in 1844, he asserted that Americans were "too corrupt, imbecile and slavish," in their dependence upon demagogues, and predicted that "we shall sink lower and lower in National degradation." Translated into specific terms, his apprehensions meant that he did not fear violations of the Bill of Rights but only assaults upon the rich.

An amazingly frank article in the first issue of *The American Law Magazine* (Philadelphia, July, 1843) goes straight to the point. Personal liberty, trial by jury, the franchise, liberty of conscience, of speech and of the press—these, the writer says, are not even topics for discussion in the United States. Indeed, the matter-of-fact way it is assumed that these concepts are protected by "their own democratic affinity" brings us back to the question of what is liberal and what conservative in America, for the piece goes on to contend that the real concern of society is the protection of property, that it is property that "eminently stands in need of every parchment barrier . . . thrown around it" for its preservation. Democracy, says this writer, is incurably hostile to the possessions of the few; since it now appears that the authors of the Constitution failed to place sufficient safeguards around private property, "it must go far to detract from the reputation which those great and good men have acquired for wisdom and foresight." It is surely a commentary on the age, in which we might suppose that threats to estates, whether in the form of revolutions or of income taxes, were unthinkable, that the legal mind was prepared to go so far as even to blame the Constitution itself for not providing the sort of inhibition upon threats to property which lawyers declared the democracy intended. In our eyes the debate of 1830 and 1840 may even appear comic; yet it not only has implications for the great discussions of later decades, but it prefigures lines of social conflict. Out of unity arises diversity, though perhaps nobody on either side, in either of the classes whom Parsons found "contending," had any notion whatsoever of starting a war. After all, everybody agreed that the great victory—freedom of speech and of opinion, above all religious liberty—had been won. Only a few cranks yet called in question the sacred rights of property. Why, then, this nervous hysteria among the lawyers?

In general, they were reluctant to confess their reason—more embarrassed than, let us say, the literary exiles of the later nineteenth century. It was not a matter of being Whigs or Democrats: it was a question of their discomfort about where, in America, the source of power resided. "Power," said James Walker in 1852, "is human will"; in America we have had to learn, though with pain, that one generation cannot bind another, that the majority can do no wrong. Here we confront a terrifying conflict within the Common Law which the profession had so wonderfully vindicated: "Certainly the architects of it did not intrust the preservation of property to those who might have an interest in its destruction." So effective was the triumph of the metaphysical lawyers of the nineteenth century, we forget how real to them was the possibility that the Jacksonian majority might override the immunities of property. They were children of the romantic past, and cited the French Revolution as a defeat of reason which might be repeated in America by a spirit of anarchy in which "the right of personal property is ever openly insulted and entirely prostrated."

As events moved on, the profession was reduced (when not arguing specific cases) to dire predictions. These become a part of the climate of sensitivity in the period; eventually they color the curiously fatalistic complexion of the Civil War, in which the South fought for a cause legally foredoomed. The "conservative" planters charged against a constitutionalism which had long since been formulated as a check on precisely such violence as theirs.

In the public forum, as I have said, the mood of hopeless-sounding pessimism in which Story would write to Kent or to Choate hardly dared appear; the customary formula became a conditional warning. "If the period should ever arrive," said *The United States Law Intelligencer* in 1830, when barriers erected by the Constitution can be overridden by a majority, then must the citizen be without redress. Often when this ominous threat is voiced, there lies behind it a specific controversy; this particular article is a discussion of the Providence Bank Case, in which Story's opinion had declared, "That government can scarcely be deemed free, where the rights of property are left solely dependent upon the will of a legislative body, without any restraint." The changes that could be rung on the "if" clauses were infinite, and the ubiquity of them in the decades before the war surely reveals the deep-seated insecurity. "If the legal profession should become so incompetent, so corrupt," as to impair the absolute right of the possessor, said Thomas Clerke in his exposition of Blackstone in 1840, "it would invite all the evils of despotism." "If the legislature can take the property of A and transfer it to B," declared Justice Bronson in 1857, "they can take A himself, and either shut him up in prison or put him to death."

It appears that most of these conditional clauses were directed against state legislatures; generally the prophets clung to a distinction between these bodies (which might be corrupt) and the people (whose instincts were fundamentally sound). As Daniel Webster proudly remarked in 1820, in no country was property so equally diffused, wherefore every man is interested in preserving the present state of things, because "while he cannot see what he might gain, he sees clearly what he might lose, by change." Behind these warnings lurked a fear that somehow the people themselves, even in this prosperous America, might break loose, that the beast might spring, that property would be invaded, not by a legislature passing confiscatory laws, but by the mob. In Charlestown, Massachusetts, in 1834, the specter became real; a crowd of otherwise law-abiding citizens, worked into a rage against the mounting Catholic immigration, sacked and burned the Ursuline Convent. Judge Peter Thacher, in his charge to the grand jury, revealed what actually had long been the secret dread of jurists: a tendency toward popular violence had been growing in other cities, said Thacher, though Boston had hitherto not been infected: "in the destruction of the Ursuline Convent, on Mount Benedict, it was seen, that a portion of the people could wage war, equally against political liberty, the sacred rights of property, and religious charity." That he was more occupied with the second than with either the first or third of his causes Thacher revealed by turning his indictment of the rioters into a charge against the conspiracy of laborers; in this charge emerged the hitherto unspoken admonition of the law of property:

Why are not all the fruits of the earth equally rich and wholesome? And why towers the oak in grandeur to heaven, while the shrub at its base is trodden under feet? Will vain regrets, and still vainer discontent change the course of nature? The policy of the law preserves equality of political rights among the citizens; but equality of wealth and condition cannot exist among men, so long as they are divided into the provident and improvident, the idle and diligent.

Memory of the Charlestown riot continued for years to haunt not only the conscience of Massachusetts but of Protestant America; the latter was torn, and genuinely torn, between its "Know-Nothing" instincts and the lessons which the lawyers had impressed upon it. A hostility to Popery, though in itself an admirable disposition, which in its zeal resorts to violence would, said an orator to the alumni of the University of Pennsylvania, provide a model for those who hold that property should be equally distributed:

If it is allowable for the people to pull down a place of worship, or to hang up a dozen individuals for supposed misdemeanours, there can be no crime in making equal the measure of human enjoyment. . . . The moment that the law is violated for any purpose, or under any pretence, and the violation is acquiesced in, its sanctity is gone, and through its broken arches and dilapidated walls the spoiler may enter upon the fairest portion of the heritage.

One may say that here, rather than in the Girard Case, the inherent opposition of the law to the Revival came into the open. Certainly the lawyers made an impressive gesture by putting aside their religious predispositions and by arraying themselves solidly in condemnation of the Charlestown rioters. George Ticknor Curtis was in 1847 still worrying himself and the Commonwealth of Massachusetts over the lesson of Mount Benedict:

Property itself is among the grand instruments by which the world is enabled to emerge out of Barbarism, by which Christianity is sustained and propagated. He that has none is benefited and blessed by its institution and preservation. . . . The state that does not protect the rights of property, to the full extent of earthly power, especially against open and public violation, loses sight of its own highest policy, and breaks its contract with the individual, and weakens that of all its members.

It is hardly an insight into the complicated abolitionist controversy, yet this point is to be borne in mind, that the lawyers—having become the pontiffs of this society—developed an obsessive horror of what abolitionism would effect toward creating "Mobs," so that, even when their moral inclinations were opposed to slavery, they fell into the trap, set by their own confusion, of condoning antiabolition mobs in their wish to check all mobs whatsoever. The crux of their confusion was, obviously, not their disposition for or against emancipation; they were caught in a cleft stick between their conscience and their professionalism by their commitment to the proposition that the purpose of the law was not to enforce freedom but to protect property from legislative, popular, or fanatical invasion. They and the nation were betrayed into the Civil War not by a spirit of equivocation (even though Daniel Webster or Judge Thacher often seem pretty far gone into outright prevarication) but by what was on the whole noble, the maintenance of legalistic negation. If this became tragedy, and many men died for it, there is a certain grandeur about the lawyers' restraint. As professionals, they would not demand what the evangelicals tried to demand from ordinary men, more than men can emotionally respond to. The result was that while abolitionists called the Constitution a covenant with hell, hundreds with a property stake in the society, or maybe only with a hope of some day having such a stake, filled the ranks of the Union armies.

2.

JUDICIAL INDEPENDENCE

From the Revolution well into the next century, a campaign was steadily waged in the several states to remove the property qualification from the suffrage. There is no need to repeat the familiar story except to note that the contest of the jurists against the democracy at the polls was also a part of their struggle against the popular election of judges. The student can readily see, if once he recaptures the mood which Hoffman, Kent, and Story imparted to the profession in the 1820's, how the double movement, which to them seemed a single conspiracy—the removal of the property qualification for the franchise and popular election of judges—would appear a revolution, not so abruptly violent as the French Revolution, but bound to be in the long run more devastating. What is amazing—this seems not yet sufficiently appreciated—is the relative ease with which both objectives were obtained despite the lawyers' magisterial assurance that the accomplishment of either one, let alone of both, insured the ruin of the Republic.

The property qualification need concern us little, for it soon became obvious that in Jacksonian America the argument had little validity outside one or two cities, and not much even there. Webster was right in saying in 1820 that most Americans could acquire enough property to qualify if they wanted to make the effort. James Kent at the New York Constitutional Convention in 1821 delivered himself in the grand manner of his favorite classical orators, seeing a Cataline under every bush. Universal suffrage, he said, will jeopardize the rights of property; the history of every age proves that the poor covet the plunder of the rich, that the majority tyrannize over the minority, and that "the indolent and profligate" will cast the burden of society upon the industrious and virtuous. *"There is a tendency in ambitious and wicked men to influence these combustible materials."* Ergo, only he who already owns some property—the more the better—should be allowed to vote. At the Massachusetts Convention in this same year, identical arguments were produced, although Story introduced an amusing variation by pointing out that experience in America already had shown that property did not stay too long in any one family, that the second or third generation dispersed it, and so we should not fear a permanent plutocracy. To us, in retrospect, the path of the juggernaut seems to have been irresistible, though we ought to remind ourselves that it *was* contested. Still, in 1859 Henry W. Warner would tell the fiftieth reunion of his class at Union College that paupers and vagabonds could now not only vote but be elected. He did not claim that property makes men wise, but he thought it did indicate orderly habits, that it was "a highly conservative element in a state system"; he could only lament, "We *had* it largely in our system, but we have thrown it away." As an episode in the life of the mind—apart from the political squabbles—this about summarizes the story. Grave doubts would arise, after the Civil War, among even such stalwart democrats as Gideon Welles and Walt Whitman about the absolute validity of universal suffrage, but by then it was clearly too late to find a road back. The lawyers of the 1840's had definitely lost their case; this may in several senses be taken as their most enduring achievement.

While the historian insists that they were bound to yield before the march of Jacksonian democracy, we must also point out, for the history of the mind, that they quickly became confused in their own thinking by their tardiness in recognizing the transformation of the very concept of property which was taking place under their own ministrations. Several times in the *Commentaries* James Kent confessed that while mostly in America we talked of the laws of property as applying to real property—and in this respect were still "under the control of principles derived from feudal policy"—wealth was already centered not in land but in corporations. In 1827, and perhaps to the end of his days, Kent could not comprehend the revolution, but only shake his learned head with the lamentation, "we seem to have no moral means to resist it, as was done at Rome, by the unshaken determination of the Emperor Trajan." Jackson was no Trajan. Simon Greenleaf in 1834, at his own inaugural, was less perturbed; the present, he announced, is no longer the age of solitary and individual effort, but of "copartnerships of the mercantile world"; all the more reason, he concluded, why the power that would move this complication of machinery should be "the all-pervading influence of law." Hesitantly and gropingly the courts did begin in this period to discover a few foundations for corporation law—in this endeavor Taney's Charles River Bridge decision is again a landmark—but on the whole I think it fair to say that before the Civil War what they chiefly did was to confuse the notion of property to such an extent that the original philosophy of a property qualification for suffrage fell apart of itself. Kent could die in the assurance that Marshall's decision in *Marbury* v. *Madison* was the greatest of all time "in favor of constitutional liberty, and of the security of property in this country."

The jurists therefore retained, so to speak, only one bastion from which they could resist change: they fought to the end against the popular election of judges. Everything that the emerging profession had contended for—its erudition, its scholarship, its inviolate morality, its self-respect—seemed here at stake. The long, heroic struggle to impress upon the democracy the infinite difference between the learned, competent lawyer and the pettifogger would, they were sure, all be lost if Natty Bumppos and David Crocketts could choose their judges, for they would be certain to call upon the pettifoggers.

Whether in the first decades of the new century the populace was already muttering against the lordly security of judges, or the lawyers, sensing their disposition, endeavored to forestall them, by 1820 defenders of the system gave every appearance of an organized band. The generalissimo, here as elsewhere, was Kent. An independent judiciary, he wrote in the first volume of the *Commentaries,* is the only kind fitted to expound our Constitution: "It is only by the free exercise of this power that courts of justice are enabled to repel assaults, and to protect every part of the government, and every member of the community, from undue and destructive innovations upon their chartered rights." Timothy Walker's widely used textbook of 1837 shows how the argument had become perfected: judges appointed for life are placed beyond the reach of fear or favor; from their secure elevation, all disturbing influences are removed, "they are left to the calm and fearless exercise of their unbiassed judgments; and there is a life before them in which to perfect themselves for duty." In the year Walker was published, John Sergeant pleaded earnestly with the Convention of the State of Pennsylvania that he would yield anything "rather than go home with the slightest apprehension, that any human being should be tried for his life, his liberty, his property, or his reputation, by popular clamour or the popular will."

The plea was by 1837 indeed becoming frenetic, for the movement for election of judges had emerged from the murmuring stage to open advocacy, with an ordered argument which threw another strong and disturbing light on the unsteadiness of the foundations of American law—those which Kent and Story had so earnestly striven to prove were solid as granite. *The Democratic Review* in 1848 (the year in which, to the utter dismay of men like Rufus Choate, the judiciary of New York did become elective) summarized the case of the insurgents: We had borrowed the principle of an independent judiciary from England, and plainly the state of affairs which caused it to triumph there never existed in the United States. In England the judges must be independent of the Crown, but "does it follow, therefore, that our judiciary should be appointed for life, when we have neither king nor aristocracy to dread?" Far from there being anything to dread in the possibility of popular clamor inflicting injustice upon men or property through elected judges, the fact is that throughout the land there is jealousy and distrust of the present judiciary. Unless it be reformed, "greater evils and heavier calamities will weigh down the spirits of our people." How can anyone argue that the most important functionaries of the government, who have to decide questions involving life, liberty, and property, "should hold their appointment from, and be responsible to, some other authority in the state than that of the people themselves"? Even in Massachusetts the conservative bar trembled as George Hood of Lynn stood on the floor of the Constitutional Convention in 1853 and declared that whoever opposes an elective judiciary has no sympathy with democracy, "knows nothing of those sublime and pure principles of democratic liberty, which are but the reflex of the great system of Christianity itself."

Filled by the gusts of such oratory, the sails of the principle of election swelled. Pennsylvania was conquered in 1850 and from that year the abolitionists became powerful champions as they contended persuasively that judges elected in Northern states would not dare enforce the fugitive slave law. As the popular cause won again and again, the lawyers fought a losing rear-guard action, by now generally in the form of lamentations. What can elected courts give of security or honor, wrote Horace Binney in 1859, "if the wheels of the instrument receive a twist or bias through party fear or favor, or are so ignorantly and presumptuously governed, as to let them cut and eat into each other, until they work falsely or uncertainly"? For by the approaching end of this decade the argument for an independent judiciary was belatedly developing a new dimension. Honest men in both the South and the North were suddenly becoming painfully aware of it. As *The American Law Register* put it in 1856, a black cloud is on the horizon, "the trembling of the earth and the stillness of the air are prophetic to our fears"; unless at this moment of crisis we can re-establish a judiciary independent and universal, we shall hasten into an anarchy of principles and a chaos of decisions, "till all law at last shall be extinguished by an appeal to arms." It may be doubted that had the elective principle been reversed the Civil War would have been averted, but the arguments for and against it suggest again the uneasiness of the conscience of the profession for not having saved the nation from this ghastly holocaust of property.

It must be acknowledged that the legal fraternity, in combating judicial election, were not merely protecting a scholastical code—

though this was a powerful influence. Their profession, always vigorous, often melodramatic, that their function was only to discover the law, to interpret the true meaning of statutes, never to make their decisions compulsory, was one they genuinely believed. They insisted over and over that by rendering opinions they did not *legislate*. In spite of Jeffersonian and Jacksonian objections to the Supreme Court, they clung to this conception. Otherwise they could not act as negativists. As Chief Justice of New York—before he acquired the wider discretion of Chancellor—Kent remarked in 1809 that the judicial was the feeblest department of the government (he quoted Montesquieu), and hence "is so checked, and so controlled, that it cannot essentially abuse its powers." An encomium upon him in 1838 made a special point that Kent never, whatever his passions, imagined that he was at liberty to promulgate rules from the bench. On the contrary, "He contents himself with administering the common law, as he finds it, without the rashness to presume himself wiser than the law, or the vanity of distinguishing himself by innovation." There were circumstances in America which might have persuaded the judges to treat the democracy more ruthlessly than they did. The controversial opinions of the Supreme Court are the first case in point, and none more so than *Dred Scott;* the great fact remains that the majority of the judges, state or national, felt a duty to refrain, to the extent they could, from extrapolating edict out of law. In all sincerity, wise as they fancied themselves, they strove not to be wiser than the law.

In the long run, as we know, the efforts of Jacksonian judges to define the criteria according to which they should restrict themselves became precedents. Confusing precedents, no doubt, because as Theodore Sedgwick pleaded in 1857, the idea that judges could mold law according to their own notions, making it conform to what they supposed it *ought* to be, could never have arisen "except at a time when the division lines between the great powers of government were but feebly drawn, and their importance very imperfectly understood." Sedgwick tried to hold off the strife, as well as any lawyer could, by telling the judiciary to be content with its acknowledged prerogatives, "and not attempt to arrogate an authority so vague and so dangerous as the power to define and declare the doctrines of natural law and of abstract right." Sedgwick's voice was almost the last rationality of the Kent and Story era. The lawyers had lost their case for the property qualification and for judicial independence. They would therefore have to insist upon judicial self-limitation in order to protect the courts against pettifoggers. But they confessed in advance that whether under legal demagogues or under qualified jurists, they rested their standing in the community upon the prestige of the learning with which the resplendent generation had bedazzled America.

An essential maneuver in the exquisite strategy by which the courts maintained their cause, despite the rising tide of democracy, was a prolongation of their advocacy of the Common Law into fervent adherence to the principle of judicial restraint. As long as they insisted upon this self-limitation, who could attack them—or, rather, whoever then assaulted them would not dangerously disturb the peace of the nation. Once more, James Kent laid down the lines of conduct which Roger Taney imagined that he was following in *Dred Scott*. The business of the legislature, Kent said in *Yates* v. *The People* of 1810, is to make the law, but that of the court is to pronounce it. Hence, as by the self-imposed rule of restraint a court cannot enlarge the powers of the legislature, so it cannot assume unto itself powers not given it by law. A court that would arrogate to itself such prerogatives "would soon become the object of intrigue, the slave of prejudice, the organ of party, terrible to the suitor, and destructive of the established law of the land." While democrats digested this intelligence, and unwillingly admitted that they did not want courts to be so prostituted, they learned that this rigor of discipline meant that the courts more than ever had to follow "the sober sense of the English Common Law," which the founders had "most providentially ingrafted into our system." If we depart from this plain standard, said Kent, "we set everything afloat, and our constitution becomes a mass of unintelligible matter." The point would therefore be, as was constantly insisted upon, that even an elected bench would need to be professionally qualified, nor could it vote merely the wishes of constituents. Instead of lowering the standard of qualification, said *The Western Law Journal* in 1851, election of judges demands increased learning, because "it is our boast that we live in an age of progress and increased intellectual improvement."

We take the success of the courts in defending their integrity so much for granted that we forget how in the early nineteenth century their champions believed that they barely survived the gale. The French Revolution and the Jeffersonian victory, remembered Joseph Hopkinson when eulogizing Mr. Justice Bushrod Washington in 1830, so agitated the passions of the people that the one thing which saved them was the rock of the judiciary rising above the storm: "Independent, truly independent, in all times and under all circumstances, it yields neither to the influence of the executive, nor to the clamours of the multitude." There would not have been such resort to fervent eloquence had not the orators been seriously worried, as when for instance Choate pleaded for the tenure of judges at the Massachusetts convention by asserting that they had to be acquainted not only with statutes, "but that other ampler, that boundless jurisprudence, the common law, which the successive generations of the State have silently built up."

The only mystery was why Choate should suppose that, in recent years, this building up of the Common Law in Massachusetts had been silent. That the Commonwealth had become wealthy was indisputable. No less obvious was the way in which even a popularly elected judiciary could and must preserve its independence. *The American Law Magazine* in 1843, in an article on "The Security of Private Property," summed up thousands of pages by saying that an independent judiciary was the sole guarantee of American liberties against the "tyranny" of either the executive or the legislature. In our eyes there may yet have emerged no really sizable "tyranny" from either of these branches; however, citizens of the Republic were preternaturally sensitive, and so those who feared the lawyers had no choice but to endorse them. Most eminently in this country, Theodore Sedgwick concluded, liberty could exist only in fellowship with law. However glorious our past, however alluring our future, "it is vain to suppose that American freedom can be maintained except just so long as our people shall exhibit the capacity justly and intelligently to administer, and the disposition steadily and loyally to obey, the government of WRITTEN LAW."

Laws in written form were chiefly laws regulating property. And clearly there would not have been so much talk about property in the period had there not existed a strange foreboding. "The tenure of property," ventured John Whipple in 1851, "is more frail than most men here imagine." Hundreds of lawyers publicly grieved that "under the magic name of equality, the abominable doctrines of agrarianism are beginning to be openly avowed"—and by "agrarianism" they meant some mysterious attack upon property. By 1850 their worry became more concentrated. George Ticknor Curtis—who had denounced the Ursuline Convent outrage as a desecration of property—set the tone for the next decade of anxiety:

To cultivate this fair and noble country; to adorn it with all that wealth and art can bring; to expand its civilization, its intellectual and its religious culture; to cherish fraternal sentiments towards every part of it; to hold fast by the fundamental principles of its civil polity, and to hold it firmly in that course of progress which those principles have marked out for it; in a word, to cherish and to cling to the Union,—this, this is our comprehensive duty.

No greater falsification can be imposed upon a majestic folk struggle than to present the American Civil War in doctrinaire Marxian terms, to see in the North a militant uprising of bourgeois capitalism. Yet there can be no question that the legalists of unification had, ever since the Revolution, done a thorough job of making the reign of law in the country one with the inviolability of property. The North did not have to fight the South in order to preserve its property rights, but only to maintain the rule of the law. The law could not prevent the war, which was a count against it, but it could survive. Kent, Story, and the great theorists of the Jacksonian era had made that much certain.

CHAPTER SEVEN

Codification

To the student of the common law, law reform is the most hackneyed and repulsive, or the freshest, deepest and most absorbing theme. It is not the *esprit de corps* that makes him dread a popular reform. It is no fear of attacks on the judiciary or the profession, but the feeling that the body of the people does not know how to construct the edifice they desire, that they do not know how to use the tools. It is like the feeling of a mechanic or an artist when he sees some novice wasting his time, spoiling his tools, destroying his materials, and making a botch of his work, and a fool of himself. But a true reform, based on a knowledge of the wants of the people, the means to supply them and the best mode of their application, is always welcome. . . . No class has such control over not only the pecuniary affairs, but the peace, the order, harmony and proper tone of feeling of society, as the lawyers. No class should be, and none is, so confidently trusted as they are to do any work legitimately professional. It is only where people of other callings, led by some false prejudice, attempt to carry out some vague plan to effect, they know not what, that the people have to fear.

—"Advancement of the Law by Lawyers," *The Law Reporter*, August, 1848

1.

RATIONAL AND SCIENTIFIC SUBLIMITY

In 1791 the legislature of Pennsylvania, finding themselves bewildered by their total ignorance of what constituted the laws of the state, appealed to James Wilson, by then an associate justice of the Supreme Court. He was delighted to assist them, and promptly explained what was necessary. It sounded very simple, very easy to accomplish. The point was that in Pennsylvania jurisprudence the Common Law was actually the greater part, local statute the lesser, but nobody knew which was which. What more obvious than for Wilson to formulate a

rational digest, arranging the several subjects into alphabetical order, and under each heading to collect all relevant laws, both statute and Common, into "a natural series, and to a just form"? Wilson was a product of the Enlightenment, and his enthusiasm (a word he would frown on) for this project glowed with the spirit of his century:

It is high time that law should be rescued from this injurious imputation [of obscurity]. Like the other sciences, it should now enjoy the advantages of light, which have resulted from the resurrection of letters; for, like the other sciences, it has suffered extremely from the thick veil of mystery spread over it in the dark and scholastick ages.

Prophetically enough, while Wilson assumed that the legislature of a state founded on Jefferson's Declaration would encourage every effort to emerge from "scholastick" blackness, that body got into an angry debate, refused to appropriate anything for the undertaking, and poor Wilson died with his project barely commenced.

The story is indeed prophetic, though in ways which the participants of 1791 could not have understood. For Wilson the issue was only rationality, and to his eighteenth-century temper there could not conceivably be any objection, among citizens who had expelled George III, against bringing their body of law out of medieval murkiness. However, Wilson may be accused of the kind of naïveté which doctrinaire rationalists of his time often displayed. Perhaps he did not know of the rather brutal lesson that had already been administered in Virginia to the archapostle of American rationalism, Thomas Jefferson. The House of Delegates, inspired by the same confidence that exuded from the Declaration and by the same assurance which Wilson retained in 1791, voted on October 12, 1776, for a general revision of the laws. Jefferson at that time thought, as Wilson later was to suppose, that the work could quickly be done. The digest should and would be drawn up "with a single eye to reason, and the good of those for whose government it was framed." A committee was appointed, composed of men as learned in the law as could then have been assembled in the newborn states—along with Jefferson were Edmund Pendleton, George Wythe, George Mason, Thomas Ludwell Lee. But even this combination of geniuses found the task beyond their competence.

As Jefferson, with characteristic ruefulness, years later recounted the sad experience, the group had reluctantly to decide against framing the whole body of the law into "a code, the text of which should become the law of the land," because they, no less than Wilson's pupils, were pragmatic enough to realize, once they came to grips with the problem, that "every word and phrase in that text would become a new subject of criticism and litigation, until its sense should have been settled by numerous decisions, and that, in the meantime, the rights of property would be in the air." Jefferson's report on these cogitations, though written as late as 1809, when the issue of codification was showing itself not even scotched, let alone killed, displayed in its concluding phrase the ominous portent of the approaching debate.

Jefferson's manner of continuing the story, though possibly not historically precise, is even more prophetic. He says that the committee thereupon decided not to meddle with the Common Law—meaning the law "preceding the existence of the statutes, further than to accommodate it to our new principles and circumstances"—and then, to demonstrate how unrepentant he remained, he relates that the committee did have the courage to attempt a systematization of the statutes of Virginia, leaving out "everything obsolete or improper," reducing the whole to a moderate compass in the language of plain common sense, "divested of the verbiage, the barbarous tautologies and redundancies which render the British statutes unintelligible." Opposition to the importation of English law into the wilderness was not a monopoly of the David Crocketts. Jefferson, the intellectual, did strive, however, to make an exception for the decisions of Lord Coke, whose language in his opinions was so simple "as to make it safest not to change words where the sense was to be retained." But at precisely this point the fatal divisions arose: Pendleton would not agree with Jefferson; Lee died, Mason resigned, and the hodgepodge report was fiercely attacked by the "conservative" side of the legislature. A legal transition, unsatisfactory to all, was accomplished in Virginia only in the 1790's.

Several states did with varying degrees of efficiency issue digests of English statutes considered as still functioning in the independent sovereignties, but among the people, or at least among their spokesmen in legislatures, there was a strange reluctance to permit law to be systematized—a recalcitrance which men like Wilson found altogether mysterious, and which for them could not be adequately explained by Jefferson's fear that the composition of a new "Institute" would threaten property.

At first we too may find it odd that a democracy pervaded by a deep distrust of the Common Law should so object to making it rationally coherent. Indeed, it is fascinating to consider how, during these and subsequent decades, the ambivalence persisted between hostility to the intricacy of the Common Law and at the same time reluctance to abandon it as constituting the bulwark of rights and liberties.

Denouncers of the Common Law fulminated against its internal contradictions, its incoherencies, and above all its offering of a veritable invitation to clever lawyers to manipulate it in such a way as to extend their power over the whole society. No matter what his qualifications, any "scoundrel pettifogger," said John Neal in an address to Waterville College in 1830, regards laborers and farmers as beneath him in the scale of being; the lawyers have so bullied us that for their benefit we are building a fortress:

> . . . the *lawyers of America*—the *unanointed* rulers of the land—the law-givers by trade—the law-makers and the law-expounders—two offices wholly incompatible with each other, and at war with the first principles of our constitution—*yet always united here;* the lawyers of America—a body of men who, with all their acknowledged wisdom and virtue—acknowledged by themselves, if not by others, every day in the year, in every speech before every jury of the country—are satisfied to follow in the footsteps of a barbarous age forever, and who, notwithstanding their ostentatious patriotism wherever they are allowed to open their mouths, are in the daily habit of recognizing the Judges of Westminster as the interpreters of *our* law—as the perpetual legislators of America therefore—in other and plainer language, as the *Rulers* of this great Commonwealth of Nations.

It was this sort of oratory that voiced the sullen, defeated, but still-rumbling scorn of the Common Law. On the other hand, along with the grumbling, there often came, and sometimes in the same speech, not a demand that the Common Law be systematized, but a perverse glorification of the Common Law. A good example is a discourse of Philip Lindsley's at Nashville, a year after Neal's blast, which commences by calling the Common Law an "interminable, incomprehensible, labyrinthian mystery of torture and extortion," but which ends by extolling it as "this intricate and beautiful science, the very perfection of written reason," its only imperfections the result of its having fallen into the hands of "pettifogging smatterers" through the passive laziness of a populace unwilling to exert themselves to "detect and discountenance" quackery. A mentality which could simultaneously relish the exciting disorder of the law and still call it the perfection of reason not surprisingly found itself bored by the prospect of James Wilson's rational digest. Had Pendleton and Wilson succeeded in persuading the Revolutionary generation to systematize American law, one great joy of life would have been snuffed out, since the society offered no amusement more absorbing than the courtroom.

Yet there was also a mounting, sober argument that such frivolity might shortly become an expensive luxury. An Illinois justice in 1848 agreed that the Common Law originated out of the laws of natural right, but for Americans the problem had increasingly become "Is the Common Law only clay in the hands of the Courts, to be moulded and shaped by them to suit their wills?" America could outgrow the pettifoggers. Was the real danger, which could not be banished either by anger or irony, that the inconclusive character of the Common Law should become the instrument—in spite of repeated professions of judicial modesty—of rule by judges? Even as the sanctions James Wilson had evoked faded into the dying twilight of eighteenth-century rationality, a new anxiety arose out of the context of romantic freedom, which sometimes employed the older forms but which gave them an emphasis that would have bewildered Jefferson: unless the American Common Law could be regularized the democracy would find itself enslaved not to pettifoggers but to professional intellectuals.

American discussion could have wandered interminably on this darkling plain had it not been confronted by, as usual, a new invasion of ideas from England. This time the assault was headed by a single name—Jeremy Bentham. Because the reigning opinion in the United States, largely formed by the Revival, condemned him sight unseen, his influence on the Republic was curiously oblique. But Bentham did coin the word "codification," and though few Americans understood what he meant by it, yet if only by planting a slogan in the mind of America, Bentham marked it as decisively as did Immanuel Kant with the equally baffling term of "Transcendentalism."

Abusing Bentham was for several years a game at which both ministers and jurists played with gusto. While the first denounced Utilitarianism as a philosophy for pigs, the second, at their mildest, found his legal manner "repulsive and unconciliating," and called him a jurist of Laputa. In their more outspoken moments, they said he was "so thoroughly mad that we really think it would be no injustice to shut him up and keep him on bread and water until he should be brought by depletion, to some tolerable measure of common sense." "God preserve us," cried such a liberal as George Bancroft in 1827, "from the extreme remedy of general codification!"

Yet it may be that Bentham had a profound effect in America because the more he was excoriated, the more publicity codification received. A few were bound to note that his scorn of "Judge and Co." often sounded like a sophisticated version of Natty Bumppo's objection to legal artifice, and believers in democracy found a special appeal in the idea of a digest speaking in a language familiar to everybody, from which the father of a family might so teach his children as to "give to the precepts of morality the force and dignity of public morals." Furthermore, though Bentham himself was ridiculed in America, Brougham for some reason was not, and his famous speech on law reform to the Commons in 1828 was reprinted throughout the country. From Brougham and not from Bentham, it seemed to Emory Washburn in 1856, had flowed that spirit of reform which has pervaded English jurisprudence, embracing alike the interests of commerce and the arts, "while it has moulded and fitted these to the prescriptive rights of birth, and the rents and burdens of the tenantry of the soil." Reform was not the monster that codification threatened to become, especially as Americans could smugly insist that most of the abuses arraigned by Brougham had already been reformed by their procedures. As for those things which American lawyers had imported but which Brougham denounced—such as special pleading—competent critics had arisen in the nation, and our reform was proceeding comfortably. "The general character of the change," said *The American Law Magazine* in 1844, "is from subtlety to common sense, from form and technicality to reason and justice." Some reviewers of Brougham would lament that American law had advanced too recklessly, while others would boast of its progress, but both sorts would find in the spectacle of natural evolution conclusive proof that no such a priori apparatus as a code was remotely called for.

This persuasion was immensely strengthened by the lawyers' pride in what appeared to them to have become their speedy and unprecedented coming of age. They could brush aside such sneers as Neal's about their congratulating each other on their advances in wisdom and virtue because they were confident that this was exactly what they had done. They had achieved it precisely because they had resisted the temptation to make a premature doctrine out of their experience. "A legal system," said *The American Quarterly Review* in a tribute to Hoffman, "should never be manufactured for a nation; it should grow with its growth; be the spontaneous product of times and circumstances; and be modified from season to season, as the exigencies of the case require." In this sense, the truth is precisely opposite to what the mobs suppose, for through this legal self-restraint the people in effect are the legislators. Instead of being an instrument of reaction, the Common Law, seen in the proper historical perspective, is profoundly democratic. "Gentlemen in their closets cannot chalk out a rule which, anticipating all contingencies, or suiting all modifications of society, will expand or contract to fit the one or meet the other." By obvious implication, the author associated the effort at codification with an aristocratic plot.

Ringing a further subtle change on this strategy, another writer in the *Review* in 1829 asserted that the splendid success of the American jurists in the last thirty years had so upset the balance of the last two centuries that English jurists now devoutly studied American procedures to learn how to effect the reforms advocated by Brougham. "Their eyes are now turned to the legal profession of this country, as those who were the first to advance into the great field of philosophic jurisprudence." The multitudes who had denounced Story for being obsequious to Ellenborough may have blinked at receiving this intelligence, but the writer serenely went on to ask where, near perfection as we were, we should seek for improvement, and answered triumphantly:

Not in the schemes of the Benthams, for they are full of doubts and contradictions. Not in the specious power of a code, for a change so vital would shake our institutions to the centre, and create an amount of litigation almost as intolerable as intestine war.

To avoid, then, intestine war, we must continue to regard our principles for accommodating the Common Law as "the best practical system of jurisprudence invented by men." A passage of this sort goes far, it seems to me, toward accounting for the ferocity with which even the mildest mannered of the lawyers fought the whole idea of codification.

All the same, certain factors in the situation obstinately pointed toward codification. There was, for one thing, the success of Edward Livingston in codifying the rules of procedure and of criminal law in Louisiana. He built upon the Code Napoleon, which scholars of the Civil Law insisted was a quite different thing from what Bentham had in mind, even though Livingston was one of the few American lawyers who professed admiration for Bentham. Even Chancellor Kent admired Livingston's achievement. Charles Watts wrote that, having been educated as "a black-letter lawyer," he had been taught to worship the intricacy of the Common Law and to believe "that it was only men who had not industry or ability to master their profession" who would complain. Since his removal to Louisiana, his experience had imparted to him "the most decided and warm preference or superiority to the civil law as there practised over the Common Law as it exists in the Atlantic States." Ironically enough, the great textbooks, by their concerted effort to impose a logical structure upon their materials, became in effect drafts of codes. Hoffman could still be courteous in his 1826 volume; while standing firm on his belief that the entire jurisprudence of a country could never be reduced to a written code, he found good sense in Bentham, and had no fears that the Common Law would suffer were it corrected by principles "which originated in the Roman Digests, the Codes of the French empire, that of Louisiana." Within a few years so hospitable a tone became more difficult to maintain; the pundits who had originally demanded that ignorant candidates submit to the immense discipline not only of the Common Law and equity, but of the Civil Law, had increasingly to insist that for an American the Civil Law was only an intellectual relaxation which should never be seriously considered integral to his own system.

The debate became acrimonious as advocates of codification made their cause an indictment of the Common Law and thus confirmed the worst suspicions of the populace. William Sampson caused a sensation of terror when he defended the Journeymen Cordwainers of New York on the ground that the Common Law arguments against unionization should not apply, and publicly regretted that however immense the advantages gained by independence, "one thing should still be wanting to crown the noble arch—A NATIONAL CODE." Sampson carried the war into the very citadel of respectability with his *Discourse Upon the History of The Law* in 1823, which, after his slashing and jaunty Irish abuse of the Common Law, stoutly concluded that the only way we could escape the evils of special pleading or achieve certainty was by a complete codification. Only then, he asserted, to the horror of James Kent, will the law itself be cited instead of particular cases; only then "The law will govern the decisions of judges, and not the decisions the law."

Lawyers who about this time had been congratulating each other upon crushing the boorish American distrust of both law in general and the Common Law in particular were aghast to find the movement for codification becoming a political agitation. They could perceive it only as a still more serious threat to the arcana of their profession, because it was conducted not by ignorant Davy Crocketts or romanticizing pioneers like Natty Bumppo, but by trained lawyers. William Rawle in Philadelphia picked up in 1824 where James Wilson had left off thirty years before, and called for a reduction of "the uncertain corruscations of Pennsylvania equity, to the safe and steady light of chancery." In New York so revered an elder as Gulian Verplanck, than whom none could be more solid, heard himself accused of betrayal of his country because he suggested timid appreciation of Bentham. In South Carolina the movement for codification became indeed a legislative reality rather than a Benthamite fantasy, and was focused sharply in a masterful declamation by Thomas Smith Grimké, delivered to the Bar Association in Charleston on March 17, 1827, under the formidable title *An Oration on the Practicability and Expediency of Reducing the Whole Body of the Law to the Simplicity and Order of a Code*. In Massachusetts Robert Rantoul, in his oration at Scituate in 1836, wherein he treated the Common Law as though it were one of George III's intolerable acts, predicted that "All American law must be statute law." The point being that statute law *can* be codified!

Rantoul conveys to us little besides impassioned rhetoric, but Grimké, both in his *Oration* and in his solidly reasoned *Report* to the Senate of South Carolina, also in 1827, made the substantive plea for codification. So it should be noted that in 1831 Grimké had the courage to stand forth in defense of science against the South's devotion to literary classicism, and that his two sisters, Sarah and Angelina, after his death in 1834, moved to the North, became Quakers, and vigorous abolitionists. Before that drama, their brother was in 1827 consuming himself, and no doubt hastening his end, by fighting for codification.

Thomas Grimké was not so fiery a foe of the Common Law as either the Irish Sampson or the Yankee Rantoul; he protested against those who called it a chaos of absurdity and injustice, and admired its great "standard rules and maxims." He pleaded only that it be "redeemed from the bondage of a barbarous state of society and accommodated to the enlightened, benevolent, practical spirit of our own times." Yet this was enough to open him to the charge of being an enemy not merely to the Common Law but to all law and order. Despite these accusations, Grimké predicted that the "accommodation" could be made: "That it will be done, I believe." And the ground upon which he based his confidence makes him the most interesting of early codifiers.

Grimké advanced those "considerations of expediency" which his "fellow labourers in the cause of reformation" also stressed—that codification will substitute method for confusion, will base law upon principle rather than precedent, serve as a check upon irresponsible legislation, present the law in clearness and simplicity. He complained that no one mind could any longer cope with the mountain of reports, digests, cases; that unless order could be imposed upon the flux, law would be dissolved into chaos. He argued that such aids as Viner's abridgment and Comyn's *Digest* were in substance codes of English law, that the American constitutions were codes of the political and parliamentary departments of the Common Law. "And why should not the *civil* branch of the Common Law be systematized, under the influence of the same science and the same common sense?"

These were, by Grimké's time, standard contentions. However, Grimké was shrewd enough to reject two claims that usually figured in the propaganda: that with a simple code every man could be his own lawyer and that a code would diminish the number of lawsuits. What gives distinction to his eloquence is his emphasis upon "science."

There is no group, he boasted, who behold with more delight than does the bar "the admirable results, which are flowing from the application of the principles of science, to the various arts and trades, under the influence of mechanic institutions, in Europe and America." Should not men who rejoice so much over "the accelerated march of mind" put to work in their own subject "the creative power of order and principles"? In short, Grimké embodies that faith in the Enlightenment which so dignified the Revolutionary leaders, but he carries it into the nineteenth century through his intoxication over the success of applications of principles to facts. The great revelation of modern education has become for him man's ability to comprehend that the endless variety, the seeming perplexity, of nature can be reduced to simple and harmonious systems. Now the one noble task remained of likewise reducing the jungle of the law; for the description of that prospect Grimké dared employ *the* magic word:

To the eye of the Poet and Painter, the natural world appears invested with a sublimity, characterized by the awful and majestic. . . . But the harmonizing magic of Philosophy gives a new elevation to the sublime, and a fresh interest to the loveliness of Nature. All, that man can know of physical existence, above, around, beneath him, has been systematized.

Grimké here was deliberately rejecting the prevailing ideal of the sublime, or, rather, projecting a sublimity beyond the sublime, one which capped the awful, the majestic, the irregular, with the systematized rationality of Science. He called the great names not of poets but of Copernicus, Kepler, Newton, Laplace; he cited the increasing marvels of practical science. If only lawyers had been of the same spirit, we should not have been imposed upon by the Atlantis of Plato, the Oceana of Harrington. At last in this century we are moving into the era of "experimental wisdom." In this spirit the laws of the Republic and of the states should be organized into codes; then jurisprudence would surpass all poetic philosophical phantasms of the sublime.

By contrast with Grimké, opponents of the reformation, in their obstinate retention of the Common Law as sublime *because* confused —as beautiful *because* as chaotic as human nature—who treasured the Common Law precisely for having grown at haphazard through the caprices of history, and who loved the heterogeneous collections of the yearbooks—appear downright poetic, though that is hardly an adjective to be applied to James Kent. Yet to look a little deeper, Grimké, even while seeming to carry the banner of science, is in fact elevating science into a realm of magnificence with all the accents of a "romantic" paean. He was possibly unique among the reformers in finding here his central appeal, and we may doubt that so resonant a statement had much effect outside South Carolina. Still, the fact that an impassioned Southerner could see this glory in the idea of codification, that he could rise to such heights of eloquence—and could identify the cause with the concept of a sublime Science—helps to explain the dedication with which he and a few other lawyers threw themselves into a crusade for the codes.

2.

SCIENTIFIC AND AMERICAN PRACTICALITY

In the early 1820's codification could still be discussed without hysteria. Grimké's invocation of the scientific analogy impressed a profession which was not only finding hitherto undreamed-of fascinations in patent law but was also, with rather dazed amazement, beginning to realize that the progress of technology was causing an exciting revolution in the law of commerce and business. For a short, happy period codification was a professional problem without political implications. Even James Kent, in his first volume in 1826, with ceremonial bow to Francis Bacon, admitted that the torrent of reports had become overwhelming, that the spirit of the age demanded simplicity, and that a compendium of American law upon the model of Comyn's *Digest*, "executed by a like master artist, retaining what is applicable, and rejecting every thing that is obsolete and inapplicable to our institutions, would be an immense blessing." Kent may have been gently insinuating that his own *Commentaries* were substantially such a digest; he was not yet, at any rate, at that stage of outrage against the very idea of a code which inflamed his otherwise serene old age, and which Fenimore Cooper, patently drawing Kent's features in his Squire Dunscomb of *The Ways of the Hour,* described in 1850.

While equanimity still prevailed, Henry Dwight Sedgwick analyzed William Sampson in *The North American Review* with a judiciousness which was not thereafter, on this topic, to distinguish that patrician journal. Sedgwick went along astonishingly (considering the audience for whom he was writing) with the "Hibernian" theses of Sampson (though he confessed his distaste for that temper). Yes, originally the Common Law was the "bloody code of barbarians"; yes, it was cultivated in a manner to impart an air of mystery, "inasmuch as its reasons and principles were not to be found in the existing state of things"; yes, it was and is founded solely on the principle of authority, despite the fact that in every other branch of "intellectual effort" —principally the sciences—veneration for precedent has proved "one of the principal barriers to human improvement." In special pleading the Common Law has become a curse, and in real estate it is sheer confusion. As to wills and inheritance, so long as the struggle between precedent and reason continues, "legal opinions must be dubious to a perplexing degree, inasmuch as the result in any given case will depend more on the character and turn of mind of the judge, who is to decide it, than upon any general principle."

All this, and more, Sedgwick would concede—everything that Sampson and Grimké adduced. He even went so far as to suggest that we should no longer depend upon modern English decisions in either equity or in Common Law because, since our Revolution, we should have been, and by 1824 even more must be, creating our own jurisprudence. Though Sedgwick well knew that some of his eminent colleagues were becoming apprehensive, he submitted that, at least for the larger and wealthier states, there were commanding reasons for putting the laws "into *written codes.*" With a kind of bland innocence which contrasts sharply with Grimké's vehemence, Sedgwick noted that simplification, order, arrangement, and efficiency were "taking place in every other branch of human knowledge and effort," and so thought it likely that the law should not be exempt from the operation of "beneficent" principles otherwise universally prevalent.

Even as Sedgwick wrote, the age of legal innocence was coming to a close; codification was on the way to becoming a party banner. In retrospect, the controversy appears all the more insane because the partisans of codification were contending for what they presented as the inherent rationality of the epoch, while their opponents accused them of endeavoring, like the Jacobins of France, to put to the guillotine the very paradigm of reasonableness which had painfully been evolved in the contentious history of the Common Law. It is not accurate to say that all the champions of codification were Jacksonians. Hundreds of Democratic lawyers remained as hostile to the notion as were Cooper and Kent. And it must be recorded, considering how he has been maligned, that in this miserable contest, Joseph Story showed himself a man of principle rather than of party.

Story was the foremost advocate of legal scholarship; yet as early as 1821 he saw that something had to be done "to avert the fearful calamity, which threatens us, of being buried alive, not in the catacombs, but in the labyrinths of the law." The notion of a digest had early become familiar to him; he did not blench at the idea of a code, and defended Livingston's work against disparagement "by the exclusive admirers of the common law." For Francis Lieber's *Encyclopaedia Americana* in 1835 Story wrote a trenchant article, disagreeing with both advocates and foes of codes, yet contending that "much may be done to simplify the principles and practice of the law by judicious codification." The next year, when Rantoul's agitation became so strong that Governor Everett, who detested the scheme, had to act, Story served on a commission which, though advising against wholesale regularization, did point out certain areas, such as criminal law, property and personal rights, contracts, where a code might be not only feasible but desirable. However, Story was a broad-gauged and exceptional man.

The fact that such advocates of codification as Sampson and Rantoul were also friends of labor meant for most members of the profession that there was a link between the two causes. Indeed, Frederick Robinson told an assembly of the trades unions of Boston in 1834 that lawyers themselves were a combination, and so had no right to complain about combinations of labor; he added for good measure that judges should be made responsible to the people by periodic elections. This same Robinson scandalized Rufus Choate by addressing to him an open letter:

Whenever a system of plain and equal laws have been proposed, the brotherhood of the bar have always with one consent, in the legislature, in the newspapers and every where, represented it as chimerical, as the scheme of levellers; that the English Common Law is the height of perfection, and that the united wisdom of the world could not produce its equal. But if we will be governed by our own reason, and not by the dictation of interested men, we shall find that a plain, equal, humane, and concise code of civil, and criminal laws, could easily be made and compiled by disinterested legislators.

At any rate, Robinson went on, we could hardly have anything worse than the present system. By the time codifiers were thus speaking, the lawyers had banded together and were striking back.

We should not be surprised that as early as 1818 Daniel Webster sensed the danger and warned, "It yet appears to us to be among the idlest and weakest theories of the age, that it is possible to provide, beforehand, by positive enactment, and in such manner as to avoid doubts and ambiguities, for all questions to which the immense variety of human concerns gives rise." This thesis would continue to be the principal bludgeon of the opponents, and as time went on, the tone in which it was spoken became increasingly shrill in spite of many efforts to prove that codification was not revolutionary or to amend the slogan to innocuous "consolidation." The professionals were not deceived. John Anthon's *The Law Student* of 1850 (a textbook widely used for a decade or more) summarized their matured conviction that destruction of the Common Law "by a set of stiff apothegms, dignified by the name of code, would be a national calamity."

In resisting the threat of codification lawyers reiterated all the arguments that had been used or were still being used to win American consent to the Common Law, though against would-be codifiers they had to resort to several emphases that were mildly embarrassing. Hoffman, always a generous intellect, could conceive that a code achieving comparative certainty might be a blessing, but the real danger was that such a revolutionary undertaking would fall into "the unholy hands of visionary and rancorous politicians," would become the instrument of "the horde of levellers"—which was enough to cause the democracy to suspect that they too ought to be codifiers. "The *Common Law*," declared William Sullivan, "will not submit to the trammels of 'codification,' " and if citizens asked why not, George Bliss came up with an answer which others also would find useful: "I fear that efforts to build up a system of law, without resort to the common law, would prove like attempts to frame a system of theology, while revelation is discarded." From either the moral or intellectual point of view, demanded Henry Warner of the New York Law Institute, "Who, that wishes well to our jurisprudence, either in point of science or practice, would exchange the common law, the precious common law, for a patch-work code?"

Naturally such spokesmen refurbished the lawyers' contentions that the Common Law grows with life itself, and that by contrast a code would turn out to be a Procrustean bed. There is, said Henry Wheaton to the New York Law Institute, a false attraction in the ideal of uniformity which, as Bacon—potent name!—had remarked, binds hand and foot those who are shallow in judgment. But experience is complex. It is the part of madness, exclaimed *The United States Monthly Law Magazine* in 1851, to suppose that a time will ever come when law will not be intricate, not have its technical rules, its conflicting analogies; but still worse, "Those who indulge the pleasing hope of making the law so simple, that every man will be his own lawyer, may rest assured that such hopes will never be realized this side of Utopia." Aside from the fact that codes themselves—as French procedure demonstrates—require "construction," the American demand is a device of ignorance. Codification is a ruse of the pettifogger, and under the charge of confusion in the law is masked "a superficial knowledge, a merely *practical* knowledge of law—a knowledge sufficient to fill the mind of the student with perplexities and doubts, but which does not extend to a comprehension of those great principles and illustrative analogies by which such difficulties are removed." It is obvious therefore that legislatures would be too ignorant ever to frame a coherent code, even if they tried. In fact, history shows that codes—those of Justinian, of Napoleon—are the work of despots. "The Spanish Inquisition was a very simple, energetic court." Was this what codifiers wanted?

On the other hand, was it not evident that the Common Law (adapted in the skilled hands of the profession to American conditions) "has been, under God, and next to the bounty of Providence, the chief source of all the blessings that are enjoyed—of all the happiness and prosperity that exist, throughout this widespread and flourishing country"? In its free and "genial" spirit the Common Law is "analogous to that which is beginning to prevail in commerce," and which is rapidly making the United States the richest nation on earth. The founders of the Republic were men of business, knew that the common concerns of life should be left to men's own notions, and "that there might be such a thing as endeavouring to regulate these matters with too much precision, and they saw that the attempt would defeat itself." This was exactly what codification, by its inherent nature, endeavored. As for Grimké's eloquent invocation of modern science, *The North American Review* dismissed it with a wave of the hand: "One may as well think of composing a system of natural philosophy, which shall be perfect, and without the possibility of further improvement, as a code of laws, to which advancing society is to be chained."

Thus we suspect that the resistance to codification sprang from a variety of motives—on the lowest plane from the lawyers' desire to monopolize a profitable mystery, on the highest from an intellectual vision of infinite extensibility. Yet very close to the heart of its inspiration was a conception of American civilization. The legal organizations of this country, state and federal, said *The North American*, are unique; they have resulted from our appropriation of the Common Law; they are eminently practical. In the end of it, the argument against the codes became an attack on Grimké's idea of the sublime. He and his ilk, said *The United States Law Journal*, attempt to dazzle the public with dissertations on Civil Law, the code of Justinian, the code of Napoleon, and a whole army of codes, but we know what their effects have been in foreign lands. We may say without fear, "they will not do in this country." Grant to codification all its advocates claim for it—"its sublimity and its consistency;—to all of which by the way, if we had time, we could easily show that their title is exceedingly questionable,—we claim for the common law all the merit of superior solidity and usefulness." And to this grand conclusion the weight of the profession came, after their voyaging in the once-uncharted seas of equity and the Civil Law. In elegance and refinement, the French have many advantages, "but in what is really valuable, they are always behind-hand. They wear the ruffle but we wear the shirt."

3.

DAVID DUDLEY FIELD

Joseph Story could marshal all the arguments against the inutility of a code, but then ask the still-persistent question: "Because we cannot form a perfect system, does it follow that we are to do nothing?" While there were thousands who answered that we could and should do nothing, there were a stubborn band who contended that we could do something, could even do much. As the debate increased in acrimony, the war was waged with verbal violence up to the eve of that war in which violence of arms interrupted the milder hostilities. Yet even that war could not settle the controversy. It behooves us to ask, as the conclusion to our analysis of the prewar legal mind, what actually was the issue? In some respects, as we have seen, the legal mind was amazingly homogeneous; differences between Whigs and Democrats did not sunder it into ideological factions. But united though the profession was on principles of scholarship and in hostility to pettifogging, when it confronted the challenge of codification, a deep division opened. We cannot separate the two proclivities solely on the basis of temperament or of attitudes toward social reform. It is impossible to say that one was radical and the other conservative. We can say, with fair certitude, that the crevasse which opened within the fraternity represented a division between two opposing ideals of America. At bottom, the dispute over codes was a dispute over the identity of the nation.

This division by no means aligns provincial codifiers against cosmopolitan opponents. Many Americans were inflamed against the codes when they learned that Jeremy Bentham had the effrontery to offer President Madison his services to codify American law. At the same time, many of the codifiers were students of the Civil Law and, though of course patriots, were disposed to think more of regularity, harmony —ultimately of "sublimity"—than of Americanism. Furthermore, several gusts of passion swept across the field which had little to do with the major problem, but which agitated emotions on both sides. Of these, the strongest was the profession's detestation of the overnight scholar, and their readiness (as in Story's report to Governor Everett) to make sure that if codes were to be adopted, they should be prepared by experts, not by hacks. In America, the issue was further complicated by a perplexity as to the shades of meaning that differentiated Bentham and Brougham: some who detested the radicalism of Bentham still found charms in the meliorism of Brougham. Allowing nevertheless for these distractions, we are forced to realize that the noisy debate was basically a contest between nationalism and cosmopolitanism. The moment we thus perceive it, we recognize that it was *the* American problem—most obviously, as we have seen, in Protestant piety, yet equally pressing in education, in theology, and above all in literature —and sufficiently disturbing even in the fields of science and technology to create difficulties in international communication.

This is not to say that codifiers muted their technical cry that the Common Law was far more complex, more abstruse than necessary, and consequently an uncertain bulwark. One of the most telling indictments, William Price's *Paragraphs on Judicial Reform in Maryland* (1846), gladdened many a patriot heart by announcing—more boldly than any back-country critic had yet ventured to complain—that the Common Law was incoherent because the principles of it are never *"allied"* to each other. "There is no cohesion among them—each separate postulate stands alone and apart from all the rest." Clearly, Price argued, the only remedy was a written code: "Codification is the only corrective, and sooner or later it must and will be resorted to."

William Price, being a distinguished lawyer, scored effectively by indicating that this state of confusion forced upon judges the very action which the entire profession had publicly renounced, that of legislating by interpretation rather than by expounding statute. Under the present anarchy—which men like Hoffman and Story had presented as the perfection of reason—what it amounted to, according to Price, was simply that "Our lives, our fortunes, our good names, must be trusted to the Judges."

This sort of argument supplied sinews to the campaign for codification. Possibly it is a revealing comment on the decade of the 1850's—that curious decade in which the intellectual momentum of the previous years carried on, sporadically, but in which younger minds seem petrified in anticipation of slaughter—that on all sides jurists conceded that reform of the law was inevitable. Often apologists were vague, and seldom went so far as positively to advocate a code, but almost all agreed that "simplification" was indicated. *The Demo-*

cratic Review in 1851 said that the age was gone in which the main end of jurisprudence would be the creation of an abstruse science. "It is now demanded, that the prime object of the law and its ministers, shall be, to mete out speedy and exact justice between man and man; that judges shall disregard the technicalities and crotchets of a scholastic age, and make forms yield to substance." *The Law Reporter* in 1851, having fought for years against every suggestion of change, admitted defeat by noting that the desire for legal reform had become so strong "among all classes in this country" that the profession itself must now join the movement. *The United States Monthly Law Magazine* chimed in with this warning: "The anti-reforming lawyer must be prepared to meet with a series of disappointments, as point after point is carried against him," and concluded with what several distinguished men—such as Horace Binney—took to be an epitaph on fifty years of heroic endeavor:

THE INTERESTS OF THE PROFESSION, (that idol to which many a good man has been sacrificed,) are not longer thought to be furthered in leaving the cobwebs of our halls of justice untouched, but in sweeping them away.

Much of the demand for reform, for codification, carried to further lengths Grimké's contention that the law should fall into step with the march of science. This contention had various implications, but for lawyers it meant that, momentarily, they had no capacity to deal with the indisputable fact of the century, that the whole field of human intelligence had lately displayed an unexampled panorama "of beauties and perfections" which had strewn everywhere "practical good to all mankind." Since reform had laid hold of everything "except that which guards and protects our property and rights," was it not entirely logical that law should no longer stand immobile "while every other science known to man is greatly indebted to our enterprize and industry." Yet soon in America it became evident that exhortations of this sort—differing from the orations of Bentham and Brougham in England—came not so much from a conception of scientific clarity as from a national particularism.

Sadly enough, these proclamations increase in number and fervor during the 1850's—as the nation hovers on the brink of disaster. The Common Law, says one magazine in 1850, is feudal in origin, but in it are combined both Saxon and Norman elements. Hence we must pick and choose: "The republican institutions of America naturally tend to revive with vigor those principles of Saxon law which sustain to the utmost the rights of the individual." So we must repudiate the Norman contributions. Yet even then, since "the Saxon swineherds would have trembled at the restless spirit of commercial enterprise which characterizes America," we must redact Saxon bequests in the light of that system called the Civil Law—and this we can do only by codification. In the next year *The United States Monthly Law Magazine* proclaimed the hope, the only hope jurists could offer, for preservation of the Union: "National, not sectional, in its character, and universal, if not in the obligations it shall impose, at least in the respect it shall win from the civilized world." Could a national code thus transcend sectionalism and hold the Union together, then to it would adhere the greatest of adjectives, which never could properly be applied to the heterogeneous pile of the Common Law:

The task of its accomplishment, will devolve upon those who see, in the science of law, something more than the mere means of acquiring a livelihood, or even wealth; who see in it a profound and sublime philosophy.

This, then, should be the American future, the American accomplishment: a legal "sublime" systematically fashioned out of harmony instead of through contradiction, permanent and stable instead of wracked by doubt and uncertainty. Yet the student gets a whiff of death in these chants about legal sublimity as he does not in the sincerity of Grimké: there is something artificial, something desperate in the appeals, as though the speakers knew in their secret hearts that the opportunity was fading for America to find its sublime expression in jurisprudence; that it would be in the surge of infantry brigades at Gettysburg.

Until that time, the central battlefield for the legal war was New York. Governor DeWitt Clinton as early as 1825 told the legislature that the whole system of law required revision into a complete code "embracing those improvements which are enjoined by enlightened experience." Since Clinton was a Jeffersonian (although in the free-for-all politics of the state he was opposed more by Van Buren than by the Federalists), and because he stressed the value of a code as preventing "judicial legislation, which is fundamentally at war with the genius of representative government," Federalists and Whigs made anticodification a party position. Some Democrats countered by urging Clinton's cause all the more strongly: Benjamin F. Butler, in his inaugural address at the University of the City of New York, cited as one of the grand conceptions of Bacon "that the common law should be reduced and systematically digested." Since the unregenerate lawyers considered Bacon enlisted on their side, words like these only inflamed passions the more. As a Democrat and a Jackson man in the 1820's, Gulian Verplanck, in a book on contracts, praised codification so strongly as to bring abuse upon himself; once he had left Jackson because of the "Bank War," he discoursed sagely on the evils of codification. "We must not, we cannot," he said in 1839, "even dream of casting away the meaning of words by the example of things."

The most comprehensive debate on the issue came at the New York Constitutional Convention of 1846. Campbell P. White introduced the resolutions which expressed the essence of the Democratic contention; a committee on the judiciary should be appointed

to inquire into the expediency of providing in the constitution for a systematic and thorough reform of courts of law and equity—for a simplification and reduction of the antiquated, artificial and ponderous forms of legal and equitable proceedings.

Ultimately, White announced, we must codify the mass of unwritten law in order that litigation may be diminished and—this is what dismayed those who had fought for equity—that there may be "the extension of the right of trial by jury to all practicable questions." In a paradoxical manner which defies historical analysis, those who invoked the Civil Law and equity in their denunciations of the Common Law argued that if their ideas were vindicated in codes, then juries—that is, the democracy—would have more rather than less to say in crucial decisions.

As a step in this direction, the reformers made clear that they wanted to abolish every distinction between law and equity. "We should use some term descriptive of the judicial power generally," they said, meaning that the legislature should discard the vestiges of English practice, and instead supply a purely native wisdom. Today we may not realize how anguished were the cries which arose from the other side of the assembly, the most unhappy being from Ambrose L. Jordan, of Columbia University. The reformers' effort to merge law and equity was, in Jordan's estimation, a plot against the Common Law—"a system which, since our first existence as a people, has constituted the law of the land—a system derived from our mother country, venerable for its antiquity, and admirable for its wisdom, and its adaptation to the condition of a free people." Jordan recited all the then-conventional laments that the Civil Law—upon which the codifiers presumed to rest their case—was the creation of despotisms; wherefore he and other opponents advanced the tremulous contention that even though the Common Law had been imported from England, it had become, thanks to its marvelous versatility, an American way of thought. "Theories and abstractions," said *The American Jurist,* "which rest upon nothing real, are no longer esteemed." Codifiers, this argument ran, were theorists, lingering disciples of "the philosophical doctrines of the last half of the eighteenth century." Yet even though few American writers had heard of Savigny and of the historical conception of law as the creation of custom rather than of legislation, before the Civil War there is nothing in the American literature of an out-and-out evolutionary philosophy. Reiterated statements that the Common Law was "malleable" seldom come to explicit historicism. On the contrary, opponents of codification planted themselves upon the rational patriotism of an irrational but native development, and so challenged codifiers to wage war with them on the issue of legal allegiance. This the codifiers were more than ready to do. The most eager of them was the man to whom codification became a religion of patriotism, David Dudley Field.

Field was anything but a radical. Like Kent, he was a scion of Connecticut Puritanism who became more of a New Yorker than the New Yorkers. He was, when he put his mind to his practice, a successful lawyer. He cherished the highest standards of legal probity and never could sufficiently condemn the "revolting doctrine" of Brougham that an advocate must carry zeal for his client to the point of forgetting that there is any other person in the world. Nobody, not even Story, more upheld the ideal of scholarship. A true lawyer, Field said, must know the law in all its departments, "he must have comprehended the greatness of the whole, the harmony of its parts, and the infinite diversity of its particulars." He excoriated the apprentice system for training lawyers because it turned out an undisciplined, half-educated creature, "the transcriber of legal formulas, the promoter of neighborhood litigation, the unsafe guide, the hopeless bigot"; he grimly declared that the present eminent men in the profession were not produced by the system but in spite of it.

When he came to the traditional view of the relation of law to property, Field was the most "conservative" of the lot. The primary purpose of the law, he wrote, is to govern property; wherever there appears material capable of appropriation, "whether it be solid earth or flowing water; whether it be the product of the soil, or the workmanship of man's hand, there comes the law, and gives you the rule by which you may take it, use it, and transfer it." Law as the arbiter of property was, in his view, the foundation of "industry, refinement, liberty, civilization." To begin with, Field's passion arose out of his rage against the chaotic state of the law: "a system more clumsily devised for the accomplishments of its end, and more inconvenient in practice, could scarcely be imagined." Special pleading especially disgusted him, for it prostituted the noble science to a "paltry learning."

As his fury mounted—he was, oddly enough, not an emotional man in the ordinary sense of the word—he acquired a language of invective: the Common Law is artificial, complex, technical, full of obsolete terms, so burdensome as no longer to command the respect of society. Because of its crudity, equity had to be devised, but that in turn has become so artificial as to be equally absurd. Field commenced his agitation in 1839 with an open letter to Verplanck, his theme one which he would not cease to belabor until his death in 1894:

This young State, with scarcely two millions of people, and republican institutions of the most democratical character, administers justice to its citizens with less certainty and promptitude than even the old overburdened kingdom of England, with fifteen millions of people, whose commerce and whose colonies encircle the world.

He early became convinced that the distinction between Common Law and equity was utterly false, "little more than a play upon words." The simplification which partisans of equity claimed for it was a delusion. Where then was succor to be found? The answer had come to him by 1840: a code was "the natural relief of a people from the burden of an incongruous, obscure, and overloaded jurisprudence." He appeared so indubitably the advocate in New York that when, following the action of the Constitutional Convention, a commission was appointed to revise procedure, he was inevitably made its head. His Code of Procedure was enacted in 1848, and by January, 1850, he completed codes of civil and criminal procedure. But by this time the opposition was highly vocal. "My life was continual warfare," Field recollected. "Not only was every obstacle thrown in the way of my work, but I was attacked personally as an agitator and a visionary, in seeking to disturb long settled usage, and thinking to reform the law, in which was embodied the wisdom of ages." Even so, as chairman of a second commission, appointed in 1857, he produced a massive organization of the whole body of state law, which he submitted in 1865. His enemies in New York were able to block the adoption of his later codes and to prevent acceptance of more than fragments of his great code; but eventually his civil code was enacted in twenty-four states, the criminal one in eighteen; he had an effect in England, Malaya, and India, and in his last decades spoke his dream of putting the laws of all nations into one gigantic international code!

In persuading the Convention of 1846, Field said that the need was for a "radical" reform, going back to first principles, breaking up the present system, and reconstructing the components into "a simple and natural scheme of legal procedure." Actually, however, as his friend

Judge Edmonds said of Field's first code, "nothing novel or startling has been introduced," and above all nothing proposed "that is calculated to impair the rights of property or to interfere with the enjoyment of liberty or the pursuit of happiness." Field himself pleaded "that none of the changes which I have recommended can prejudice in any respect the rights of the parties," but would only make the assertion of these rights less dilatory and expensive. To defend his codes, Field used arguments the profession had long since devised. He invoked not only the standard of scholarship but that of comparative study: the average lawyer is the "only man of science who does not look beyond his own commonwealth," and should be ashamed of himself as he measures himself against the student of comparative anatomy. Field as much as Story believed in the plastic character of the law, and dismissed as contemptible the charge that codes would prove a strait jacket to progress. His program was a simple one: instead of the random maze of rules, "to have these rules collected, arranged, and classified; the contradictions reconciled; the doubts settled; the bad laws eliminated, and the result written in one book, for the instruction and guidance of citizen and magistrate, lawyer and client." This did not mean sacrificing the wisdom of the ages, or pretending that law was not a growth within specific conditions. Field gladly admitted, "An original system of jurisprudence, founded upon mere theory, without reference to national characteristics, habits, traditions, and usages, would be a failure." While Field fully comprehended the purport of Savigny, he found therein no reason that a factitious historicity should impede the cause of systematization.

Why then, we ask, did the profession react so vehemently to "the Field Codes"? There are, of course, the reasons which professional colleagues adduced on purely professional grounds. In these, all the stale arguments for the flexibility of the Common Law were paraded. Had the crux of the argument, up to the Civil War, been only a matter of the simplicity of codes versus the malleability of precedents, the entire contentious episode would be only a sad footnote to a period of vigorous intellectual exertion.

Something more was involved, something which from the beginning we have seen haunting the jurists even when they were strenuously endeavoring to talk law as pure law, and not let it become contaminated by the nativistic resistance of a Natty Bumppo. David Field during the 1840's was a close associate of a group of New York littérateurs who styled themselves "Young America." The most important pupil of this fraternity, which in the main made more noise than sense, proved to be Herman Melville, though the little band also

had an effect upon Whitman. They were all Democrats and nationalists; yet being learned in European literature—at least in contemporaneous Romantic writers—they were not Know-Nothings. Field proclaimed his alliance with them by publishing, in *The New York Review* for April, 1841, a discussion of the works of one of their revered
prophets (now forgotten), William Leggett. Field's notice, though of
course nothing so strident as Whitman's "Preface," throws at least
some light on the sources of his codifying impulse. Americans, he said,
continue still to write like Englishmen; but eventually writers such as
Leggett will show that our political condition must recast our ideas
about government—even more, "that it will modify our tastes, enlarge
our sympathies, and in no inconsiderable degree remodel our social
condition." Field's extracurricular writings—if so they may be called
—are rare enough to make each word resounding, and it may be
that because of his friendship with Evert Duyckinck and Cornelius
Matthews he struck the patriotic pose with a bit more bravado than
he really felt. Still, he pointed an accurate finger at what in literary
creation—not to mention in religion, science, and the law—was the
predicament of the American: "Not being provided with a literature
of his own, the American is subjected to two opposite systems of training; one from books, the other from the life he sees around him."
Field may have derived some inspiration from Bentham, even more
from Brougham, but he preferred to insist that his zeal for the codes
arose out of an empirical use of his own eyes, regarding the American
scene as it actually existed. Whoever wishes to speak to the American
people a language they can understand, Field continued about Leggett, "must have studied much that the schools of Europe do not
teach." In literature a bold spirit was required, a readiness to receive
any truth, to search for it in hidden places, and a strong sympathy
for all other citizens. "Why," he asked—and here we do get a fore-
shadowing of Melville and Whitman—"should we disregard the
obvious and necessary consequence of this new state of things in the
economy of the world? why persist in applying here the customs and
maxims which belong to Europe?"

This transplanted New Englander would not have written this way in
New York, at the age of thirty-six, unless the virus of intellectual
nationalism—or at least of independence—had entered his veins. From
the insight afforded by the review of Leggett one can perceive that
Field's passion for simplicity was not merely the desire of an efficient
lawyer to have things tidied up: it was his way of fulfilling the promise
of the Republic. To him the Common Law was as much a foreign levy

upon the pristine continent as were for Whitman the academic "rhymes and rhymers." It was, Field declared,

a most artificial system of procedure, conceived in the midnight of the dark ages, established in those scholastic times when chancellors were ecclesiastics and logic was taught by monks, and perfected in a later and more venal period, with a view to the multiplication of offices and the increase of fees, was imposed upon the banks of the Hudson and the quiet valley of the Mohawk.

This lofty language shows what was working in David Field's heart: the Hudson and the Mohawk—the realm of Natty Bumppo—versus the dark ages, scholastic times, monks, venal England. Men like Robert Baird were no longer apologizing to Europeans for the voluntary system as creating a shambles among our churches but were proudly exhibiting it as an original contribution of American genius; so the age was ripe "for a code of the whole of our American law. The materials are about us in abundance, derived from many ages and nations; and we must now have a system of our own, symmetrical, eclectic, framed on purpose." In monarchies, for obvious reasons, a special class, a guarded elite, arrogates to itself all interpretation of the laws; but here the people are sovereign, elect all officers ("even the Judges themselves," Field could note with satisfaction) so that the creation of a lawyer class, bullying the democracy into submission by the bedazzlements of their erudition—"that this should happen in a republic, where all the citizens both legislate and obey, is one of those anomalies which, however susceptible of explanation, seem at first sight incredible."

Roscoe Pound paid tribute to Kent, Story, and their allies for having held the fort for the Common Law so long and so valiantly that by the time of Field it had become the bastion of American jurisprudence, that by then not even Field could raze it, even in California. They saved us from premature codification which in Pound's view would have become a shirt of Nessus. Of course, for Dean Pound the Common Law was as much a religion as codification was for Field. And since the problem of systematizing our statutes is still with us, if only as a matter of convenience, we can hardly assert that Field lost his cause entirely, though I suppose most legal thinkers would now agree that his ideal is not realizable in its total sweep. For the story of America in the 1850's these later considerations are matters of technique. They no longer pertain, unless by accident, to what for Field and his opponents was the major concern, which was nothing more or less than the establishment of an identity for the nation. Field was, for instance, prepared in 1844 to fight for Oregon. In a quarter of a century, he said, there will be populous cities around Puget Sound, which will trade with the Orient, awaken the Asiatic mind, open Japan to modern civilization. There is no evidence that Field ever essayed to write poetry, or that he set any store upon Whitman, but when he made his appeals for the codes, thematically he anticipated Whitman. "Your canals, your railways, your incalculable wealth, your ships cutting the foam of every sea, the enterprise of your merchants, the skill of your artisans, the fame of your ancestors"—all these David Field would invoke to persuade the Republic that its destiny depended, not upon these forces, but upon an ordering of them within the codes. The codes, "instinct with the free spirit of our institutions, should become the guide and example for all nations bearing the tie of our common language."

Because after the Civil War Field dedicated himself to the cause of international law, it is difficult to label him merely a nationalist. Yet the spirit in which he approached the global problem was like that of Mark Twain's Yankee in Camelot—he wanted to "fix up" a messy European confusion. On one level he generally writes in so plebeian, so flat, a style that the modern student becomes wearied, and prefers the sounding periods of Kent, the flourishes of Story. Yet occasionally Field shows the dedication within him, and then the grandeur of his vision emerges. Hence it seems more than coincidence that in 1855, the year of *Leaves of Grass*, Field should so slough off his Yankee reserve as to write,

a CODE American, not insular but continental, as simple as so vast a work can be made, free in its spirit, catholic in its principles; and that work will go with our ships, our travelers and our armies; it will march with the language, it will move with every emigration, and make itself a home in the farthest portion of our own continent, in the vast Australian lands, and in the islands of the southern and western seas.

Practitioners of the Common Law considered themselves as thoroughly American as anybody; yet it was consistent with the patriotism of such a gentleman as Story—or of Longfellow and Lowell, for that matter—that America acknowledge her relation to the mother country by gradually adapting to local situations the English skills, either in the Common Law or in prosody. Only thus did they believe America could become a civilization, by remaining within the context of an international culture, certainly not by seeking for a phantasmagorical personality within its own undisciplined bosom. Let the world admire Natty Bumppo as a dream of individualism, but let him remain a dream. The great fact about David Field is that, in his often pedestrian way, he entertained the dream with deadly seriousness. Everything in our government and our society, he said, proceeds from the idea of equality. "Would to Heaven," he exclaimed, "that there might arise some master-spirit," who would teach this mighty doctrine as it ought to be taught, showing the people how it abases none but elevates all, "how this equality, not of strength, nor of genius, nor of external circumstances, but in rights and essential attributes, is the peculiar doctrine of the American people, their ornament, their glory, the foundation of their strength, and the chief source of their prosperity."

Here, as the nation stumbled into Civil War, seemed to be the one debatable issue in the law. After that war, it appeared suddenly to have become merely a matter for round-table discussions among lawyers, and the glory had departed. Possibly it was already departing in the 1850's, and men like Field and Theodore Sedgwick were striving to create a sublime idea from which sublimity had already been subtracted by the progress of technology. Compared with the palatial steamboats, the roaring railroads, the Atlantic cable (which David Field's brother laid in 1858), wherein was the majesty of a code, or even of the Common Law? Among the many respects in which the Civil War brought down upon the American drama a violent curtain, the way in which it terminated a stupendous era of legal thinking is one of its poignant tragedies, if not indeed its most poignant.

BOOK THREE

SCIENCE—THEORETICAL AND APPLIED

CHAPTER ONE

Technological America

The two inventions—the development of latent heat, which produced the steam engine, the modern lever of mechanical power, and especially of navigation by water and transportation by land,—and the development of galvanism, which produced the magnetic telegraph—seem to have been designed mainly for our country. A population spread over an immense extent, and migratory in habit and tendency, is enabled to hold immediate intercourse in one shape from the remotest distances, and personally to visit and become familiarly acquainted through the length and breadth of the land without loss of time, material expense or fatigue. . . . A new world expands in wealth and wisdom, over regions newly redeemed from the hunter and his game, and shares with more advanced civilization in distant regions, its own exhaustless and invaluable resources.

—JOSEPH R. INGERSOLL, 1848

1.

AMERICAN PHILOSOPHES

St. George Tucker, being a virtuous eighteenth-century Jeffersonian, suffered not a few pangs of conscience at having brought forth an edition of Blackstone; but in one emphatic respect he could feel his guilt assuaged. Despite all Blackstone's antidemocratic quirks, on one point the great man had been firm, that wherever knowledge is the monopoly of the few, tyranny will usurp the prerogative. This ringing affirmation provided Tucker with a welcome sanction for expounding the scientific rationalism of Virginia: science discloses all the operations of "the machine," from which it followed, since the diffusion of letters among the populations of the West, that "those nations which have been most eminent in science, have been most distinguished by freedom." At the very beginning of the century, this foremost legal spokesman for the democratic faith could thus commit the cause of freedom to scientific progress. Whether or not Tucker knew in 1803 precisely what he was doing, he was in fact prophesying what then doubtless presented itself as a gradual ascent to American felicity, but which, in the next sixty years, became a torrential rush of progress that subjected the young Republic to an ordeal of intellectual adaptation beyond any conceived by revivalists or imagined by legal theorists.

Tucker could still happily use "science" and "letters" as interchangeable terms. Both were activities of philosophy, and the great "philosophes," to the extent that they were known in America, had conclusively shown that "natural philosophy" comprised all the pursuits of disinterested leisure. So far, in spite of the political involvements of a Jefferson or a Franklin, the Americans had sustained the posture of disinterestedness.

So, while the transformation of colonial America into a nation commences with the shout of the Revival and then proceeds apace through a greedy appropriation of legal science to suit the native circumstances, for some time there lingered among the most self-conscious intellects a calm of spirit which was still of the eighteenth century. Henry Adams composed a dramatic paragraph on the landing, in the New York of 1867, of his father and John Lothrop Motley, describing them as bric-a-brac of the eighteenth century, hideously out of place in the America of business and the ghetto. Actually, by that time the tone and manner of the Enlightenment had long since vanished from the society, and Adams was stretching his rhetoric to score a sentimental point; yet it is true that in the first decades of the new century words were frequently spoken and printed which please us by exhibiting an utter innocence of the calendar. For instance, in 1813 William Barton published a eulogy of Rittenhouse, making much of the circumstance that the natural scientist—"equally with the teacher of religion and morals"—extends the benefits of his researches beyond the frontiers of his own country. Truth, he pleaded, is everywhere the same, wherefore the philosopher must pre-eminently be considered a citizen of the world; at the same time this need never detract in the slightest degree "from that spirit of patriotism which ever stimulates a good man to contribute his primary and most important services to his own country." Thus could Barton justify his writing about a scientist who happened also to be an American.

It followed that a philosophe in America need not sacrifice his cosmopolitan breadth when he dealt with the flora and fauna of this continent. In Barton's view, as in Benjamin Franklin's, there could be no question of producing some uniquely American scientific doctrine. In science, as compared with religion and law, such distinctions simply did not exist. American discoveries would be contributions to the international Enlightenment. A physician, Edward Miller, felt no sense in 1805 that he was betraying the national honor by congratulating the country for coming into being in an "inquisitive" age. The present period, he could say, is one of those distinguished eras to which posterity will look back with profound interest, "and of which it will expect a just account from all such as have it in their power to assist and accelerate the progress of discovery and improvement."

This sense of the epoch inspired one of the major productions of the early Republic, the Reverend Samuel Miller's *A Brief Retrospect of the Eighteenth Century*, which was anything but brief, consisting of two large volumes which were published in New York in 1803. Miller's aim was to acquaint the democracy with the immensity of the "mass of improvement" wrought in the preceding century. He expresses a proper American, and ministerial, disapproval of certain tendencies in speculative philosophy and in fiction, but he himself, Calvinist product of the epoch, takes immeasurable delight in reporting, at remorseless length, the triumphs of "Mechanical Philosophy," under which rubric he enumerates chemistry, natural history, medicine, agriculture, geography. Though Miller is careful never to praise the licentious freedom of France, he actually manages to combine a righteous censure of Voltaire with an approbation of an age in which the elements of literature and science "descended from the higher classes of society, and from universities, to the middle, and, in some instances, to the lower orders of men." In fact, he adds, even to females! As Charles Caldwell would say, at Louisville, Kentucky, when asked in 1832 to celebrate the birthday of Washington, the biography of Washington, important though it be, is of less consequence than the scientific advances made within his lifetime: that was "an aggregate into which most that enters belongs to the sublime."

If, then, the glory of the century could be so sanctioned, and a new America be received into the community of sublimity, it seemed obvious that science in America would be similar to, even hopefully someday might rival in profundity or extent, the science of Europe. Just as the Connecticut poets dreamed of an American Milton—or, at their most extravagant, of an American Watts—John Coxe told the Philadelphia Medical Society in 1800: "Let me hope, that many whom I now address, are destined to attain an eminence, as great as Newton, Bacon, Boyle, and all those other illustrious characters, who rank so high in the annals of science."

Inevitably, while aspirations of this sort were consoling provincial inferiority, the question arose in the proud national mind as to why

America had not already produced Newtons and Bacons. A lyceum lecturer in 1820 might valiantly remind the people of the obstacles against which their fathers had contended—the necessities of subduing the soil, inducements to trade, Indian wars, the dissimilarity of the colonies—but he gingerly came round, though protesting he intended no offense, to the statement that the colonial culture had been so dominated by the clergy, who suffered themselves "to be often led astray with a propensity for jejune and useless disquisitions, and a zeal for theological controversy," that the best intellects among the laity were rendered "unable to cultivate, with any considerable prospect of success, the field of general study." By "the field of general study" he specifically meant the array of sciences listed by Samuel Miller. Because we have been obsessed by theology, he further ventured, our most creative minds, from whom we ought to have received "bold and vigorous excursions into the paths of literature and science," who were fully qualified to have reached "some of the loftier recesses of intellectual discovery," have instead been forced to follow "in the eccentric steps of their predecessors."

As late as 1820 there survived just enough of the spirit of the Enlightenment still to inspire a few such anticlerical jibes. Shortly thereafter they were to be silenced, and those champions of science who still nourished hostile feelings toward the clergy found it wiser, as evangelical orthodoxy came to dominate the intellectual scene, to place the blame simply on colonial conditions—the forest, Indian wars, and "foreign" tyranny. Not unnaturally, said the first issue of *The American Journal of Science* in 1818, purely intellectual and speculative sciences, which required only books, teachers, and study, had been cultivated rather than those which demand physical demonstrations, instruments of research, material specimens. Hence we have done respectable work in theology, jurisprudence, civil policy, but we have yet to make any mark "in the sciences relating to material things."

Recently scholarship has sought to determine the amount of scientific knowledge that actually was current in the colonies. This tender documentation has made much not only, for instance, of Cotton Mather's awareness of inoculation but of fragmentary explanations of Newtonian physics in the simple language of the almanacs. I. Bernard Cohen declares that in eighteenth-century America the sciences "flourished," and that in the declension of the early nineteenth century this fact was obscured. Yet for many years into the latter period, a litany of self-congratulation regularly was run through on ceremonial occasions which conventionally acknowledged that the founders, though hindered by physical difficulties, had none the less included names precious to science: "FRANKLIN, RITTENHOUSE, JEFFERSON, BOWDITCH." To this incantation was frequently added the name of Godfrey, robbed by English jealousy of all credit for his discovery of the quadrant!

Yet it was rapidly becoming evident that this recital could sustain national self-respect for only a short time. Samuel Miller confessed that the spirit of the American people had already shown itself ominously *"commercial,"* and predicted that men of science should here expect "little reward either of honour or emolument." The bleak prospect for emolument quickly became not so much a worry as an enforced recognition of the fact, which Simon Newcomb was to sum up in Henry Adams's monumental review of the century of American independence (*The North American Review,* January, 1876) by asking "why the growth of the tree planted by Franklin was so slow and stunted." In 1814, DeWitt Clinton—thus early displaying the courage which deserves more than the ritualistic veneration occasionally afforded him in the State of New York—bluntly informed his constituents that when Americans stumble into the fields of science, "the master spirits, who preside over transatlantic literature, view us with a sneer of supercilious contempt," and consider our few productions—even those of Franklin and Rittenhouse—"as Oases in the regions of Africa; deriving their merit less from intrinsic beauty and excellence, than from their contrast with the surrounding deserts."

To be sure, in these misty decades, while men who considered themselves at least amateur philosophes—Jefferson, Madison, Monroe—presided over the Republic in what they thought an effulgence of light, ceremonial orators could still assert that there were "living Artists" to be added to the venerable list. Jeremiah Van Rensselaer, delivering his public lectures on geology in 1825, chided such self-congratulations by remarking that they could all remember "when the *terms* of science were scarcely understood among us." By this time there were several voices penetrating the haze of complacency, although the more they seemed to support the last of the philosophes in the White House, John Quincy Adams, the less seemed the possibility of their ever being noticed by the cohorts of Andrew Jackson. Nevertheless, on November 13, 1826, at the opening of the Medical College in Charleston, South Carolina, Stephen Elliott asked where in all the country, and "more particularly in our section of the United States," was there a man in any branch of science who could feel himself upon a level with European practitioners? Anger burning through his Ciceronian periods, he declared that Americans scarcely yet lived in the past century, and as for the present: "We stand around this great arena of human enterprize and mental exertion rather as spectators than as actors." We know nothing of firsthand research, we trust to digests in magazines. In a complicated but still-vigorous sentence, Elliott formulated the problem for science in America as it was to be confronted for several decades:

If in the mechanic arts the ingenuity of our country, if in legislation and in commerce the unrivalled freedom of our institutions have given us a high rank and a distinguished name among nations—it would show that the talent of our country only wants opportunity and the means of action to become equally illustrious in the higher walks of science.

Or rather, as high-minded friends of science liked to phrase the problem, America needed only opportunity and means of action to be delivered from enslavement to mechanic arts or to the merely "speculative" sciences. The haunting question, however, which lurked behind this assurance was more troubling: supposing the economy does produce the opportunities and means; is there enough talent in the Republic that can be lured from the countinghouse, let alone from the pulpit and the law office, to then dedicate itself to the creation of a reputable scientific discipline in these states?

The most stirring speeches of the young Republic were resonant with a confidence that the pause between the pioneer age of Franklin and Rittenhouse and the glorious one about to dawn would be brief. The unquenchable Joel Barlow issued at Washington in 1806 a Prospectus for a national institution (dreaming, as so many Jeffersonians then were, of what ultimately emerged as the Smithsonian). "What a range," he exclaimed, "is open in this country for mineralogy and botany!" And for the other sciences no less: chemistry, anatomy, mechanics, and hydraulics. The prospect for America was immense; all that was needed was intelligence:

Could the genius of Bacon place itself on the high ground of all the sciences in their present state of advancement, and marshal them before him in so great a country as this, and under a government like ours, he would point out their objects, foretell their successes, and move them on their march, in a manner that should animate their votaries and greatly accelerate their progress.

There could be no question about foretelling the success of science in America; as one journal said in 1812, "Standing, as it were upon the shoulders of our transatlantic rivals, we may hope to catch new views of the prospect before us, which will enable us to shorten the road to ultimate perfection."

It was not only in the Revival that a doctrine of "perfectionism" emerged; the revivalistic mentality was sibling to the technological. The Lyceum lecturer of 1820 saluted the new era as America's emergence from infancy into manhood, when it would no longer be entangled in childish delusions: "The intellect will neither be warped by the subtleties and mystifications of speculative refinement, nor will it grovel in the sensualities of bestial voluptuousness." (We may pardonably wonder, amid these prognostications, how the reputation of Franklin managed to survive at all.) We must acknowledge that these prophets were inspired by the most exalted of motives. Yet few of them realized how fatally they were committing the nation to so resplendent a vision of the future as to make any falling short of the goal of ultimate perfection seem grievous failure. And they continued to speak of the technological era in terms in which science and literature remained interchangeable. DeWitt Clinton, for all his pragmatic vigor, in 1814 was still speaking the language of St. George Tucker. Our energies have indeed, he said, been directed so far toward wealth rather than knowledge; but how can we ignore the true implication:

Our enterprising spirit, as exhibited in the fisheries, in navigation, and in commerce, is the admiration of the world; and if it had soared to the heavens in pursuit of knowledge, instead of creeping along the earth in the chase of riches, America would have been as illustrious in the rolls of fame as those states where literature has seen her augustan ages.

Clearly, if the United States did not soon produce some such age, it would fail its mission and have to live with a chiding conscience. Here still another wrinkle of doubt could have, or should have, formed on the brows of the prophets: were they quite sure that once American energies were diverted from fisheries, the scientific paradise then achieved would merit the adjective "augustan"?

2.

SCIENCE AS A FORM OF CONTEMPLATION

Colonial Americans who wanted to learn the wonders of the new science, and who themselves had no laboratories and at best only an elementary mastery of mathematics, naturally seized on popular summaries. The vast majority of these were expositions of Newtonian physics, which invariably maintained the tenets of theism from the evidences of design in the solar system. Hence, when the Republic achieved independence, the dominant conception of science entertained by the educated classes was one of passive contemplation of the divine perfection revealed in the order and coherence of Nature. As Frederick Dalcho phrased it before the South Carolina Medical Society in 1805 (his manner of conceiving the subject would continue for several decades to be less affected by later developments in the South than in the North): the pursuit of scientific information, while an honor to the country, is of even greater advantage to individuals.

The human mind, vast and capacious in its resources, is bounded by no limits but the GREAT FIRST CAUSE, and yields to no impediments, but the disorganization of matter. The heart expands with virtue and benevolence, as the mind extends its information.

For this grandiose symmetry there were several adjectives regularly employed—majestic, magnificent—but only one was truly adequate: "sublime."

In one sense, all American discourse on the sublimity of science is but a pale reflection of European imports, which continue to be a permanent factor in the background of the American intellect throughout our period. Bishop Paley's *Natural Theology*, first published in London in 1802, was reprinted endlessly in America, used as the standard text in the colleges, and assiduously conned by the self-educated. In the 1830's, the Bridgewater treatises were extensively republished in this country, and from 1849 on there was a large sale of the Bohn Library translation of Humboldt's *Cosmos*. To mention only these few, and yet to note with what weight of authority they imposed themselves upon the provincial mind is to underscore the problem that mind faced in summoning itself to its national identity.

George Logan, addressing the Tammany Society of New York City in 1798, told the politicians that the regularity of Nature extended to the smallest particles of matter, and that thus from the most stupendous to the most minute there prevailed "order, proportion, fitness, and congruity." Nicholas Collin had already informed the Philosophical Society, which showed no disposition to argue, that the sagacity by which man traced the intricate path of the moon was "sublime," and asked why he should not now explore the source of the tempest. Edward Cutbush in 1811 spoke still as a man of the previous century when he saluted natural science "as the most sublime and refined species of drama," especially since in it the entertainment is produced "not by fictitious scenery, but by real exhibitions of the operations and changes of nature." Thus we have steadily with us, as a sort of ground-base to the technological progress, a persistent reiteration of this eighteenth-century theme. "The contemplation of the universe," said James Leib in 1830, "is the sublimest poetry." In 1835 Thomas Dick pleaded for a general dissemination of scientific information among the masses by calling the objects of study sublime and, ignoring Pascal, asserting, "The vast and immeasurable spaces . . . convey august and sublime conceptions."

The almost automatic carry-over into the nineteenth century of this ideal of sublime science is a factor so fundamental to the life of the mind in the nation that today it is generally ignored. Yet if we are to understand the later history of that mind, we must fully appreciate two inheritances from colonial subservience: the Enlightened theory of science, coming to these shores with incalculable prestige, taught Americans to conceive of it as consisting in an aesthetic contemplation of a perfected universe, and then to salute the comprehension of this universe (mainly through a grasp of Newton's system) as providing an entrance into the cosmopolitan culture of the West. To adore and to understand were first of all an escape from provinciality, and not a patriotic assertion.

And yet it was patriots who made the assertion, children of the Enlightenment who never for a moment supposed that they had to prove their mettle by proclaiming their nationality. Charles Peale, advertising his Museum in 1799, was untroubled by separatist scruples. It was enough for him that "philosophy" should conduct its votaries in America as in Europe "to the temple of religion: contemplate the objects and productions of nature as the great and marvelous works of Almighty God." Science, being a contemplation of wonders long since expounded, should enable Americans to look upon God "without superstitious terror," enable them to approach Him "without fanatical familiarity or mystical enthusiasm." Such was the spirit in which the thrust of modern science was received by the new Republic, and from that time on the rationalization for what we may call a spectator attitude of humble acquiescence has remained a problem for the scientific intelligence.

An interesting sidelight on the power of the concept gleams in the customary treatment throughout the period of Franklin's kite experiment. Augustus Woodward in 1816 expressed what had become the formula: America has made but one philosophical discovery, yet that "must be admitted to be one of the most important and sublime, which has ever been accomplished by human genius." From the vast literature of tribute we would gather no notion that Franklin was, in his own phrase, a "leather-aproned" man who tinkered and invented; rather, in the language of Robert C. Winthrop we behold a figure as majestic as Archimedes, or even more so: sending up his kite and deliberately drawing down upon himself the bolts of heaven, Franklin "presents a picture of even greater and nobler sublimity." He might incidentally aim at the good of mankind, but primarily he was enacting an "exhibition of moral and physical heroism."

A basic tenet in this structure of thought was, as John Craig said upon opening a course entitled "Experimental Philosophy" in 1819, "Of all the sciences, astronomy is the most sublime." Benjamin Silliman dedicated himself to becoming the first professional chemist in the country, but prefaced his lectures by saying, "Astronomy is, not without reason, regarded, by mankind, as the sublimest of the sciences." Occasionally celebrants of astronomy, as, for example, John Quincy Adams, for whom it was a form of religious worship and who suffered ridicule over his passion for "lighthouses of the sky," had to take cognizance of popular objections against the inutility of the science. Joel Poinsett, speaking on behalf of the Smithsonian in 1841, reprimanded the utilitarians for calling astronomy mere "star-gazing," and spelled out its practical effects, that it has carried along in its progress the physical and mathematical sciences, "as well as contributing to the advancement of the mechanic arts, and, in this respect, acting as the pioneer of civilization." Yet on the whole the American public displayed an astonishing readiness to read, or in the lyceums to listen to, interminable praises of astronomy as the one science sufficient unto itself. It is, said a lecturer in Lynchburg, Virginia, in 1837, the queen of the sciences because it is the only *"perfect one."* All others will modify or wholly change the expression of their laws, but, he orated,

How different is it in physical astronomy! Here our first conclusion is our last. Here particulars have been completely subjected to generals, effects to causes. . . . The only remaining work for future astronomers, is to determine with the extreme of accuracy the consequences of its rules, by the profoundest combinations of mathematics; and the magnitude of its data by the minutest scrupulousness of observation. . . . All the phenomena of this science depend upon a *single law.*

Passages of this sort, of which there are hundreds, reveal the special satisfaction the multitude found in panegyrics to astronomy. They needed to have no knowledge of their own, or to make the slightest exertion of mind; they could simply sit passively and admire, feel themselves inwardly excited at no cost to themselves. There is no science, as another speaker informed a class of "Young Ladies" in 1833, "more calculated to exalt the soul and fill it with sublime conceptions of the great Author of nature, than Astronomy." Even John

Quincy Adams usually concluded on this note of mental exhilaration: the sublimest of all contemplations for an energetic mind is "the structure of that universe, of which itself is an imperishable, though an infinitely diminutive atom." The very fact that astronomy was *the* perfect form of contemplation made it somehow comfortable—a fixed point in a world of accelerating change. And at the same time, it flattered the intelligence of the simple by telling them that even their intellects were somehow commensurate with the universe. "What, indeed, can be more astonishing," rhetorically asked Alexander Young in his eulogy on Nathaniel Bowditch, "than that a being like one of us, endowed apparently with no higher or different powers, should be able to obtain so minute and accurate a knowledge of those distant planets?" In this way Bowditch, being one of us, vindicated democratic self-respect.

As in so many other areas of the mind, if we wish to discover what the majority of citizens endorsed as profundity of thought, we must consider the orations of Edward Everett. No other orator so elegantly presented platitudes to the populace, because no one else so fervently believed them to be exertions of the brain. He was as true to form on astronomy as on the Battle of Gettysburg, and in 1857 was still expounding at St. Louis the spectator concept of the pageant as though nothing in his own century had in the slightest disturbed the equilibrium of the Enlightenment. While the phenomena of the heavens do indeed tax the highest powers of philosophical research, Everett said, the happy fact remains that they "are also well adapted to arrest the attention of minds barely tinctured with scientific culture, and even to touch the sensibilities of the wholly uninstructed observer." The complexities of chemistry, physiology, geography are lost on the common understanding, "but the unspeakable glories of the rising and the setting sun; the serene majesty of the moon, as she walks in full-orbed brightness through the heavens . . . these are objects which charm and astonish alike the philosopher and the peasant." Everett's ability, on the slightest provocation, to sing the glorious effects on the human psyche of astronomy—"The soul becomes great by the habitual contemplation of great objects"—and the never-failing readiness of his audiences to absorb this rhetoric speak volumes for what throughout the Republic was the unshakable conviction that this was the perfect science. Against this passivity, this mood of self-congratulation without curiosity or criticism, the aspiring naturalists, chemists, geologists, even the young physicians, had endlessly to contend. And as very quickly the inventor would become a folk hero, those who labored in other sciences had an increasingly difficult task getting a hearing for experiments or speculations which offered no immediate practical benefits nor filled the soul with such caressing emotions as did astronomy.

Yet it must be stressed that the people of the new nation were not unique in their veneration for a science which they could revere without understanding its details. The image of science which the eighteenth century bequeathed to America bespoke an international community and a sense of a rational cultivation superior to the random impulses of untutored nature. Self-respecting citizens of the Republic, though so occupied in farming or in acquiring wealth that they had no time for unproductive meditation, still could, in rare moments of relaxation, assure themselves that in their high estimation of science as sublimity, especially in their nodding agreement to all tributes to astronomy, they too were part of civilization. Every assertion that they, or their spokesmen, were not savages in the forest, that they participated in the universal intellect of Europe, was a way of reassuring themselves against their unsettling fear of appearing eccentric. Over and over again they applauded the remark that the Indians had shown themselves incapable of scientific thought, and so nervously agreed with John Fairbanks in 1812 "that the natural state of man is that of civilization; because in this state his dignity is advanced, and his faculties improved, which furnish him with powers the savage cannot possess."

3.

NATIONALITY WITHIN UNIVERSALITY

Happily the scientific creed which eager Americans took from Europe gave them gracious permission to be, within reasonable limits, themselves. It was not incompatible with membership in the concert of Europe for the budding scientist to pay attention to the particular phenomena of his country or even of his limited locality. The early exhortations suggest that there existed an apprehension among the learned lest, in their pride of military victory, they should become in natural philosophy too chauvinistic and so expose themselves to ridicule. In 1789 Nicholas Collin, after acknowledging to the American Philosophical Society—which body was especially determined that it should not be accounted a merely provincial assembly—that philosophers are citizens of the world, and the fruits of their labors are freely distributed among all nations, went on to affirm it to be their duty, in the highest sense, "to cultivate with peculiar attention those parts of science, which are most beneficial to that country in which Providence has appointed their earthly stations." The virtuoso was in the most gratifying of positions: where the theologian, the lawyer, and above all the poet were torn between the patriotic urge to be original and caution lest forced straining for particularity should result in grotesque caricatures of the accumulated sagacity of mankind, the scientist had not only the leave but a positive injunction to cultivate his own garden. He alone need not worry about appearing to be a provincial boor.

In the universe of science, Collin assured Philadelphia, patriotic affections are "conducive to the general happiness of mankind, because we have the best means of investigating those objects, which are most interesting to us." John Ewing lectured for years at the University of Pennsylvania, officially upon Newtonian physics, but in the course of expounding a cosmos in which nationality was an irrelevance he contrived to indicate how he, and such friends as Jefferson and Peale, could conscientiously foster an *American* science without deserting the attitude of a true philosophe:

When you survey the extensive fields of useful knowledge, which are opening to your investigation, through the unexplored deserts of this new world, and the improvements that are daily making by the sons of science, you must naturally feel your hearts swell with an honest and laudable ambition, to distinguish yourselves amongst the most celebrated inventors of those useful arts, which have a tendency to exalt the understanding, alleviate the miseries of human nature, and promote the happiness of mankind.

Where the literary enthusiast appeared presumptuous in calling for an American Milton, Benjamin Shultz in 1795 could temperately venture to predict that in America "a genius equal, if not superior, to a Buffon, a Linnaeus, or a Spallanzi" could plausibly arise when "European habits shall no longer influence our various pursuits." John Coxe obviously exceeded the bounds of sobriety when he dreamed of an American Newton or Bacon, but Shultz's targets were more attainable.

For, as Benjamin Barton said in 1798, this age was above all one of natural science: "The mind of LINNAEUS has effected more than the combined intellects of all the naturalists of any preceding century." And if there was a science in which the provincial observer could make contributions to universality by concentrating upon his restricted field of vision, it was botany, and to almost the same extent zoology. "Even the *nomenclature* of our productions is extremely imperfect," said Barton, and this blank in the history of science gave him pain. But, already in 1798, "This pain, however, is daily diminished, for something is daily added to the stock of our knowledge."

Indeed, in this area of exploration the efflorescence of talent in the first five or six decades of independence remains even today a subject to marvel at. The names of the two Bartrams and Audubon are familiar to most students of American history, but few are aware of the monumental works of—to name only a few—James DeKay with his *Zoology of New York;* Stephen Elliott and his *Sketch of the Botany of South Carolina and Georgia;* Lewis R. Gibbs's *Catalogue of the Phaenogamus Plants of Columbia, South Carolina, and Its Vicinity;* John Bachman, a Charleston minister, with his *The Viviparous Quadrupeds of North America;* Dr. Edmund Ravenel's *Echinidae, Recent and Fossil, of South Carolina;* Samuel Latham Mitchell's lectures on a wide range of topics, including a *Synopsis of Chemical Nomenclature and Arrangement,* and *The Present State of Medical Learning in the City of New York;* Alexander Wilson and his *American Ornithology.* John Edwards Holbrook, a Charleston physician whose hobby was zoology, published *North American Herpetology* in 1836–1838, and lived to be told by Agassiz that he had "first compelled European recognition of American science by the accuracy and originality of his investigations," and that Europe had "nothing which could compare with it." That certain Europeans, notably Constantine Rafinesque, could enter freely into the American enterprise, leave it and then return to it, only confirmed the fact that the more nationalistic its motivation the more it secured an American position in the international conference. Chiefly relying upon the acknowledged fame of these naturalists—most of whom were not professionals, but pursued their studies in time taken from their professions—John Quincy Adams in 1843 permitted himself to glow, as much as an Adams could, with pride:

We have been sensible of our obligation to maintain the character of a civilized, intellectual, and spirited nation. We have been, perhaps, over boastful of our freedom, and over sensitive to the censure of our neighbors. The arts and sciences, which we have pursued with most intense interest, and persevering energy, have been those most adapted to our own condition.

Adams spoke these words on the occasion of laying the cornerstone of an observatory in Cincinnati, being careful at the same time to remind his hearers that the science of the eternal heavens was as much adapted to our condition as that of our plants and birds. He would hardly have spoken with such affected ingenuousness had he not been fully aware that in the science of astronomy the tension between patriotism and universality could not easily be dissipated. Gouverneur Emerson, dedicating a monument to Thomas Godfrey in 1843, was openly inviting trouble by his insistence that as a scientist he was a "cosmopolite," ready to honor all who promote useful discoveries: "In relation to such matters, the empire of science should be regarded as universal, and not subject to the restrictions imposed by geographical circumstances." There were gatherings in which an avowal of this sentiment could have been shouted down as treason.

If the tension between nationality and cosmopolitanism in the American mind had been merely the oversensitiveness of a society-in-the-making to the censures of such critics as Marryat, Basil Hall, and Mrs. Trollope, Adams's summary would have subdued the passions. But the truth of the matter is that national pride had been so mobilized as to become insatiable. Compliments to a few naturalists who had observed or portrayed indigenous species were not enough to assuage a vanity only too painfully aware that in general studies America had not lived up to its opportunity. What it should have done, what every moment it had to demand of itself, was to create a science equal in majesty to the colossal expanse of its landscape. A handful of practicing naturalists could possess their souls in patience while identifying and classifying a lonely specimen, but a legion of orators were demanding that the American genius achieve at a single leap a scientific comprehension as much more compendious than that of feudal Europe as the continent was more extended than those congested lands. Into the American eagerness for scientific distinction was injected, bit by bit, the dangerous persuasion that an intellect tutored by nothing more than the grandeurs of Nature could easily dispense with the rigors of Old World discipline. Consequently, the more it became apparent that in the United States there appeared few, if any, whose minds were a match for the professionals of Europe, the more embarrassment grew, and the more a compensatory scorn for the purely contemplative, the traitorously cosmopolitan intellect increased.

It all began innocently enough with the naturalists' persuasion that in America there must exist innumerable plants, birds, insects which no Linnaeus or Buffon had catalogued, and that hence even an amateur would make contributions to the categories. The American Academy of Arts and Sciences in Boston commenced operation in 1780, modestly addressing itself to an ample field in which the ingenious might "expatiate" during their leisure. This is, it remarked in the first volume of Academy *Memoirs* published in 1785, an extensive country, with a rich variety of soils and streams wherein "the citizens have great opportunities and advantages for making useful experiments and improvements," whereby—in the spirit of the Enlightenment—"the interest and happiness of the rising empire may be essentially advanced." The progress from this sober moderation to the thunder of the scientific patriots was rapid, bewildering, and strident.

We may note the beginning of the shift in, for example, Samuel Smith's address on education to the American Philosophical Society in 1797, which probably saw no nationalistic distortion in his concluding that the opportunities for research on this continent "could not fail to elevate the United States far above other nations" on earth. But cosmopolites might have become genuinely perturbed by 1808 when a writer in *The Medical Repository,* expatiating on the wide field for investigation, said it had too long been fashionable for Americans to seek scientific news from transatlantic regions, that now they are learning "to turn their backs to the east, and direct their views to the inviting and productive regions of interior America." After the Treaty of Ghent, however, such tentative essays at scientific isolationism would come to sound tame indeed, while the atmosphere echoed with the ever-stirring word "sublime." Everything in this nation, asserted a lyceum speaker in 1820, is colossal. Nature here "retains her native and unsophisticated charms, and towers on high in all the picturesque splendour of beauty, and in all the grandeur of sublimity." In that year Dr. Daniel Drake, who was a man of scientific sobriety, was telling Cincinnati that our scientific future should be scaled to the physical expanse of the continent. "Let the architects of our national greatness," he solemnly said, "conform to the dictates of science; and the monuments they construct will rise beautiful as our hills, imperishable as our mountains, as lofty as their summits, which tower sublimely above the clouds."

Though for decade after decade these exhortations had tacitly to confess that the scientific accomplishment of this nation lay still in the future, this admission seldom inhibited rhetorical grandiloquence. Albert Barnes, speaking on Literature and Science at Hamilton College in 1836, told the enthralled students that the freshness and vastness of Nature in America filled the soul with grand conceptions and so invited it to successful investigations. "It seems," he concluded, "almost as if God, in favor to science and the enlargement of the human mind, had reserved the knowledge of the western world, until almost the last felicitous investigations that could be made had been made in the old world." In so short a time, only ten years after the death of Jefferson, the naïve self-satisfaction of America had created this image of its scientific personality.

Assurance was constantly reinforced by a reiterated contention that American society was the one in the world most congenial to scientific exertion. To modern eyes the voluminous literature upon this theme is the most monotonous as well as the most unfortunate in the era, but we can never understand America without a realization of the terrible power of the argument. A good example—if only for its phrasing of the typical—is a speech by Thomas Jones to the Franklin Institute in 1826, for by then the observation had become stereotyped and could safely be delivered en bloc to the "mechanics." Our institutions, asserted Jones, admit of no degrading distinctions, our disposition is outraged by any attempt to make useful pursuits odious, our country permits the human mind to exert its native energies. Jones spoke of Bacon, Newton, Linnaeus, and summed up his case by noting that these would have been even greater men had they been presented with the opportunities now offered to the rising mechanics of Philadelphia: "How would they have been aided in their progress, and have been relieved from days of toil and nights of vigilance, in attempting to obtain a knowledge of the first principles of science."

Occasionally, we sadly note, even the most sanguine had to lament that so far the "inducements which are held out by commerce" appeared to have temporarily seduced the scientific intellect, but they usually came round to the inspiriting conclusion that once this boundless empire should be populated, "the collateral pursuits of natural sciences, will keep pace with, or follow closely upon, the steps of these improvements, and the golden era of our intellectual history will then have commenced." The important point to be made was that in a republic the mind enjoys an uninterrupted use of its powers—"unallowed by the grossness of superstitious reverence, and unshadowed by the awe of the tyrant's frown." In this land, then, "we have reason to look for the highest efforts of genius." It might be too much to suppose that the democracy would soon produce a Shakespeare, but what more plausible than that it would astonish degenerate Europe with a Newton or a Laplace? There seemed abundant proof "that the glowing anticipations we form of our meridian glory, are not mere discolourations of youthful fancy."

In view of what most foreign visitors, especially Tocqueville, charged against the nation, we should note that a few apologists were sufficiently aware of the issue to attempt refutation of the idea that a democracy was inherently suspicious of science. Frances Wright D'Arusmont, in the month after Jackson's inauguration, went out of her way at the opening of the Hall of Science in New York to deny that there existed any mood of intellectual cowardice among the populace. "The spirit of enquiry is abroad; the dawn of a brighter day is kindling in the horizon, and the eyes *of the people* are opening to its observa-

tion." Madame D'Arusmont did strike, or half strike, a somewhat foreboding note in acknowledging a "common persuasion" that science
might be the private preserve of only trained scientists, but she dismissed
any such imputation as merely an attempt "by the crafty and the superficial to palm upon society deficiency for skill, or error for truth."
In the security of this confidence, countless American orators announced, as did Richard Harlan at the University of Pennsylvania in
1837:

What may not be expected in a country like our own? where the monstrous
forms of superstition and authority, which tend to make ignorance *perpetual,*
by setting bounds to the progress of the mind in its inquiry after physical
truths, no longer bar the avenues of science; and where the liberal hand of
nature has spread around us in rich profusion, the objects of our research.

Thus Nature and the social order wonderfully jibed together, and
made certain that in science, if not in literature, America should advance to a resplendent future. Only a slight question persisted: where
and how were the brains to be trained for this performance? Granted
that the people were not so suspicious of mathematical ability as they
were of skill in the law, still even they had to admit that Newtons
could not, like officers in the Revolution, be summoned ready-made
from the plow.

The hope seemed to lie not so much in educational institutions as in
the societies. These would prove the instruments of a democratic culture, would strike the proper balance between provincial ambition and
recognition of the cosmopolitan fraternity. Through them Americans
might modestly claim a place which they could eventually justify by
actual performance. Benjamin Franklin had pointed the way: the
American Philosophical Society, founded in 1743, had, though contending with initial discouragements, vindicated Franklin's purpose.
In Boston, the American Academy of Arts and Sciences in 1785 could
define the aim more precisely. Scientific societies, it pronounced, may
bring together persons ready to supply each other with hints of progress, publish their discussions, and excite a spirit of emulation that
will enkindle the sparks of genius which otherwise in this America
"might forever have been concealed." Societies could, in short, be
both national and international, and lead the Republic into a
scientific haven. Through these associations, continued the Boston
Academy, "knowledge of various kinds, and greatly useful to mankind,
has taken place of the dry and uninteresting speculations of schoolmen." Through them, "solid learning and philosophy have more increased, than they had done for many centuries before." Thus adver-

tised as engines of social betterment, and thus blessed by the Philadelphia and Boston precedents, the savants of innumerable localities organized themselves into institutes, societies, academies, and supplied the tumultuous democracy with lanterns of learning, generally more flickering than resolute, but always endeavoring to keep alight even a smoky torch of learning.

One might plausibly argue that the societies did yeoman service for the cause in America not by supporting scientific research (which they could seldom afford) or by encouraging speculation (for they seldom knew enough to recognize worthwhile endeavor), or even by their publications (though many of these were of inestimable value in sustaining lonely workers), but chiefly by bewailing the outcast state of scientific activity in America. By lamenting what the nation lacked in comparison with Europe, the society orators continued to prod the nation to recognition that it belonged to the larger culture. In Europe, Stephen Elliott told the Charleston Literary and Philosophical Society in 1814, "the pursuit of science has long been a cherished and a fashionable occupation." With this reminder Charleston was induced to construct a museum. When Theodoric Beck eulogized the career of Simeon DeWitt before the Albany Institute in 1835, he explained how as against Europe our means of investigation were limited and partial, our men of ability scattered over a large country, that while we have an abundance of talent we have no arsenal of data. His aim was clearly to stimulate, if only for the moment, discontent among the burghers with the inadequacies of Albany's accommodations. The histories of the several institutions founded in these years have been recited; most of them are poignant, and some are tawdry. Yet among even the most forlorn of them, let alone the Philadelphia and Boston undertakings, there always shines something of that persuasion which DeWitt Clinton imparted to the Literary and Philosophical Society of New York in 1814, that even so humble an association might prove an instrument for paving the way to the "sublime result" of making the United States "the chosen seat, and favourite abode, of learning and science."

4.

UTILITY WITHIN UNIVERSALITY

The intellect of the philosophe, in either Europe or America, never actively despised the application of scientific principles to ordinary affairs of life. Thomas Jefferson himself complained to Thomas Ewell in 1805 that professional chemists wrote unintelligible nonsense to each other, "while the arts of making bread, butter, cheese, vinegar, soap, beer, cider, &c, remain unexplained." Yet the disciple of the Enlightenment was apt to be nervously apologetic about the practical consequences of his knowledge. A last stand, or nearly the last, of this attitude was made by James Dean at the University of Vermont in 1810. The original vision granted to human foresight seldom, according to Dean, exhibited the least promise of ultimate application; while the philosopher should neglect no prospect of promoting the convenience of society, he should think first of "the pleasure of the investigation, or the gratification of curiosity," and so "when utility presents itself," it should be treated like fame accruing to the man of merit, something that comes unlooked for, if it comes at all.

One consequence which we may find appealing was that in the Revolutionary generation there is displayed a disposition to account for the useful results of science as a proof of mankind's inherently benevolent nature. Machines that save human labor are not profit-making devices but benefactions to the race. The explorers of science, noted Samuel Miller, have, while principally concerned with gratifying their liberal curiosity, incidentally contributed to "the abridgment of labour; the increase both of expedition and elegance of workmanship, in manufactures; and the promotion of human comfort, to a degree beyond all former precedent." Men like Peale and Jefferson found endless satisfaction in the prospect of scientific agriculture because it would ameliorate the condition of man. "To produce the best effect of labor with ease," exclaimed Peale, "how vastly important!" In that spirit Jefferson scorned to patent his moldboard, wishing it to be a gift to civilization; Peale likewise refused to patent his windmill.

Yet even before these two sages had left the scene, commentators were showing signs of anxiety over a shift of emphasis. Timothy Ford told the Charleston Society in 1817 that he would not insult it by predicating the inducements to the cultivation of science "solely upon the grounds of mere utility," but he also resented in its name an English sneer that Americans have made some few advances in chemistry, but always "in connexion with some *useful* and *gainful occupation*," that they "have not yet found leisure to pursue it as a science of *amusement*." Ford's anger, however, is directed not at the charge of excessive utilitarianism, but at the idea that Americans could not combine successfully *both* the practical and the disinterested. Rapidly thereafter speakers on similar occasions are reduced to protesting that they do not undervalue "the natural and mechanical sciences," and wish well to the comfort of mankind, but after all the main function of science is moral and aesthetic. Walter R. Johnson published in the *Journal* of the Franklin Institute in 1828 a noble but obviously doomed series "On the Combination of a Practical with a Liberal Course of Education," and in a still more noble speech of 1831 contended, "It may be important to subdue the physical elements, and make them subservient to our wants and conveniences;—but much more so, to subdue the chaotic elements of human society to the form of a well regulated community." The pathos of this and a thousand other idealistic protestations is in their all being confessions that the world of science in America had become radically reoriented: there was simply no longer any place in it for the large and benevolent conceptions of a Peale or a Jefferson.

In 1829 Jacob Bigelow published in Boston a book entitled *Elements of Technology*. It should be honored as a major document in American intellectual development; it has not been so esteemed because, of course, the technological revolution already extensively under way when Bigelow wrote has proceeded at such a pace that his little book seems rudimentary. Yet it is indeed curious that the highly industrialized society of twentieth-century America can be bullied by humanistic professors into remembering Emerson's *Nature* of 1836, or even to cherishing the candlesticks and spinning wheels of our preindustrial past, and yet will not bother to salute in Bigelow a prophet more relevant to the later economy than either Emerson or Jefferson. Young Dr. Bigelow in effect declared the independence of the nineteenth century from the eighteenth—of the practical, materialistic, hardheaded, utilitarian age from that of ideology and benevolence. He lived to remember, in 1867, that in 1829 the very term "technology" was unknown and that he had been accused of crass barbarism. In the later year he could note that there was a thriving Massachusetts Institute of Technology, and that applied science had advanced "with greater strides than any other agent of civilization; and has done more than any science to enlarge the boundaries of profitable knowledge, to extend the dominion of mankind over nature, to economize and utilize both labor and time, and thus to add indefinitely to the effective and available length of human existence." Though some passages in his expressed satisfaction with his age seem to come from the philosophes, his appreciation of the saving of human labor has nothing in common with earlier benevolence: Bigelow's calculation is tough and rudely commercial. In his delight over having proved a true prophet, there is no occasion for him ever to mention that Emerson was related to the age, or for his paying any mind to the animadversions of a Henry Thoreau against the march of technology. Of what profit could it be,

Dr. Bigelow and the Boston of his time might well have asked, to give heed to impotent whimpers against "whatever may tend to increase the facilities of subsistence, and the welfare of those among whom we live"?

Bigelow's boldness in announcing the new era, along with his gracious tribute to history for having borne him out, obscures the slow stages through which the gospel of science was, in America, converted to stark utilitarianism. Looking back from the mechanical order that ultimately prevailed, these tentative struggles may seem not worth recounting; yet they are memorable in the history of American thought. What I find most striking in these endeavors to come to terms with the process is the insistence that mounting devotion to technology is compatible with the universal, the cosmopolitan character of the scientific intellect, and no mere glorification of the nation. Only thus could the national conscience afford to become nationalistic, relieved of responsibility for proving itself benevolent toward mankind in general, and concentrate upon improving American technology, trusting other peoples to look out for themselves.

We perceive how the new voice answered to the echoes of the old in a lecture by Robert Fulton given in Washington on February 17, 1810, on—of all things—"Torpedoes." The inventor of the steamboat, having triumphed over his long ordeal of ridicule, was now listened to with solemn attention, whatever he published read with excitement. Fulton's conception of the scientist was of no philosophe but of an "inventor silently laboring in his cabinet," one who receives the "appellation of a projector," toward whom the sneers of contempt "are in proportion to the magnitude of the object which he has in view, and its range beyond the limits of vulgar understandings." Benevolence has somehow evaporated while Fulton depicts the man of science as one at war with the inertia of mankind, one who is right when all the rest are wrong. Strong enough to bear the contempt of society, founding his theories on the laws of Nature, he it is to whom mankind is indebted for not remaining as uncivilized as the aborigines of the American forest; "This to a man of science is a consoling reflection." Fulton may, as even his friends would admit, have been a bit soured by his own experience; but he presented himself and his confreres as a type quite different from Franklin with his kite. He taught the public no longer to envisage the scientist as the worshipper of cosmic order, but as the hero who sacrifices himself for a specific invention from which the community will eventually profit enormously, but which the generality have been too stupid to recognize. What then are to be the relations between technology and democracy? With the mere breathing of this question there opened a prospect which Jefferson had never so much as imagined.

The conception of science as primarily a form of contemplation was inevitably transformed into a more activist ideal by the lure of the vast continent, especially after the philosopher Jefferson had purchased "Louisiana." Partisans of science were bound to see it as a challenge to the conquest of the wilderness, though it is remarkable that they moved cautiously toward this argument, as though reluctant to cast loose from the moorings of pure natural philosophy. Yet they, like the lawyers, had to align themselves on the side of a future which would be artificial, urban, and comfortable, which would not be diverted by Natty Bumppo's lament for the desecrated forests. In 1817 a society formed in New York for the encouragement of domestic manufactures endeavored to project the Jeffersonian dream of human felicity into a world where men would not sit under their vines and fig trees, but would go forth to shops and factories:

There cities, towns, and villages, centres of intersecting orbits through which domestic commerce will revolve, shall rise and flourish. And whilst the plough shall trace the silent furrow, the mill shall turn, the anvil ring, and the merry shuttle dance. The exhaustless stores of mind and matter shall be this nation's treasury. Adventurous man, triumphing over the obstacles of nature, shall search the recesses of the stubborn mountain. The sounding tools, and the voice of human speech shall wake the echo in the vaulted space; where from the beginning, silence and darkness reigned; and the rich ore shall quit its hidden bed, and sparkle in the upper day.

To any demurrer that however eloquently the vista was presented, what really was proposed was that science enter into the service of economy, the answer would be that by furnishing the Republic with factories, science would make of the nation "a proud promontory, whose base is in the deep, whose summit strikes the clouds; the storms of fate may smite upon its breast, the fretful ocean surge upon its base; it will remain unshaken, unimpaired—type of duration—emblem of eternity!" The problem, however, still eluded the rhetorician. Could this technological majesty join with the starry heavens above and the moral law within to form a peculiarly American trinity of the Sublime?

Another decade more, and the question would be radically altered into a query as to whether the stars and the moral law could any longer keep up with the dazzling light of applied science. We should not be surprised that the lawyer in whose mighty intellect we have seen the heritage of the eighteenth century refashioned to the needs of nineteenth-century America would also be the one to announce a happy reconciliation of the mind to applicability. Judge Joseph Story

informed the Boston Mechanics' Institute in 1829 that the outstand-
ing characteristic of this age is "the superior attachment to practical
science over merely speculative science," averring that this is true
even in metaphysics! The jurist was, if anything, more blunt than the
physician: until recently, Story declared in Bigelow's vein, scholars
"looked with indifference or disdain upon the common arts of life, and
felt it to be a reproach to mingle in the business of the artisan," but
when at last they grasped the idea that applied science led to financial
reward, they began "to devote themselves practically to the improvements of the arts." And a good thing that was, according to Story.
Both art and science have prospered by this victory of common sense.
"The manufacturer, the machinist, the chemist, the engineer, who is
eminent in his art, may now place himself by the side of the scholar,
and the mathematician, and the philosopher, and find no churlish
claim for precedency put in." Story, from Harvard, could tell an
audience of factory laborers that this "fortunate change in public
opinion" has made it not only profitable but honorable for them to
ply their trades, and to tell them that hereafter they would instruct the
scientists rather than the scientists them, because in manufactures the
wit of man is tasked to invent "cheaper, thriftier, or neater combinations." He does not say anything about wages.

Story, the very type of the legendary "conservative," is here, as
elsewhere, the classic liberal of his century. In 1836 a Congressional
Committee investigating the Patent Office produced a report which
gives a sort of official sanction to the technological era. It points out,
in flat chronological narrative without any apostrophes to sublimity,
that the War of 1812 had been a blessing because of the immense
impetus it imparted to American manufactures. Since then, it recounts,
the development of "human ingenuity" in this country has been more
spectacular than in any other period of recorded history—including
ancient Egypt. The congressmen were prepared to be as amazed and
reverent as any philosophe before the infinite perfection, but the glory
they beheld was no longer the Creator's simple plan of the universe,
but man's boundless knack for inventing. For them science had become nothing but technology; they had no sense that in marveling
over the miracle they lost what the true savant would have considered
the heart of the matter:

Who can predict the results, even in a few years, of that spirit of enterprise
which pervades the Union, when, aided by the Genius of Invention, and
propelled onward by powers which she alone can bring into exercise? The very
elements are submissive to her will, and all the endless combinations of mechanism are subservient to her purposes.

In this atmosphere, the language of a Franklin, a Rittenhouse, even of a Samuel Miller, becomes desiccated, and if it survives at all, it is only that the dried husks may be filled with a new moisture. "American industry and enterprise, guided," according to the congressmen, "by American ingenuity and intellect," have achieved in thirty years "what would have taken Europe a century to accomplish."

There is no need here for reciting an inventory of inventions and mechanical improvements which daily staggered the imagination of Americans in the early nineteenth century. Men like Bigelow and Story delighted to intone the list, as ultimately did Walt Whitman. Because the catalogue continued, and is still continuing, to expand, these technological dithyrambs from the age of Mr. Justice Story may seem merely quaint; but examined for their rhetoric rather than for their comprehension of the processes of change, they remain case histories of the growth of the American mind, as important for modern analysis as debates in the Congress or as literary creations.

Most instructive, I should say, was the quantity, range, and repetitiousness of the celebration of the glories of steam. Words ring countless descants upon the majestic theme—not to any particular mechanism activated by this marvelous "motive agent," but merely to steam itself—the pure white jet that fecundates America. The imagery frequently becomes, probably unconsciously, sexual, and so betrays how in this mechanistic orgasm modern America was conceived.

The parabola of language may be said to spring from Thomas Fessenden's *Compendious View of Some of the Most Useful Modern Discoveries and Inventions* of 1810, a bold assertion of utility, albeit still so contained within the framework of the Enlightenment as to vouchsafe only a bare mention to the steamboat while praising at length the cotton gin. Yet he did say that the most valuable gift philosophers have given to the arts of life is the steam engine, and this because, in contrast to the compass, the telescope, gunpowder—which were "productions of chance"—steam was from the beginning "the result of reflection," with every subsequent improvement being "the effect of philosophical study." Indeed, during the next three or four decades, the legend of James Watt and the teakettle was inflated in America to proportions as great as that of Washington and the cherry tree. And the stupendous conquests by steam grow with the legend:

It is on the ocean, it is on the rivers, it is on the mountains, it is in the valleys, it is at the bottom of mines, it is in the shops, it is every where at work. It propels the ship, it rows the boat, it cuts, it pumps, it hammers, it cards, it spins, it weaves, it washes, it cooks, it prints, and releases man of nearly all bodily toil.

It annihilates space, brings the world to a unity, and all this mighty power is acquired by a "scientific" knowledge of the air we breathe and the water we drink "so as to make these familiar objects work for man."

Clearly the progression from Fessenden to this 1846 *Discourse of the Baconian Philosophy* by Samuel Tyler was, at least rhetorically, an intoxicating revel. And other voices joined the chorus. Steam "as a motive agency" is the greatest triumph of human ingenuity, Charles Fraser told the Mercantile Library Association of Charleston in an address on *The Moral Influence of Steam*: "it seems to be rather the effect of discovery than the discovery itself, that so widely distinguishes it from all others."

While sectional animosities augmented in the nation during the 1840's, spokesmen from both sides appealed to possible forces of union; and just as on each side they invoked the Revival, so also they called upon the conciliatory offices of steam:

Something was wanted to give a practical effect to the prominent theory of our government. The philanthropist regarded it as the last experiment of rational freedom, and trembled for the result. But an agent was at hand to bring everything into harmonious co-operation, to vanquish every obstacle, to crown all enterprise, to subdue prejudice, and to unite every part of our land in rapid and friendly communication; and that was *steam*.

These words were spoken in Charleston, South Carolina.

At the same time that steam was proving incapable of warding off secession, in New York there appeared a massive two-volume summary of *Eighty Years' Progress of the United States*, in which steam still reigned as the presiding goddess—and in which the Confederacy could have, and should have, read its doom. The scene presented was one which not even Fulton in his wildest dreams had pictured, for not only are ships propelled by steam, "not alone in the large manufactory, the gallant steamer, and the rushing car, does the vapor of water show its strength and usefulness, but thickly strewn about our cities and villages, delving in mines, driving the rattling press, it helps all trades, and multiplies the power of man a thousand fold." Under its magic touch, so an agrarian South might have learned, cities have sprung up, "and everywhere we see traces of the king of motors—steam!" And the king of motors took precedence over the queen of the sciences, and utility fought the war which astronomy could never have won.

For the galloping triumphs of steam (our two volumes predicted that the time would come when steam would no longer "frighten horses in our cities . . . for there will be no horses to frighten") there remained only one term through which the human mind could encompass the marvel. "Its introduction and gradual improvement," said James Renwick in his *Treatise on the Steam Engine* in 1839, "have required inventive talents of the highest order, and the exertions of genius the most sublime." It has already surpassed the brilliant conceptions of poetry and the wildest fables of romance. Even so, it promises "to fulfill yet higher destinies." As another acolyte of the machine expressed it, "These are only the precursors of other still more sublime accomplishments reserved for human genius—the dawnings of that perfection which futurity will unfold."

Steam was a particularly rewarding theme for such chants because it appeared to contain an especial affinity for America. Or at least after 1807 patriots talked as though it had, even though America had not actually invented the engine. They more than compensated by exclaiming, "The honour of converting the agency of this wonderful machine into a new channel;—of applying its energies to the propelling of vessels on the water;—was reserved for a native of our own country—for an individual on 'the wrong side of the Atlantick;'—for the American Archimedes;—the immortal Fulton." Henry Clay's "American System" could hardly have been conceived without the aid of the machine, and so he above all other orators elevated it to glory. Contrasting it with the struggling, barely moving keelboat, Clay described the gay, cheerful and "protected" passengers (in all these panegyrics the appalling number of explosions and the slaughter of innocent passengers were discreetly not mentioned) as the steamboat rushes past the outmoded contraption whose "scanty cargo is scarcely worth the transportation." And, revealingly, the beauty of this spectacle for Clay is that both artificial economy and natural sublimity coincide in the American victory: "Nature herself seems to survey, with astonishment, the passing wonder, and, in silent submission, reluctantly to own the magnificent triumphs, in her own vast domain, of Fulton's immortal genius!"

Celebrants of the steamboat always dilated on its immense utilitarian consequences, its bringing the inhabitants of the world near to each other, spreading the influence of religion, civilization, and the arts; but from the beginning, down to the great scenes of Mark Twain, the steamboat was chiefly a subject of ecstasy for its sheer majesty and might, especially for its stately progress at night, blazing with light through the swamps and forests of Nature. The *Claremont* was described by some who saw her in the night, said Fulton's biographer in 1817, "as a monster moving on the waters, defying the winds and tide, and breathing flames and smoke." Almost always there is explicit delight that in this device man has overcome Nature. As a salutation in *The American Journal of Science* in 1818 put it, this creature, stronger than the largest animal, more manageable than the smallest, propels itself "against the currents, the winds, and the waves, of the ocean," and so on the very bosom of these most overwhelmingly sublime of natural elements establishes "the luxuries and accommodations of the land." For this *Journal,* from its inception fighting for the independence of the American mind, resisting the currents of enthusiasm from abroad which elevated the heart above the head with its "romantic" praises of Nature against civilization, staked out its battle lines by calling the steamboat "that legitimate child of physical and chemical science." Nor with Fulton as its model need the *Journal* submit to any charge of gross materialism, for in 1806 Fulton had refused a profitable invitation from the War Department because, intent upon his engine, as he wrote to the Secretary, "I labour with the ardour of an enthusiast." As steamboats extended their sway from the great rivers to the Atlantic, there were many who with intentional malice exclaimed over what "a magnificent FACT" is an ocean vessel: "How completely such a floating palace transcends the wildest dream of which the builder of the gigantic Pyramids or even Archimedes himself might be supposed capable."

Less spectacular than the steamboat, but still offering similar possibilities for literary improvement into another demonstration of the intellectual majesty of applied science, was the factory. Here also the revolution in rhetoric and in mental attitudes is as violent as that in the economy. Hamilton's *Report on Manufactures* in 1791 may not have been quite as prophetic as later historians have made out, but for something over two decades it seemed entirely chimeric. The dominant, or the dominantly vocal, thinking was enunciated by Jefferson in *Notes on Virginia,* that "artificers" were the panders of vice and instruments for the destruction of liberties. As late as 1813 Theodoric Beck, addressing in New York a society for the promotion of "Useful Arts," assumed that no patriot could for a moment wish "that the United States should become, in the strict sense of the word, a manufacturing country," for the disease, vice, and "diversified forms of misery" in those parts of England "from whence our hardware and cloths are obtained, are sufficient to make the most sanguine advocate of manufactures tremble."

While the change that transformed the national intellect thereafter may be told solely in terms of technology and financial opportunity, in its own terms it made its way through two dawning recognitions: one, that the machine was compatible with piety, and two, that the factory was a victory for pure science and not a degradation of the mind. John Griscom in 1819 told of his marveling within a manufactory of cotton goods in Manchester at the genius which could bring into subservience to mankind so many opposing movements. "Can it be possible that any man can contemplate such a train of machinery . . . and regard all this as the offspring of thought and reflection, and yet remain a materialist!" As this mode of thought developed, it utilized little or nothing of Hamilton's tough realism, but instead tried to smuggle the cause of manufactures under the canopy of Jeffersonian intellectualism. A Philadelphia magazine devoted its short life between 1812 and 1814 to pleading the cause of applied devices because they "would extend knowledge of all kinds, particularly scientifical." It advanced courageously out of the Enlightenment, expecting the universe of the philosophes to be strengthened, never in the least overturned. The "tradesmen of Great Britain," it declared, meaning the factory owners, can now "furnish more profound thinkers on philosophical subjects, more acute and accurate experimenters, more real philosophers thrice told, than all Europe could furnish a century ago." The writer, probably Thomas Cooper, dared to hope that Americans might construct factories so they might also learn a bit of "mathematical and physical science," but doubted that they would do much because of their unfortunate penchant for political disputation. It may well have taken considerable courage for William Duane in 1811 to tell the people of Pennsylvania that the legislature should not feel it any derogation of their republican independence to borrow ideas from European nations in order to improve roads and factories, and thus to give to the "rising youth, of both sexes, the foundation of knowledge, love of country, virtue and industry; they can so direct the energies and resources of this commonwealth."

When we seek to comprehend the processes of the American intellect, in this as in later phases, we must dwell upon the curious fact that the technological transformation of an agricultural society into an industrial economy was symbolized in such propositions as "The time has already [1814] arrived, when a general diffusion of the knowledge of Europe on these subjects, cannot fail of being highly interesting and beneficial amongst us." Analyzed into its components, this statement tells us volumes about that hesitant period, though even it is exceeded in revelation by the speech of another short-lived society in New York "for the Encouragement of Domestic Manufactures," this time in 1817, which grandly exhorts the "artificer and philosopher" to combine their endeavors, "to walk by the side of practice," in order that in factories America may follow its destiny: "The head that conceives, will soon find the hand that can execute, and nothing of the stock of intellect will go to loss." Was there any reason, therefore, why a republic which already had an Eli Whitney and a Fulton should cower in chagrin because it had not yet a Newton? "The power of generalizing will follow as of course."

In fact, the nation might say—virtually did say—that it could boast one as great as Newton, though in a different way—Francis Lowell. His feat of memory, of going through English factories, divining and retaining in his head the plans of secret machines, seemed to his fellow-citizens an act of patriotic espionage beyond all conceivable merit. When he got his textile mill operating in Waltham, he brought to behold it one of his backers, Nathan Appleton, subsequently to be father-in-law to the sweet Longfellow; Appleton sat staring at the spindles, struck dumb before this manifestation of the sublime. Lowell, the customary eulogy ran, was a man of genius; if Michelangelo gained imperishable fame as the man who placed the pantheon in the heavens, then "surely the thought of bringing the workshops of Europe to our shores, and of doing it, was as great, and of more importance, to millions of our race."

As the progress of industry more and more demonstrated what benefits it could confer on the populace, its defenders needed less and less to fear frank assertion of its claims against the still-dominant agricultural interest. "Manufacturing may innocently be inoculated on the agricultural system, without endangering the morals of the people," insisted Edmond Genet in an address in 1821 before the Agricultural Society of the County of Rensselaer on new sources of wealth. And we may look to the added advantage that by encouraging our own manufacturies, we will "cure the vices of foreign luxuries."

The time has come, said Joseph Story in 1829, when the mechanic and manufacturing power will form the great balance between commerce and agriculture, "between the learned profession and the mere proprietors of capital; between the day laborer and the unoccupied man of ease." Though Jacksonians would sneer that such words only showed how Story's concept of justice was subservient to the Whig program, even they could not deny his open assertion that this "practical science" was not only a source of pleasure, a means of securing rank and reputation, but also "one of the surest foundations of opulence." Spokesmen for New England rather gingerly advanced their claims to keep time with the whirling mechanisms, but when we find that in the 1830's Edward Everett felt he could safely adorn this revolution with the pomposity of his oratory, we may comprehend how thoroughly economic insurgence had solidified its position: it was no longer vulnerable to the fragile darts of a Henry Thoreau. These ingenious and useful *"arts,"* Everett declaimed, are both the product and the cause of civilization, and they "form the difference between the savage of the woods and civilized, cultivated, moral, and religious man." Everett was no longer to be intimidated by the charge that these engines were the creations of merely the last few vulgar years. On the contrary, "there is also a great deal, of which the contrivance is coeval with the ancient dawnings of improvement"; and Everett could conclude, as though he had indeed completed a heroic exertion of his own intellect, that "the moral and social improvement of our race, and the possession of the skill and knowledge embodied in them, will advance, stand still, and fall together."

His was a lapse into the atmosphere of his boyhood to suggest even remotely the possibility of "fall." Yet it is a revealing one, for it shows how even Everett was not yet entirely comfortable with what had been wrought. Through the opacity of his sensibility we discern what the pioneers of industry thought they were doing for the nation and what the masses were being persuaded to accept, even though with muted lamentations. Speaking in 1838, he reminded his audience that twenty years earlier the whole area of the city of Lowell comprised but "two or three poor farms." Not more rapidly was the palace of Aladdin reared by the genius of the lamp than was "this noble city of the arts" built by "the genius of capital." For years Everett, and after him his lesser colleagues, was adept at reciting the splendors of Lowell: "the palaces of her industry . . . her churches . . . her school-houses . . . the long lines of her shops and warehouses . . . the comfortable abodes of an enterprising, industrious, and intelligent population . . . her watery Goliaths, not wielding a weaver's beam, like him of old, but giving motion to hundreds and thousands of spindles and looms." But as generally happens in the effusions of Everett—what makes him, precisely because of his mediocrity, one of the rewarding witnesses of the time—he betrays that he is defending a conservatism which, by its very dynamism, is transforming the country into an awesome monster—and that the instinctive wisdom of the democracy distrusts it. He gives the plot away—except, of course, that it was never a deliberate conspiracy—when he goes out of his way to excoriate those who have denounced the "capital" that has been the agent of this beneficent creation. Such critics wage war against a system spreading plenty throughout the land, and what is this

but to play, in real life, the part of the malignant sorcerer, in the same Eastern tale, who, potent only for mischief, utters the baleful spell which breaks the charm, heaves the mighty pillars of the palace from their foundation, converts the fruitful gardens back to their native sterility, and heaps the abodes of life and happiness with silent and desolate ruins?

Everett's device of presenting the industrialization of America, especially that of New England, as a miracle from *The Arabian Nights* was ingenious, but his resort to such a fable almost leads one to suspect he had his inward doubts as to whether Lowell was quite real.

A similar mixture of incredulity, excitement, and apprehension informs the countless lyric paeans to the glorification of the factory. Because most of our classic literature of these years is hostile toward, or at least resistant to, the machine, we forget against what a background of loud hosannas Thoreau and Melville wrote. The interior of a cotton mill, said Samuel Goodrich in 1845, reduces the beholder to admiring wonder:

The ponderous wheel that communicates life and activity to the whole establishment; the multitude of bands and cogs, which connect the machinery, story above story; the carding engines, which seem like things of life, toiling with steadfast energy; the whirring cylinders, the twirling spindles, the clanking looms—the whole spectacle seeming to present a magic scene in which wood and iron are endowed with the dexterity of the human hand—and where complicated machinery seems to be gifted with intelligence—is surely one of the marvels of the world.

The dedicated advocate of scientific agriculture, Henry Colman, constantly adduced the triumphs of technology in his speeches at country fairs as a means of overcoming the farmers' reluctance to tamper with Nature by the use of fertilizers. And adding his voice to the celebrations of the factories of Lowell, Colman in 1836 extolled operations which, by the simple revolution of a wheel, wrought ends never to be effected by human power: "and all this, with an exactness and precision absolutely perfect, I may properly add, sublime." Furthermore, let none confound the majesty of this spectacle with that of mountains or cascades, for it has a nobler splendor. In the harmony and the subordination of parts to the whole, "where each part retains its place, performs its duty and supplies its contribution," the machine constitutes a picture of the ideal society; and so he concluded, "The moral spectacle here presented is in itself beautiful and sublime."

Indeed, one of the more moving manifestations of the American mind was its long effort to maintain a belief that moral benefactions were conferred by the mills and factories. The prized showpiece was the Lowell system for recruiting, supervising, and improving young ladies off the farms, an experiment which, it was being said even into the 1860's, proved that "a factory entailed no degradation of character, and was no impediment to a respectable connection in marriage." There were, to be sure, occasional low murmurings about the prospect of "industrial feudalism," as Frederic Lincoln admitted to an audience of Boston workmen in 1845, but this can be avoided by the improvement of each individual to his full capacity. Assuredly, it was no answer to destroy the machinery: "If the physical resources of the country are becoming so greatly developed, the more necessity then, that those of man should be brought forward and carried to perfection." (Again, it is worth our notice, "perfection" is attainable through *both* the machinery of the Revival and that of the factory!) The ideal of America as a frontier and agricultural society was still so strong that even when intoning their chants, admirers of the factory had to move with caution. There may be much truth, said Lincoln, in Jefferson's assertion that cities are sores upon the body politic, "but he must be a bold reformer who would advise us to demolish our edifices, or plough up our streets." The hiss of the serpent and the scream of the wild bird which would then be heard over the ruins, Lincoln ventured to surmise, "would be far less pleasant to the senses than the hum of industry, or the noise of traffic."

We can, in fact, observe the Jeffersonian mentality coming to terms with the industrial—and in the act of reconciliation admitting surrender—in the readiness of John Pendleton Kennedy to salute the factory and the factory worker as achievements of intellect—"the higher work of the higher intellect, and each kind in its degree, partaking of the dignity inherent in intellectual pursuits." Whereupon he yielded even further, abject even beyond apparent necessity. Hereafter men will find less urge to make lawyers or doctors of their sons, for the glories of those professions afford no renown greater than those of the steamboat and the cotton mill:

When I look upon this vast enginery, this infinite complication of wheels, this exquisitely delicate adjustment of parts, and this sure, steady, and invariable result shown in the operation of the perfect machine; when I contemplate the tools and implements by which it is made, the abstruse mathematics that have been employed in them, and the extraordinary acuteness of the intellectual power that has invented and contrived them—I am lost in admiration of the genius that masters the whole.

Thus the patron of Poe, who in *Swallow Barn* blessed the genial, slow-moving idyl of the Virginia plantation, acknowledges the victory already won a decade and a half before Appomattox. Even so, we must note that Kennedy in no way cringes before an inhuman contrivance;

he retains his dignity, as his America strove to keep its own dignity, by enlisting the factory into the cause of the mind, by voluntarily placing the banner in its hands, as though those grasping hands had not already rent it. He was convinced that for every hundred men capable of making a figure in professional life, "you will not find more than one who is able to comprehend and apply the intricate science and practical detail belonging to the highest branches of architecture and enginery." We may find this deplorable treason to American principles or admirable recognition of fact, or a bit of both; whatever it be, it exemplifies the kind of reasoning by which the mind in America signalized its uneasy alliance with the technological revolution.

There was for a moment some hesitation about admitting canals into the empire of intellect. Digging a ditch would at first sight seem a merely physical exertion when compared with Francis Lowell's stupendous feat of mind. The great Robert Fulton endeavored in 1814 to make the inclusion of ditch-digging irresistible by saying that he then intended to give all the aid in his power to the "sublime" enterprise of the Erie Canal—"for I deem that a sublime national work, which will secure wealth, ease and happiness to millions." He encountered in this undertaking the same sort of opposition, or, rather, ridicule, he had fought against with the steamboat. A committee of the legislature, headed by Gouverneur Morris and including DeWitt Clinton and Stephen Rensselaer, observed that canals would freeze in winter as easily as lakes, but supposed, heavily ironic, that champions of these useless projects intended to supply water "by their depth of intellect," thaw ice by "their warmth of imagination," all the while "insisting that whatsoever they think proper to approve of is sublime." In due course apologists for the committee were to declare that Morris had used the language of fancy and imagination instead of "the cool course of argument" (he had thought the alignment exactly the reverse!), and explained DeWitt Clinton's signing of the report by the fact that when he had studied in Columbia College in the 1790's, "Science had not yet taken its just and proper standing by the side of Literature." Happily, according to his biographer, Clinton was led by such pleas as that of Ferr Pell in 1816 to perceive, in "the cool method of philosophic discussion," that the canal was "a stupendous and sublime work," and thus called for the highest statesmanship. All might have been lost, proclaimed *The Mechanics Magazine* in 1833, "had not the soaring genius of a Clinton, in defiance of the vulgar prejudices of the day, predicted and finally executed a work that will command the admiration of ages, and stand a cenotaph to perpetuate his name to a grateful posterity." For several decades after his death the name of Clinton imparted almost a magic aura, not for any of his political deeds, but because he was believed to have wrought the miracle of the canal almost singlehanded.

The completion of the Erie Canal authenticated the stamp of sublimity. A report of the passage of the first boat on October 22, 1819—from Rome to Utica—described the ringing of bells, the roar of cannon, the acclamation of thousands of spectators, and could only conclude that "the scene was truly sublime." Charles Haines, addressing himself in 1821 to the subject of the New York canals, felt it proper to begin with a review of the great events of the age—"the reign of Napoleon, the reign of George III, and the reign of Alexander of Russia," but he went on to ask, "yet, where is there a work of their hands which will compare in grandeur and utility with the great Western canal?" A South Carolina advocate for a proposed canal westward from Charleston was so carried away by prospects of sublimity that he foresaw eventually "internal communication with the Pacific ocean" through the Missouri River, with the East India trade anchoring at the mouth of the Columbia River and merchandise carried all the way across the continent to Charleston by this sublime web of canals!

Once canals were absorbed into the universe of mind, they like the factories encouraged a few brave spokesmen frankly to refuse any longer to utter apologies for the supposed poverty of the American mind. Did we live amidst ruins, remarked Cadwallader Colden in his 1825 *Memoir* on the New York canals, were we everywhere confronted with evidences of present decay, we might be as little inclined to look forward as are Europeans; but our canals flow into the future. Therefore we should indulge in no foolish laments over the rude wilderness. Thanks to canals, "Instead of uncultivated wilds, we shall be surrounded by a country yielding all that is necessary to the comfort of man." Even as Cooper, upon returning to Jacksonian America, was expressing his horror of American restlessness, George Wharton was telling the alumni of the University of Pennsylvania that it was a glory of America that there everything erected by man is periodically pulled down: in this country we consider "that rivers were made by the Almighty for the purpose of feeding navigable canals." The naiads of classical poetry may be shocked at this, but in our philosophy the only question is how the space between two points can best be annihilated. "The line of beauty is any thing but a curve; and the windings of a river are regarded as evidence of the ignorance and want of foresight of dame Nature." And finally Henry Thoreau, taking with his brother the canal from Billerica to Chelmsford in their week on the

Concord and the Merrimack, could remark that "Nature will recover and indemnify itself and gradually plant fit shrubs and flowers along its borders. Already the king-fisher sat upon a pine over the water, and the bream and pickerel swam below."

The railroad was not, unfortunately, an American invention, but this lapse in the providential design was quickly corrected, according to the literature, because "we, in this country, may boast of our superiority, not only in the extent to which the system has been carried here, but also in the admirable formation of its various lines," as well as of our improvements in "the structure and management" of the locomotive engine. On the Pennsylvania railroad, beyond Altoona, the track ascends one hundred feet to the mile, and so short are the curves that the locomotive is visible from the fourth car during parts of the climb, and this at the speed of thirty miles an hour: "No other nation in the world can show so great a triumph of civil engineering as this." Yes, we commenced by imitating English models, "but American genius is destined always to rise superior to imitation, and it is, in fact, only when it so rises, and trusts to its own gigantic plans, that the true power of American character shows itself." Literary prophets had been proclaiming this revelation for several decades, but if according to general opinion the results in the arts were, by 1860, confusing, technological patriots could point to indisputable successes. The English engineer imitates Egyptians and Romans, and so works artificially, but "The American imitates nature, with whose great works he is in constant communication, and, like a spider, constructs a bridge light in appearance, but sufficiently strong to withstand the tempest and the storm, and bear with easy vibration, double, nay, triple, the load put upon it." Significantly, this account concludes: "Only an appreciation of the grandeur of such a fall as that of Niagara, could fit a man to construct the bridge that spans its river"—significantly because it shows that down to the crash of the Civil War the mind in America could happily interpret the railroad and the factory not as rejections of natural grandeur but as legitimate offspring of its spontaneity.

Above all, the force of Nature, the majesty of Niagara, were transmuted into machinery and locomotives by passing through the brain of man. The American railroad was a creation both of vital impulse and of mathematical intellect, of heart and head, here fused harmoniously, as poets had yet singularly failed to accomplish (or at least so wrote a hierophant in 1857 who obviously had never heard of *Leaves of Grass*). There never before was such an achievement, sang Charles A. Drake of St. Louis, never such a creation in any land, requiring such an exhibition of human power as the race had never before put forth. His language speaks for what the revolution had wrought within the deepest consciousness of the nation:

It was by concentration, action, and transformation. Concentration of thought, purpose, will, means, and men—not futile and impotent, but quick with life, and taking shape in action, and that action tending, not to rebuild and perpetuate the old and decayed, nor to hem in what is, so that it should never be ought else, but to transform it into something better, and in the transformation to make it give forth new qualities, and put forth new and more exquisite beauties.

An orator who in 1841 commenced his address by exclaiming, "What varieties of elocution are not blended to make railroads sublime!" was not reproving his predecessors but girding himself to surpass them. For the next twenty years hyperbole outdid itself. Edward Everett may just possibly have heard echoes of Mike Fink and Paul Bunyan, though we may be sure he would resent any insinuation that he went to school to the tall tale; still, the stupendous panorama of the American railroads carried his classical rhetoric far into the realm of popular extravagance. In the West, steam communication invites personification:

Here we should be taught to behold him, a Titanic colossus of iron and of brass, instinct with elemental life and power, with a glowing furnace for his lungs, and streams of fire and smoke for the breath of his nostrils. With one hand he collects the furs of the arctic circle; with the other he smites the forests of Western Pennsylvania. He plants his right foot at the source of the Missouri —his left on the shores of the Gulf of Mexico; and gathers into his bosom the overflowing abundance of the fairest and richest valley on which the circling sun looks down.

Here was surely a creature to roam the land of the mythologized Davy Crockett, who released the sun from an ice pack and returned to earth with a piece of daylight in his pocket. The public speech of the period everywhere resounds with these addresses to the railroad—the steam horse who mounts the Alleghenies "and awakens the slumbering echoes of hill and plain with his shrill whistle, at once the signal of his power and the paean of a mighty conquest in the march of engineering science." The similarity between such cadences and those of both the tall tale and of Whitman reveals the temper of the times in a manner which must again and again be brought home to the historian and social analyst, and above all to the critical interpreter of American literature.

It is therefore significant that Edward Everett, pronouncing upon the "beneficial" influence of railroads, felt obliged to contradict William Wordsworth, who had held that the seclusion of the Lake Country would be ruined by the panting locomotive. He was mistaken, said Everett, with an implied admonition to recalcitrants nearer home; though the quiet of a few spots may be disturbed, a hundred quiet spots are made accessible, and while the bustle of the depot may invade some shady dell, many "of those verdant cathedral arches, entwined by the hand of God in our pathless woods, are opened, for the first time since the creation of the world, to the grateful worship of man by these means of communication!" Repeatedly we have to ask whether this sort of speech was mere fretwork embellishment of the iron rail or whether it played a more essential part in the intellectual development. Chief Justice Taney's opinion in the Charles River Bridge Case resorted to no such argument, and decided against the old turnpike corporations simply because their claims would prevent the states from availing themselves of improvements "which are now adding to the wealth and prosperity and the convenience and comfort of every other part of the civilized world." But we may properly doubt that such a prosaic decision could have been rendered and accepted had not the atmosphere been permeated with the mystique of the railroad as something more wild and unimaginable than the most lurid creation of *The Arabian Nights*—"our modern locomotive engine, with its mile length of loaded cars, rushing over river and valley and through the very bowels of the mountain, making its scared echoes reverberate with its warning scream." The sublimity of the beast was entirely compatible with its utility, for in that very union was the guarantee that railroads opened to America an unlimited horizon, since nothing could be "more beautiful than a community made happy by well directed labor." For so profound a romantic as George Bancroft the railroad proved that mechanics, science, Nature, and genius could come together in a single triumph which, in its ultimate meaning, was a work of art. Michelangelo, he said in Cincinnati in 1857, held that all forms of beauty lie hidden in the marble, awaiting the hand of the sculptor. So the eye of Latrobe saw the capacity of the mountain and, scoffing at the ravine, "gave himself no rest till commerce had carried its safe and easy pathway in triumph over the mountain top, and proved to the world that there are no difficulties which true enterprise cannot surmount—that nature herself is in league with genius." In this philosophy, which dreamed of all things possible on earth if not in heaven, there was no remotest chance that things could mount the saddle and ride mankind, for man's conquest of the mountain was not a violation of Nature but an embrace.

Every year, every month, brought forth some fresh advance of technology, but the next major one was truly an American achievement. Morse's telegraph "stands alone in its brilliancy, and reflects more of honor upon the age and country which gave it origin, than has been derived from any other of the results of physical science." For a while, however, it evoked a transitory perplexity, as with this writer in *De-Bow's Review* of 1846, because it was a victory *over* the powers of Nature. The steam engine was a wonder for mankind, but there was nothing in it which refused to accord with our preconceived notions of natural possibilities. But in the applications of the electric battery there is something "so gigantic and stupendous," something so far beyond "all the conceptions which had ever entered into the brain of philosophy before," that refuge had hastily to be sought in the one concept which might still prevent the mind from riot and preserve Nature as a friend: "Can we conceive of anything more sublime or grand?" Miraculous, inexplicable as the experiment did at first appear, on second thought it too could be made to demonstrate the union, in technology, of Nature and the intellect, at least the intellectual genius. "Let us not forget," continued *DeBow's* in 1853, "that a fragmentary knowledge of our new electric telegraph had existed in the human mind for hundreds of years; it needed only a master mind to unite the elements; a master hand to forge the mechanical instruments, to show the wondering world the perfect work." Michelangelo again, but this time in the person of American Morse, who earlier had practiced colossal sculpture! A few dour souls, chained by formal logic to the prosaic earth, might be so staggered by this invention as to say, with Calhoun, that "the subjugation of electricity to the mechanical necessities of man would mark the last era in human civilization," but they obviously were merely confused. They missed the great point, which after a few years of adjustment the dominant American voices were able to repeat interminably, that the telegraph was indeed the supreme achievement of applied science because its end was "not the modification or transportation of matter, but the transmission of thought."

As soon as the telegraph proved a success, ardent imaginations commenced to dream of its extension into a transatlantic cable. Thoreau snorted that the great invention would serve only to convey across the ocean the intelligence that Princess Adelaide had the whooping cough; but nobody paid him any heed, and the public waited in assured expectation that the shores would be linked together and eventually "the entire earth shall be incircled, and every important city connected by the wires of the magnetic telegraph." Even in anticipation, prophets were considering as already proved the thesis that nobody could set "bounds to the inventive powers of the human mind" save God Himself. In 1858 there seemed to be some doubt whether even He could. Cyrus Field's cable showed, wrote Charles Francis Briggs, "that nothing is impossible to man, while he keeps within the sublimely imperious orbit of Nature's laws." Joseph Henry kept his language under sober restraint, simply pointing out to the Council of New York City that the cable sealed the definition of the nineteenth century as that in which "the application of abstract science to the useful arts, and the subjection of the innate powers of the material world to the control of the intellect as the obedient slaves of civilized man" were accomplished. Such a concurrence of circumstances and energies would not have happened at any other period. Less scientifically sophisticated admirers of the cable were thrown back upon a kind of superstitious awe. The Reverend Ezra Stiles Gannett exulted from the pulpit of the First Church in Boston that now we saw the ultimate in man's power over Nature, that "the swift-winged messenger of destruction, the vital energy of the material creation," is brought under our control, and asked in rapture, "Who shall now describe the circle within which human ability must confine itself?" Science seizes upon the mysteries that formerly surrounded us; nothing can baffle its persistent scrutiny. With obvious relief Gannett announced that the cable closed the era of speculative inquiry, inaugurated that in which "mind asserts its superiority over matter, not in a spirit of self-admiration, but for the sake of enriching life." Neither Gannett nor his congregation realized that if he was correct, then by the same token they had come to the close of an epoch in religious thought as well as in metaphysics.

5.

THE BOUNDLESS PROSPECT

A few years after Samuel Miller's backward look at the eighteenth century, a somewhat altered style of retrospection began to appear in the discourse of the learned. The Commissioners for the University of Virginia exemplified it in 1818: instead of contemplating the philosophical range of the Enlightenment, they commiserated with that age because in a mere fifty years scientific advances had rendered the elements subservient to man beyond all the dreams of the philosophes. In the 1830's this gambit of rehearsing the glories of the last fifty—or sixty or seventy—years becomes standardized ritual, and with the passing of time, the pity extended to the ignorance of the fathers came to embrace the times when the fathers had been gloating over their progress beyond their grandfathers. Phi Beta Kappa meetings were considered particularly propitious occasions for hailing the last half-century as an era of wonders and asking, "Who that, in the beginning of it, should have predicted the progress we have made, would not have been set down as a madman?" There came to be a kind of caress in the mere recital of the advances which lulled audiences into a glow of self-gratification—machinery, steam, gaslights; geology, physiology, even phrenology. "Within the memory of man"—this was ever the invocation—"labor has been superseded; expense abridged; time saved; public comfort enhanced; national wealth increased; education promoted; and the welfare and happiness of man exalted." At a Massachusetts cattle show in 1838 Henry Colman described his recent tour into Ohio in the hope of encouraging stubborn farmers to move into the new century:

What mighty triumphs of art and labor were here! What a moving of the affections! What an expanding of the imagination! How many beautiful and splendid visions have floated before the mind, which were here surpassed by the great realities. Here were mountains levelled and valleys filled. . . . Here were rivers, hundreds of miles in length, flowing at man's pleasure, and in channels formed by his hands. . . . Such are the great results of intelligent, concentrated, persevering labor; achievements of our own times, and scarcely a quarter of a century old.

Art and labor, the affections, the imagination, and a massive reconstruction of Nature: the "reality" of the revolution had even this early created a sublimity so vast as to make the astronomers' sublime seem pallid. The year 1850, marking the half-century, gave rise according to Dana to thousands of sermons praising not the Revival but the marvels of science, so that "it was in fact a scientific jubilee."

In 1836 Henry Laurens Pinckney brought the full dignity of his name to inform the literary societies of the University of North Carolina, *This is the age of Science,* and to declare in a South where the ideal of the gentleman still looked to classical languages that antiquity had no science, whereas the present is illuminated with a flood of light. In this decade and the next, there is little to distinguish the tone of these exhortations according to their sectional source. Samuel Ward in 1837 told the Stuyvesant Institute that in this age the "sublime prophecies" of Bacon and Galileo were being realized, that a great enthusiasm is enkindled through Europe—and America. "Thus, gushing from a few primitive sources of knowledge, has the placid stream of science swollen into a majestic river; its waters fertilizing the soil, and its resistless current affording a thousand new and living powers to the arts of life."

Even so, several more years of this vaunting were to pass before, in 1853, a Horace Mann, by then the most powerful figure in American education, would be bold enough, or callous enough, to reduce our "literature" to what had been written "before the truths of modern science were discovered; the idea that there is an order of nature." Since that concept has been "received into the mind," he prophesied in *Thoughts for a Young Man*, nothing will be more different than "what the same genius would write before being imbued with the spirit of science, and after being so imbued." *The Dial*, brave venture on behalf of transcendental mind and letters, barely struggled through four years. One might almost say that in the ninth volume of *The New Englander*, in 1851, Daniel March was dancing on its grave. There was nothing transcendental in his vision: never in the whole history of the world has the spirit of investigation been so widely at work, exploring "with the light of modern intelligence amid the fossil remains and the mouldering archives of the past," torturing substances in furnaces, scrutinizing the processes of germination and reproduction, analyzing even the embryo. Never before have numberless eyes been on the watch night and day "to discover and publish to the world the causes of those [phenomena] which have been hitherto familiar in fact, and inexplicable in nature." To men like Mann and March, this was *the* reality of the age, and they lost no opportunity to impress upon the national intelligence the vastness of the change it had witnessed.

Awareness of the transformation became even more awe-struck as the prophets began themselves to glimpse and to impart to others the notion that if, by looking back fifty years, they could be so amazed by recent achievements, they might also peer ahead into a future of technological progress truly without limit. In an address of 1848 daringly entitled *Agency of Steam Power in Promoting Civilization and Christianity*, Rufus Clark concluded that if while in its infancy steam power "is accomplishing such wonders, what may we not expect when it reaches maturity, and has the aid of a longer experience in its application to the arts?" In metaphysics and poetry the infinite was a speculative term, its content merely negative. The outer boundary of which theologians and mystics have spoken, said Mann, is that of their vision, but not of Nature's works. "It was only in the infancy and poverty of knowledge that men claimed to have reached its *Ultima Thule*." Or, as Pinckney carefully insisted, it is the "peculiar property" of science to refuse all boundaries, so that even the elevation of the present must be regarded as a point from which "it will continue, with undazzled eye and unwearied wing, to ascend to greater and still greater heights." Wing might not weary, but eyes had a difficult time to keep from being dazzled. We may be sure that Everett was happy to describe the vista, over and over again: there is no final goal; the sciences "are moving powers, animated principles; they are instinct with life; they are themselves the intellectual life of man." Mark Hopkins, like Horace Mann, saw the challenge to education in science: "Already have the dreams of imagination been transcended, and yet the impression and belief is, that we have but just commenced this grand career." Boundless, illimitable, unending—Pisgah: how incessantly, how beautifully these words are sounded throughout these decades. And with the obbligato, as *DeBow's* exclaimed about the telegraph, "We cease to limit the powers of the mind." Often, alas, the assertion was made by those who reached the limits of their mental powers in the assertion itself, but in many instances the proclamation was a notice served that the mind no longer needed to apologize for devoting itself to utility, that, in fact, such seeking for practical improvement was *the* true life of the mind. In the euphoria of this revelation, few partisans of science any longer gave any attention to what Emerson called the "noble doubt" or Whitman "the terrible doubt of appearances." In America, more generally than anywhere else in the world, circumstances gave assurance that the mind was perfectly commensurate with the phenomena. "The internal connection existing among all phenomena," dogmatized John Leconte in 1857, "renders it certain, that every discovery in sciences prepares the way for higher conquests, and forces upon us the conviction, that when thousands and thousands of years have passed, untrodden paths will still be opened to the scientific observer, leading him to an illimitable world of thought." Leconte, a pious man, would still speak of an inscrutable divinity as the source of cosmic order, but, as we shall see in greater detail, the language of contemplation was becoming pale. The real vitality was not in natural theology but in such phrases as "there is no resting place, no pause." As the intellect cultivated nimbleness and leaped from invention to invention, there seemed no longer any point in asking whether the mind, shut up within the senses, could cope fully with objective reality.

Astonishingly early in the century, when to the historian's eye the technological revolution was barely beginning, there had been anticipatory tremors of its approach. Thomas Cooper, assuming one of the newly founded chairs of chemistry at Carlisle College in 1811, put a wholly fresh accent upon the old adage "knowledge is power," making it mean that now we can compel every object around us to contribute "to our pleasure, to our profit, to our comfort, or to our convenience." In a very short time, this sense of an onrushing technology became explicitly equated with the national destiny. Is it nothing, sternly demanded Gulian Verplanck in 1818 of European critics of the United States, to have in less than half a century reformed law, improved the science of political economy, and "to have augmented the power and comforts of civilized man, by miracles of mechanical invention"? An orator before a medical society in 1816 already placed the hope of the scientific intellect of all mankind in this emerging America: should a second night of moral darkness ever descend upon our civilization, here in America "may science flourish with luxuriant growth, under the fostering patronage of a free people; and from hence may burst forth those radiations of intellectual and moral light, which we are taught to believe will, at one period, illuminate and bless every portion of our globe." Occasionally in the early decades a propagandist would remind Americans that scientific genius "has a universality which elevates it above all human jurisdictions," that it belongs to the whole of humanity and cannot be monopolized by any one country. Americans might continue to import their technology from abroad, especially from England, as witness the textile mills and the railroad; but all the time the serene belief was waxing that it was the proper feeling of nationality diffused among American naturalists "which has impelled them to study and examine for themselves, instead of blindly using the eyes of foreign naturalists, or bowing implicitly to the decisions of a foreign criticism."

By 1835 this scientific nationalism had become so strong that many were convinced that the nation had now surpassed all of Europe put together. The historian of science may be appalled or at least amused at such conceit in a world which contained a Liebig or a Mendel, but Edward Mansfield at Miami University in Ohio was troubled by no such reflections:

The philosophers of England have distinctly declared, that there the cultivation of science is on the *decline;* the German mind is occupied with romantic poetry, and metaphysical subtleties; the French have lost the genius of the Institute; and are, as, with few exceptions, they ever have been, occupied upon the *details*, rather than the *foundations of knowledge*. It is in America, that the great additions to science and social improvement must be made.

Foreign observers, such as Mrs. Trollope and Charles Dickens, threw their hosts into paroxysms of rage by their general tone of condescension and particularly by their ridicule of the American propensity for bragging. Mansfield may be doing no more than that; yet for the social history of American technology, let alone for the history of the American mind, the proliferation of such declamations is a more profound manifestation. It speaks an ever-expanding discovery of the national destiny. As John Pendleton Kennedy gazed upon an exhibition in New York of the products of American industries, he beheld the ingredients not merely of present but of future glory:

There are the materials from which, I trust, for many an age to come, the sinewy toil of a sturdy, independent, and intelligent people may earn them competence, strength, and virtue, and, through these means, continue to the world that most glorious of empires,—a free republic unerringly converting to the best use the talents with which God has endowed it, and mastering the most hidden as well as the most open resources of a territory as exhaustless in moral and physical treasures, as it is wide in its expanse.

So, Kennedy (very much a gentleman) continued, the stranger who comes to spy out our land and confines his inspection to the aristocratic elements will not read the true spirit of the land, and will see in its tremendous dedication to producing articles of utility and comfort only vulgarity.

There is, said Henry Baldwin in 1834, an "inventive creating spirit" informing the industry of the country, "which does not wait the slow and tedious march of time for its development." It is a "giant growth." What a "gigantic" theater is the future of this nation, cried the good Dr. Francis in 1841; "What scope for the man of science! . . . Imagination is lost in the colossal prospect." It is absolutely certain, said George Gifford to the American Institute in 1849, that the Republic "will soon be the grand laboratory of the world, and command the entire frontier of the dominions of science." It will seize the most outward posts of discovery and "wrest them from all other nations, and still further on through ages to come." Page after page in this vein was printed, the number increasing with the years. Wearied though the modern student may become with much reading of such boasts, the mentality of the period and the heritage it fashioned for its posterity cannot be understood without them, nor can the features of those who, like Thoreau, rebelled against the torrent be clearly discerned except when seen in the light reflected from this blaze. As Kennedy said at yet another exhibition of American manufactures in 1851, we blend our admiration with the sentiment of pride: "Our applause is seasoned and refreshed by a wholesome patriotism."

Plan for Book Three,
Chapters Two through Seven

[As was his custom, Perry Miller prepared what might be called a scenario, or working script, for whatever he was writing. His plan for the remaining chapters of Book Three, "Science—Theoretical and Applied," follows in exactly the form in which he had sketched them out.]

CHAPTER TWO

From Agriculture to Chemistry

1.

THE RELUCTANCE OF NATURE

General awareness at end of Revolution (cf. S. Miller) that immense changes have been wrought in 18th century in agriculture.

Hence agriculture most effective of appeals for science.

Incipient, often open, conflict of scientific advocates with rooted tradition.

In addition to farmers' conviction that old methods are traditional wisdom, is also pervasive conviction that agriculture—unspoiled by brain—is *natural* state of mankind.

Amount of this in Jefferson—or supposed to be?

Confirmation c. 1800 by American fact.

From 18th-century concept of agriculture comes mounting insistence that improved agriculture is *benefit to society* (esp. Jefferson).

In name of this ideal scientists challenge the American farmer.

They bound to assume monitory tone, telling farmers what they should know but don't know, and chiding them for their ignorance.

Farming population, though not organized as such, makes sullen replies, puts up brute resistance, to these charges.

314

Practical farmers say scientific notions are fantasy:
> dreamed up by city folks
> are intellectual instead of real down-to-earth
> amount only to "book-farming"
> just don't know the simple facts of the occupation.

Popularizers of science obliged to renew, to expand, plea to the farmers.

They have to appeal to experiment, to prove their case by conducting experiments.

By 1820 or circa, advocates of science have to protect their cause against fakes, agricultural quacks, etc.

Also—most difficult—to contend that science of agriculture must not be enslaved to empirical habits.

(This apt to become most resented insult to the farmers who pride selves on traditional wisdom)

Hence contention of agricultural intellectuals that progress is itself a projection of experience, is experience systematized.

Hence it is *not* "book-farming," speculative, theoretical, intellectual at all.

Steadily growing assertion of the scientists in this debate—though they never come quite into the open with it—is that because agriculture is or can be made a science, then conclusion must follow that
> Mind is equal to Nature.

2.

THE VITALITY OF NATURE

Advocacy of scientifically directed improvements in agriculture inevitably invokes aid of chemistry.

At first, circa 1800, the chemistry summoned to aid is systematic, theoretical, ideal—is anti-"empirical."

In short time, early decades of the century, realization comes that chemistry is on the march, making fabulous progress, while astronomy and physics—the two sciences most revered by 18th century—seem relatively immobile.

With this comes ecstatic discovery that America is the providentially appointed field for the expansion of chemistry.

18th-century ideas about chemistry thus are rapidly being transformed, broken up.

Silliman, for all his great services, is clinging to 18th-century conception (hence the use of chemistry for religious argument), a belated child of the Enlightenment.

As chemistry becomes more complex, and especially as it is enlisted in the cause of agriculture, chemists have to insist that it is compatible with an empirical approach to Nature.

It is consistently stripped of its speculative or theoretical pretensions. Rapidly disowns them.

So, in this science emphasis upon utility; results:

with effect, by end of the period, that chemists have become the most professional of all scientists in America and have utterly reversed the 18th-century inheritance and in essence are saying that Nature is so dynamic, so vital, so rushing pell-mell, that mind can only grab bits and pieces of it as it passes, constructing rules for incidents.

Mind is not equal to Nature. (cf. C. S. Pierce)

CHAPTER THREE

The Religion of Geology

1.

REPHRASING THE ARGUMENT FROM DESIGN

Period begins with retention of conventional 18th-century forms of theism proved from design—"Nature's simple plan."

Hence little or no sense of science as antagonistic to religion. Instead, almost everywhere, among Deists and Revivalists alike, assumption usually is one of perfect harmony.

Further, there is a pronounced tendency to identify scientific mind and attitude with Protestantism, against superstition, etc., of Catholicism.

Apprehension grows through middle of the period, that science is becoming self-sufficient, will dispense with religious concern or even actively oppose Christianity.

Scientists hint science a firmer revelation than Bible, etc.

Apprehension becomes anxiety.

Threat assumes specific form—"utilitarianism."

The steady triumph of the "empirical" over the systematic promises to end all use for concept of theism from design.

2.
TEMPORALIZING THE COSMIC DESIGN

Both religious leaders and the pious scientists clearly endeavoring to find some formula which will demonstrate that science and technology are actually confirming the proof that divine providence governs the world.

But need to advance the concept not in static but in developmental terms.

So railroads, telegraph, cable can be identified with the march of Christianity.

The science which now satisfies ideally both necessities—for a static order and within it growth and change—suddenly becomes geology.

It seen afresh as *the* sublime science instead of astronomy.

Appeases the scientists' demand for inductive method, factual, non-speculative, and yet tells how God operated through time.

(Americans so sure, they were not much bothered by dispute between Wernerians and Huttonians)

Furthermore, geology proves of immense utilitarian value, though with none of utility's dangers. Hence is really the strongest scientific ally of Christianity.

However—

as celebrants of pious geology enlarge upon the glories of their subject, they uncomfortably find themselves in increasing danger

of not actually praising God's operations through the geological eons,

but of boasting the powers of the human mind, which, in a day of tremendous technological achievement, is now able to give laws to these remote eras.

So, out of efforts to find religious security in geology, which is the science above all others set within a framework of time, the period comes reluctantly and full of vague forebodings to the threshold of the Darwinian age, when the conflict of science with religion suddenly will become a real issue.

CHAPTER FOUR

Mind and Nature

1.

THE HUMAN BRAIN

March of technology excites increasing admiration for man, his ability to master Nature. Developments in agriculture, geology assert ability of mind to comprehend all Nature. Chemistry asserts, gradually, that mind can achieve only fragmentary glimpses.

Thus in 19th-century intellect a crisis takes shape, for a long time unnoticed, which emerges finally as crucial question: what is relation of mind (brain) to object.

Note: story of this struggle can be told with no reference whatsoever to Emerson's *Nature* or to any Transcendental wrestling with duality. Little or no influence within circles of science and orthodox theology of Kantian idealism. Through almost all these regions "Common Sense" metaphysics prevail, and epistemological "realism" is untroubled. For what, historically speaking, is the main stream of American intellectual activity the problem was not any terrible doubt of appearances—appearances were real—but of adjusting the conception of mind to a reality which was racing dizzily through a process of transformation.

2.

THE HERITAGE OF THE ENLIGHTENMENT

The idolization of Linnaeus.

Hence in infant American science, reigning ideal is classification. This is supreme operation of MIND.

Newton in fact was a classifier.

Baconian method (induction) is only for documenting classes.

Ruled out are hypotheses, guesses, brilliant but shallow theories.

Ideal is slow, steady, patient observation—no place for genius in popular, literary sense.

Hence best suited to a democracy. Everybody can be scientist, at least in comprehension.

Reason then not a faculty—gives no laws of itself—but is arranger of facts and ideas.

Mind cannot classify all universe—in that sense is not equal to totality of things.

However, though classifying mind falls short of absolute knowledge, order and system of scientific classification gives insight into SUBLIME (refer back to I, 2—do not repeat).

Prospect of still more to learn is itself road to the SUBLIME —Rittenhouse.

Argument is that through induction (via close observation through senses) scientific classifications truly approach the SUBLIME. Claims of intuition, imagination, wild genius to beholding it are false.

Last positive stand of science as majestic taxonomy in C. W. Peale's vain effort to get state support for his failing museum in 1816.

His claims a last summation of the philosophy, although pieces of it are endlessly repeated in orations and pep talks for decades thereafter. But c. 1820 a subtle, pervasive transformation is under way in the nation's sense of or feeling for science.

3.

SUBJUGATING THE ELEMENTS

Shift of emphasis, intermittent, seldom fully aware of revolution, yet always more and more excited by technological achievements.

Wherein, science comes more and more to mean, not just the incidental utilities of general principles, but actual *conquest* of physical Nature. E.g., figure of DeWitt Clinton.

In this conception, Mind, the creator of technology, becomes itself an object in space and time, an object to itself, not merely the spectator of Nature's simple plan. All this while, in these realms, no Transcendental correspondence of mind and Nature, but rather a study of Mind in operation as a phenomenon comparable to railroad, telegraph.

Celebrations of this concept, such as e.g. those of Edward Everett, protect tremulous American intellect from Transcendentalism, giving new but still "realistic" version of relation of mind to object.

Orthodoxies all reassured (why the nervousness?) that technological triumph is demonstration of triumph of mind over matter.

Issue is not any longer how much knowledge the nation gains, but how it uses such knowledge. Philosophy obviously is handmaid of the arts.

The transition is from the real to the possible. Classification is for bold new combinations.

One of first signs is refashioning of the image of Bacon and inductive method. Bacon even more the name to conjure with, as he is made to signify not passive reception of facts of Nature, merely arranging them in classifications, but inducting from facts the forces behind the array, and then using knowledge of these forces for compelling nature to submit to human (intellectual) mastery.

This new cluster of aggressive concepts around image of Bacon is explicitly hostile to all forms of Transcendentalism, to anything smacking of *a priori*.

Most resolute of inductive scientists, in name of Bacon, announce Linnaeus now obsolete. Begin fight for "natural" system of biology against artificial classification. Asa Gray vs. Agassiz. Gradual taking shape of idea of the *dynamic*.

Changes in concept of mind at work in science produce a new evaluation of *analogy* as fundamental intellectual device. Cautious about misuse, and again no Emersonian nonsense, but in marked contrast to the lawyers' profound distrust of analogy in legal thinking, these popularizers salute it as hitherto (in 18th century) neglected instrument.

Inductive philosophy thus not hostile to beauty, ideals, etc. By condemning Transcendentalism it preserves balance of intuition and logic. It, and it alone, imbues phenomena with a spiritual and poetical significance. It can safely say that mind knows nature in knowing itself.

Here, oddly and ironically enough, way is prepared in many circles for reception of Hegelian idealism—e.g., St. Louis—because effort of scientists to assert that mind is equal to totality of things, but not in language of Emersonian correspondence, points toward concept of dialectical process in Nature to which key is found in working of Mind.

This development supported all along the way, though with increasing emphasis, that plain, solid science is real, and is always to be set in opposition to romance, fiction, fancy rhetoric, etc. Division between the scientific and the poetic is steadily widened throughout period, until bifurcation is radical, and an intellectual civil war exists which would have been inconceivable to Jefferson.

Result—much nervous, inconclusive discussion of relation of

science to arts. Incessant efforts to assure nation that its success in technology does *not* mean lack of aesthetic taste.

But—carried into technological age is 18th-century hostility to notion that scientist is genius. With stronger emphasis, contention always is that scientific achievement is patient labor, not flash of inspiration.

Hence, America, led by Science out of Colonial isolation into National magnificence, has discovered, more than anybody else, the TRUE SUBLIME behind the obvious SUBLIME of the immense pageant of Technology. This is MIND itself.

Here is major impulse in sudden fascination of many peoples with various "sciences" of Mind, whether Transcendental and Idealistic analyses or popular fads:

> Animal Magnetism
> Spiritualism
> Phrenology.

Gradually taking shape, though in this period entirely derivative, is concept of "Psychology" as a science. No original work done, but the term domesticated in America.

Central fact, however, is general conviction that ultimate Sublimity in the creation is human Mind (especially when dependent entirely on sense impression), because it can demonstrably cope with infinite expanse of Nature, can keep pace with further and further discoveries, can follow the dynamic flow.

CHAPTER FIVE

The Scholar and the Artisan

1.

EMERGENCE OF THE UTILITARIAN

Original premise, in thinking of Revolutionary Generation, that Science has practical effects—improves, adorns, embellishes daily life. Easy assumption that the theoretical and practical go hand-in-hand. Little or no uneasiness about conflict between them, or even possibility of dual allegiance.

(Here refer back to I, 4, where this idea must be treated very briefly. At this point show how axiomatic it was at end of century, how innocently, so to speak, it expanded through first two or three decades of 19th century.)

Genial tone—improvements in technology all one with improvements in legislation, law, etc.

Around 1830, tone changes: insistence upon utility, practical science, becomes strident. Lifting it up, with explicit or implicit denigration of theoretical scientist, shows that popular sensibility is taking sides.

In part a manifestation of Jacksonian revolution. The pure scientist is identified with luxury, elegance, snobbishness, whereas practical scientist—inventor—is down there working with common people. Applied science is moral. Mechanics have minds. Practical science is plain, homespun; science in general is diet of epicures. Axe, hammer, trowel call for as much Mind as calculating an eclipse.

This theme most emphasized in addresses to societies of working men.

Tremendous support given to mood of hostility against theoretical science by wide diffusion of hostility to "scholasticism" and "middle ages."

Prevalence of this denunciation one of most striking and revealing phenomena of age. Medieval scholastic becomes a bogey-man, upon whom all American doubt of self can be discharged.

In this vein, Bacon appears as the deliverer from cobwebs, sophistry, and syllogism.

In 1830's serious students of science become really aware that this utilitarianism now constitutes a threat against dignity and integrity of the subject.

2.

CONFUSION

In initial dismay, advocates of science look about in bewilderment, start crying, no, no, this is not what Bacon meant at all.

Situation gets more complicated when poets, classicists, Transcendentalists begin attack on science and technology as in itself vulgar, materialistic, etc. Scientists have to answer that this is false, sentimental charge.

Then they must endeavor to free themselves of any contagion of this protest in order to protest against excessive utilitarianism in the name of ideal of pure, disinterested, idle scientific speculation or experiment.

But difficulty grows of making clear-cut distinction between theoretical and practical.

Apologists carry on 18th-century argument that pure science, even if at moment it seems unproductive, will eventually translate its principles into machines. But tone is now not the confident meliorism of Enlightenment, but defensive. Pleading with the democracy to try to understand that basic research should be respected, on argument that eventually, someday, it would justify itself in terms the people imposed.

Similarly, apologists restrain denunciation of utility on consideration that America still has the immensely practical problem of subduing the Continent; so may be allowed extreme devotion to "things" for a while, because after material order is established the nation will then be able to devote itself to elegance and culture. This again and again a transparently nervous contention.

Most concentrated and sustained effort is to present, over and over, some reassuring version of just how the two, theoretical and practical, work together.

But, apologies have to reveal, usually inadvertently or unwittingly, that there does exist in the country a deep, angry, sullen hatred of the concept of intellect maintained by the advocates of pure, unproductive science. The democracy and the religious community both sense that it is their enemy.

3.

THE SMITHSONIAN INSTITUTION

All the aspects of this issue brought out in the Congressional debates and measures over handling of Smithsonian bequest. The Congress has to face the problem of pure science versus applied, of intellect versus practicality, and in its discussion, over twenty years, the issue was luridly dramatized.

4.

THE 1850'S

Even though, thanks largely to JQA, Marsh and above all to Henry, the Smithsonian was saved from utilitarianism, the argument continues through this decade; yet in language that seems to show a complete bewilderment, the issue more beclouded than ever.

On the one hand, continued plaint of pro-science [men] against vulgarization of utility becomes a stereotyped whimper, carries less and less conviction.

On the other, more positive claims are made for utility, though even these show little courage, and appear to be mainly satisfactions with continued progress of railroads, telegraphs, etc. On eve of Civil War, while technological transformation still under way, the American mind is utterly unprepared for the strenuous demands about to be made upon it.

CHAPTER SIX

The Oath of Hippocrates

1.

THE PROSPECT FOR MEDICINE

c. 1800 widespread recognition that medicine in US is in primitive state, but immense confidence that profession will develop.

Resolution to build schools, etc.

In medicine as elsewhere the new nationalism is expressed in firm determination of doctors to build up a science and a dignity befitting the Republic.

In this spirit, solemn proclamation uttered that medicine, though in past was largely conjecture, has now at last become an authentic science.

Doctors share reverence for Linnaeus, attempt a classification of diseases—nosology.

They hold their principal enemy is "empiricism."

Rush inspired to doctrine of unity of all diseases in one basic disease in effort to give scientific respectability to practice, against the prevalence of empiricism.

However, medical mind also venerates Bacon, and in first decades is insisting that through observation and induction the science is steadily advancing.

In the name of devotion to "utility," doctors rally around the slogan of no system, no theory, and even no hypothesis.

Rush's ideas and his "heroic" treatment soon abandoned as a foisting of system upon the open Baconian method.

Gradually the issue which will bedevil the profession is foreshadowed: is freedom from system, from tyrannical generalizations, not bound to lead eventually to an avowed empiricism? If so, medicine is not a science and the pretensions of the doctors are pompous and dangerous. A people profoundly suspicious of lawyers easily turn same suspicion upon doctors, with even greater hostility because doctors will not only take their money but also their lives.

2.
A SEARCH FOR AN IDENTITY

The very sense of immense progress being made becomes by around 1830 a disturbing factor:

On the one hand, pride in advances;

But at same time lesson brought home that what profession holds and does today will be obsolete by tomorrow, so that practices of any one moment may well be proved murderous.

Discussion and debate take on new urgency in 1830's, as various leaders try to defend claims to scientific respectability, meanwhile endeavoring to teach themselves and the country that this is compatible with constant rejection of old methods as new ones prove superior virtue.

Haunting concept of "uncertainty" cannot be shaken off.

Uncertainty aggravated by disputes among the schools of belief—e.g., the "chemical" versus the "vital."

Recognition slowly forced upon the profession that mere anti-system is not enough, that if it is only aggressive stand the doctor can take, then indeed he does lapse into empiricism.

Hence greater need than ever for medicine to define its relation to other sciences, especially chemistry.

And thus to compare its state with them. Is it more insecure than they, is it in same condition of advance, or is it not at all a science as they are?

Painful discovery, and then constant re-discovery, that the making of medicine into a solid and reputable science not only is a much more difficult task than was dreamed of at the beginning of the century, but furthermore is becoming every day more difficult by the increase of empirical data.

This calls for reassertion of loyalty to the Baconian method. But always, this cry for more intense observation, more rigorous induction, says it is not empiricism and at same time is not system, theory or hypothesis.

Yet another thought intrudes: perhaps we had better check blanket condemnation of theory—or at least admit function for hypothesis, as long as we do not permit it to become a theory.

Immense amount of energy devoted to striking a balance, or a series of balances, between generalization and concrete fact. A precarious stance.

Bewilderment of the profession about just what it is conveyed to the public in a myriad ways. Result: the doctors increasingly alarmed in 1830's, 1840's about what they take to be increase in "quacks." Quacks are empiricists gone mad, not necessarily dishonest, and even more dangerous when honest.

Chief attack by homoeopathy, which challenges the orthodox most severely by itself appearing as pure science, against the muddled "empiricism" of the learned.

Confusion confounded by the heresy of Bigelow and Holmes, preaching self-limited diseases, advocating that physician do as little as possible, and give virtually no medicines.

In 1850's no real resolution of the problem. Yet the doctors have somehow prospered, and can call down upon themselves the blessing of the SUBLIME.

CHAPTER SEVEN

The Triumph of Technology

The forlorn hope: that technology, by binding the continent into a unit of railroads and telegraph and steamboats, will prevent any split.

Actually, "Science" itself moving so rapidly in 1850's toward specialization, it no longer has any such unity to preach as Jefferson and Peale supposed it did. The Enlightenment is far away. Science and its applications simply put weapons and machines at the service of armies.

Hence ironic effect of Civil War, which begins to be seen by only a few before 1865: the real result of the conflict is not so much the humbling of the South and abolition of slavery, but a tremendous impetus given to accelerated subjection of natural continent to the mechanisms of technology.

The Nine Books of the Whole Work

In a letter to Harcourt, Brace & World of February 28, 1963, Perry Miller presented the following as "the list of sections as now constituting the plan for *The Life of the Mind in America: From the Revolution to the Civil War*."

PROLOGUE	The Sublime in America
BOOK I	The Evangelical Basis
BOOK II	The Legal Mentality
BOOK III	Tension: Technology and Science
BOOK IV	The Battlefield of Democracy: Education
BOOK V	Freedom and Association: Political Economy and Association
BOOK VI	Philosophy
BOOK VII	Theology
BOOK VIII	Nature
BOOK IX	The Self

Acknowledgments

While working on *The Life of the Mind in America,* Perry Miller talked to many of his colleagues, seeking the advice and criticism of those in fields where he felt himself distinctly less than an authority. He would, I know, want his thanks expressed particularly to Mark De-Wolfe Howe, to Donald Fleming, to Kenneth Lynn, and in a special degree to Alan Heimert, who assisted him in much of the research. He would also wish his deep appreciation expressed to the D and R Fund, the Bollingen Foundation, and the Institute for Advanced Study for generous support of his research. No scholar does his work without libraries. The libraries of Harvard University, the Boston Public Library, the New York Public Library, the Massachusetts Historical Society, and the American Philosophical Society were unfailingly generous and helpful. And finally, perhaps his greatest debt was to the students who, over the years, in seminars and in his course on romanticism in America, stimulated him, challenged him, and explored with him wherein the sublime prospect of the nation lay.

E.W.M.

Index